Theory On Gender / Feminism On Theory

SOCIAL INSTITUTIONS AND SOCIAL CHANGE
An Aldine de Gruyter Series of Texts and Monographs

EDITED BY

Michael Useem • James D. Wright

Theory On Gender / Feminism On Theory

Paula England
EDITOR

ALDINE DE GRUYTER
New York

About the Editor

Paula England is Professor of Sociology at the University of Arizona. Her research interests include occupational sex segregation, the sex gap in pay, and the integration of sociological, economic, and feminist theories. She is the author of numerous journal articles on these topics, and is the author of *Comparable Worth: Theories and Evidence* (Aldine, 1992). She has testified in federal court as an expert witness in discrimination suits.

Copyright ©1993 Walter de Gruyter, Inc., New York
All rights reserved. No part of this publication may be reproduced or transmitted in any form or by any means, electronic or mechanical, including photocopy, recording, or any information storage or retrieval system, without permission in writing from the publisher.

ALDINE DE GRUYTER
A division of Walter de Gruyter, Inc.
200 Saw Mill River Road
Hawthorne, New York 10532

This publication is printed on acid-free paper ∞

Library of Congress Cataloging-in-Publication Data
Theory on gender/feminism on theory / Paula England, editor.
   p. cm. — (Social institutions and social change)
  Includes bibliographical references (p.   ) and index.
  ISBN 0-202-30437-X (cloth : alk. paper). — ISBN 0-202-30438-8 (paper : alk. paper)
   1. Feminist theory. I. England, Paula. II. Title: Theory on gender. III. Title: Feminism on theory. IV. Series.
HQ1190. T48   1993
305.42'01-dc20   92-27886
                                                 CIP

Manufactured in the United States of America

10 9 8 7 6 5 4 3 2 1

Contents

List of Contributors

Ben Agger

Department of Sociology
State University of New York
Buffalo

Elizabeth M. Almquist

Department of Sociology
University of North Texas

Janet Saltzman Chafetz

Department of Sociology
University of Houston

Norman K. Denzin

Department of Sociology
University of Illinois

Carol Diem

Department of Sociology
University of Arizona

Dana Dunn

Department of Sociology
University of Texas-Arlington

Paula England

Department of Sociology
University of Arizona

Sarah Fenstermaker

Department of Sociology
University of California
Santa Barbara

Nancy Folbre

Department of Economics
University of Massachusetts
Amherst

Debra Friedman

Department of Sociology
University of Arizona

Miriam M. Johnson

Department of Sociology
University of Oregon

J. Miller McPherson   Department of Sociology
                                       University of Arizona

Linda D. Molm   Department of Sociology
                                       University of Arizona

Cecilia L. Ridgeway   Department of Sociology
                                       University of Iowa

Beth Anne Shelton   Department of Sociology
                                       State University of New York
                                       Buffalo

Lynn Smith-Lovin   Department of Sociology
                                       University of Arizona

Joey Sprague   Department of Sociology
                                       University of Kansas

Nancy Tuana   Program in Humanities
                                       University of Texas-Dallas

Kathryn B. Ward   Department of Sociology
                                       Southern Illinois University
                                       Carbondale

Candace West   Department of Sociology
                                       University of California

Christine L. Williams   Department of Sociology
                                       University of Texas-Austin

John Wilson   Department of Sociology
                                       Duke University

Mary Zimmerman   Department of Sociology
                                       University of Kansas

Preface

By 1988, when I conceived the idea for this volume on sociological theories, my intellectual interests had become interdisciplinary to an unusual degree. In part I attribute this to having started my career in the mid-1970s when there was still little written on gender in sociology. I also attribute it to working at the University of Texas–Dallas, which had institutionalized interdisciplinary graduate programs. I had been reading a lot of economics, political theory, philosophy, and developmental and clinical psychology. I approached all the fields except economics in a receptive mood. In contrast, I learned the neoclassical paradigm "kicking and screaming," as I engaged in debates with economists about occupational sex segregation and comparable worth. While I still regard neoclassical positions on these issues as misdirected, I see now that I absorbed some of economists' sensibilities on the battlefield.

This learning was all to the good. But I was so immersed in interdisciplinary dialogue that I had begun to see my own discipline of training, sociology, in a blurred fashion, as an orientation to "social structure" that, however vaguely defined, seemed to distinguish most sociology from, say, economics or psychology. I feld a need to clarify my understanding of each of a number of sociological theories, as well as what they can say about gender. I also wondered if something analogous to the feminist critiques I was reading of theories in other disciplines was apt for sociology. What better way to learn about this, I thought, than to edit this volume. It was a way to persuade some smart people to write the papers I needed to read. I decided to select authors who have worked in the theoretical tradition they discuss here because of my bias against dynamite; even the most deconstructive of criticisms is more effective when done by one who has intimate familiarity with the perspective. Still, this choice did mean that authors might be too easy on theories in which they had a vested interest. Because of this, and my love of the back-and-forth of dialogue, I settled on a format for the volume that includes debate.

In writing my introductory chapter, I reigned myself in from revealing how I adjudicate the explicit and implicit debates between authors in the volume. I decided it would be ungrateful and reductive to summarize the volume with a scorecard. (The reader who is curious about my opinions is referred to my past and future writings!) Instead, I offer my thanks to all the authors whose papers appear here. Their efforts have sharpened and deepened my understanding of the uses and limitations of sociological theories.

The more I study gender, the more I recognize two distinct ways in which societies disadvantage women: through discouraging women's participation in stereotypically male activities that are highly rewarded, *and* through the failure to recognize the contribution of, and thus to value and reward, the activities typically done by women. One example of the second is the discriminatorily low pay accorded to predominantly female occupations, thematized in the issue of comparable worth. Another example is the failure to properly value and reward the important work of providing nurturing emotional support.

In recognition of the benefits of emotional work, I want to thank three wonderful people whose love and companionship have been sources of strength and creativity for me during this project. I thank Nancy Tuana, whose intellect I revere, who I regard as a mentor in matters of feminist theory, and who inspires action. I thank Nancy Vining Van Ness, who talks with me about things out of fashion in the academy, supporting me in developing links between my personal healing, political visions, and spirituality. And I thank my husband, Dale Conner, whose loving acceptance of my successes, limitations, and changes gives me a deep sense of safety and comfort.

Paula England

PART I

Introduction

Chapter 1

Sociological Theories and the Study of Gender

Paula England

How do various sociological theories understand gender differentiation and gender inequality? Are these theories infused with masculinist bias that needs to be redressed with insights from feminist theory? To address these questions, I asked a number of authors to write chapters on the strengths and limitations of theoretical traditions within which they have worked to understand gender. Each of these chapters provides a brief introduction to the theory, explains its implications for gender, reviews relevant empirical research, and comments upon sexist biases or other limitations of the perspective. To examine possible biases of the methods used by sociologists, I invited two coauthors to write a paper on feminist debates about methodology. To provide dialogue on all these topics, I asked four additional scholars to comment on the papers in the volume, and asked authors to reply to the comments.

The organization of the volume is as follows. This introductory chapter is Part I. It provides a brief summary of each of the chapters, and some highlights of the debates between the commentators and chapter authors. My summaries are necessarily partial and selective; they are intended merely to suggest the flavor of what follows. Part II, "Theoretical Perspectives on Gender," presents ten chapters. Theoretical positions covered in these chapters include Marxism, world system theory, macrostructural theories, rational-choice theory, neofunctionalism, psychoanalytic theory, ethnomethodology, expectation states theory, a poststructural version of symbolic interactionism, and network theory. Part III, "Dialogue and Debate," begins with a paper on feminist debates about methodology. The section then continues with four essays, each of which comments upon several of the previous chapters. The four commentators include two sociologists, a philosopher, and an economist, all conversant with work in feminist theory. Following each of the four essays are replies by the authors whose chapters were commented upon by the essay. This section demonstrates the diversity of opinions about how sociological theory illuminates the study of gender, and how feminism can inform sociological theory and methods.

Part II begins with Shelton and Agger's chapter, "Shotgun Wedding, Unhappy Marriage, No-Fault Divorce? Rethinking the Feminism-Marxism Relationship." They argue for a revised Marxism that retains the essence of Marxism and speaks to women's oppression as well. They differentiate their position from liberal and radical feminism, from orthodox Marxism, as well as from the "dualist" and "capitalist-patriarchy" perspectives commonly labeled socialist-feminist.

They read Marxism as a theory of capitalism that sees exploitation to occur when producers do not control the means of production and thus have some of the value of what they produce taken from them. In Shelton and Agger's scheme, these producers include those who nurture humans in the household (those who do "reproductive labor") as well as those who work for a wage. Reproductive labor produces the current and next-generation labor force, and thus makes a necessary contribution to capitalist profits. Unlike orthodox Marxists, they see homemakers to be exploited by capitalism. That is, just as all paid workers have surplus value extracted by capitalists so that they are not paid for a portion of their labor, so too do homemakers have surplus extracted from their work. However, in Shelton and Agger's view, homemakers are even more exploited than paid workers since they receive *no* pay. They also see women to be exploited more than men as paid laborers, because discrimination is a profitable "divide and conquer" strategy.

Shelton and Agger think it important to look for one structuring principle that explains the social totality. Socialist-feminists of either the dualist or capitalist-patriarchy school tend to see two such principles, patriarchy and capitalism, although they differ on how merged the two are. Shelton and Agger see the logic of capitalism to be the overriding structuring principle; patriarchy receives equal billing as consequence but not as structuring principle. They see who owns or controls capitalist firms to be more structurally crucial, more consequential, than who calls the shots in the household, although the latter is an important consequence of capitalism in their scheme. They propose that Marxism and feminism be merged into a rejuvenated Marxism that differs from orthodox Marxism in that it expands the traditional Marxist notions of class and exploitation in a way that includes homemakers in the exploited working class, but retains a commitment to totalizing theory with one structuring principle.

They review research done by Shelton and others that documents the reciprocal links between women's position in the paid labor market and in the household. Women's responsibility for the household negatively affects their wages as well as the hours they spend in paid employment. Lower earnings, in turn, lead women to do more household work and to have less power relative to men. They argue that women's subordinated position in both the labor market and the family makes their rate of exploitation higher than men's, and that this benefits capitalism. Thus, they believe that these reciprocal links between women's subordination in the household and the paid labor market can be explained in terms of the logic of capitalism.

In her comment on their chapter, Folbre, a socialist-feminist economist, argues that Shelton and Agger are overconfident of the ability of Marxist theory to provide an explanation for women's oppression. For her, any theory called "feminist" must recognize conflicts of interest between men and women within households, and collective interests based on gender that cross class lines, and are thus in tension with some class interests. She thinks that Shelton and Agger downplay this tension too much. In reply, Shelton and Agger argue that to separate out class and gender interests into separate "battles" inevitably leads to liberalism.

On this same theme, Wilson, a sociological theorist working within the Marxist tradition, takes issue with Shelton and Agger's belief that one can explain all of women's subordination to men in terms of capitalism—even when it is redefined to consider homemakers as producers of surplus value and thus members of an exploited working class. Although Wilson himself has worked within the Marxist tradition, he argues that patriarchal structures predate capitalism and survived in state socialist societies, and that it is doubtful that sex discrimination in labor markets can be explained entirely as a strategy to divide and conquer the working class. Further, he asks how capitalism can explain men's inclination to impose an arrangement whereby wives do more than their share of housework even when employed, even if it could explain their economic power to do so. Shelton and Agger respond that capitalism changed and intensified the nature of patriarchy. Since today's male dominance is in the interest of capitalism, they see it as explicable in terms of the logic of capitalism. Since they see men as a whole to benefit less from women's oppression than do capitalists, they find it more fruitful to focus on capitalism and all the forms of domination it engenders as the enemy than to invoke a separate theory of patriarchy.

Ward's chapter is aimed at "Reconceptualizing World System Theory to Include Women." World system theory is a derivative of Marxist theory, and focuses on the links between nations that have developed as capitalism, since the sixteenth century, has gradually encompassed the

globe, incorporating more and more nations into an international economy. Core nations control capital and the design of production while
peripheral nations provide raw materials and the cheapest labor. Theorists argue that these relations of dependency between core and peripheral nations lead the latter to experience low rates of economic growth,
distortion of their economies toward extraction and production for the
core, and higher internal income inequality.

Most theorists in the world system tradition have taken what Shelton
and Agger call the orthodox Marxist position on domestic labor. In this
view, as their husbands become wage laborers, women who are homemakers are seen to be incorporated into capitalism with class interests
consistent with those of their husbands. Homemakers are not seen to be
themselves exploited or to have important interests distinct from those
of men of their class. Ward's earlier work attempted to add women into
world system theorizing without altering the theory fundamentally. Her
research showed that incorporation of a less developed nation into the
world system, as measured by levels of commodity concentration and
foreign investment, negatively affected women's share of employment,
and increased fertility.

Ward now believes that a fundamental rethinking of the theory is
needed to capture the way gender, race, and class interact in a holistic
manner. She believes that current versions of world system theory fail to
explain why the informal and household sectors, in which women often
work, have expanded rather than contracted as nations and regions are
incorporated into the world system. Similarly, in her view, the theory is
unable to explain discrimination against women in formal economies, or
disparities of male and female power within the household. Less optimistic than Shelton and Agger about the adequacy of even rejuvenated
derivatives of Marxism to avoid androcentric bias, she suggests that
scholars go back to the drawing board. She advocates drawing upon
diverse data sources to formulate theories of the middle range that start
with poor women of color in peripheral nations, since she believes their
experiences are the least well understood, the most marginalized, in
current theories.

Commenting on Ward's chapter, Wilson disagrees with her contention that Marxism, from which world system theory derives, cannot
explain the expansion of informal and household labor as nations are
incorporated into capitalism. Wilson sees one of the contradictions of
capitalism to be the simultaneous expansion of wage labor and nonwage
labor, the latter presumably because of the pauperization and/or commodity fetishism caused by the former. However, Wilson agrees with
Ward's contention that sexism in less developed nations cannot be
explained entirely as an effect of the capitalist nature of the international

economy. Yet he wonders if she should not assess the relative magnitude of the contributions of the dynamics of capitalism and sexism. In response, Ward argues against hierarchizing categories of oppression since this often leads to one being completely ignored as the theory progresses. In this vein, she notes that Wilson ignores her arguments about race.

Folbre agrees with the spirit of Ward's desire to transform theories, but does not see that a new conceptual framework has been offered. She suggests that theorists focus on the coalitions engendered by overlapping collective interests arising out of positions in systems of production and distribution.

Where world system theory emphasizes the relations between nations in the world economy, the "Macrostructural Perspectives on Gender Inequality" reviewed by Dunn, Almquist, and Chafetz take nations (or other geographical aggregates) as units of analysis. Theories operating at this level of analysis examine how various characteristics of such systems affect each other. The level of gender inequality (on any of a number of dimensions) varies across nations and regions, and they believe that macrostructural theories are needed to explain this variation. They see macrolevel processes, either material or normative, as affecting microlevel processes more than vice versa.

The authors review propositions from a number of macrostructural theories aimed at explaining variation in systems' level of gender inequality. Some theorists see world view to affect the level of male dominance. In this view, greater gender equality results when societies privilege cooperation over competition, see nature as friendly rather than threatening, and see male and female gods and humans to be part of rather than above nature. While cross-cultural comparisons support this correlation, theorists differ on the causal order: Does such an ideology affect male dominance, does male dominance affect the ideology, or both?

Most theories and research in this tradition find that women have more advantages where they are more involved in nondomestic production. Increases in complex technology and surplus production are believed to increase gender (as well as class) inequality, at least prior to advanced industrial societies. Women's status is higher where they control more of the means and distribution of production. There is a link between the extent of women's penetration into high-level occupational positions and their share of political positions, although it is not clear which is causally prior.

In her comment on the chapter by Dunn et al., Molm reiterates a concern noted by the authors themselves: Many of the propositions advanced by macrostructural theorists have not been tested because of lack of comparable data on many of the indicators across nations. Folbre is critical of this literature for presuming that the effects of nation, race, and class are additive rather than interacting with gender. She also sees this research tradition as too atheoretical, as macroempiricist rather than macrostructural. In their reply to Folbre, Dunn et al. agree that their perspective is eclectic, drawing upon a number of broad metatheories, but do not see this as a defect. They defend an inductive, quantitative approach to theory building, starting with additive relationships, with a goal of adding the complexities of interactions later.

In "Feminism and the Pro- (Rational-) Choice Movement: Rational-Choice Theory, Feminist Critiques, and Gender Inequality," Friedman and Diem argue for the utility of sociological rational-choice theory in illuminating gender inequality.

They begin by defending rational-choice theory against various feminist critiques, some of which were made by Kilbourne and me in a 1990 paper. We argued that a separative rather than emotionally connected self is both assumed and glorified in Western thought. We argued that this masculinist bias ignores emotional connections that both men and women experience, but that are often emphasized more by women because of gendered socialization and role assignments. We took neoclassical economics to be the paradigmatic form of rational-choice theory, and argued that several assumptions of neoclassical theory involve assuming the separative nature of the self and, thus, are biased.

One such assumption is selfishness. However, Friedman and Diem point out that rational-choice theory assumes self-interest, which does not necessarily imply selfishness, and can include altruism. A second assumption made by most economists is that interpersonal utility comparisons are impossible (that is, we cannot know which of two persons is "happier" or has more utility). Friedman and Diem argue that sociological practitioners of rational-choice theory do not necessarily disallow interpersonal utility comparisons and that, in any case, allowing such comparisons does not necessarily imply an empathic or altruistic self. A third assumption is that preferences (tastes) are stable and exogenous to the system under analysis. Since this seems to imply that tastes are not affected by social processes, we argued that it downplays connections and assumes a separative self. Friedman and Diem argue that rational-choice theorists assume exogenous tastes as a simplifying assumption because no adequate theory of preference formation yet exists. They do not see this assumption as embodying a separative bias since preferences may change for reasons other than social interaction.

Other feminists have accused rational-choice theory of "blaming the victim." The idea is that seeing women's plight as a result of their own choices seems to blame them for their subordinate position. Friedman and Diem argue that this is a misunderstanding of rational-choice theory. Since the theory sees all choices as made within constraints, women are not entirely responsible for their outcomes or even their choices; their choices are a function of both their preferences and of constraints.

Friedman and Diem argue that rational-choice theory explains outcomes by the rational actions of purposive agents. These agents are assumed to be subject to external constraints in the form of institutional forces (such as rules, laws, policies, and norms) and in the form of opportunity costs. Agents are assumed to make the choice that, given these external constraints, best advances their goals (whether these goals are selfish or altruistic).

As an example of an explanation consistent with rational-choice theory's contention that institutional constraints matter, they discuss Brinton's work on gender differences in human capital formation in Japan. The absence of social security leads parents to rely on their children for support in old age. Other features of the institutional landscape are internal labor markets in firms combined with sex discrimination in access to jobs on mobility ladders. These institutional facts mean that parents will find providing education for sons more in their self-interest than providing education for daughters.

Another key concept in rational-choice theory is opportunity cost. The opportunity cost of choice X is the value of the other option you will forgo if you choose X. They interpret arguments presented by Gerson in *Hard Choices* in terms of opportunity costs. Comparing women that started out with the same aspirations, those women who happened into an especially good job were less likely to have children. This can be interpreted in terms of the greater opportunity cost of leaving employment to care for children experienced by women with better jobs.

Rational-choice theorists also believe preferences are consequential. Freidman and Diem hypothesize that if most men hold preferences for even a weak level of segregation, this may aggregate into extreme occupational sex segregation. The process they describe is analogous to one hypothesized to explain the speed with which neighborhoods sometimes "tip" from having all white to having all black residents.

Folbre's comment on Friedman and Diem's paper focuses on their contention that rational-choice theory does not assume selfishness, and that even the "free-rider" problem can be understood as a desire by rational agents to engage in collective action only when it is efficacious, rather than as a result of selfishness. Folbre agrees that the self-interest assumption does not necessarily imply selfishness. But she notes that economists often add the auxiliary assumption that actors' utilities are independent (e.g., that my happiness is independent of, or not affected by, your happiness), which she believes to sneak the selfishness assumption in through the back door. Folbre argues that Friedman and Diem may underestimate the extent to which the level of altruism affects whether collective action occurs. Folbre argues that precisely because most actors are reluctant to act until they can be sure that their efforts will make a difference (as Friedman and Diem emphasize), a few altruists who act on strictly moral basis without regard for consequences may be necessary to get the ball rolling in any social movement. In their reply, Friedman and Diem contend that many rational-choice theorists, including economists, *have* pursued and will continue to pursue models that allow interdependent utilities. Freidman and Diem also contend that it is fruitless to argue about whether we should assume humans to be selfish or altruistic; they see the important questions to deal with what institutional arrangements bring forth behavior that we regard as socially responsible.

In "Functionalism and Feminism: Is Estrangement Necessary?" Johnson argues for "neofunctionalism" as a loose organizing perspective for the study of gender. The functionalism espoused by Parsons in the 1930s–1960s started with the question of how we can explain patterned order in social life. It understood structural change within an evolutionary model. Johnson argues that Parsons did not assume that everything we observe is functional, but rather that processes, such as structural differentiation, that turn out to be functional for a society or subsystem are likely to persist because they work. Nonetheless, structural strains may persist as well. On the microlevel, Parsons believed that socialization in the family generally led to the internalization of values consistent with societal structures, but that strains and inconsistencies between the family and societal structures might exist as well.

Johnson defends Parsons's distinction between instrumental action which moves a system in its environment, and expressive action which contributes to internal integration of the system, for example, by increasing group solidarity. Parsons saw breadwinning as instrumental and homemaking as expressive, and saw each role as equally important to the system. He saw this division of labor by sex as functional for marriages because it prevented divisive competition between husband and wife. Johnson criticizes Parsons for overemphasizing the degree to which values are consensual and ignoring relations of domination. An example of this is his failure to note that what was holding marriages together was women's financial dependence as much as affective solidarity. However, she thinks it is useful to retain the distinction between instrumental and expressive roles, and not to assume definitionally that expressive roles carry less power. She argues that social systems may vary in whether the nurturant work she calls expressive brings those who perform it high levels of power and rewards.

In her comment on this chapter, Tuana, a philosopher interested in feminist theory, argues against Johnson's tendency to see instrumental and expressive action as entirely distinct, even opposite. She argues that expressive actions, by increasing group solidarity, often contribute to getting the instrumental task done. Then why are they themselves not seen as instrumental as well as expressive? Tuana finds the instrumental/expressive dichotomy reminiscent of the reason/emotion dichotomy so common in Western philosophy. Tuana argues that feminists should attempt to transcend these dichotomies that have been linked to male and female. As she sees it, the need is not simply to disassociate the dichotomies from male and female (as in demonstrating that women, too, can be rational and instrumental, and men can be expressive), although this is needed. Nor is the solution merely to increase the value given to the traditionally female side of the dichotomy, although this too is worthwhile. Tuana believes that transcending false dichotomies entails showing that the two supposedly oppositional or separate concepts are actually entwined parts of the same process. In her reply, Johnson states that she did not intend a dichotomy, and that some of her past work shows that most women see themselves as both instrumental and expressive.

In her own work, Johnson has attempted to keep what she sees as the merit of functionalism, the focus on how multiple levels—biological, psychological, social, and cultural—interpenetrate each other. However, she includes a focus on the dominance relations ignored by earlier functionalists. In this spirit, she offers her view that the interactional sequences in families most responsible for perpetuating male dominance are fathers' interactions with daughters, which encourage them to become subordinate wives. She argues that mothers act in a nurturant way that is fairly undifferentiated by sex of child, thus teaching both boys and girls a common humanity and working against male dominance. She sees the male peer group to be the major factor socializing males into orientations of dominance over women.

Functionalism has been characterized as inherently conservative. But Johnson argues that this need not be so if neofunctionalists add the question of "Functional for whom or what?" In his commentary on Johnson's chapter, Wilson protests that adding this question undermines the whole causal logic of functionalism. He further argues that social reproduction is a goal of the powerful, not a system need. In her reply, Johnson argues that social reproduction is *both* a goal of the powerful and a need of any system, even a utopian one, and that many Marxist and other critical theories ignore the latter.

Williams's chapter discusses "Psychoanalytic Theory and the Sociology of Gender." Her focus is on sociological uses of object relations theory. She notes that Parsons drew upon object relations theory for his theory of how individuals internalize cultural norms and values. In the 1970s, Chodorow revived this notion and infused it with a more critical spirit. She argued that the structural arrangement by which women do the primary caretaking of children creates internalized, unconscious desires in sons and daughters that reproduce male dominance and female mothering independent of conscious intentions. In this view, when women mother, all children have an initial attachment to and identification with a female. Because boys have a caretaker of a different sex, achieving gender identity encourages emotional separation from the mother. The developmental process of individuation from a female caretaker encourages a boy to define himself in terms of rejecting whatever he sees as female, thus increasing the salience for males of a gender identity that emphasizes difference from and rejection of femaleness. For girls, given a same-sex caretaker, gender identity and individuation are not as mutually reinforcing. Thus, in this view, males grow up with an internalized need to emphasize separation rather than connection, and with misogynistic tendencies to define themselves in opposition to whatever is female; females grow up with an internalized need for emotional connection, which often leads to a desire to mother. Chodorow emphasized, however, that these arrangements cause great pain, especially for women, who seldom find the emotional intimacy they want in relationships with men, and who are the victims of men's misogyny. Williams argues that this misogyny is institutionalized in the public sphere wherever men have the power to realize and enforce these unconscious needs, resulting in sex segregation of activities, and a general devaluation of women as well as their domestic and paid work. The theory suggests that this cycle will only be ended when children have both men and women as equally participating parents in their early life, yet it also implies that it will be terribly hard to get men to be coequal parents.

Williams reviews research findings for which she believes this perspective provides a useful interpretation. Rubin's interviews with married couples showed that many women are frustrated by men's disinclination to talk or listen when the topic is feelings. Fox Keller argues that men have defined good science in terms of the separation between the knower and the known as a result of their psychological need for separation rather than because this enhances knowledge. Williams' own research shows that women in a male profession are treated much worse than men in a female occupation. Williams sees all these pieces of research to be consistent with her theoretical perspective in that they suggest women's desire for emotional connection and men's desire for separation and an identity that emphasizes their difference from and superiority to women.

In Tuana's comments on Williams' chapter, she argues that psychoanalytic theory may explain how parts of the gender system are reproduced, but that interactional dynamics and men's economic power may contribute as well. Regarding the latter, while psychoanalytic theory may explain men's desire for distinguishing themselves from women, it cannot explain why they have the power to carry this out. Williams replies by agreeing with Tuana's suggestion that understanding is enriched when we embrace multiple theories, and is hindered when we see theories as rivals competing for the place of the "one true theory."

In her comment on Williams' chapter, Folbre labels as indisputable the general claims about women's greater internalized tendency to value emotional connection made by object relations theorists. But Folbre protests that advocates of the theory have not presented evidence showing that having had female (as opposed to male or both sex) caretakers is a major cause of this difference. In the absence of such evidence, we could just as easily conclude that biology, cognitive learning, or sex-differentiated reinforcement histories are the cause of these differences in disposition. In response, Williams points out that many sociologists disagree with the contention that women and men have deeply internalized differences in desires for connection and separation that are not merely a product of more immediate situational factors. Indeed, several authors in this volume (Molm, Smith-Lovin and McPherson, West and Fenstermaker, and Friedman and Diem) express disagreement with this contention. Williams argues that the psychoanalytic notion of the unconscious helps explain orientations that have more persistence across varying situations than is consistent with reinforcement or other social learning theories.

The next three papers all focus on how processes of face-to-face interaction affect the gender system. The first, by West and Fenstermaker is "Power, Inequality, and the Accomplishment of Gender: An Ethnomethodological View." They reject the notion that gender is the result of internalized social norms that are learned early in life and change little thereafter. Rather, they argue that gender is accomplished through ongoing interaction with others. They distinguish between sex, one's biological classification as female or male; sex category, one's social identification as a male or female; and gender, which they define as conduct that is accountable to normative conceptions of womanly or manly natures. As we interact with others, they believe that we are "held accountable" by others to display gender in conformity with our sex category. Our sex category is generally consistent with our biological sex, but need not be, as in the case of a woman "passing" as a man.

As an example of how this accountability affects behavior, aspirations, and affect, they review Fenstermaker's research on the disproportionate amount of household work done by women, even in marriages where both partners are employed full-time. They argue that this seemingly irrational and inefficient division of labor is intelligible when we see it as the interactional accomplishment of gender display.

At first glance the ethnomethodological view may strike some readers as indicating that people follow consensual, internalized norms about how men and women are both supposed to act, similar to the Parsonian view. The ethnomethodological view of gender is different from this, however, in that what can pass as "accountable" action for one whose sex category is woman is situationally specific and is subject to variability and negotiation. As an example of this point, they use Hurtado's discussion of how white women and women of color have been held accountable to normative conceptions of "essential" womanly nature in very different ways—women of color seen as drones and appropriate objects of sexual aggression, white women as fragile, childlike subservients to be protected.

In their comments on this chapter, both Tuana and Wilson, in slightly different ways, raise the question of why the authors see sex category to be omnirelevant, or why the fact of being held accountable for behaving in accordance with our sex category is invariant—even if the definition of what constitutes womanhood or manhood can vary situationally. West and Fenstermaker reply that the power of their framework does not depend on a theory of origin—of how it came to be that being held accountable for gendered behavior that corresponds to our sex category is relatively invariant across situations. They believe that one strength of ethnomethodology is in showing that, despite this invariance, many other seemingly transsituational properties of social life—such as what behavior will count as accountable to one's sex category—are local, variable, situationally achieved processes. They believe that this perspective affords a new understanding of the mechanisms through which women's subordination and inequality are maintained.

Ridgeway's chapter also focuses on small-group interaction. She discusses how expectation states theory illuminates "Gender, Status, and the Social Psychology of Expectations." The theory focuses on processes of interaction that occur when a group sets out to perform an instrumental task. (In this research tradition, "instrumental" action is conceptualized much the way it is in Parsonian functionalism, discussed in Johnson's chapter.) According to the theory, participants in task-oriented groups form expectations about the relative value of their own and others' contributions. Ridgeway argues that, in our society, these expectations are based on shared cultural beliefs that those who are white, male, educated, older, or in a higher status occupation are generally more instrumentally competent. These characteristics of individuals that affect expectations about the value of their contributions are called *status characteristics*. The focus is on shared beliefs that affect expectations of who is more competent; the theory has no implication that men are *actually* more competent or that women internalize less of a desire for instrumental action in early socialization.

The theory asserts that actors with status characteristics leading to higher expectations, e.g., men, are more likely to speak up initially. In addition, others will give men more opportunity to participate and more positive evaluations. This, in turn, will reinforce men's sense that it is appropriate to take charge in the discussion or activity. Through a kind of self-fulfilling prophecy, actors with highly valued status characteristics will become more and more influential over group decisions.

Unlike ethnomethodologists, researchers in this tradition have generally used quantitative analysis of data collected from laboratory experiments. Despite the difference in methods, the two perspectives share a belief that the way gender plays out in interaction is situationally specific. Thus, Ridgeway argues that the extent to which being male is a status characteristic varies across situations. While expectations generally favor men, this is not always true. Ridgeway argues that gendered expectations are more likely to be activated when the task is stereotypically associated with either men or women (e.g., football or cooking), when the group includes both males and females, or when a group of all one sex comes together within an organization where the persons in positions of authority are largely of the other sex. It is the fact that gender is not always activated as a status characteristic that makes the theory situational.

Molm's comment on Ridgeway's chapter notes the contention of expectation states theorists that the salience of gender to expectations is situationally variable. Initially this led researchers to assume that gender is only relevant in mixed-sex groups. But the literature has continued to add more and more situations in which gender is seen to affect expectations, as noted above. The continual addition of these new conditions runs the risk of weakening the theory's situational specificity. But this specificity is the very thing that distinguishes the theory from conventional socialization analyses that see beliefs or dispositions to be deeply internalized and thus relatively constant across situations. Ridgeway responds that she does not find this trend toward adding situations in which gender is seen to affect expectations to be severe enough to contradict the situational nature of the theory. However, she concedes that the way in which gendered expectations affect interaction in same-sex groups is yet only dimly understood.

Commenting on Ridgeway's paper, Wilson criticizes expectation states theory for having a presocial notion of the self that is brought to group interaction. Ridgeway, in contrast, sees the theory as radically

social since the selves brought to interaction are assumed to hold a
socially shared belief about who is competent, and the analysis of interaction documents how conceptions about self and other are derivative
from social interaction. Wilson also criticizes the experimental method
used by researchers in this tradition. He argues that it maintains a rigid
emotional separation between researcher and subject of research. In
response, Ridgeway defends this as one, though not the only, valid
method for gaining understanding.

In "Sexuality and Gender: An Interactionist/Poststructural Reading,"
Denzin merges an interpretive version of symbolic interactionism with
the poststructural emphasis on texts to analyze gender. Like ethnomethodologists and theorists of expectations states, symbolic interactionists see gendered identities as an interactional production. The focus
is on how identities are formed from meanings arising out of interaction.
Thus, our gendered identities and our notions of what it means to be
male or female are formed and change through interpretations made in
interaction.

Symbolic interactionism shares the situational emphasis of ethnomethodology and expectation states theory. What meanings and
interpretations make sense to actors are seen to vary with and be
negotiable in the specific context of the interaction. Some symbolic
interactionists, including Denzin, take this to mean that deterministic
predictions are not consistent with the theory.

Denzin explains poststructuralism as a theoretical position examining
how our notions are constructed in and through language and ideology.
Poststructuralists adopt the method of deconstruction, the critical analysis of texts such as books, articles, verbal statements, pictures, and
movies. The goal is to ascertain the meanings that are implicit in them,
and how these were constructed by the author. Texts are a locus of
power, in Denzin's view.

Denzin advocates blending these two perspectives and using qualitative methods to study cultural meanings and lived experience. He thinks
it is useful to focus on turning point experiences (epiphanies) that cast
formerly dimly understood aspects of reality into sharp relief. These
epiphanic moments, in his view, can lead to either deepening internalized oppression or rebellion. For example, on the occasion of a
particularly severe beating, a battered woman may see the nature of her
marriage in sharp relief, and either become more hopeless about her
victimization or experience a new resistance. Either way, epiphanic
moments are occasions where we can see individuals working back on
the gendered order through the meanings they give things.

Wilson's comment on Denzin's paper protests the location of women's oppression in texts. Wilson sees the texts to reflect rather than create the order of class and gender relations. Denzin's reply argues that to contest class and gender relations, it is necessary to change how they are interpreted, although he does not argue that this is all that is necessary. He argues that Wilson's realist epistemology encourages hegemonic constructions that make it harder for actors to produce new interpretations.

In "You Are Who You Know: A Network Approach to Gender," Smith-Lovin and McPherson argue that small differences between males and females in early childhood or early adulthood are transformed, via differential networks, into extreme gender inequalities as the life course proceeds. Homophily by gender in early ties to playmates leads boys and girls to move into sex-differentiated, largely one-sex networks early in life. These network connections encourage later network ties to be sex differentiated. These sex-differentiated network locations, accentuated by women's child rearing responsibilities and the effects of this on further network location, push women into more kin-related and men into more occupationally relevant networks. This affects the information, opportunity, and taste formation experienced by men and women. Smith-Lovin and McPherson do not see gender-differentiated dispositions to be deeply internalized in early life. Rather they see men and women's behavior to be a more situational response to their current set of network ties.

Smith-Lovin and McPherson review research consistent with this perspective. Networks show considerable homophily by sex in childhood and adulthood. Voluntary organizations typically have very skewed sex ratios in one direction or the other, so they are a source of as well as an effect of sex-segregated networks. Compared to men, women have fewer network ties to non-kin, yet it is precisely non-kin ties that are most useful in finding jobs. Having children reduces the number of cross-sex network ties women have, yet network positions to other women are less useful in locating well-paying jobs than are ties to men. Given women's smaller networks containing persons with less occupationally helpful information, it is not surprising that women use networks less than men to find their jobs. Overall, Smith-Lovin and McPherson argue that the social role an individual is in (e.g., occupation, homemaker, voluntary organization member) affects the network ties s/he will develop, *and* that network ties determine information and preference formation that facilitate entry into different social roles. Gender inequality is reinforced through these mechanisms.

In their comments on Smith-Lovin and McPherson's chapter, both Folbre and Molm remark that the authors go a bit too far in their attempt to explain gender differences without using individuals' choices as a causal force. To this Smith-Lovin and McPherson plead guilty; they believe that choices are so narrowed down by the structure of network ties that the remaining choices explain little variance; they only look important from the subjective view of those making them.

Molm notes that their argument is focused on effects of being in same-sex networks. She agrees that sex-segregated networks have powerful effects, but believes that the authors have slighted the importance in perpetuating male dominance of cross-sex ties in which men bring more resources and power to the relationship. Such cross-sex ties between men and women occur in dating, marriage, and on the job. Smith-Lovin and McPherson reply that differential power is itself often determined by differences in the two parties' other network ties.

All the chapters discussed above apply one theoretical perspective to gender inequality, with only passing references to methodological questions. To provide more discussion of methodology, Part III begins with Sprague and Zimmerman's chapter, "Overcoming Dualisms: A Feminist Agenda for Sociological Methodology." They argue that both positivism and some prior feminist approaches to methodology have erred in seeing each of the following pairs as dichotomies: object and subject, rational and emotional, abstract and concrete, and quantitative and qualitative. Positivism and many feminist theorists have simply differed in which side of each dichotomy they chose to valorize, positivists choosing the first and feminists the second in each case. They argue that a better approach for feminist critics of positivism is to see each of these dualisms as a tension that we should strive to integrate in the research process. They argue that this is consistent with the emphasis in feminist theory on challenging false dichotomies. To do this entails not only disputing the link of the dichotomy to gender (that men are one way, while women are a distinct and sometimes opposite way). It also entails showing how things presumed to be entirely separate or oppositional are really always combined, and most beneficial when combined, despite some tension between them.

In her discussion of Sprague and Zimmerman's paper, Tuana acknowledges that knowledge has been distorted by reflecting the viewpoint of dominant groups. Yet she questions assuming that those on the margin (e.g., women) have a *privileged* access to reality, a less distorted view, rather than merely a different view. She also raises the question of "which margin" is relevant. Do lower class lesbian women of color have the most privileged standpoint because they are marginal on four dimensions? In their response, Sprague and Zimmerman note that they prefer to refer to dominated groups as "frontline actors" in getting things accomplished rather than as marginal. They also note that the notion of a standpoint should be seen as a position from which to view the situation with all one's analytical training in force, not necessarily synonymous with the empirical view of people who hold that position. While they agree with Tuana that all viewpoints are partial, they see the choice of what standpoint to adopt as necessarily political.

Molm's comments on Sprague and Zimmerman show her agreement with their desire to decouple the dualisms discussed from male and female. However, Molm finds their proposed integration problematic— too heavily weighted toward the subjective, emotional, concrete, and qualitative side of the dualisms. Molm does not see the equation of objective and rational with the scientific method as sexist, as long as these notions are decoupled from gender. She argues that the important way in which sexism has affected sociology is not in definition of the scientific method, but rather in which topics are chosen for analysis and given high status. Thus, the study of labor markets has higher status than the study of the family since the latter is seen as women's realm, and so on. In their reply, Sprague and Zimmerman criticize Molm's acceptance of the very dualisms they set out to integrate. They see both sides of each duality as equally valuable, yet she characterizes their suggestions as too heavily weighted toward one side. When Molm argues that emotional, subjective, and qualitative methods have *greater* potential for injecting gender bias into research than methods seen as opposites of these, Sprague and Zimmerman protest that she is holding to the very dichotomies they sought to integrate, and privileging one side of them.

The discussion above has highlighted some of the criticisms made of each chapter by the four commentators' essays. However, the authors of these essays did not merely criticize papers; they also attempted to bring the papers commented upon into dialogue with each other, and to advance their own view. A summary of these aspects of the four essays concludes this chapter.

Tuana is a philosopher, interested in epistemology and feminist theory. Her theme is that we should abandon the search for the "one true theory." Rather we should see various theories as differing lenses upon a complicated reality. This is not to say that one can never dispute a theorist's arguments or a theory's implications, but that it would be more fruitful to stop pressing for a single true theory. Accordingly, she uses her essay to show how each theory she discusses provides a lens through which to see both the gender system and other theories about the gender system. She believes that alternating between each theory as a lens on others helps us to find the truths and limitations of each perspective.

Molm is a sociologist who does experimental work to develop social exchange theory. She devotes most of her essay to showing how the four substantive papers she discusses, those offering a macrostructural perspective, a network perspective, expectation states theory, and rational-choice theory, can be put together into an integrated view that takes us a long way toward understanding gender inequality. Such integration can take the form of macro-micro linkages when generalizations at one level of analysis are exogenous inputs to theories operating at another level of analysis. For example, macrostructural perspectives, operating at a macrolevel where societies or other geographical aggregates are units of analysis, may tell us the conditions under which sexist ideology or a particular gender division of labor is most likely. Institutionalized forms of these macrocharacteristics may be assumed by theories operating at an interactional level. For example, expectation states theory takes the cultural belief that men are generally more competent than women at instrumental tasks as a given, itself unexplained by the theory. Its focus is then on how the theory says that this belief plays out interactionally. Similarly, rational-choice theorists may take some macrolevel institutional constraints as given, and study results of individual choices under these constraints, sometimes including how these choices reproduce old or form new institutions. Network theorists take some initial gender differences in information or behavior as exogenous and study how this produces more gender differentiated worlds via network processes.

Links between micro and macro are also thematized by Folbre's commentary. Folbre is an economist who attempts to combine neoclassical, Marxist, and feminist theories in her work. She sees structural constraints as one determinant of the choices individuals make (their preferences being another determinant). On the other hand, such choices, in aggregation, are inputs into the formation of structures. She rejects any attempt to see either the micro-to-macro or macro-to-micro direction as less fundamental. She argues for a focus on how structural conditions (including laws, norms, distributions of property) create overlapping vectors of collective interests and identities based on gender, race, class, and nation (and probably other distinctions), and how coalitions are (or are not) mobilized to reproduce or change structures involving production (in the household and the firm) and distribution.

Wilson is a sociological theorist with special interests in the Marxist tradition. He argues that to contribute to theory, feminism must somehow steer a course that avoids both essentialism and nominalism. If everything about current gender arrangements is a simple, relatively unmediated consequence of biological or other "essential" differences between men and women, there is no need for social theory and no chance of social transformation. On the other hand, Wilson argues that if what the theory sees as determinative of gender inequality is some social location in which men and women could potentially change places, then no claim can be made that gender (or patriarchy) is an irreducible social structure. Thus, he thinks that an irreducible difference between men and women must be maintained in the theory, and the various ways that social structures can mediate them must be discussed. Wilson also advocates an epistemology he calls "social realism," which rejects the positivist limitation of ontology to the observable, but stays with the Enlightenment commitment that one true theory can eventually be found by a combination of praxis and intellectual work.

Despite all the variety of viewpoints in the chapters that follow, the reader will note one commonality. The application of each theory to gender starts by assuming some initial difference in how males and females behave or are treated. This initial difference is, itself, unexplained by the theory. Generally the authors are silent about what biological or social forces produced this difference historically or developmentally. This assumed difference is generally not a core assumption of the theory—after all, few of these theories were devised with special attention to gender. Rather, the assumption of some initial difference is necessary for practitioners of the theory to apply it to the topic of gender. Other practitioners of the same theory might apply it to gender differently, choosing a different initial difference to work through the logic of the theory. (Analogous starting assumptions would be necessary to apply these theories to any other topic.) An assumed difference is sometimes that women, not men, do child rearing. We see this in the papers focusing on Marxist, world system, psychoanalytic, and network theories. The assumed starting point may be beliefs about men's and women's relative competence at instrumental tasks, as in expectation states theory. It may be the belief that there are two fundamentally different sexes, as in the ethnomethodological treatment offered in this volume. It may be small sex differences in children's information and network-formation tendencies, as in the network theory presented here. For other theorists, the initial difference may be variable, with the theory producing a variety of if-then statements, as in the presentations of macrostructural and rational choice theories offered here. In each case, the theorizing then takes the form of working this initial difference through the processes the theory thematizes, producing a conclusion about the result for gender of these initial differences in a social system that operates in the way posited by the theory.

The reader may become frustrated, wondering at the end of each chapter whether it is not this initial assumed difference on which the argument hinges, even though this difference is itself unexplained by the theory. This is partly true, but there is no way out of the dilemma. In part this is because few of the theories here purport to be explanations of the historical origins of gender inequality. In part it is because every theory, even a theory of origins, must have assumptions to derive conclusions. The important thing to note is that the argument advanced never turns *entirely* on the initial assumed difference. Otherwise, the theory would contribute nothing. What each theorist contributes is clarification of how the social processes at the core of the theory determine what, if anything, will be made of this initial difference. Beyond this similarity, the theorists focus on very different aspects of social processes. My hope in assembling this volume has been to contribute to dialogue that enhances our understanding of the forces that produce, reproduce, and challenge gender inequality, and of the strengths and limitations, including gender biases, of sociological theories.

PART II

Theoretical Perspectives on Gender

Chapter 2

Shotgun Wedding, Unhappy Marriage, No-Fault Divorce? Rethinking the Feminism-Marxism Relationship

Beth Anne Shelton and Ben Agger

The question of how feminism relates to Marxism has been asked and answered so many times that yet another discussion of it may seem redundant. Yet we believe that the question of the feminism-Marxism relationship, while posed often, has been addressed inadequately. Most of the work pertaining to this issue assumes that there is some essential difference between feminism and Marxism and that the relevant project is to mend fences. While we are not opposed to fence mending in general, we do not believe that feminism and Marxism are fundamentally different or opposed traditions. Given that Marxism and feminism can be conceived as a common theory of oppression, at least with respect to gender, we reject the prevailing readings of class and gender, Marxism and feminism, that address them as distinct perspectives and then try to reconcile them.

We also reject the orthodox-Marxist perspective that dismisses unwaged labor as unimportant, but preserve what we regard as the essence of Marxism. Marxism is an analysis of exploitation in capitalism, where exploitation is defined as the appropriation of surplus value from its producers, including people (mainly women) who engage in unwaged domestic labor. This exploitation is possible where individual producers (and reproducers) do not control the means of production. Thus, workers are exploited to the extent that they produce value (in the form of commodities) for which they are not paid. Every workday is then composed of a paid and an unpaid part. In our analysis, we extend the definition of the workday to include unpaid household labor as well as that part of the workday spent "on the job." In this sense, women's unpaid household labor, in reproducing labor power, produces surplus value, just as surplus value is produced by so-called productive labor. The reproductive work performed in the household is fundamentally the same as productive work, except that it is completely unwaged rather than partially unwaged. Thus, unlike orthodox Marxists who see unpaid household labor as essentially outside and irrelevant to capitalism, we see it as surplus labor (i.e., labor that produces surplus value).

Our version of Marxism allows us to understand both women's and men's productive and reproductive labor. It also makes clear that while men may benefit from women's labor, at least in the short term, capital exploits women's labor, both waged and unwaged, just as it does men's.

What is at stake here is more than intellectual coherence or innovation. Marxism and feminism are perspectives on the empirical world. As such, how one theorizes the relationship between them has implications for what empirical questions are deemed appropriate or important as well as for how the empirical world is interpreted. This is not to say that one can "test" any of this. Rather, we argue that Marxism and feminism are worldviews and theories of practice that frame the interpretation of evidence. Marx and Engels (1959, p. 245) were correct when, in the final thesis on Feuerbach, they said that the aim of theory (or science) is to change the world; as such, a theory's validity is proven by the extent to which it is successful in changing the world, not in terms of whether data support the hypotheses derived from the theory (i.e., positivism).

Marxism and feminism are political practices as well as theories. As such, they theorize and oppose oppression. The academization of Marxism and feminism has proceeded so far that they have become merely symbols of affiliation. Indeed, Marxism and feminism are generally accepted as modes of scholarship, literatures, degree programs, and academic journals (see Jacoby 1987). One claims Marxism or feminism on the basis of what one has read, the courses one has taken and teaches, the journals to which one subscribes. One of the hottest commodities in the American university today (at least on the fringes) is feminist theory. By the same token, so-called Marxist theory abounds. What is at stake in this reflection on the Marxism/feminism relationship is more than scholarship. At issue is politics. Where Marxism and feminism are jealously divided by territorial concerns they cannot combine to fight their common enemy. What we address here is that common enemy. While many feminists would argue that "male Marxism" is as problematic as male non-Marxism, there is a difference between noting the sexism of men and acknowledging the theoretical and political commonality between Marxism and feminism. Women/feminists can find a theoretical and political home within Marxism and men/Marxists can find one within feminism.

Our interest in this paper is to reconceive Marxism and feminism as the same discourses, the same theoretical, empirical, and political practices in terms of how they deal with gender. This reconceptualization may seem strange to most people on the left, who assume that Marxism and feminism are different theories and practices, the one of and by men and the other of and by women. But we want to challenge this conventional assumption because we oppose this dualism, both in terms of empirical analysis and political practice. In only a few decades, American Marxism and feminism have become alien to each other, indexing the extent to which incorrect assumptions about gender politics have gotten out of hand.

The argument about the identity of Marxism and feminism has been elaborated before (see Agger 1989a, 1989b), albeit in the terms of recondite European social theory. In this paper, we want to restate that argument with reference to the two dominant formulations of the relationship between Marxism and feminism now current in American intellectual life as well as in terms of the empirical and political implications of our perspective. Below, we describe and reject the dualist and the capitalist-patriarchy perspectives on Marxism and feminism and propose our own position on the Marxism and feminism relationship. We recognize that left feminism is, in fact, somewhat more diverse than we are supposing for the sake of argument. Nevertheless, it is clear that most left feminists fall into, or somewhere nearby, either the dualist or the capitalist-patriarchy camp.

A Note about Left Feminism

By left feminism we denote any intellectual and political perspective sympathetic to both Marxism and feminism. Of course, the dominant strain of feminism in the United States today is what Jaggar (1983) has called liberal feminism. This is the National Organization of Women (NOW) feminism that attempts to reduce male domination through rational discussion among women and men, to remove legal barriers to women's work force entry, and to ensure their equal treatment in the paid labor force (Friedan 1963). We join those who regard liberal feminism as procapitalist, only improving the situation of middle- and upper-middle-class women by affording them somewhat greater opportunities for career mobility but not significantly changing the plight of women of color, working-class women, working-class men, or Third World men and women.

Left feminism is also distinct from so-called radical feminism (e.g., Firestone 1970). Radical feminism essentially disregards issues of class or capitalism, focusing instead on male power and male-dominated culture as a source of women's oppression. Radical feminists attack patriarchy, especially the patriarchal family, as the sole system of domination. Unlike liberal feminism, radical feminism rejects the male-centered family as oppressive in its own terms. Radical feminists view men and women as classes, or sex classes (Firestone 1970), fundamentally opposed in their common interests. Unlike left feminism, radical feminism does not regard the relationship between family and work as particularly important. Instead, radical feminists argue that women's subordination in the household is somehow prior to, and more important than, their subordination in the paid labor force. Moreover, they see women's subordination in the household as a function of patriarchy, rather than capitalism.

Radical feminism reconceptualizes women's domestic activity as productive in its own right, suggesting a valuable line of argument for left feminists who want to understand women's oppression in the same terms that we understand men's oppression, that is, in terms of the value that women produce in the household. In addition, oppression can be understood in terms of the relationship between productive and reproductive activity. By valorizing housework and sexuality, radical feminists valorize the whole sphere of reproduction as politically salient, an insight that is central to left feminism. Where liberal feminism views what transpires in the household as essentially irrelevant economically and politically (e.g., to be merely a topic of role renegotiation for women and men), radical feminists politicize and economize the family, albeit without understanding the full theoretical, empirical, and political implications of this move. The valorization of household labor has taken fullest form in the Wages for Housework movement (e.g., James and Dalla Costa 1973), which in certain respects could be categorized as radical feminist as well as left feminist.

Left feminists reject liberal feminism for endorsing capitalist gender relations, while they reject radical feminism for ignoring capitalism altogether. The political impact of left feminism in the United States is negligible for the same reason that the political impact of any coherent left perspective is insignificant (see Kann 1982): Marxism is regarded as a foreign, totalitarian movement best equated with Soviet terror (Agger 1989b). By the same token, radical feminism, with its attack on the patriarchal family, is typically caricatured as the province of maladapted women. It is even arguable whether liberal feminism is a particularly credible perspective in post-Reagan America, especially given the conservative attack on hard-won reproductive rights as well as the seeming "post"-feminism of the post–baby boom generation of women. Although a majority of Americans seem to favor legalized abortion under certain circumstances, it is a real question whether most Americans, even women, identify themselves as feminist in the sense that they challenge some of the fundamental definitions and practices of hetero-sexist gender relations today.

As a result, we want to check the tendency on the left to solve political problems theoretically, through self-reproducing academic nitpicking. Left feminism is virtually nonexistent in contemporary America; at best, it is relevant to a few academics and fringe political groups. Thus, for us to reconceptualize the Marxism/feminism connection has very little political salience. Indeed, one of the most damaging outcomes of liberal feminism is its blithe progressivism—its assumption that, in fact, women are making progress in the same inexorable way that the Enlightenment *philosophes* assumed that people and societies would advance since the seventeenth century. In fact, data indicate that women are still overrepresented among these in poverty, earn less than men, and are occupationally segregated. As we just noted, it is doubtful that even liberal feminism as a political theory has made much lasting headway in the United States.

Part of what it means to be a left feminist involves a good deal of empirical skepticism about the inevitability of gender and class "progress," especially in light of their recent reversals. Although left feminism is a theory of practice, frequently left feminists must conclude that transformative political action is structurally blocked by huge global forces. In this sense, left feminism is as much an analysis of what is going wrong as it is an action plan. This disqualifies left feminism only if we allow optimism to become a theoretical category in its own right. A serious student of the Left recognizes that the story of the Left is much more a story of defeat than of triumph (see Jacoby 1981). But at least we can claim to have asked some of the right questions at a time when the mainstream's idiocy (e.g., "you've come a long way, baby") suffocates nearly all critique. There are few on the American left, either male or female, who can resist the temptation to view the world through rose-colored lenses. This optimism, combined with intellectuals' hubris, has produced a thousand essays on the occlusions and opportunities of a feminist Marxism or a Marxist feminism. The existence of these essays does not erase the fact that they are typically read by only hundreds, not hundreds of millions.

Dualism

The first species of left feminism's articulation of the Marxism/feminism relationship to be considered here is dualism, a version of left feminism in some respects closer to radical feminism than to the Marxist feminism that we propose below. Dualists (Delphy 1977, 1984) suggest that women's oppression and class-based oppression are essentially separate, especially in the sense that they pertain to different spheres (Walby 1986). Some dualists suggest that patriarchy and capitalism are in conflict in the sense that patriarchy wants to keep women at home while capitalism wants them to work outside the home (Walby 1986, p. 57). Thus, they suggest, there is a certain inevitable tension between patriarchy and capitalism as social systems of domination. Others (e.g., Hartman 1979a, 1979b) see patriarchy and capitalism as analytically distinct but as mutually reinforcing. We should note that other scholars (e.g., Fraser 1989) use the term *dualism* to describe what we call capitalist-patriarchy feminism, discussed below. We retain the term *dualism* because we think it best characterizes the position on the class-gender interaction typical of theorists like Delphy.

Dualists argue that, although analytically distinct, capitalism and patriarchy nevertheless occur together in history. For example, the United States is both a patriarchal and a capitalist social order, requiring dualists carefully to disentangle patriarchy and capitalism as systems of oppression that impinge differentially on individual women's lives. It is suggested that some women are more oppressed by capitalism than by patriarchy, where, for instance, they participate in the paid labor force and they have relatively egalitarian relationships in the household. Other women are more oppressed by patriarchy, where they are exploited as much as men in the labor market but are responsible for all of the work in their household.

Dualist left feminism is especially compelling where it seems to counter the male Marxism that virtually ignores women's oppression in the household, instead concentrating only on exploitation in the paid labor market. Although it is true that male Marxism has been historically and theoretically inured to sexism as a central basis of contemporary oppression, this does not mean that the household and labor market operate according to different logics. Dualist left feminism usefully draws attention to the household as a vital region of experience, a public sphere worthy of consideration by political theorists (Fraser 1989). But in valorizing the household as a site of sexual politics, many dualist left feminists, like liberal feminists, exaggerate the extent to which the capitalist labor market operates according to a nondiscriminatory logic of reward (Jaggar 1983). Even among those who see patriarchy as supportive of capitalism, it is a mistake to see the subordination of women as a consequence of patriarchy rather than capitalism (e.g., Hartman 1979b) as if patriarchy and capitalism are different systems or structures.

Their argument goes this way: Given the logic of capitalism, over time women will be treated like men in the paid labor force. What instances of sex discrimination there are are merely vestiges of traditional patriarchal ideology. In a certain sense, to be sure, capitalism is sex-blind and color-blind: People's worth is equivalent to the value of their labor power, in Marx's terms. But this prejudges the issue. We prefer to view women's economic discrimination in the paid labor force as a structural outcome of advanced capitalism—a systematic way for capitalism to hierarchize the work force in order both to divide and conquer the proletariat (Engels's notion of a labor aristocracy) and to increase profit on the backs of women (people of color, deskilled labor, the lumpenproletariat, workers in the Third World, workers in the informal economy). That is, women's economic disadvantage in the paid labor force creates a division between women and men that is useful in forestalling the development of working-class consciousness. At the same time, the low pay of sectors of the working class allows for more profit, at the expense of super exploited members of the working class (i.e., women).

Where women are not treated the same as men in paid labor, according to dualists, this is because patriarchal ideology holds sway in the workplace (extended from household roles). Indeed, men are conceptualized as a different sex class (to use Firestone's (1970) radical-feminist terminology) from women, to whom their interests are opposed. This leads dualist left feminists to focus on issues of wage discrimination as if these issues were not part and parcel of capitalism itself (which rewards workers differently from capitalists). Where dualists view the logic of capital as essentially sex-blind, we regard it as the *same* logic that hierarchizes men over women in the patriarchal family. Marx did not understand this, partly because the proletariat in the mid-1800s was largely composed of men. Only later did Engels (1948) (unsuccessfully) theorize women's oppression. To assume, as dualist left feminists do, that capitalism operates differently from the patriarchal family in the sense that it rewards men and women equally is, we believe, empirically and theoretically false. Although the realms of household and paid work are not exactly identical in late capitalism, we maintain below that they operate according to exactly the same logic of devalorization-of-otherness that subordinates women, people of color, fractions of male labor, and members of the informal economy.

In effect, dualist left feminism suggests that capitalism and patriarchy are two quite separate systems, often seen as separated by the distance between household and economy. Delphy (1977, 1984) talks about the "household mode of production" as if it is different from the market mode of production. It is very difficult for dualists to analyze society as a totality given their view that men's and women's worlds are separate, a view in part owed to both radical feminism and postmodernist feminism (e.g., see Weedon 1987). Although it is true that men's and women's life experiences markedly differ in certain respects, we believe that to suggest that there are separate worlds for men and for women is both empirically and politically unfruitful. Men and women share the same world, albeit unequally.

As for the dualist contention that women and men may inhabit the same world but have different interests, thus requiring the differentiation of patriarchy from capitalism, this is both true and false. Certainly working-class men (like virtually all men), who expect unpaid household labor from their wives, in some sense exploit them directly. But we believe that it is more fruitful to conceptualize this double oppression of women (once in the household, a second time in the paid labor force) as a function of capitalism, which requires unpaid household labor in order to reproduce men's and children's labor power. Although individual men may be seen to benefit from the sexual division of labor, this is less important structurally and politically than the fact that capitalism benefits; indeed, capitalism organizes gender relations in such a way that women and men accept that household labor—women's work—will not be waged.

This is very much a matter of emphasis. Dualists concentrate on how individual men benefit from patriarchal capitalism; we prefer to focus on how oppressed groups are hierarchized and divided in order for them not to recognize and act against their common enemy. Patriarchal ideology that justifies the bourgeois family is certainly a factor in overall domination. But this ideology is not composed by all men but merely by the custodians of patriarchy and capitalism, the busy scribes who write advertising, science, religion, journalism, and popular culture, portraying oppression as socially necessary and inevitable. Although individual men benefit from patriarchy, to put the emphasis here diverts attention from the larger structures of capitalism within which women and men are pitted against each other.

One of the most serious weaknesses of dualist left feminism is that it does not suggest a coherent vision of an alternative social order. In large measure, this is because dualism does not sufficiently indict capitalism but only argues that capitalism and patriarchy are *different* systems of oppression. In this respect, dualists are perhaps closer to being radical feminists than they are to being left feminists. To them patriarchy, not capitalism, is the main problem. Although dualist left feminists like Delphy do not approve of capitalism, capitalism is seen primarily as men's problem, where patriarchy is *the* problem for women. Dualists are led to conclude that women's oppression is more or less equivalent to male dominance in the household. Hence, the solution to women's oppression in paid labor is simply to do away with patriarchy, as if that will somehow liberate women in paid labor from the caprice of men who willfully discriminate against them on the basis of an ideology of male supremacy, extended from the household to the labor market. But if we eliminate the patriarchal family and sex discrimination in paid labor, what remains? What remains is capitalism, only shorn of the remnants of gender inequality.

Capitalist-Patriarchy

Capitalist-patriarchy feminists accept that capitalism and patriarchy are separate but connected social formations; they are functionally interrelated in the sense that capitalism is useful for patriarchy and patriarchy is useful for capitalism. [Eisenstein (1979, 1981) is a capitalist-patriarchy theorist.] Perhaps the majority of left feminists hold this view, as Jaggar (1983) and Donovan (1985) suggest. These left feminists are more explicitly Marxist than are dualists, who remain closer to radical feminists in their view of Marxism.

One might even say that the capitalist-patriarchy version of left feminism is the official marriage of Marxism and feminism. This version of Marxism-feminism has a place for class and a place for gender. It is understood by capitalist-patriarchy theorists that patriarchy preceded capitalism and remains somewhat separate from it today, especially in the way in which traditional sexist ideologies predominate both in the household and market spheres. Unlike dualists, capitalist-patriarchy theorists recognize many points of complementarity between capitalism and patriarchy, although, unlike us here, this complementarity is understood mainly in terms of functional interrelatedness rather than in terms of dialectical interweavings to the point of indistinguishability. These capitalist-patriarchy theorists offer the useful insight that housework, which is done primarily by women, is an economic contribution to capitalism (Benston 1970; James and Dalla Costa 1973). Socialist feminists expand Marx's labor theory of value to include both waged and unwaged labor, refusing to accept a separation of public and private spheres. They argue that there is no "private" sphere.

Like dualism, capitalist-patriarchy theory assumes that capitalism and patriarchy are clearly differentiable but historically connected systems of oppression. Like dualism, this makes some metaphysical leaps, notably in terms of how analysts distinguish between capitalist and patriarchal phenomena. Although a good deal of energy has been expended in defining their differences, we feel that these have been exercises in scholasticism given the permeability of the boundary between the two sets of phenomena. We do not believe that it is correct to view capitalism and patriarchy as separate orders of being, regardless of how and in what ways the two systems are connected analytically.

Capitalism and patriarchy are at best theoretical constructs. But many Marxists and feminists give them undue ontological substance without carefully evaluating the assumptions implicit in the concepts. We agree with capitalist-patriarchy theorists that it is not fruitful to conceptualize capitalism and patriarchy as antagonistic forces. But we disagree that it makes sense to conceptualize capitalism and patriarchy, or class and gender, as separate systems, structures, or practices given how much they have in common. Whether or not they are distinguishable is largely a rhetorical problem; we can define anything into or out of existence. After all, what the left understands to be an inherently antagonistic social order—capitalism—is conceived by neoclassical economists as a benign, stable, well-functioning, and equitable matrix of exchange relationships. Data cannot settle this argument. It is the role of theory to construct the world in broad strokes that enable us to understand the empirical particulars comprising it. We cannot simply search for entities called "capitalism" and "patriarchy" as if that would solve the substantive problems haunting a left-feminist approach to the complexly interwoven structures of domination.

Although we accept the capitalist-patriarchy critique of dualist left feminism, agreeing that class and gender oppression are compatible and interconnected, we, like Jaggar (1983), seriously doubt that a more unified feminist Marxism or Marxist feminism sufficiently sheds the hidden dualisms of liberalism to theorize creatively. Indeed, feminism's relatively scanty philosophical foundation (compared to Marxism's) makes it very difficult for any self-professed feminism to be any but a partial theory of society and thus a partial political practice. In other words, we worry that even the most radicalized left feminism fails to break with the individualism underlying almost all of Western philosophy, leading variously to pluralism, political liberalism, methodological individualism, and interest group theory.

The problem with this interest group approach to social theory is that it fails to understand the complex interlinkages and mediations structuring the social totality and making victims similar. It is the essence of Marxism to resist interest group theories, like Weber's, that fail to recognize structuring principles of the social totality. Of course, in today's trendy postmodern philosophical climate, it is no wonder that many feminists (e.g., Weedon 1987) have flocked to postmodernism and poststructuralism as epistemologies with which to reject Marxism yet again. Derrida, Lyotard, Barthes, Foucault, and the so-called French feminists (Irigaray 1985; Kristeva 1980) reject Marxist "metanarratives" (Lyotard 1984) in favor of the "small stories" told by people occupying different "subject positions" that are judged to be inherently incommensurable, as such resistant to totalizing analysis and political practice. Instead, as with all liberalism, victims occupying these putatively heterogeneous subject positions are supposed to tell their own "stories," the "narratives" that empower them to change their own lifeworlds (Habermas 1984, 1987).

Left Feminism's Latent Liberalism

In this sense, most feminisms—left, right, and center—unfortunately reject Marxism's stress on totality, on global explanation and transformation. We would argue that Lyotard's (1984) aversion to Marxist "metanarratives" is yet another articulation of Bell's (1960) original end-of-ideology thesis, according to which class conflict has been overcome in the direction of a postindustrial cornucopia of limitless goods and services. Postmodernism is not significantly different from liberalism, embracing the chic cynicism and irony characteristic of the 1990s.

In this way, we suspect that left feminism needlessly gives up a perspective on the social totality that explains the global structures of domination in terms of their common features and functioning. The separation of capitalism and patriarchy almost inevitably accompanies an interest group pluralism and liberalism that advocate piecemeal redistributive changes. The understandable feminist critique of orthodox male Marxism gives way to a rejection of the very totalizing that makes Marxist historical materialism such a politically relevant perspective. That Marx missed or misunderstood the oppression of women does not mean that we have to give up Marxism's claim to totality. It signals rather that we must rethink Marxism in terms that improve its grasp on the totality, notably by incorporating perspectives from feminism, critical theory, and various interpretive theories developed in response to changes in capitalism simply unforeseen by Marx.

At this point, we reach the most important fork in the road. And, again, discourse plays a telling role. Most left feminists argue that Marxism is incomplete, requiring a feminist addition from the outside. Feminists disagree about how much weight Marxism is to be given in the feminist-Marxist synthesis. Dualists clearly give Marxism less weight than do capitalist-patriarchy theorists. But we wonder whether it makes sense to formulate a model of oppression in which feminism explains part and Marxism explains part. Domination cannot be parceled out into disconnected fragments not joined together in a coherent structured totality. Marxism and feminism cannot be successfully joined without being blended to the point of indistinguishability.

Against Hyphenation

The argument that we simply want to subordinate feminism to Marxism assumes that feminism and Marxism are different. While most Marxists and feminists resolve the domestic-labor debate differently, theirs are not fundamentally different perspectives. We believe that Marxism is the more global and agile analytical strategy because it offers a perspective on the interrelatedness of the totality. Marxism transcends particularism in a way that feminism does not. Whether that ignores the particularities of women's experience and objective reality is another question. We are convinced that Marxism in its best sense is feminism (and that feminism can become Marxism once it learns not to hyphenate itself). The hyphenation of Marxism and feminism is not simply a rhetorical move; it separates men and women who should be united in the conquest of their common enemy. As Rabine (1983) has argued, the hyphen dividing Marxism and feminism conceals secret hierarchy— either Marxism over feminism or feminism over Marxism.

This leaves us as Marxists and feminists curiously opposing the Marxism-feminism integration. We endorse feminism as theoretical and political practice; we oppose the notion that feminism is a distinctive perspective on oppression that somehow stands on its own against Marxism. Feminism and Marxism are profoundly different where Marxists try to explain everything and feminists only the plight of women. Feminists of all sorts will proclaim that Marxists have always ignored women. Although true, that is no reason whatsoever to jettison Marxism, a perspective on totality in which women have a central place. The logic of Marxism includes women just as it includes people of color. What we seek is a new Marxism, not a hyphenated Marxism-feminism that pretends that Marxism is "about" working-class men and feminism "about" women. The only kind of Marxism that ignores parts of the totality is precisely the interest group Marxism of Weber—his well-named conflict theory, according to which plural groups' conflicts will be everlasting (see Agger 1989b). In many respects then, the Marxism that left feminists try to hyphenate *is not Marxism at all*.

Can there be another Marxism, that includes women? There can be another Marxism if we recognize that Marxism is *not* simply a theory of class but a theory of everything, including women. Marxism is a theory of gender oppression *if* we understand Marxism to be a theory and critique of the hierarchy of productive over reproductive activity. For Marxists to "wage" housework conceptually is extremely easy and has been done (e.g., Benston 1970; James and Dalla Costa 1973). Although individual male Marxists may refuse defensively to valorize all of the historically unwaged reproductive activities millennially done by women, the logic of Marxism readily enables us to valorize these reproductive activities. Let it be said again: Housework produces surplus value in that it produces workers. A part of every paid work day, it is surplus labor. That is, it is labor that is not compensated. In reproducing labor power, other things are produced in the household (e.g., transportation), and the household serves important cultural and ideological functions for capital as well. Marx (1973) wrote the *Grundrisse* precisely to develop a theory of reproduction. He only failed to recognize that household labor is perhaps the most important form of reproduction. Engels's (1948) *The Origin of the Family, Private Property and the State* is an unsuccessful effort to economize household labor, failing to theorize women's unwaged household labor correctly and to issue a relevant agenda of sexual-political changes.

Admittedly, all sorts of Marxists deny the relevance of housework to Marx's theory of surplus value (see Smith 1978). That says more about them and their sexual ideology than about Marxism itself. One might object that there is no Marxism apart from Marxists. But there are Marxists who endorse feminism politically and who use essentially feminist categories in order to rejuvenate Marxism as the most enduring theory of totality. Whether we call ourselves Marxists or feminists is somewhat beside the point, even acknowledging that such naming exercises are inherently political. What matters most is the way in which we accommodate Marxism to emancipatory theories and practices historically outside it, including feminism and critical theory.

We solve the problem of hyphenation by our understanding of Marxism as including a theory and critique of the hierarchy of value over valuelessness as part of the logic of capitalism. Of course, feminism can also claim to be the theory and critique of all such hierarchies—at least a feminism that relentlessly totalizes, refusing to be only a "voice" of women or a "story" told by members of a special interest group. Indeed, we feminize Marxism with feminist resources: After all, it was feminism that said that the personal is political or, in Marxist parlance, that seemingly valueless activity produces (and is robbed of) value. Housework is political because housework contributes to capitalist political economy.

Empirical Implications of a Feminist Marxism

Our theoretical unification of Marxism and feminism has empirical implications as well. Traditionally, sociologists have treated the economy and the household as if they were not only analytically distinct but empirically separated. The result is empirical research on women's and men's participation in the labor market without adequate (or often, any) consideration of the implications of, or for, the household division of labor. Women's status as deskilled, nonunionized, underpaid workers both reflects and reproduces their status as caretakers in the household. The only real difference between women's paid and unpaid labor is that one brings direct economic returns in the form of a wage and the other does not. They are the same in that they both help reproduce capitalism and patriarchy.

Women's status in the household makes them more exploitable in the paid labor market, while their exploitation in the labor market reinforces their subordinated position in the household. Those empirically oriented sociologists who fail to see these ties fundamentally misunderstand both the paid and the unpaid—the public and private—spheres.

Empirically, women's responsibility for the household negatively affects them in the labor market in three ways. Women's time spent on unpaid household labor represents time they do not have to spend in paid labor. Thus, women's position in the household has a negative impact on their paid labor time (Firestone and Shelton 1988). Reduced hours in paid labor have both a direct and indirect effect on earnings. Part-time workers, or even those who work fewer overtime hours, are less likely to be viewed as committed to the paid labor force and thus are less likely to be promoted and rewarded in other ways. Women's responsibility for the household and for child care also has an impact on their educational attainment, affecting choice of major as well as the timing of education, which in turn has an impact on women's labor force participation.

Women's role as caretakers in the household also carries over into the labor market, where they are viewed as helpmates, working as children's teachers and service workers. Both because of the work involved as well as because women do this work, these positions are rewarded less than male-typed occupations. Finally, even when women work full-time and in jobs similar to men, they are rewarded less than men (Blau and Ferber 1986, p. 175). This reflects the view that women are less committed to paid labor, at least partly because of their presumed commitment to home and hearth. Housework and child care time also affect women in the labor force through their impact on work continuity. Women's movement into and out of the labor market means that they sacrifice job ladder seniority that men do not.

The nature of women's labor market experiences also affects their position in the household. Women's lower earnings and their concentration in the pink-collar ghetto mean that they have fewer resources with which to resist the imposition of household and child care chores (Blood and Wolfe 1960; Ericksen, Yancey, and Ericksen 1979). Men's greater power resulting from their labor market resources can be used in the household in order to resist efforts to redistribute household responsibilities (Ross 1987). Women's lower earnings in the paid labor market also mean that, from the perspective of the household, it is more economically rational for a woman to forfeit paid labor for household labor than it is for a man to do so (Becker 1981). That is, it will cost the household less to forfeit a woman's earnings than to forfeit a man's earnings. In this way, women's subordination in the labor market reinforces their subordination in the household.

It is clear from the empirical evidence that it is impossible to understand the "choices" women make about the labor market without understanding their roles in the household (Coverman 1983). At the same time, the nature of women's participation in the paid labor force and their earnings have an impact on their position in the household. Women with subordinate positions in the labor market are more likely to have subordinate positions in the household. Thus, even a basic empirical understanding of the household division of labor and of women's position in the labor market is impossible without focusing on both.

The Marxism we propose thus allows us to offer an interpretation of women's and men's roles in the labor market and in the household that avoids the ad hoc interpretations that are common. While there are certainly microlevel processes that affect particular women's and men's housework and paid work time, the general pattern that we find is consistent with the interpretation that we offer. Women's subordinated position in the labor market, and their labor in the household, means that their rate of exploitation is higher than men's. That is, women perform more labor for which they are not remunerated, thus producing more surplus value than men. This clearly benefits capital and is therefore understandable in terms of the logic of capitalism. This interpretation of women's labor allows us to understand it without reference to men's benefits. Of course, men benefit from women's unpaid household labor, and they may benefit from reduced competition in the paid labor force, but the logic behind women's position is the logic of capitalism; it is not necessary to see women's subordination as a product of patriarchy. A feminized Marxism can provide a better theoretical understanding of women's subordination than can the theory of patriarchy, whether seen as separated from or tied to capitalism. In addition, this feminized Marxism offers a theoretical rationale for empirically examining the relationship between the household and the labor market instead of doing so based only on empirical relationships.

What all this means strategically is unclear. As we said in the beginning, the sectarian quarrels over the pedigree of one's emancipatory theory mean next to nothing in this age. It is understandable that left women refuse to claim Marxism when most Marxists are antifeminist. But that is no reason not to interrogate the possibility that feminism is so deeply rooted in Western liberalism, dualism, and pluralism that no amount of its seeming radicalization will help it replace Marxism as the most relevant emancipatory philosophy of our time. That is not to defeat feminism with Marxism. We are feminists. But inasmuch as Marxism is the more total, if incomplete, emancipatory theory and practice, we conceive of feminism as a moment in a rejuvenated, feminized Marxism. The fact that few (male) Marxists subscribe to this feminized Marxism only underlines the need for serious articulation of these two emancipatory perspectives. The orthodox-Marxist position on the domestic-labor debate is proof positive that sexist Marxism is no different from sexist non-Marxism.

References

Agger, Ben. 1989a. *Fast Capitalism: A Critical Theory of Significance*. Urbana, IL: University of Illinois Press.
———. 1989b. *Socio(onto)logy: A Disciplinary Reading*. Urbana, IL: University of Illinois Press.
Becker, Gary. 1981. *A Treatise on the Family*. Cambridge, MA: Harvard University Press.
Bell, Daniel. 1960. *The End of Ideology*. Glencoe, IL: Free Press.
Benston, Margaret. 1970. "The Political Economy of Women's Liberation." Pp. 279–92 in *Voices from Women's Liberation*, edited by Leslie B. Tanner. New York: Signet.
Blau, Francine D. and Marianne A. Ferber. 1986. *The Economics of Women, Men and Work*. Englewood Cliffs, NJ: Prentice-Hall.
Blood, Robert O., and Donald M. Wolfe. 1960. *Husbands and Wives*. Glencoe, IL: Free Press.
Coverman, Shelley. 1983. "Gender, Domestic Labor Time, and Wage Inequality." *American Sociological Review* 48:623–37.
Delphy, Christine. 1977. *The Main Enemy*. London: Women's Research and Resources Centre.
———. 1984. *Close to Home: A Materialist Analysis of Women's Oppression*. London: Hutchinson.
Donovan, Josephine. 1985. *Feminist Theory*. New York: Ungar.
Eisenstein, Zillah (ed.). 1979. *Capitalist Patriarchy and the Case for Socialist Feminism*. New York: Monthly Review Press.
———. 1981. *The Radical Future of Liberal Feminism*. New York: Longman.
Engels, Friedrich. [18] 1948. *The Origin of the Family, Private Property and the State*. Moscow: Progress Publishers.
Ericksen, Julia A., William L. Yancey, and Eugene P. Ericksen. 1979. "The Division of Family Roles." *Journal of Marriage and the Family* 41:301–13.

Firestone, Juanita, and Beth Anne Shelton. 1988. "An Examination of the Effects of Women's Work on Available Leisure Time." *Journal of Family Issues* 9(4):478–95.

Firestone, Shulamith. 1970. *The Dialectic of Sex.* New York: Bantam.

Fraser, Nancy. 1989. *Unruly Practices: Gender, Discourse and Power in Social Theory.* Minneapolis: University of Minnesota Press.

Freidan, Betty. 1963. *The Feminine Mystique.* New York: Dell.

Habermas, Jurgen. 1984. *The Theory of Communicative Action*, Vol. 1. Boston: Beacon.

———. 1987. *The Theory of Communicative Action*, Vol. 2. Boston: Beacon.

Hartmann, Heidi. 1979a. "Capitalism, Patriarchy and Job Segregation by Sex." Pp. 206–47 in *Capitalist Patriarchy and the Case for Socialist Feminism*, edited by Zillah Eisenstein. New York: Monthly Review Press.

———. 1979b. "The Unhappy Marriage and Marxism and Feminism: Towards a More Progressive Union." *Capital and Class* 8:1–33.

Irigaray, Luce. 1985. *This Sex Which Is Not One.* Ithaca, NY: Cornell University Press.

Jacoby, Russell. 1981. *Dialectic of Defeat.* New York: Cambridge University Press.

———. 1987. *The Last Intellectuals: American Culture in the Age of Academe.* New York: Basic Books.

Jaggar, Alison. 1983. *Feminist Politics and Human Nature.* Totowa, NJ: Allenheld and Roman.

James, Selma, and Mariarosa Dalla Costa. 1973. *The Power of Women and the Subversion of the Community.* Bristol: Falling Wall Press.

Kann, Mark. 1982. *The American Left.* New York: Praeger.

Kristeva, Julia. 1980. *Desire in Language.* New York: Columbia University Press.

Lyotard, Jean-Francois. 1984. *The Postmodern Condition: A Report of Knowledge.* Minneapolis: University of Minnesota Press.

Marx, Karl. 1973. *Grundrisse.* London: Allen Lane.

Marx, Karl, and Friedrich Engels. 1959. *Basic Writings on Politics and Philosophy.* Garden City, NY: Anchor Books.

Rabine, Leslie. 1983. "Searching for the Connections: Marxist-Feminists and Women's Studies." *Humanities in Society* 6(2/3):195–221.

Ross, Catherine E. 1987. "The Division of Labor at Home." *Social Forces* 65(March):816–33.

Smith, Paul. 1978. "Domestic Labour and Marx's Theory of Value." Pp. 198–219 in *Feminism and Materialism: Women and Modes of Production*, edited by Annette Kuhn and Ann Marie Wolpe. London: Routledge and Kegan Paul.

Walby, Sylvia. 1986. *Patriarchy at Work: Patriarchal and Capitalist Relations in Employment.* Minneapolis: University of Minnesota Press.

Weedon, Chris. 1987. *Feminist Practice and Poststructuralist Theory.* Oxford: Basil Blackwell.

Chapter 3

Reconceptualizing World System Theory to Include Women

Kathryn B. Ward

Gender and World System Theory

In this chapter, I explore the contributions of world system theory to our understanding of gender and consider the possibilities for reconceptualizing world system theory to include gender. In doing so, I draw on some of the feminist critiques of sociology and sociological theory. First, I examine the origins and development of world system theory as a critique of modernization theory. Second, I review literature on women in development, which is largely absent from the world system perspective. I propose a synthesis of the two literatures, and assess the resulting empirical applications. Third, I discuss other researchers' attempts to add gender to world system theory via the household but without fundamental modification of the theory. Fourth, I consider some of the proposed extensions or modifications of world system theory, in particular, issues of incorporation, the role of the informal sector, and the connections between women's formal and informal labor and housework, and redefining definitions of work and resistance. Finally, I argue that world system theory needs to be recast and suggest some possible avenues for making the perspective more inclusive of gender, race, and class.

Origins and Tenets of World System Theory

World system theory emerged in the 1970s in response to prevailing modernization theories that were prevalent in economics and sociology in the 1950s and 1960s. These theories posited that the experiences of the currently developed countries provided the blueprint for the socio-economic development of currently developing countries. Developing countries needed to follow the path of the currently developed countries, which reflected a movement from agriculturally based economies to industrialization and eventual development of a service-based economy. Development was an individual nation-state phenomenon where each country was responsible for its development efforts. Some researchers (Inkeles and Smith 1974) argued that modernization could be achieved by men's adoption of certain so-called modern ideas prominent in currently developed countries, such as ideologies of individualism and the work ethic. These values were remarkably consistent with what capitalist employers preferred in their male employees. However, such research ignored the question of whether women's adoption of such values was necessary for modernization.

In contrast, Latin American scholars generated theories of dependency in the 1960s. Their later merger with world system theory in the 1970s drew a different picture of development. [See Chase-Dunn (1989) for an excellent synthesis of these theories.] The dependency perspective examined exploitive relationships among nation-states that led to development of some countries or regions and underdevelopment of others. For example, in his early works, Frank (1969) argued that socioeconomic ties to urban areas resulted in the underdevelopment of the rural periphery because capital and raw materials flowed toward the core, and the periphery received little or no return. Likewise, colonial ties to industrializing countries meant underdevelopment for colonies or agriculturally based countries because raw materials flowed toward the industrializing centers. In return, the periphery received more expensive finished goods, resulting in unequal exchange and barriers to socioeconomic development of the periphery (Galtung 1971; Emmanuel 1972; Amin 1975).

World system theory has located the origins of the capitalist world economy in what Wallerstein (1974; 1979) has termed "the long 16th century," from 1450 to 1600. (For an alternative view that locates the origins of the world system in the East, see Abu-Lugod 1989.) From that time on, capitalism was the international form of economic organization, which gradually encompassed the entire globe. These processes of incorporation led to the increased commodification of production and transformation of farmers and artisans into proletarianized workers who sold their labor power. In peripheral areas, cash crop production expanded, while indigenous industrial activity declined (Wallerstein 1989). Eventually, the world system evolved as a single system of economic production organized through an international division of labor of nation-states and regions. This system differed from earlier world empires, which were single systems of political rather than economic organization.

Currently within the world system the core nations such as the United States, Germany, and Japan control the capital and design of production, while the peripheral nation-states provide raw materials and sometimes also cheap labor power. Core nations emerge via military and capital conquest, state-sponsored development, and protective trade legislation, which results in flows of capital and materials from their peripheral colonies and affiliated countries. Core states use their military and political powers to protect their economic interests at home and abroad. Meanwhile, countries in the periphery suffer underdevelopment: lower relative rates of economic growth, distortion of economies that are oriented toward extraction and production for the core, and higher internal income inequality (Bornschier and Chase-Dunn 1985; Chase-Dunn 1989).

Wallerstein discusses a third group of countries: the semiperiphery. The semiperiphery functions as an intermediary or sometimes as a competitor in relations among core and peripheral nations. However, this category often mixes three types of countries: socialist countries, countries ascending to core status, and countries descending from core status. For example, the previously socialist nation-states often have competed with core nations for materials and resources from the peripheral nations. Further, several countries have ascended from peripheral to semiperipheral status: Brazil, India, and South Korea. Finally, earlier core nations such as Portugal and Spain have lost their hegemonic status and now reside in the semiperiphery.

The world system has gone through periodic crises marked by global economic restructuring. These are often modeled in the form of long waves or Kondratieff economic cycles (Chase-Dunn 1989, p. 50), where economic activity increases and falters over forty to sixty years. Core countries, which achieve a certain hegemonic form of control/power in the world system during these cycles, are gradually replaced by other core powers. For example, the United States has been a hegemonic power for much of this century, but has lost much of its competitive control to other countries such as Germany and Japan, paralleling the experiences of Spain and Great Britain in past centuries.

These changes/crises are related to specific patterns of socioeconomic relationships. Researchers have identified phases of classical economic dependency, associated dependent development, debt dependency, and the growth of the informal economy and their connection to the new international division of labor (Bornschier and Chase-Dunn 1985; Evans and Stephens 1988; Portes, Castells, and Benton 1989; Fernandez-Kelly 1980; Chase-Dunn 1989; Gereffi 1989). Classical economic dependency refers to the international division of labor from colonial times to the present in which the core nations extract agricultural products and raw materials from their (former) colonies in the periphery and then return finished goods to the periphery. Such economic relationships result in the underdevelopment of peripheral industrial facilities, because core nations either destroy local factories or discourage their growth.

Over time, many peripheral countries move to a strategy of associated dependent development or import substitution. In this phase, peripheral nations use foreign investment of bank and transnational corporation capital from the core to build capital-intensive factories producing goods oriented toward the domestic market. These activities keep alive markets for heavy machinery from the core while the peripheral nations develop their own production facilities. However, as Bornschier and Chase-Dunn (1985) note, this strategy leads to continued underdevelopment, especially when capital/profits flow from the periphery's factories to the core. More recently, Gereffi (1989) notes how many semiperipheral countries, especially in East Asia, now manufacture heavy machinery and chemicals for export to the West.

Rising labor costs and declining capital costs in the core together with low labor costs and high capital costs in the periphery produce another form of global restructuring: labor-intensive factories in the periphery that produce exports in electronics, pharmaceuticals, clothing, etc. for the core and other countries. Here, core corporations control research, design, and capital-intensive facets of production in core countries. Then these corporations use the periphery and sometimes the ascending semiperiphery (NICs or newly industrializing countries) as locations for labor-intensive assembly work for export. Other production roles of peripheral countries include subcontracting by local firms for internal markets and supplying components for assembly in computers, drugs, and automobiles (Gereffi 1989).

International financial institutions also support such investment strategies in response to the international debt crisis/dependency. Many peripheral and semiperipheral nations have paid more and more of their export earnings to service debt incurred to pay for import substitution facilities, the costs of the 1970s energy crisis, and the more recent economic recession (Debt Crisis Network 1987; Wood 1988).

At the same time, export-oriented industries are very competitive and many countries have a hard time meeting their debt obligations, especially under austerity programs that mandate the reduction of imports and the increase of exports. For example, the export-oriented industries often need import parts for assembly, thereby creating problems in meeting the conditions of austerity programs (Glasberg and Ward 1990).

Ironically, under this investment strategy, while the clothing and textiles industries once stimulated economic development for core development, now these industries have been relegated to the highly competitive peripheral market, where limited capital is generated for debt service and domestic development efforts (Chase-Dunn 1982).

At the same time, export-oriented development strategies are accompanied by increased participation in the informal economy, especially in countries with strong subcontracting roles (Castells and Portes 1989); Gereffi 1989; Portes and Sassen-Koob 1987). Portes and Sassen-Koob define the informal sector as:

> All work situations characterized by the absence of (1) a clear separation between capital and labor; (2) a contractual relationship between both; and (3) a labor force that is paid wages and whose conditions of work and pay are legally regulated. . . . The informal sector is structurally heterogeneous and comprises such activities as direct subsistence, small-scale production and trade, and subcontracting to semiclandestine enterprises and homeworkers. (1987, p. 31)

These latest developments in global restructuring require a reexamination of the informal economy and its role in the world system. The Marxist roots of world system theory embodied the assumption that with the deepening of the world system and the commodification of production, the so-called precapitalist forms of the informal economy would disappear and all production would be incorporated into the world system. Instead, researchers such as Portes et al. (1989) have noted the amazing resilience of the informal sector and its growth over time in core, semiperipheral, and peripheral regions and countries.

Increasingly, capitalists and employers have informalized industrial and service production to deal with the economic crises of the 1980s. Castells and Portes (1989) analyze several causes and related consequences of this restructuring. First, employers and some male managerial workers use the strategy of informalization of assembly work by shifting production sites from established factories in the core to more informalized factories such as *maquiladoras* and to household-based assembly or production. (*Maquiladoras* refer to clothing and electronics factories on the U.S.–Mexico border that circumvent U.S labor legislation and wages.) Second, employers use informalization to increase their competitive flexibility in the global economy because smaller shops permit product design and assembly to change more rapidly to meet market demand. Third, competition among nations to attract industrial investment results in decreasing or negligible state regulation of industries. As a consequence, informalization increases in countries receiving such investments. Fourth, with global and regional economic crises and pursuant unemployment in the formal labor sector, many workers seek some form of economic remuneration in the informal sector. Many workers, particularly men, have gone into the informal sector, where they perceive that they can make more money by setting up subcontracting networks. Finally, workplace dynamics become more heterogeneous as class positions blur and as employers use statuses based on gender, age, and race/ethnicity to divide and exploit labor in the informal sector.

Where Are Women in All of This?

The theories discussed above provide a structural context for the operations of the global economy and the world in which we live and produce. Unfortunately, gender is missing as a central construct in most of these perspectives. Modernization theory assumes, but never tests, two propositions: (1) As women adopt modern values, they participate in development efforts, and (2) women in currently developing countries follow the path of women in the currently developed countries as they enter into the formal labor force via service and clerical positions (traditionally women's occupations).

Likewise, world system theory, consistent with its Marxist roots and orientation toward commodification of labor, assumes that women are incorporated as their households are incorporated into the world economy (Smith, Wallerstein, and Evers 1984). Accordingly, when the male head of household enters into proletarian labor or production for exchange, then the household is incorporated. Many theorists perceive the labor of women in housework as subsistence labor or production for use value. They relegate this labor to precapitalist relations or ignore it because it is not seen as production but merely as reproduction of the capitalist labor force through procreation and nurturing those household workers who work for pay (Fernandez-Kelly 1989). [For more discussion of Marxist debates on the status of household labor, see Shelton and Agger in this volume and Collins and Gimenez (1990).] Furthermore, such theorists argue that the situation of male dominance or control over access to valued economic resources is a capitalist phenomena. They fail to trace roots of male dominance to preexisting conditions. Also, such theorists erroneously assume that the liberation of women will occur with the rise of socialist forms of economic organization.

In fact, world system theorists and others in international political economy perspectives exclude the role of women in the global economy. First, these perspectives exclude the vast and growing literature on the effects of so-called development on women's status relative to men's and on the centrality of women's labor to the operation of the world system. For example, when Wallerstein (1989) discusses the introduction of cash crops and the decline of local industries as signs of incorporation, he fails to note the voluminous literature indicating that women in West Africa and Asia were negatively affected by this form of incorporation (Boserup 1970; Sen and Grown 1987). Second, world system theorists assume that women are only incorporated as members of households and fail to acknowledge gender differences in formal and informal sector participation. They impose male definitions of work on women's socioeconomic participation. As a consequence, such researchers dismiss women's household and informal sector participation as nonproductive labor. Finally, they overlook women's active roles and resistance to the processes of incorporation and women's resulting marginalization or exclusion from paid labor and inclusion on the margins of economic activity (A. Scott 1986; Ward 1990b; Ward and Pyle forthcoming).

I consider these themes below in the context of more general feminist critiques of sociology. These critiques have categorized sociologists' responses to feminist critiques as taking three basic forms: (1) "add women and stir," or using race and gender as additive variables tacked on to a theory; (2) modifying the theory to remove or alter problematic sections that ignore gender; and (3) recasting/transforming theory to put gender at the core (Stacey and Thorne 1985; Ward and Grant 1985, forthcoming; Grant and Ward forthcoming). I suggest that rather than giving women viability in world system theory only through the household as some world system adherents have done (Smith et al. 1984), world system theory needs to be recast totally to incorporate gender and race at its center. To begin with, I examine and critique the two most frequent strategies used to add women to world system research: adding women in development and bringing in the household.

Linking Women in Development Strategy

With the publication of Esther Boserup's (1970) classic book on women's role in development, researchers throughout the world began to document the disparate effects of socioeconomic development on women's status relative to men's. Research showed that development differentially affected women's and men's access to valued resources such as education, work (both formal and informal), and social and political institutions. (For reviews of this literature, see Ward 1984, 1988; Ward and Pyle forthcoming; Tinker and Bramsen 1976; Tiano 1987a; Fernandez-Kelly 1989; Enloe 1989.) For example, when colonial administrators introduced cash crops, men had greater access to and control over cultivation of new crops, while women farmers continued subsistence production that supported their families and communities. In many places, colonial and development officials educated men about new crops while women remained in the fields. More recently, the Green Revolution and global restructuring of food bypassed or displaced many farmers, in particular, women, in South Asia (Friedmann 1990). Women traders' routes were displaced by new distribution networks imposed by colonial officials, global markets, and mechanized routes (Boserup 1970; Ward 1985b).

The arrival of capital-intensive manufacturing industries has often displaced women from industrial jobs in small indigenously owned firms. Women industrial workers were not rehired in many countries until the arrival of export processing industries, for example, textiles, shoes, garments, electronics, and pharmaceuticals. In the meantime, women found work in the expanding service industries or in the informal economy of agricultural, trading, domestic, and food services. As a consequence, many women had less access to cash-generating activities precisely when incorporation of their region into the global economy made access to cash necessary for household survival. This limited access especially affected those women who were expected to support themselves and their households economically, for example, women in the Caribbean, West Africa, and parts of Southeast Asia.

Much of this research on women in development retains problematic assumptions from developmentalist or modernization perspectives. These researchers are correct to acknowledge that women have been displaced by these processes, but they err in believing that reinvolving women in development processes and projects on a country-by-country basis provides an adequate solution (Beneria and Sen 1981; Ward 1988, 1990b; Fernandez-Kelly 1989; Moser 1989). Theorists pay little attention to the processes of the world system or to how the operation of the world system is linked to the marginalization of women during development. Meanwhile, like many other social scientists (Acker 1990), world system theorists assume the world system is gender-blind in its operation.

In my earlier book and research (Ward 1984, 1985a, 1985b), I sought to merge theories on the world system and women in development with my research on the status of women and fertility in the world system. In the 1970s, many researchers were puzzled about why levels of fertility remained high in currently developing countries. They began to examine links between the status of women and fertility. Meanwhile, other researchers such as Boserup (1970) and Tinker and Bramsen (1976) were exploring the effects of development on women. I hypothesized that the effects of the world system, through the consequences of classical economic dependency and foreign investment, had negative effects on women's status relative to men's. I defined women's status as women's share of educational, economic, political, and organizational resources. In turn, women's marginalized status meant they had less control over their fertility and, hence, levels of fertility remained higher than expected.

I tested these hypotheses with aggregate-level data from 126 countries. I found that a country's incorporation within the world system, as measured by levels of commodity concentration and foreign investment, negatively affected women's share of the labor force and women's share of the agricultural and industrial sectors. Greater diversity of trade structures (a mixture of raw and finished goods) positively affected women's share of the labor force. Later tests of these relationships using data measuring change over longer time periods (from the 1960s into the 1980s) have supported these conclusions regarding effects of underdevelopment on both women's share of the labor force and fertility. Clark, Ramsby, and Adler (1991) found that dependency affected the growth in women's share of the labor force from 1960 to 1985. Further, during this same time period trade and investment dependency negatively affected changes in women's share of agriculture and manufacturing (Clark 1990). Likewise, Kim (1990) found similar effects of dependency on changes of women's share of the labor force from 1965 to 1980.

As for fertility, the measures of commodity concentration and investment increased fertility slightly in 1975, while birth control programs and economic development decreased fertility. The status of women, as measured by women's share of the labor force, had negligible effects on fertility. London (1988) retested the relationships proposed by Hout (1980), Nolan and White (1984), and my research (Ward 1984), and found that measures of dependency were related to smaller declines in fertility between 1960 and 1984, net of the effects of birth control programs and economic development. Women's share of the labor force in 1965 did not significantly affect fertility.

Thus, women's so-called incorporation in the world system frequently means marginalization within the capitalist economy whereby women have limited access to the formal labor sector and to the money that is increasingly necessary for survival. However, cross-national aggregate-level data on women's labor force participation are notably inaccurate and fail to capture women's extensive economic participation in the informal sector and the household (Dixon 1982). Nevertheless, numerous case studies support these findings about women's marginalization from the formal labor force. These studies also provide important insights on conditions of women's work that only rarely are reflected in official labor force statistics or in accounts of the world-system: the connections between women's formal labor, informal labor, and household labor (Ward 1990b).

Unfortunately, research on women's status in the process of development remains largely unincorporated into most writings on the world system and international political economy. For example, in Evans and Stephens's chapter on international political economy in Smelser's *Handbook of Sociology* (1988), gender is mentioned only in two footnotes. In Shannon's (1989) overview of world system theory, my research is literally placed in a box and remains unintegrated into the critique of the theory. The Smith, Collins, Hopkins, and Muhammed (1988) volume on racism and sexism in the world system recognizes many of the omissions, but the insights of this volume are rarely cited by world system theorists such as Wallerstein, whose third volume (1989) on the world system continues to neglect issues of gender. A few male researchers have begun to cite one or two references to work on gender, but only in a list of "-isms." These issues are rarely or never addressed in their empirical analyses (for exceptions see Clark et al. 1991; Clark 1990; London 1988; Chase-Dunn 1989; Ramirez, Weiss, and Tracy 1979; Harvey 1989).

The Household/Housewives Strategy

When gender is considered by some of the world system theorists, they most commonly pursue a strategy of studying households in the world economy (See Smith et al. 1984) rather than recasting world system theory to put gender at the center of analyses. Household-oriented world system research attempts to deal with the anomalies of the persistence or re-creation of informal sector labor and unwaged housework in the world system, with the household as the basic unit of analysis. While this perspective acknowledges, in part, the contribution of unwaged labor to the reproduction of the labor force and the capitalist system, unwaged labor and housework still are perceived as being products of capitalism rather than distinctive phenomena properties with their own logic (Wallerstein 1984; Smith 1984). Male dominance over women is seen as a recent social construction of capitalism (Smith 1984).

Four problems exist with this household approach to gender. First, it ignores the divergent socioeconomic interests of women and men within a household (Wolf 1990a, 1990b, 1992; Wong 1984). The divergences are accentuated by underdevelopment. Second, studying only households in a context of accumulation and exchange ignores the dialectics between women's formal and informal labor and housework. It also ignores women's and men's different experiences in the informal sector. For example, most women enter the informal sector for survival while many men enter for mobility (Schmink 1986; Ward 1990a; Ward and Pyle forthcoming). Third, this perspective ignores the existing literature on the disparate impact of underdevelopment on women's access to valued resources relative to men's. Fourth, adding women merely as housewives ignores theoretical holes in world system theory such as the persistent presence of precapitalist forms of informal and household labor despite incorporation within the global economy.

When world system theory incorporates women, they come in as appendages of men in households. Household decision-making is assumed to consist of joint decisions of wives and husbands. This strategy ignores one of the main insights from women in development research on households: Contrary to views of "new home economists" such as Gary Becker (1981), there is more than one utility function in the household. Men and women in the same household often have divergent productive and reproductive interests and socioeconomic contributions (Roldan 1985, 1988; Acker 1988; Bruce 1989; Stichter 1990; Collins 1990; Blumberg 1989; Wolf 1990b). Fernandez-Kelly (1989) calls these "overlapping circles of production and distribution." Women's interests and positions relative to capital are obscured behind the facade of household, or male, interests. Rather than being benevolent dictators (Wolf 1990b), men often use their disproportionate power and violence against women to enforce these so-called joint arrangements (Mies 1986; Barry 1979). Government-sponsored development programs solicit industries that do not hire women and interfere with their wife and mother roles (Pyle 1990a, 1990b). By merely reformulating women's roles as an extension of their household position or by defining women's interests by the position of their husbands, researchers ignore inequality between women and men *in* their households as well as in the economy (Wolf 1990b; Hossfeld 1988, 1990; Pyle 1990b).

Divergent interests include divergent contributions. In many cases, women contribute up to 100 percent of their earnings to the household, while men keep a substantial amount for their personal consumption (Beneria and Roldan 1987; Blumberg 1989; Bruce 1989; Stichter and Parpart 1990). Women's total contributions to the household through their informal and formal sector activities and housework provide *most* of the subsistence for many households (see, for example, Narotzky 1990). These contributions also vary by race and class. Poor or working-class men spend less time in the household and contribute less to household maintenance than do more economically advantaged men (Gimenez 1990).

Second, the overemphasis on exchange and accumulation in world system theory obscures how women's socioeconomic roles in waged and nonwaged labor and housework are intertwined. Sokoloff (1980) calls this relationship the dialectic between women's home and market work, because women's position in the household shapes their position in the market and vice versa. Other researchers have noted that women's formal and informal labors are frequently defined as an extension of women's work within the home and hence are lower in status and pay than comparable labor by men. Working-class husbands may also devalue women's contributions (Narotzky 1990). However, many scholars now concur that the public/private division is an ideological invention by men that ignores the interconnections of the two spheres in women's lives (Rosaldo 1980; J. Scott 1986; Smith 1974, 1979; Thibault 1987) and experiences of women of color and working-class women, who have always worked outside the home and in the informal sector.

I argue that the boundaries between women's formal, informal, and household labor are much more permeable for women than for men. Men's labor tends to have clear boundaries between labor performed in the home and outside the home (Ward 1990a). Many men have much clearer demarcations between various types of work. For example, in California's Silicon Valley some unemployed minority men refuse to set up informal shops in their homes because they do not perceive these activities as work (Hossfeld 1990). At the same time, their spouses or partners are working a triple shift of up to fifteen hours per day in some combination of formal, informal, and household labor to ensure survival. Massiah (1989) and Heyzer (1989) describe similar scenarios for Caribbean and Asian women.

Many women enter the informal sector for household survival, while men may enter to boost their wages relative to the formal sector—a relationship ignored by discussions such as Portes and Sassen-Koob's (1987). Many men enter the informal sector as subcontractors, where they control the labor of women who are at the bottom of the subcontracting pyramid as sewing machine operators, assemblers, and distributors (Truelove 1987, 1988, 1990; Harvey 1989; Ward 1990b; Ward and Pyle forthcoming). And even where women are entrepreneurs, they are the most economically and politically vulnerable (Fernandez-Kelly and Garcia 1988). This vulnerability also varies by class and ethnicity. Chicana and Mexicana women workers in assembly work in Los Angeles experience greater economic vulnerability than do Cuban women who work in immigrant enclaves (Fernandez-Kelly and Garcia 1990).

Third, the Smith et al. (1984) focus on the household ignores how women have been systematically denied access to formal waged labor under the global economy, with the exception of limited employment in transnational corporations. Further, one third of the world's households are headed by women, and in some countries this proportion is closer to 50 percent (Moser 1989). These women cannot depend on men for sustenance. For example, in Belo Horizonte, Brazil, Schmink (1986) finds that female heads of household and poor women are more likely to be in the informal sector than are single women and married women. Meanwhile formal labor and development projects often exclude women heads of households. When women are employed, their employers pay them less than men, assuming that these women will pool wages with a husband (Hossfeld 1990; Narotzky 1990; Acker 1988).

Finally, as von Werlhof (1980, 1984, 1985, 1988) and Mies (1986) have argued, the omissions of women's socioeconomic experiences highlight two major theoretical problems in world system theory. By ignoring women's informal and housework labor, researchers have ignored the anomalies or theoretical holes presented by the continued presence of these so-called noncapitalist activities. Further, the emphasis on exchange production has led to male biases in how *work* and *households* are defined in their theories. It has also led researchers to ignore increases in male dominance in women's everyday lives that are exacerbated by underdevelopment. In this way, important facets of the operations of the global economy are obscured.

Some debate remains about whether informal sector work and male dominance predate the arrival of the capitalist world system (Smith 1984). I believe that socially constructed male dominance/control over valued resources in formal and informal sectors and in the household existed before capitalism. This male dominance was transformed by the emergence of the capitalist world system. In many situations where women had substantial power vis-à-vis men, male hegemony was externally bolstered by colonial administrators and transnational corporations (Nash 1988b). Male dominance has been maintained by men's monopoly creating the rules in the workplace and organizations (Reskin 1988; Hacker 1989; Acker 1990; Pyle 1990b), by violence against women (Barry 1979; Mies 1986; Enloe 1989), and by men's control over relations of production, distribution, and reproduction (Hartmann 1976; Beneria and Sen 1981; Ward 1984; Acker 1988; Fernandez-Kelly 1989). Furthermore, the Marxist overemphasis on exchange/accumulation/class cannot account for these continuing processes of male domination or the gendered nature of production where formal, informal, and housework labor are intricately linked (Acker 1988; Fernandez-Kelly 1989; Ward 1990b). I believe that this overemphasis reflects the conscious inability of world system theorists to comprehend the entirety of women's lives beyond stereotypes of women as breeders and feeders and beyond theoretical assumptions that regard women's labor as nonproductive work. Some researchers have taken these critiques seriously. How have they gone about modifying these theories?

Attempts at Modification

A number of recent studies represent a transition from "adding women and stirring" to modification or what Thibault (1987) calls deconstruction of world system theory (Ward 1984, 1990a, 1990b; Ward and Pyle forthcoming; Mies 1986; Nash and Fernandez-Kelly 1983; Fernandez-Kelly and Garcia 1988, 1989, 1990; Fernandez-Kelly 1989; Sassen-Koob 1985; Friedmann 1990).

What do these studies contribute to modification of world system theory? One important line of analysis is how and when women are actually incorporated in the world system. According to earlier definitions of incorporation via the formal sector, women have been incorporated only sporadically into the global economy, in particular through work in transnational corporation (TNC) plants (Nash 1983; Nash and Fernandez-Kelly 1983; Sassen-Koob 1985; Mies 1986; Ward 1988, 1990b; Ward and Pyle forthcoming). Although some view this employment as enhancing women's opportunities (for example, Lim 1978, 1983a, 1983b, 1985, 1990), I believe that this is a short-run view because women's incorporation through TNCs is temporary and selective (Elson and Pearson 1981; A. Scott 1986; Ward and Pyle forthcoming). In the long run, these jobs reflect the continuing control of women's productive roles by men because employment in TNCs is transitory and provides low wages relative to subsistence costs. Male managers perpetuate control over women working under already hazardous conditions (Ward 1988). When TNCs move on to other export processing zones and/or women are fired, they drop out of formal labor force statistics because they return to the informal sector, to subcontracted industrial assembly work in the home, to the sex trade (Enloe 1989), or to domestic service or housework—forms of work that do not provide direct incorporation into processes of exchange or accumulation. (For a review of the recent literature, see Ward and Pyle forthcoming.) Further, with the increasing automation and capital-intensive production of early TNC recipients (for example, South Korea), women are once again excluded from industrial employment (Yoon 1990).

However, only a small proportion of women work in TNCs. For most women greater contact or incorporation with the world system or global economy has often meant their *exclusion* from access to valued socioeconomic resources introduced by the world system (Boserup 1970; Ward 1984, 1988). Meanwhile, women meet their subsistence and survival needs through informal and household labor and some formal work. Such labors make a rather large economic contribution or an estimated 66 percent of the work hours performed around the world (Leghorn and Parker 1981).

At the same time, each day women resist pressures of socioeconomic marginalization (Aptheker 1989). Women of color often resist by surviving violence and a wide variety of other oppressive conditions in their countries, work, and households and teaching their children survival skills. Supportive alliances with other women have also contributed to survival (Collins 1990; Giddings 1984; Dill 1986). Working-class women use numerous economic survival strategies such as the triple shift, where they combine formal, informal, and household labor to ensure survival of their household despite male unemployment and/or low male economic contributions. In many work situations, women have creatively used the sexist, racist, and classist stereotypes of managers to better their own positions (Hossfeld 1990; Aptheker 1989; Freeman 1989; Lamphere 1987; Ong 1987; Peña 1987; Yelvington 1991; Bookman and Morgen 1988; Westwood and Bhachu 1988). For example, in Silicon Valley women told their managers that they needed hormone breaks—up to two to three times per day. When a racist manager told a group of Mexicanas to work quickly like a group of Asian women on an assembly line, the Asian women coworkers slowed down (Hossfeld 1988, 1990). Some Malaysian women have used possession by spirits to resist factory rules (Ong 1987). And finally, many women have taken part in organized resistance through unionization and demonstrations against governments and structural adjustment programs, thereby transforming their lives and empowering themselves (Nash 1988a,b; Aptheker 1989; Van Allen 1976; Ward 1988; Kingsolver 1989; Kamel 1990).

I propose that these activities, in conjunction with the continued prevalence of informal sector and household labor, constitute an important form of women's resistance to incorporation. I believe that we need to redefine our notions of work, resistance, and incorporation to encompass the range of women's labors and the realities of how most work is being done around the world. For example, Von Werlhof (1985) notes that waged laborers are scarce relative to the numbers of laborers in the informal sector and in housework. Much if not most of production of food, goods, and subsistence around the world is being provided by informal/unwaged labor and housework. And the informal sector is growing rapidly rather than disappearing as predicted. Von Werlhof (1985) questions the overemphasis on exchange and accumulation in capitalist production. She argues that our theories of production should be based on consideration of the most prevalent patterns of production, those in the informal sector and the household, and should acknowledge, women's central role in such forms of production. Mies (1986) supports this position and argues that theories of political economy should be based on women's production of and for life rather than men's expropriation of resources generated by other people. Further, she traces how the subordination of women's labor by men's sometimes violent expropriation provided the model for the violent subjugation of colonies by colonial/core powers. Women in the periphery are doubly (or triply) exploited. These relationships are replicated by the language used by world system theorists to describe colonialization: penetration, conquest, untouched or virgin land. (For discussion of other examples, see von Werlhof 1985; J. Scott 1986; Ward 1988.)

On the basis of the evidence and arguments above, I would argue that world system theorists have failed to modify their concepts (such as production, accumulation, or incorporation) to accurately depict women's status. As study of the prevalence of the informal sector and housework continues, we may rediscover that much of the world's population is only tenuously connected with the world system through some vague articulation of subcontracting, marriage, and occasional waged labor. This is likely the case despite Fernandez-Kelly's (1989) assertions of the utility of world system theory for understanding gender. Race and ethnicity also mediate incorporation as Hall (1986, 1989) has demonstrated for the U.S. southwest. Race/gender groupings may constitute a safety valve for the global economy and also a source of resistance to incorporation. Given these problems, and the failure of world system theory to give a central place to women's work, I believe that now we must start the process of reconstructing/recasting process (Ward and Grant 1985; Thibault 1987).

Reconstructing/Recasting

"After modifying, bending, and pulling at theories to make them work after women were abruptly added to them, feminists began to question whether or not there is something more problematic" (Thibault 1987, p. 9).

How should we go about reconstructing our theories on the political economy of gender/class and development? First, we need to do our research differently, because we need to look at gender, race, and class in a holistic manner that emphasizes the totality of what women and men do to survive. Thus, our new theory or theories need to explain the intertwining of women's and men's labor in the formal and informal sectors and in the home. The best attempt to locate women's work at the center of theory building has occurred in the work of Mies (1986) and

Mies, von Werlhof, and Bennholdt-Thompson (1988), as well as among younger women researchers who are sympathetic to world system research but recognize its limitations.

Second, Fernandez-Kelly (1989) and Acker (1988, p. 477, 1990) propose that all socioeconomic processes are gendered and reflect asymmetries of power. To this, I would add the interacting effects of racial asymmetries (Enloe 1989). These researchers suggest that we look at the overlapping relations of production and distribution of resources within households and families. Further, gender-based conflict over power marks much of family, work, and organizational structures (Acker 1988, 1990). Von Werlhof (1985) notes that, although working-class men have limited control over their lives, they still have more control than do most housewives. Hartmann (1976) describes how men have greater organizational control and how this has shaped women's access to waged labor. Reskin (1988) argues that occupational integration and pay equity will not decrease the female-male wage gap. During periods of socioeconomic change, men still make the rules, dominate the best paid occupations, and construct the pay evaluation systems. Based on these redefinitions of gender and class we can explore the following questions: How are the relations of production gendered in the allocation of work, authority, wages, and class positions and how does this shape economic, social, and political institutions? When do women of certain classes and race/ethnic characteristics use the triple shift and other resistance strategies?

Finally, we need to explore the seemingly taboo topic of violence by men against women and by white men against people of color. Such violence occurs in the household, in workplaces, and elsewhere. How does this contribute to the social control of women? How are these patterns of violence replicated in racial, colonial, and dependent relationships (Barry 1979; Giddings 1984; J. Scott 1986; Mies 1986)? How does this benefit economic and political elites (Enloe 1989)?

What are the sites/techniques for developing holistic theories of gender and of the global economy? I question the utility of world system theory insofar as it describes a single economic system, particularly if gender and race are missing as central components of the theory. As we examine the feminist critique of existing paradigms, we discover that the "add women and stir" approach does not work. [See, for example, Aptheker's (1989) experiences in attempting to apply Marxist theory to women of color.] Developing these theories will require multifaceted and interdisciplinary work with the most new information being generated by women's studies scholars, especially those from currently developing countries. I suggest that we concentrate on middle-range theories rather than all-encompassing theories, which seem never to place race and gender at the center. These can be developed by moving between the comparative studies of regions/countries and contextual case studies.

Historical studies are needed to trace women's socioeconomic activities over time. For example, the world system literature extensively explores the effects of changes in the price of British sailors on the development of capitalism. But what was the relationship between witches and women's resistance to emergence of capitalism (Mies 1986)? What was the relationship between the development of the sex trade in women and the development of the tourist trade and military bases around the world (Enloe 1989)? During the decline of various hegemonic powers, what were women and men of all classes and races doing in household, subsistence, formal, and informal labor activities? Case studies of household, informal, and formal labor are needed to untangle these gendered processes. This information can also be used to guide the collection of better statistical data on the entire range of women's and men's economic activities.

Once we address these questions and evaluate the results of our research relative to previous propositions, we may find that the global economy looks like a very different place—once gender and race become central kernels of our theorizing. Thus, the terrain of the global economy will be mapped via the various types of work that women and men of different races and classes engage in.

Otherwise, we may see the continuation of two parallel strands of theory: (1) international political economy where gender and race issues are ignored, and (2) women in development literature where international political economy is ignored. I propose that when theories continually fail to respond to feminist critiques, and thus to incorporate gender, race, and class at their centers, this omission results in theories that fail to fully capture the experiences of diverse groups of women and men. In response, such biased theories may continue without input from frustrated gender researchers who may pursue a more inclusive form of theory generation of their own (Grant and Ward 1991; Ward and Grant 1991). The eventual result may be two bodies of theories: those generated by the feminist critiques and those prefeminist theories that have remained unresponsive and untransformed by the feminist critiques. These implications are already apparent in world system research and in sociology more generally. They are suggested by research showing that fewer women than men call themselves theorists, that women are seldom authors or editors of theory or world system journals, and that neither so-called classical sociological theory nor world system theory is drawn upon in much of the new feminist sociology (Grant and Ward 1991; Ward and Grant 1991).

Acknowledgments

The comments of Paula England, Linda Grant, Jean Pyle, and Cindy Truelove were very useful. The research assistance of Julie Gast and Mary Lou Fuller and word processing skills of Laura Whistle Cates were invaluable. An earlier version of this chapter was presented at the Annual Meetings of the American Sociological Association, Atlanta, GA, 1988.

References

Abu-Lughod, J. 1989. *Before European Hegemony: The World System A.D. 1250–1350.* New York: Oxford University Press.

Acker, J. 1988. "Class, Gender, and the Relations of Production." *Signs* 13: 473–97.

———. 1990. "Hierarchies, Jobs, Bodies: A Theory of Gendered Organizations." *Gender & Society* 4:139–58.

Amin, S. 1975. *Unequal Development.* New York: Monthly Review Press.

Aptheker, Bettina. 1989. *Tapestries of Life: Women's Work, Women's Consciousness, and The Meaning of Daily Experience.* Amherst: University of Massachusetts Press.

Barry, K. 1979. *Female Sexual Slavery.* New York: New York University Press.

Becker, G. 1981. *A Treatise on the Family.* Cambridge, MA: Harvard University Press.

Beneria, L., and M. Roldan. 1987. *The Crossroads of Class and Gender.* Chicago: University of Chicago Press.

Beneria, L., and S. Sen. 1981. "Accumulation, Reproduction, and Women's Role in Economic Development: Boserup Revisited." *Signs* 7:279–98.

Blumberg, Rae. 1989. "Toward a Feminist Theory of Development." Pp. 161–99 in *Feminism and Sociological Theory,* edited by R. Wallace. Beverly Hills: Sage.

Bookman, Ann, and Sandra Morgan. 1988. *Women and the Politics of Empowerment.* Philadelphia: Temple University Press.

Bornschier, V., and C. Chase-Dunn. 1985. *Transnational Corporations and Underdevelopment.* New York: Praeger.

Boserup, E. 1970. *Woman's Role in Economic Development.* New York: St. Martin's.

Bruce, J. 1989. "Homes Divided." *World Development* 17(7):979–91.

Castells, M., and A. Portes. 1989. "World Underneath: The Origins, Dynamics, and Effects of the Informal Economy." Pp. 11–37 in *The Informal Economy: Studies in Advanced and Less Developed Countries,* edited by A. Portes, M. Castells, and L. Benton. Baltimore, MD: The Johns Hopkins University Press.

Chase-Dunn, C. 1982. "The Uses of Formal Comparative Research on Dependency Theory and the World-System Perspective." Pp. 117–40 in *The New International Economy,* edited by H. Makler, A. Martinelli, and N. Smelser. London: Sage.

———. 1989. *Global Formations.* New York: Basil Blackwell.

Clark, R. 1990. "Economic Dependency and Gender Differences in Labor Force Sectoral Change in Non-Core Nations." Unpublished paper, Rhode Island College.

Clark, R., T. Ramsby, and E. Adler. 1991. "Culture, Gender and Labor Force Participation: A Cross-National Study." *Gender & Society* 5:47–66.

Collins, J. L. 1990. "Unwaged Labor in Comparative Perspective: Recent Theories and Unanswered Questions." Pp. 3–24 in *Work Without Wages: Domestic Labor and Self-Employment Within Capitalism,* edited by J. L. Collins and M. Gimenez. Albany: State University of New York Press.

Collins, Jane L., and Martha Gimenez (eds.). 1990. *Work Without Wages: Domestic Labor and Self-Employment Within Capitalism.* Albany: State University of New York Press.

Debt Crisis Network. 1987. *From Debt to Development.* Washington, DC: Institute for Policy Studies.

Dill, Bonnie Thornton. 1986. "Our Mothers' Grief: Racial Ethnic Women and the Maintenance of Family." Research paper #4. Center for Research on Women, Memphis State University.

Dixon, R. 1982. "Women in Agriculture: Counting the Labor Force in Developing Countries." *Population and Development Review* 8(3):539–66.

Elson, D., and Pearson, R. 1981. "Nimble Fingers Make Cheap Workers: An Analysis of Women's Employment in Third World Export Manufacturing." *Feminist Review,* Spring:87–107.

Emmanuel, A. 1972. *Unequal Exchange.* New York: Monthly Review Press.

Enloe, C. 1989. *Bananas, Beaches, and Politics.* Berkeley: University of California Press.

Evans, P., and J. Stephens. 1988. "Development in the World Economy." Pp. 739–773 in *Handbook of Sociology,* edited by N. Smelser. Newbury Park: Sage.

Fernandez-Kelly, P. 1989. "Broadening the Scope: Gender and International Economic Development." *Sociological Forum* 4:11–35.

Fernandez-Kelly, Patricia, and Anna Garcia. 1988. "Economic Restructuring in the United States." Pp. 49–65 in *Women and Work #3,* edited by Barbara Gutek, Ann Stromberg, and Laurie Larwood. Beverly Hills: Sage.

———. 1989. "Hispanic Women and Homework: Women in the Informal Economy of Miami and Los Angeles." Pp. 165–79 in *Homework: Historical and Contemporary Perspectives on Paid Labor at Home,* edited by E. Boris and C. R. Daniels. Urbana: University of Illinois Press.

———. 1990. "Power Surrendered, Power Restored: The Politics of Home and Work Among Hispanic Women in Southern California and Southern Florida." In *Women and Politics in America,* edited by L. Tilly and P. Guerin. New York: Russell Sage.

Frank, A. G. 1969. *Latin America: Underdevelopment or Revolution?* New York: Monthly Review Press.

Freeman, C. 1989. *High-Tech and High Heels: Barbadian Women in the Off-Shore Information Industry.* Paper presented at the 15th Annual Conference of the Caribbean Studies Association, Trinidad and Tobago.

Friedmann, H. 1990. "Family Wheat Farms and Third World Debts: A Paradoxical Relationship Between Unwaged and Waged Labor." Pp. 193–214 in *Work Without Wages: Domestic Labor and Self-Employment Within Capitalism,* edited by J. L. Collins and M. Gimenez. Albany: State University of New York Press.

Galtung, J. 1971. "A Structural Theory of Imperialism." *Journal of Peace Research* 2:89–117.

Gereffi, G. 1989. "Rethinking Development Theory: Insights from East Asia and Latin America." *Sociological Forum* 4:505–35.

Giddings, P. 1984. *When and Where I Enter.* New York: Bantam.

Gimenez, M. E. 1990. "The Dialectics of Waged and Unwaged Work: Waged Work, Domestic Labor, and Household Survival in the United States." Pp. 25–46 in *Work Without Wages: Domestic Labor and Self-Employment Within Capitalism,* edited by J. L. Collins and M. Gimenez. Albany: State University of New York Press.

Glasberg, D. S., and K. Ward. 1990. "Debt Dependency and Economic Development." Paper presented at the annual meetings of the American Sociological Association, Washington, DC.

Grant, L., and K. Ward. 1991. "Gender and Publishing in Sociology." *Gender & Society* 5:207–223.

Hacker, S. 1989. *Pleasure, Power & Technology.* Winchester, MA: Unwin Hyman.

Hall, T. 1986. "Incorporation in the World-System: Toward a Critique." *American Sociological Review* 51:390–402.

_____. 1989. *Social Change in the Southwest, 1350–1880.* Lawrence: University of Kansas Press.

Hartmann, H. 1976. "Capitalism, Patriarchy, and Job Segregation by Sex." Pp. 137–70 in *Women in the Workplace,* edited by M. Blaxall and B. Reagan. Chicago: University of Chicago Press.

Harvey, D. 1989. *The Condition of Postmodernity.* London: Blackwell.

Heyzer, N. 1989. "Asian Women Wage Earners." *World Development* 17:1109–24.

Hossfeld, Karen. 1988. "Divisions of Labor, Divisions of Lives: Immigrant Women Workers in Silicon Valley." Unpublished dissertation. University of California at Santa Cruz.

_____. 1990. " 'Their Logic Against Them': Contradictions in Sex, Race, and Class in Silicon Valley." Pp. 149–78 in *Women Workers and Global Restructuring,* edited by Kathryn B. Ward. Ithaca, NY: ILR Press.

Hout, M. 1980. "Trade Dependence and Fertility in Hispanic America." Pp. 159–88 in *Studies of the Modern World-System,* edited by A. Bergesen. New York: Academic Press.

Inkeles, A., and D. Smith. 1974. *Becoming Modern.* Cambridge, MA: Harvard University Press.

Kamel, Rachael. 1990. *The Global Factory: Analysis and Action for a New Economic Era.* Philadelphia: American Friends Service Committee.

Kandiyoti, Deniz. 1988. "Bargaining with Patriarchy." *Gender & Society* 2:274–91.

Kim, H. K. 1990. "The Effects of the Modern World-System on the Changing Status of Women, 1965–80." Unpublished Ph.D. dissertation, University of Georgia.

Kingsolver, B. 1989. *Holding the Line.* Ithaca, NY: ILR Press.

Lamphere, L. 1987. *From Working Daughters to Working Mothers.* Ithaca, NY: Cornell University Press.

Leghorn, L., and R. Parker. 1981. *Woman's Worth.* Boston: Routledge & Kegan.

Lim, L. 1978. *Workers in Multinational Corporations: The Case of the Electronics Industry in Malaysia and Singapore.* Michigan Occasional Papers in Women's Studies No. 9. Ann Arbor: University of Michigan.

———. 1983a. "Capitalism, Imperialism, and Patriarchy." Pp. 70–92 in *Women, Men and the International Division of Labor,* edited by J. Nash and M. Fernandez-Kelly. Albany: State University of New York Press.

———. 1983b. "Are Multinationals the Problem? A Debate." *Multinational Monitor* 4(8):12–16.

———. 1985. *Women Workers in Multinational Enterprises in Developing Countries.* Geneva: International Labor Organization.

———. 1990. "Women's Work in Export Factories: The Politics of a Cause." Pp. 101–19 in *Persistent Inequalities: Women and World Development,* edited by I. Tinker. New York: Oxford University Press.

London, B. 1988. "Dependence, Distorted Development, and Fertility Trends in Noncore Nations: A Structural Analysis of Cross-National Data." *American Sociological Review* 53:606–18.

Massiah, J. 1989. "Women's Lives and Livelihoods: A View from the Commonwealth Caribbean. *World Development* 17(7):965–77.

Mies, M. 1986. *Patriarchy and Accumulation on a World-Scale.* London: Zed.

Mies, M., V. Bennholdt-Thomsen and C. Von Werlhof (eds.), *Women: The Last Colony.* London: Zed.

Moser, C. 1989. "Gender Planning in the Third World: Meeting Practical and Strategic Gender Needs." *World Development* 17(11, November):1799–1826.

Narotzky, S. 1990. " 'Not to be a Burden': Ideologies of the Domestic Group and Women's Work in Rural Catalonia." Pp. 70–88 in *Work Without Wages: Domestic Labor and Self-Employment Within Capitalism,* edited by J. L. Collins and Martha Gimenez. Albany: State University of New York Press.

Nash, J. 1983. "The Impact of the Changing International Division of Labor on Different Sectors of the Labor Force." Pp. 3–38 in *Women, Men, and the International Division of Labor,* edited by J. Nash and M. Fernandez-Kelly. Albany: State University of New York Press.

———. 1988a. "The Mobilization of Women in the Bolivian Debt Crisis." Pp. 67–86 in *Women and Work #3,* edited by B. Gutek, L. Larwood, and Ann Stromberg. Beverly Hills: Sage.

———. 1988b. "Cultural Parameters of Sexism and Racism in the International Division of Labor." Pp. 11–36 in *Racism, Sexism, and the World-System,* edited by J. Smith, J. Collins, T. Hopkins, and A. Muhammad.

Nash, June, and Maria Fernandez-Kelly. 1983. *Women, Men and the International Division of Labor.* Albany: State University of New York Press.

Nolan, Patrick D., and Ralph B. White. 1984. "Structural Explanations of Fertility Change: The Demographic Transition, Economic Status of Women, and the World System." *Comparative Social Research* 7:80–109.

Ong, A. 1987. *Spirits of Resistance and Capitalist Discipline: Factory Women in Malaysia.* Albany: State University of New York Press.

Papanek, H. 1979. "Development Planning for Women: The Implications of Women's Work." Pp. 170–201 in *Women and Development,* edited by R. Jahan and H. Papanek. Dacca: Bangladesh Institute of Law and International Affairs.

Peña, D. 1987. "Tortuosidad: Shop Floor Struggles of Female Maquiladora Workers." Pp. 129–54 in *Women on the U.S.-Mexico Border*, edited by V. Ruiz and S. Tiano. Boston: Allen & Unwin.

Portes, Alejandro, Manuel Castells, and Lauren Benton (eds.). 1989. *The Informal Economy: Studies in Advanced and Less Developed Countries*. Baltimore: The Johns Hopkins University Press.

Portes, A., and S. Sassen-Koob. 1987. "Making It Underground." *American Journal of Sociology* 93:30–61.

Pyle, Jean. 1990a. "Export-Led Development and the Underemployment of Women: The Impact of Discriminatory Development Policy in the Republic of Ireland." Pp. 85–112 in *Women Workers and Global Restructuring*, edited by Kathryn B. Ward. Ithaca, NY: ILR Press.

―――. 1990b. *The State and Women in the Economy: Lessons from Sex Discrimination in the Republic of Ireland*. Albany: State University of New York Press.

Ramirez, F., and J. Weiss. 1979. "The Political Incorporation of Women." Pp. 238–49 in *National Development in the World System*, edited by J. Meyer and M. Hannan. Chicago: University of Chicago Press.

Redclift, Nanneke, and Enzo Mingione (eds.). 1985. *Beyond Employment: Household, Gender, and Subsistence*. Oxford: Basil Blackwell.

Reskin, B. 1988. "Bringing the Men Back." In Sex Differentiation and the Devaluation of Women's Work." *Gender & Society* 2:58–81.

Roldan, Marta. 1985. "Industrial Outworking, Struggles for Reproduction of Working-Class Families and Gender Subordination." Pp. 248–285 in *Beyond Employment: Household, Gender, and Subsistence*, edited by N. Redclift and E. Mingione. Oxford: Basil Blackwell.

―――. 1988. "Renegotiating the Marital Contract: Intrahousehold Patterns of Money Allocation and Women's Subordination among Domestic Outworkers in Mexico City." Pp. 229–47 in *A Home Divided: Women and Income in the Third World*, edited by Daisy Dwyer and Judith Bruce. Stanford: Stanford University Press.

Rollins, Judith. 1986. *Between Women*. Philadelphia: Temple University Press.

Rosaldo, M. 1980. "The Use and Abuse of Anthropology: Reflections on Feminism and Cross-Cultural Understanding." *Signs* 5:389–417.

―――. 1984. "Notes on the Incorporation of Third World Women into Wage-Labor Through Immigration and Off-Shore Production." *International Migration Review* 18(4):1144–67.

―――. 1985. "Capital Mobility and Labor Migration: Their Expression in Core Cities." Pp. 231–65 in *Urbanization in the World-Economy*, edited by M. Timberlake. New York: Academic Press.

Schmink, M. 1986. "Women and Urban Industrial Development in Brazil." Pp. 136–64 in *Women and Change in Latin America*, edited by J. Nash and H. Safa. South Hadley, MA: Bergin & Garvey.

Scott, A. 1986. "Women and Industrialisation: Examining the 'Female Marginalisation' Thesis." *Journal of Development Studies* 22:649–80.

Scott, J. 1986. "Gender: A Useful Category of Historical Analysis." *American Historical Review* 91:1053–75.

Sen, Gita, and Caren Grown. 1987. *Development, Crises, and Alternative Visions*. New York: New Feminist Library.

Shannon, T. R. 1989. *An Introduction to the World-System Perspective.* Boulder, CO: Westview.

Smelser, N. (ed.). 1988. *Handbook of Sociology.* Newbury Park, CA: Sage Publications.

Smith, D. 1974. "Women's Perspective as a Radical Critique of Sociology." *Sociological Inquiry* 44:7–13.

———. 1979. "A Sociology for Women." Pp. 135–87 in *The Prism of Sex,* edited by J. Sherman and E. T. Beck. Madison: University of Wisconsin Press.

Smith, J. 1984. "Non Wage Labor and Subsistence." Pp. 64–89 in *Households and the World-Economy,* edited by J. Smith, I. Wallerstein, and H. Evers. Beverly Hills: Sage Publications.

Smith, J., J. Collins, T. Hopkins, and A. Muhammad (eds.). 1988. *Racism and Sexism in the World-System.* Norwalk, CT: Greenwood Press.

Smith, J., I. Wallerstein, and H. Evers (eds.). 1984. *Households and the World-Economy.* Beverly Hills: Sage Publications.

Sokoloff, N. 1980. *Between Money and Love.* New York: Praeger.

Stacey, J., and B. Thorne. 1985. "The Missing Feminist Revolution in Sociology." *Social Problems* 32:301–16.

Stichter, S. 1990. "Women, Employment and the Family: Current Debates." Pp. 11–71 in *Women, Employment and the Family in the International Division of Labor,* edited by S. Stichter and J. L. Parpart. Boulder, CO: Westview Press.

Stichter, S., and J. L. Parpart (eds.). 1988a. *Patriarchy and Class: African Women in the Home and the Workforce.* Boulder, CO: Westview Press.

———. 1988b. "Introduction: Towards a Materialist Perspective on African Women." Pp. 1–26 in *Patriarchy and Class: African Women in the Home and the Workforce,* edited by S. Stichter and J. L. Parpart. Boulder, CO: Westview Press.

———. (eds.) 1990. *Women, Employment and the Family in the International Division of Labor.* Boulder, CO: Westview Press.

Thibault, G. M. 1987. *The Dissenting Feminist Academy.* New York: Peter Lang.

Tiano, S. 1987a. "Gender, Work and World Capitalism." Pp. 216–43 in *Analyzing Gender,* edited by B. Hess and M. M. Ferree. Beverly Hills, CA: Sage.

Tinker, I., and M. Bramsen. 1976. "The Adverse Impact of Development on Women." Pp. 22–34 in *Women and World Development,* edited by I. Tinker and M. Bramsen. Washington, DC: Overseas Development Council.

Truelove, C. 1987. "The Informal Sector Revisited: The Case of the Columbian Mini-Maquilas." Pp. 95–110 in *Crises in the Caribbean Basin: Past and Present,* edited by R. Tardanico. Beverly Hills: Sage.

———. 1988. "Factories in the Fields of Plenty: Gender, Agrarian Transformation, and Industrial Restructuring in Columbia." Unpublished Ph.D. dissertation. The Johns Hopkins University, Baltimore.

———. 1990. "Disguised Industrial Proletarians in Rural Latin America." Pp. 48–63 in *Women Workers and Global Restructuring,* edited by K. Ward. Ithaca, NY: ILR Press.

Truong, Thanh-dam. 1990. *Sex, Money and Morality: Prostitution and Tourism in South-East Asia.* London: Zed.

Van Allen, J. 1976. "African Women, 'Modernization,' and National Liberation." Pp. 25–54 in *Women in the World: A Comparative Study*, edited by L. Iglitzin and R. Ross. Santa Barbara, CA: ABC-Clio.

Von Werlhof, C. 1980. "Notes on the Relation Between Sexuality and Economy." *Review* 4:33–44.

_____. 1984. "The Proletarian Is Dead: Long Live the Housewives?" Pp. 131–47 in *Households and the World-Economy*, edited by J. Smith, I. Wallerstein, and H. Evers. Beverly Hills: Sage Publications.

_____. 1985. "Why Peasants and Housewives Do Not Disappear in the Capitalist World-System." Working Paper No. 68. Sociology of Development Research Centre, University of Bielefeld, Germany.

_____. 1988. "Women's Work: The Blind Spot in the Critique of Political Economy." Pp. 13–26 in Maria Mies, Veronika Bennholdt-Thomsen, and Claudia Von Werlhof (eds.), *Women: The Last Colony*. London: Zed Press.

Wallerstein, I. 1974. *The Modern World System*. New York: Academic Press.

_____. 1979. *The Capitalist World-System*. Cambridge: Cambridge University Press.

_____. 1984. "Household Structures and Labor-Force Formation in the Capitalist World-Economy. Pp. 17–22 in *Households and the World-Economy*, edited by J. Smith, I. Wallerstein, and H. Evers. Beverly Hills: Sage.

_____. 1989. *The Modern World System III*. New York: Academic Press.

Ward, K. 1984. *Women in the World-System: Its Impact on Status and Fertility*. New York: Praeger.

_____. 1985a. "The Social Consequences of the World-Economic System: The Economic Status of Women and Fertility." *Review* 8(4):561–594.

_____. 1985b. "Women and Urbanization in the World-system." Pp. 305–24 in *Urbanization in the World-Economy*, edited by M. Timberlake. New York: Academic Press.

_____. 1988. "Women in the Global Economy." Pp. 17–48 in *Women and Work #3*, edited by B. Gutek, L. Larwood, and Ann Stromberg. Beverly Hills: Sage.

_____. (ed.). 1990a. *Women Workers and Global Restructuring*. Ithaca, NY: ILR Press.

_____. 1990b. "Introduction and Overview." Pp. 1–24 in *Women Workers and Global Restructuring*, edited by K. Ward. Ithaca, NY: ILR Press.

Ward, K., and Linda Grant. 1985. "The Feminist Critique and a Decade of Research in Sociology Journals." *Sociological Quarterly*, 26:139–57.

_____. 1991. "On a Wavelength of Their Own? Gender and the Production of Sociological Theory." *Current Perspectives in Social Theory*. 11:117–140.

Ward, K., and Jean Pyle. Forthcoming. "Gender, Industrialization, and Development." In *Women in Development in the Third World*, edited by C. Bose and E. Acosta-Belen. Philadelphia: Temple University Press.

Weiss, J., F. Ramirez, and T. Tracy. 1976. "Female Participation in the Occupational System: A Comparative Institutional Analysis." *Social Problems* 23:593–608.

Westwood, Sallie, and Parminder Bhachu. 1988. *Enterprising Women: Ethnicity, Economy, and Gender Relations*. London: Routledge.

Wolf, Diane. 1990a. "Linking Women's Labor with the Global Economy: Factory

Workers and Their Families in Rural Java." Pp. 25–47 in *Women Workers and Global Restructuring*, edited by Kathryn B. Ward. Ithaca, NY: ILR Press.

———. 1990b. "Daughters, Decisions, and Domination: An Empirical and Conceptual Critique of Household Strategies." *Development and Change* 21:43–74.

———. 1992. *Factory Daughters, Their Families, and Rural Industrialization in Central Java*. Berkeley: University of California Press.

Wong, D. 1984. "The Limits of Using the Household as a Unit of Analysis." Pp. 56–63 in *Households and the World-Economy*, edited by J. Smith, I. Wallerstein, and H. Evers. Beverly Hills: Sage.

Wood, R. 1988. *From Marshal Plan to Debt Crisis*. Sage: Berkeley: University of California Press.

Yelvington, K. 1991. "Gender and Ethnicity at Work in a Trinidadian Factory." Forthcoming in *Caribbean Women*, edited by J. Momsen. London: Methuen.

Yoon, Y. H. 1990. "Economic Development and Changes in Gender Composition in the Manufacturing Industries in South Korea, 1963–1983." Paper presented at annual meetings of American Sociological Association, Washington, DC.

Chapter 4

Macrostructural Perspectives on Gender Inequality

Dana Dunn, Elizabeth M. Almquist, and Janet Saltzman Chafetz

Introduction

This chapter focuses on theories that provide insight into the macro-level structural causes and maintenance mechanisms of systems of gender inequality. These macrostructural theories differ fundamentally from social psychological and other microlevel perspectives on gender. The latter focus primarily on the process of learning gendered self-concepts, personality, emotional, and cognitive traits by individuals, and on individual-level choices and behaviors as they reflect and affect gender roles and gender inequality. By emphasizing characteristics of social aggregates, macrostructural theories enhance the understanding of how individuals are affected by and in turn affect structure. Features of communities, metropolitan labor markets, states, and nations all affect the degree to which males and females are equal in access to a society's scarce and valued resources and opportunities. This differential access cannot be fully understood by studying only individual-level variables. Macrostructural perspectives do not deny that individual characteristics and behaviors play a role in the creation and maintenance of gender inequality; rather, they assert that the influence of macrolevel structural variables is paramount. From this perspective, individual-level variables are conceptualized as reflecting macrostructural properties and, in turn, either recreating or changing them, contingent upon stability or change at the structural level.

Since Acker (1973) first criticized the lack of attention to sex/gender as a basis for stratification, several comprehensive macrostructural theories have been developed to explain inequality between the sexes (e.g., Blumberg 1984; Chafetz 1984, 1990; Collins 1975; Sanday 1974, 1981).

These theoretical models depart from what Andersen (1988) calls the "add-women-and-stir" approach to sociological theorizing in that they were developed specifically to address issues of gender inequality. (For more discussion of the "add-women-and-stir" approach, see Ward, the previous chapter in this volume.) As a result, they are less likely to embody gender bias than other, more traditional theoretical perspectives in stratification, which were developed in a climate of male-dominated sociology.[1]

Macrostructural theories attempt to explain gender stratification both panhistorically and cross-culturally. A viable macrostructural model must be universally applicable because, by design, the theory is intended to assess the effect of features of society on the level of gender inequality. Typically, these models are multicausal and include a combination of predictor variables such as features of the organization of the family, work (both household and nonhousehold), and politics.

The panhistorical, cross-cultural, and multicausal nature of macrostructural theories causes them to be difficult to test. A thorough empirical test would require data from a wide range of societal types (hunting and gathering through advanced industrial). Anthropologists often test portions of macrostructural theories with data collected on preliterate societies (e.g., using data provided by the Human Relations Area Files). Sociological analyses most commonly employ data from industrial and advanced industrial societies (e.g., Bureau of the Census data). Problems of data incomparability across these two types of data sets compound those produced by the multicausal approach of macrostructural theories. Due to the complexity of macrostructural theories, empirical tests to date have been restricted to only portions of the models.

Defining Gender Stratification:
Conceptual and Operational Definitions

Blumberg (1978) argues that the study of stratification answers the following broad questions: Who gets what? And why? Reformulating and expanding these questions to focus on gender stratification from a macrostructural orientation results in the following: (1) Which sex gets how much of what socially valued, scarce resources? (2) What features of social structure create this sex-based distribution of resources? The answers to the first question vary enormously from one society to the next. Macrostructural theories are designed to explain why this variation occurs, based on ideas concerning the answer to the second question.

The ultimate dependent variable in a macrostructural model of gender stratification would measure women's access to valued resources and opportunities, *relative to men's*, in all spheres of life (e.g., work, family, politics). Chafetz (1984) offers a thorough (though in her own view not necessarily exhaustive) list of the conceptual dimensions of gender inequality. They include women's access, relative to that of men who are their social peers (e.g., similar in age, social class, race, ethnicity, religion), to material goods, services, education and/or training, decision-making (in both public and private spheres, e.g., politics and family), prestige, psychic enrichment and gratification, discretionary time, and life-sustaining requisites (e.g., food, shelter, medical care). Freedom from physical coercion and behavioral constraints are also included as dimensions of gender inequality.

Developing an operational definition of gender inequality that encompasses all the dimensions of inequality and is valid across all types of societies at all points in time is an extremely difficult task that remains to be accomplished. Existing empirical tests of macrostructural theories employ a number of different compromise strategies in the choice of a dependent variable to represent gender inequality. One common approach involves restricting the research focus to only one dimension of gender inequality, usually women's relative access to formal employment opportunities and rewards (e.g., valued occupational roles or wages).[2] Another approach involves using a composite dependent variable, such as that used by Blumberg (1979) in studying preliterate societies. Her dependent variable, life options, is created by combining four options: women's relative freedom with respect to initiating marriage and divorce, premarital virginity, and the exercise of household authority (p. 31). Both of these approaches restrict the analysis of gender inequality to only one sphere of life—the former to the nondomestic workplace, the latter to the family. The ideal dependent variable would combine women's relative position in these two and other relevant spheres into one measure. Researchers creating such a comprehensive composite variable must be sensitive to the relative importance or value of the various types of resources and opportunities in each of the different spheres of life. It would therefore also be necessary to assign appropriate weights to the various components of the dependent variable. In order to effectively test macrostructural theories of gender inequality, the dependent variable must be measured at the aggregate level. Macrostructural perspectives do not address the situation of individual women. Rather, they focus on the status of women, relative to men, as general categories. Appropriate units of analysis when predicting this type of patterned inequality include communities, labor markets, states, and nations.

Predicting Gender Inequality from a Macrostructural Perspective

Identifying the sources of male advantage is a critical first step in the process of building an egalitarian society. The key causal variables set forth in macrostructural theories can be classified into five broad categories: ideological, family-related, sex ratio, economic, and political. In the following sections we explore the predictors of gender inequality in each of these categories.

Ideological Systems and Gender Inequality

Ideological variables are those which measure the importance of aggregate-level belief systems and associated symbols and rituals. In large-scale, technologically and socially complex societies, extensive variation with respect to beliefs is likely to exist across individuals. Nonetheless, patterned belief systems emerge to represent the values and attitudes of large numbers of individuals, or more commonly those of elite and powerful members of the society. These patterned belief systems are posited to be significant predictors of gender inequality in the theories of Blumberg (1978), Chafetz (1984, 1990), and especially Sanday (1981).

Both Blumberg (1978) and Chafetz (1984) treat ideological variables as secondary in importance to other structural variables. Blumberg argues that an ideology of male superiority or of sexual egalitarianism is an intervening variable between "the main poker chips of power" (1978, p. 29) and women's status relative to men's. She also suggests that ideological variables are shaped, in large part, by women's position in society. Chafetz (1984, 1990) further elaborates the relationship between belief systems (which she refers to as social definitional variables) and gender stratification, borrowing from Marxist sociology. According to Chafetz, patterned belief systems emerge out of material structures (primarily economic), and serve to legitimate the existing structural arrangements. The theoretical model Chafetz proposes includes a mutually reinforcing relationship between ideological systems and notions regarding gender differentiation (gender norms and stereotypes). In other words, thought systems that depict women as inferior to men also depict sharp differences between the sexes and advocate substantial behavioral differences. These behavioral differences then reinforce and legitimate the subordination of women (Chafetz 1990).

In contrast to the theories of Blumberg and Chafetz, which suggest that ideology has only a minor independent role in affecting women's status, anthropologist Sanday (1981) depicts belief systems as a pivotal independent variable determining the degree of gender inequality in a society. Sanday's model is based on the assumption that a materialistic focus, emphasizing concrete, tangible phenomena, places the cart before the horse. She asserts that humans develop belief systems to give order and meaning to their world, and that these belief systems subsequently serve to shape that world (influence its material structure). This argument about the importance of ideology as a predictor of women's status is summed up by Schlegel in the following statement:

> People do not form social groups and productive relations and then sit down to think and symbolize about them; rather, they act in accordance with both material and social advantage and the guiding principles that give the stamp of approval—or disapproval to their actions. (1977, p. 34)

Sanday, whose work focuses on technologically simple societies, argues that a society's belief system is affected by the nature and harshness of the environment, and the mode of subsistence. Sanday thinks that dangerous, harsh environments whose economies are based on migration and the pursuit of large game give rise to "outer orientations"—a belief system that portrays nature as a hostile force to be conquered, and emphasizes competition, physical coercion, and violence. Sanday thinks "inner orientations" develop in societies where the population lives in harmony with nature (e.g., few environmental threats, stable food supply), and the resulting values emphasize cooperation, life-giving, and nurturance. Sanday posits that these two types of ideological systems exert strong and opposite influences on the degree of equality between the sexes. Specifically, she argues that an inner orientation is associated with more egalitarian relations between the sexes, an outer orientation with male dominance.

Sanday offers empirical support for her theoretical model. Deviating from the single-case, ethnographic approach commonly used by anthropologists, she employs Murdock and White's Standard Cross Cultural Sample, consisting of 186 diverse societies, to test for a relationship between ideology and women's status. Using correlation analysis, Sanday presents convincing evidence of an association between ideological orientation and inequality between the sexes. Yet this correlational evidence says nothing about the direction of the causal connection between ideology and women's status relative to men. Sanday interprets the results of the correlational tests as supporting her model, but an alternative and equally feasible interpretation would be that the degree of gender inequality influences the development of differing societal orientations—a view more compatible with the theories of Chafetz and Blumberg.

Family Structure and Gender Inequality

Virtually all theories addressing gender inequality take note of the basic biological distinctions between the sexes, and suggest that these differences contribute to patterns of male dominance. The facts that women bear children and lactate, in particular, are often depicted as disadvantages with which women must contend. A common view is that childbirth and early child care responsibilities operate to limit women's social participation, including work outside the home. It is generally accepted that in the few societies where subsistence is largely based on hunting and in the many where warfare is common, women's relative status is low compared to other societies at the same level of technological development. Because these activities involve extensive, rapid travel, stealth, and danger, women constrained by childbirth and child care activities are excluded. Functionalists (e.g., Parsons and Bales 1955) imply that excluding women from dangerous activities (e.g., warfare, large animal hunting, claiming land, felling trees) is beneficial because it enables groups to survive. If women participated in these activities and were killed or injured, the ability to reproduce the group would be lost. As a result, men become the major providers and protectors, and are able to "exchange" these contributions for higher status. This, combined with the physical strength advantage of men, is seen by some theorists to be the basis for the origin of gender inequality (e.g., Washburn and Lancaster 1968).

It is important to note that where constraints arising from childbirth and child care prevent women from engaging in nondomestic work, they remain active workers in the domestic arena. However, household work is generally devalued. Much of the work performed within the home has use value rather than exchange value. Macrostructural theorists argue that exchange or surplus production is everywhere more highly valued. Women working only in the domestic sphere are cut off from the public realm of men, and also from other women. Women's relative isolation prohibits them from forming networks of support, and limits their access to information. In contrast, men working in extra-domestic roles are able to build networks of economic exchange, and they have far greater access to information in the public sphere. These advantages derived from nondomestic employment partially constitute the basis of men's superior status (Chafetz 1984; Friedl 1975).

Most contemporary macrostructural perspectives on gender inequality go beyond an emphasis on pure biological determinism and posit complex theoretical linkages between women's reproductive role and patterns of social organization. Chafetz (1984), for example, notes that while women everywhere give birth to children and lactate, different types of family and work systems exist cross-culturally. She suggests that the different forms of family and work organization interact with women's reproductive role to create variation across societies with respect to the overall degree of gender inequality. Friedl (1975) and Nerlove (1974) suggest that women adapt their child rearing (e.g., ceasing breast-feeding, introducing solid foods, spacing children) to fit other work roles. Brown (1979) argues that women's work must be compatible with nursing and child care responsibilities (e.g., it must be repetitive, require little concentration, be easily interrupted and resumed, be nondangerous, and require little travel). Work in horticultural societies is compatible with simultaneous child care; work in the large fields of agrarian societies and with machines in factories is far less compatible with child care. Rosaldo and Lamphere summarize this view that the connection between childbirth and gender inequality is mediated by structural features: "biological facts may make certain socio-cultural arrangements highly likely, but with changes in technology, population size, ideas and aspirations, our social order can change" (1974, p. 7).

Macrostructural theories of gender inequality employ numerous indicators of family structure as intervening variables. Specific features of family structure include lineality, locality, and household division of labor (Blumberg 1978; Chafetz 1984). Matrilineal and matrilocal kinship arrangements are posited to be associated with higher status for women. When descent and inheritance systems are designed to take them into account, women are less disadvantaged in terms of access to the means and fruits of production than where other kinship structures exist. Matrilineality tends to be associated with residence patterns that also favor women—either living with the wife's relatives (matrilocality) or establishing a separate residence for the new couple (neolocality). Matrilocal living arrangements result in higher status for women because they remain integrated in familial support systems after they marry. Neolocal residential patterns are also advantageous for women in that they permit a greater degree of autonomy than does patrilocality, especially freedom from constraint and supervision by in-laws. In contrast, when newly married couples are required to reside with the husband's kin, women's contact with their family and community of origin is severely curtailed, and they often become isolated in their new residence (Chafetz 1984).

In the theoretical models of both Chafetz (1984) and Blumberg (1978), the extent to which women specialize in domestic activities (including child rearing) is an important predictor of the overall level of gender inequality. When women assume the primary responsibility for domestic sphere labor and devote large proportions of their lives to child rearing, they are disadvantaged in the nondomestic workplace. Chafetz (1984, 1990) following Friedl, takes care to note, however, that mutual causation occurs between women's investment in the domestic sphere and women's role in the nondomestic economy. High levels of domestic and maternal involvement may simply be a response to exclusion from more socially valued roles in the economy.

Sanday (1981) and Chafetz (1984) both posit a link between the degree of threat in a society, family-related variables, and male advantage. Chafetz argues that high levels of social threat (warfare) give rise to patrilineal and patrilocal family structures, which in turn contribute to gender inequality. Sanday suggests that high levels of environmental threat are associated with male dominance because such conditions are associated with a fear of uncontrollable forces, a fear that extends to women's reproductive ability. When men's fears are projected onto female reproductive roles, they attempt to control women just as they attempt to control nature. This control is then reinforced by ideological systems that favor men.

Of the various macrostructural theories, Chafetz's is most complete with respect to the relationship between family structure and gender inequality. She asserts that the structure of the workplace, ideological systems, gender stereotypes, environmental harshness, and social threat all influence family structure. Family structure (lineality, locality, and household division of labor) is then posited to have a direct effect on gender stratification. Family structure is also assumed to exert an influence on the way in which nondomestic work is organized, and to produce an indirect influence on gender inequality through this variable. While a complex theoretical model such as this is required to approximate social reality, it is extremely difficult to test.

Empirical tests with family-related structural variables as predictors of gender inequality have included marital status as an indicator of the level of women's domestic responsibilities (Almquist, Darville, and Dunn 1985; Dunn 1987, 1988; Jones and Rosenfeld 1989). The assumption is that currently married women are more likely to have greater domestic responsibilities than those who are unmarried, and that this domestic burden will detract from participation in the economy, resulting in lower overall status for married women. The presence of children in the home, particularly young children, is another indicator of women's investment in the domestic arena that has been employed in empirical tests (Almquist et al., 1985; Dunn 1987, 1988). As macrostructural theories suggest, there is a weak negative effect of the proportion of women who are either married or have children (or both) on one dimension of gender inequality: women's average occupational attainment. Almquist et al. (1985) found evidence for the negative link between family responsibilities (proportion married and the birth rate) and women's share of professional occupations, using U.S. metropolitan labor markets, U.S. states, and nations as the units of analysis. However, these family-related variables were not found to have a significant effect on two other dimensions of women's status: women's earnings relative to men's (Dunn 1987, 1988) and women's political status (share of state and national legislatures) (Almquist and Dunn 1987).

The percentage of women who are divorced is another family-related variable that has been linked to the level of gender inequality in empirical tests. This variable is also thought to tap the level of women's investment in the domestic sphere in that divorced women are assumed to have a lighter domestic workload due to the absence of a spouse. Clearly, the assumption here is that husbands do not share equally in household responsibilities, so their departure does not imply a significant reduction in their contribution to such work. Much evidence exists to support this view (Beer 1983; Cowan 1983). Ideally, researchers would control for the involvement of men in the domestic arena, but such data are not available at the aggregate level. Almquist et al. (1985) found that the divorce rate is one of the strongest predictors of women's share of managerial occupations. While a high divorce rate in a state or a labor market is associated with a larger share of managerial occupations for women, no relationship exists between the divorce rate and women's share of the professions (Almquist et al. 1985) or women's earnings relative to men's (Dunn 1987, 1988). One interpretation of these seemingly contradictory findings is that divorced women need to support themselves and do not have time to undergo lengthy professional training. They may choose managerial positions, but they are restricted primarily to the lower level, lower paying managerial jobs.

It is important to note that while empirical tests of the link between family-related structural variables and gender inequality offer some support for macrostructural theoretical propositions, these tests are limited in several respects. First, they are often restricted to contemporary industrial societies where lineage and locality variables are constant. Second, they explore only one, or at most a few, dimensions of gender inequality. Third, they often ignore the larger context of the theoretical model (i.e., links to other theoretical variables).

The Sex Ratio and Gender Stratification

The sex ratio is the number of men per hundred women in a society or other aggregate. The sex ratio is often high, with an oversupply of men and an undersupply of women, in frontier or immigrant situations. In these instances, men take on domestic activities—cooking, washing, sewing—traditionally ascribed to women and they may assume paid occupations traditionally held by women as well. Women are scarce and highly valued for their homemaking and child rearing skills; they will be somewhat constrained to focus on domestic duties and refrain from extensive involvement in paid employment (Guttentag and Secord 1983; Chafetz 1984, 1990).

Sometimes societies artificially limit the number of women through female infanticide. Harris (1974) describes how this practice fits with the warfare complex prevalent in certain preliterate societies. These groups exist in harsh and threatening environments with high population density (cf. Chafetz 1984; Blumberg 1979), and they compete with each other for land and resources, including women. Warfare involves organized raids on other groups to steal women, who are then used as prizes to induce individual men to engage in further warfare. Thus in Harris's view, an artificially high sex ratio, warfare, and the subordination of women go hand in hand.

In contemporary societies, organized warfare reduces the supply of men. Women may temporarily gain access to important production roles in agriculture and industry and acquire some control over production. However, women's gains are temporary; when men return from battle or when a new generation replaces those lost in war, men resume control (Chafetz 1990).

Guttentag and Secord (1983) point out that an unbalanced sex ratio with an excess of women makes it less likely that women will marry and more likely that they will seek paid employment. However, women will not necessarily gain access to the most highly valued work roles. This perspective is borne out in current (mid-1980s) cross-national research. A low sex ratio (more women) is connected with high rates of labor force participation for women, but with women being severely underrepresented in managerial jobs (Almquist and Dunn, forthcoming). Jones and Rosenfeld (1989) also found that the sex ratio had similar effects in their study of metropolitan labor markets.

Economic Factors and Gender Stratification

Several features of the economic organization of society influence the status of women singly or in combination. These features can be grouped in three main categories: level of technology, societal emphasis on surplus production, and the manner in which work is organized.

Level of Technology and Surplus Production

Chafetz (1984) concludes that the level or type of technology is one of the most important independent variables affecting gender inequality. Technology is intimately linked with several other variables that directly or indirectly influence women's access to scarce and valued economic roles. For example, the more sophisticated the technology, the more work and home sites are separated. The more distant work and home sites are, the less opportunity women have to participate in nondomestic work roles, especially if they are tied to home with extensive child-rearing responsibilities. Work and home are most separated in industrial and agrarian societies, less so in horticultural groups.

Further, technology determines the importance attached to physical strength and/or mobility in production. The more important strength and mobility are, the more handicapped women are, particularly if women are seen as possessing less strength than men. Technology frequently combines with degree of gender differentiation—the extent to which women and men are seen as possessing very different skills, aptitudes, and abilities—to produce severe limitations on women's opportunity to participate in highly valued work roles (Chafetz 1984).

Physical strength is very important in agrarian and early industrial societies, and many (not all) women are excluded from work roles that require it. Women are not excluded from work activities requiring strength in horticultural societies (Murdock 1936); indeed they do much of the heavy work of carrying burdens, as well as a great deal of physical work preparing and planting soil, and tending and harvesting crops. But in all types of societies, women tend to be excluded from (or seen as not fit for) work requiring (geographic) mobility. Examples include business roles that require traveling, large animal hunting forays, claiming new land in horticultural or agrarian societies, and warfare in all types of societies. Each of these activities gives men access to other important resources and rewards. The business traveler can build a profitable business; the hunter can distribute the meat outside his family and form beneficial alliances with other non-kin (Friedl 1975); men who successfully claim land can then acquire rights to control its use which exclude women. Military service may not always lead directly to property ownership as it frequently did in feudal society, but military veterans can claim a variety of services, benefits, and exemptions not open to nonveterans.

The level or type of technology is also connected to a society's emphasis on surplus, rather than mere sustenance, production (Chafetz 1984; Blumberg 1984). Lenski (1966) points out that the more sophisticated the technology, the more surplus that can be produced and the more a society emphasizes the accumulation of goods and property, especially when the society is in intense competition with other groups. Hence, in Lenski's view, each advance in the level of technology leads to an increase in the degree of class stratification, at least until the later stages of industrial society where class inequality may diminish somewhat. All the available evidence from very diverse types of societies also suggests that the more sophisticated the technology and the greater the emphasis on surplus production, the greater is the inequality between women and men, at least until later stages of industrial development (Etienne and Leacock 1980; Huber 1991; Semyonov 1980; Youssef and Hartley 1979).

Some of the mechanisms linking technology, surplus production, and gender inequality are discussed in the section on the nature of work organization below. Arguably, the most important mechanism is that the more sophisticated the technology and the greater the emphasis on surplus production, the more likely some—highly advantaged—groups of men are to own or control the means of production and the more likely all women and most men are to be excluded from ownership and control. With this exclusion, both gender and class stratification are heightened (Chafetz 1984). It is noteworthy that socialist nations have vested "ownership" in all members of the society, but control in male elites. Therefore, the former state socialist societies were about as highly gender stratified as capitalist ones. Blumberg (1978) also stresses that the more accessible the means of production are to all individuals in society, the less the stratification of all types.

The technology of hunting and gathering and of simple horticultural societies includes only simple tools, handcrafted from wood, stone, and bone. Both women and men make and control the tools required for their work: men those required for hunting and women the gathering or horticultural implements. In these technologically simple societies land is regarded as the property of the entire group, not subject to private ownership and control. Women control their own work activities in these societies, often work together in cooperative groups, and some- times enjoy the benefits of matrilineal family patterns (Martin and Voor- hies 1975; O'Kelly and Carney 1986).

The development of advanced horticultural societies coincides with the introduction of the steel-tipped hoe, increased competition and warfare with other groups (Lenski 1966), and the vesting of land own- ership in men from patriarchal and patrilineally organized families (Martin and Voorhies 1975; O'Kelly and Carney 1986). Women continue to do the bulk of the sustenance production in the gardens they farm, but they do not participate in warfare, or the claiming and ownership of land. They do not control the means of production, and their status deteriorates.

Women's status deteriorates even further in agrarian societies. Agricultural production is carried out in large fields far removed from the household. Men control the bulk of the technology, including plows and other farm implements, draft animals, and military weaponry. Women work very hard, but their productive activities are seen as secondary to those of men. Moreover, in both advanced horticultural and agrarian societies, women's reproductive roles loom large. Their task is to produce future generations of men for warfare and work, and future generations of women for work and reproduction. In these instances, women devote an enormous proportion of their life cycle to childbearing (Chafetz 1984), and the children (and sometimes the women themselves) are seen as the property of the fathers/husbands.

The transition to industrial society results from numerous, far-reaching changes in technology, and corresponds with ownership of the means of production being increasingly concentrated in the hands of a few. The best jobs in machine production in early industrial societies and in contemporary societies that are beginning to industrialize are typically reserved for men.[3] However, as industrial technology becomes increasingly sophisticated, many processes are automated, so that strength to run the machines is no longer an issue. Late industrial societies and emerging postindustrial societies demand an enormous number of sophisticated scientists and technologists as well as managers and other professionals, often more than can be produced among men alone. If women can acquire the education needed for these positions, and if barriers to their involvement in sophisticated technical and professional occupations begin to fall, then their status relative to men's begins to improve.

Chafetz (1984) also suggests a curvilinear relationship between level of technology and the degree of gender stratification. Each increase in technological sophistication brought an increase in inequality between women and men, primarily because men controlled new technologies. But some decrease in inequality is predicted as control over technology, and hence over the means of production, becomes more a matter of education and training and less a matter of ownership in postindustrial societies.

Only one variable in contemporary research reflects the level of technology in society: the proportion of the total labor force engaged in manufacturing as opposed to other industries. (The assumption here is that firms in the manufacturing sector use more advanced technology then do agriculture or services, on average.) This is a very imperfect measure of the level of technology, but results from several studies suggest the predicted curvilinear relationship. Cross-national studies from the mid-1970s (Almquist et al. 1985) showed that the prevalence of manufacturing had extremely deleterious consequences for women's share of both professional and managerial jobs. By the mid-1980s, as service industries expanded and the proportion of the labor force in manufacturing declined slightly, a high proportion in manufacturing still curtailed women's representation in managerial jobs, but not the professions (Almquist and Dunn forthcoming). Similarly, Jones and Rosenfeld (1989) found that manufacturing limited women's share of managerial and male-dominated professional jobs in 1950 across U.S. metropolitan labor markets, but that the significance of manufacturing had declined by 1980.

Nature of Work Organization

For Chafetz (1984), the nature of work organization is the single most important factor that influences the degree of gender inequality. Work organization has a mutually reinforcing relationship with four other important factors: the level and type of technology, the type of family structure, the degree of ideological or religious support for gender inequality, and the degree of gender differentiation. Chafetz identifies six specific variables that comprise the organization of work:

1. Work requiring a long attention span negatively impacts women's opportunity to be involved, especially in preindustrial societies.
2. The more women participate in work activities that are highly valued by the society, the higher their status relative to men's.
3. If women and men are engaged in work activities that are sharply segregated by sex, women may benefit but only if they have fairly exclusive knowledge of and control over that work.
4. If women workers can easily be replaced, either by men or by a surplus pool of other women, their status is lower.

5 and 6.   The extent to which women control the means and the products of their production is the most important feature of work organization that affects their status in society at large.

Blumberg (1984) argues that the extent to which women control the means of production and allocate surplus products is *the cause* of women's economic power. She also believes that achieving economic power is the precursor to gaining power in all other spheres of life. Women's participation in productive, nondomestic work activities is a precondition, but is not by itself sufficient to produce economic power. Supplying labor is less important than the demand for women's labor (see also Chafetz 1990) and the specific areas of women's expertise. In order for women to gain economic power, their work must be strategically indispensable. In turn the strategic indispensability of women's work is a function of (1) the relative size of their contribution to total output, (2) the short-run substitution costs at the margin of their labor (how difficult or costly it is to replace individual women workers), (3) the extent to which women control technical expertise, (4) the extent to which women work free from close male supervision, and (5) the extent to which women are able to organize themselves collectively.

Blumberg's and Chafetz's positions on work organization are highly similar and equally difficult to test. Women's labor force participation (LFP) rate is one variable relevant to their perspectives. However, it reflects both women's supply of labor and the demand for women's labor, making it an inadequate measure of either. Furthermore, when women's LFP rates are low (less than 35 percent of all women are employed) or even moderate (up to 60 percent), women workers are probably highly replaceable by other women who are not working for pay, or by men who are seeking jobs. Only when women's LFP rates are very high (perhaps as high as 75 percent) will women not be replaceable, and will women's status improve. In contemporary cross-national research on industrial and developing societies (Almquist and Dunn forthcoming), women's LFP rates averaged only about 25 percent. Controlling for a number of other variables, the higher women's LFP rate, the larger was women's share of total employment and of some industry sectors, notably manufacturing and agriculture. However, there was no significant relationship between women's LFP rate and their share of managerial or professional jobs. Similarly, Semyonov and Scott (1983) found that increases in women's LFP rate did not increase their share of the top jobs in the United States, net of the increase in women's share of total employment.

Political Factors and Gender Stratification

Except for Blumberg, macrostructural theorists generally ignore women's political power or political status. Sanday (1981) emphasizes prestate societies, in which political officeholding is less important. Chafetz (1990) argues that political variables are, at most, of marginal importance in understanding gender stratification, net of the effects of economic ones. Blumberg (1984) offers two propositions, one that can be tested and one that cannot. The proposition that cannot be tested is her discounting principle. Societies are composed of successive levels of power and influence. In ascending order, these are the family, social class, community, and nation. Blumberg argues that the power women gain at one level may be used to gain power at a higher level, but women's power is discounted, i.e., it is not "cashed in" at full price at a higher level of power, because of male dominance at the higher level. In the United States today, some women may have equal or greater power than their husbands in their immediate family. But this does not translate into an equivalent amount of power in community affairs, for example. As indicated, this discounting principle is intuitively appealing, but impossible to test. It is clear that the higher the political office, the smaller is women's share. That is, women are better represented in city councils and mayoral offices than they are in state legislatures and gubernatorial offices, and better represented at state level than in national offices such as congressional or cabinet posts. This evidence is consistent with the discounting principle, but it could be explained without reference to this principle.

Blumberg's (1984) second proposition involving politics states that women must gain economic power before they gain significant political power and control over life's options. What evidence is there to support this? Studies of women's representation in political office are few in number, and only one (Almquist and Dunn 1987) examines officeholding within the context of macrostructural gender theories. In the mid-1980s, there were too few women in the upper houses of state legislatures to make meaningful comparisons, but women held about 20 percent of all seats in the lower houses of state legislatures in the United States, with a low of less than 5 percent in several deep south states and a high of 35 percent in New Hampshire and Colorado. Most of the variables suggested by gender theories—birth rate, labor force participation rate, marriage and divorce rates, percentage of the labor force in manufacturing—had no direct effect on women's share of house seats. However, the larger women's share of high-status managerial and professional occupations, the larger was their share of state legislatures. This evidence is consistent with Blumberg's principle of women gaining economic power before they gain political power. However, it is equally consistent with political power affecting economic power.

Variables measuring political organization were more important in predicting women's share of state house seats than was women's occupational status. Among the political variables, the size of the legislative district was of paramount importance. The larger the district, and the more voters a representative must reach, the fewer women were elected. States with highly professional legislatures (i.e., those with high pay for legislators, those which meet continuously rather than for brief sessions, and those which spend state dollars for research) were unlikely to have very many women. States with a high level of interparty competition exhibited high turnover among legislators, and in these states, women were more likely to be elected if they could gain their party's nomination (Almquist and Dunn 1987).

These findings are not readily interpretable within the framework of macrostructural theories of gender stratification, but it is clear that the more powerful and prestigious the legislature and the greater the costs of running for office, the less likely women are to be represented within it. These findings are faintly reminiscent of Blumberg's (1984) discounting principle, i.e., that it is unlikely that women will be able to translate power and influence gained at one level into a commensurate amount of power and influence at higher levels.

Contemporary Change in Women's Status Relative to Men's

Women's status relative to men's in nondomestic work plays a pivotal role in changing women's status in the theories of both Blumberg and Chafetz. The critical issues concern the demand for and replaceability of women's labor, and the extent to which women control the means of production and the products of production. In addition, Blumberg (1984) describes collective organizing as an avenue for women to gain economic power. Chafetz (1990) looks to the impact of technological, economic, and demographic variables on the total demand for labor as the central factor explaining change in the level of gender stratification. She argues that only when there are insufficient men available for the work they traditionally perform will women gain entrance to such jobs. In turn, women's increased access to labor force positions reduces other aspects of gender inequality.

Research on change in women's aggregate status in society has barely begun, but the enormous literature on gender segregation in occupations (Abrahamson and Sigelman 1987; Bridges 1980; England 1981, 1984; England and McLaughlin 1979; Reskin and Hartman 1986; Rosenfeld 1983) addresses these issues indirectly. Predominantly female occupations are underpaid relative to other, comparable occupations that are filled primarily by men. Women do not control access to jobs or occupational knowledge and training in any field, even those in which they are numerically very prevalent, e.g., nursing and teaching. Sex segregation is a prominent feature of the occupational landscape, and remains so, despite considerable increases in the number of women in the labor force, as well as decreases in the amount of time women devote to child rearing and increases in the number of years they devote to paid employment (England and Farkas 1986).

Despite a long-term decline in the level of sex segregation in the labor force in the United States, there has not been a unilinear movement of women into high-powered and prestigious occupations. Increasing demand for labor has occurred in the service or tertiary industries, and in jobs traditionally held by women (Semyonov and Scott 1983) as much as in the highly skilled and production-controlling positions traditionally held by men. Some occupations have become significantly less sex-typed, e.g., accounting, pharmacy, real estate and insurance sales. Often these occupations have become deskilled or declined in opportunity and wages just as secretarial work did when the typewriter was invented (Reskin and Hartman 1986).

It is clear that increases in demand do predict increases in women's employment, as Chafetz suggests (1990), and there was increased movement between 1970 and 1985 of women into professional and managerial fields. In the early 1970s, women's occupational position was not a significant predictor of their share of state legislature seats (Almquist, Darville, and Freudiger 1985). Fifteen years later, women had gained a larger share of the top occupations, and the larger their share of these, the larger was their share of state legislative seats (Almquist and Dunn 1987). How much additional economic power women can gain and whether they can continue to translate it into political power and control over life's options remain open questions.

Conclusion

We have reviewed macrostructural theories and research findings concerning aggregates that address the question, what factors explain variation in the level of gender stratification panhistorically and cross-societally? The literature reviewed explains women's collective access to society's scarce and valued resources, relative to that of men who are their social peers, by using five clusters of structural variables: ideological, family, sex ratio, economic, and political. Given the complexity of both the theories and the conceptual definition of gender stratification, we noted repeatedly that empirical tests to date have employed only very few, limited, and approximate measures of the many theoretical constructs.

Among specialists in macrostructural gender stratification, there is little debate that the five types of independent variables discussed here constitute the major ones required to explain how systems of gender inequality arise and maintain themselves, and why they vary in level. There is considerable difference of opinion, however, concerning the relative importance of each, as well as the nature and direction of their causal links with one another and with the dependent variables. These differences can only be resolved empirically, yet serious methodological problems abound that make such resolution very difficult.

The research discussed in this chapter leads to several conclusions concerning the impact of the major independent variables identified in the theories:

1. Ideology and gender stratification are related, but the causal direction is unclear. Therefore, disagreement between Sanday, on the one hand, and Chafetz and Blumberg, on the other, cannot yet be resolved.

2. Marriage and fertility rates are inversely related to some indicators of women's occupational status, but not others. Virtually all theories predict an inverse relationship. Similarly, divorce rates are directly related to some indicators of women's occupational status, a relationship that all theories concerning family structure and gender stratification predict.

3. Low sex ratios (relatively few men) are inversely associated with women's labor force participation rate, but not occupational status.

4. As several theorists suggest, a curvilinear relationship exists between the proportion in manufacturing (a measure of technological level) and women's share of higher level jobs, especially the professions.

5. Occupational gender segregation has deleterious effects on women's earnings in industrial societies, because the possible mitigating circumstances Blumberg and Chafetz suggest are absent from these societies. Where women control the means of production and the products of their labor, in some preindustrial societies, gender segregation leads to higher status for women, as these theorists predict.

6. Women's share of political offices increases as their share of top labor force positions does, as predicted by Blumberg's theory.

We conclude, therefore, that some evidence exists in support of the major theories reviewed in this chapter, and some evidence seems to require theoretical refinement. Most striking, however, is the general paucity of systematic, macrostructural research designed to test these theories. This area is still in its infancy, compared to gender research that employs individuals as the unit of measurement. The future is exciting precisely because so much work remains to be done.

Notes

1. In the introduction to *Feminism and Sociological Theory* (1989), Ruth Wallace describes the "male bias" in sociological theorizing that existed prior to the late 1960s. Janet Chafetz, in *Feminist Sociology: An Overview of Contemporary Theories* (1988), suggests that more recently feminism has served to counterbalance the prevailing male bias in sociological theory building. The tensions between advocates of traditional, male-centered stratification theories and proponents of a feminist reconceptualization of such theory are described in selections in *Gender and Stratification*, edited by Rosemary Crompton and Michael Mann (1986).

2. For an example of valued occupational roles used as a dependent variable in an empirical test of macrostructural theory, see Almquist and Dunn (forthcoming). For an example of the male/female wage gap used as a dependent variable, see Dunn (1988).

3. Further discussion of contemporary developing societies is provided by Kathryn Ward in this volume.

References

Abrahamson, Mark, and Lee Sigelman. 1987. "Occupational Sex Segregation in Metropolitan Labor Areas." *American Sociological Review* 52:588–97.

Acker, Joan. 1973. "Women and Social Stratification: A Case of Intellectual Sexism." *American Journal of Sociology* 78:(January):936–45.

Almquist, Elizabeth M., Ray Darville, and Dana Dunn. 1985. "Inter- and Intra-Societal Variations in Women's Occupational Position: Three Studies Assessing Sources of Sexual Inequality in the Labor Market." Paper presented at the annual meeting of the American Sociological Association, Washington, DC.

Almquist, Elizabeth M., Ray Darville, and Pat Freudiger. 1985. "Woman's Place Is in the House: Political and Social Variables Influencing Women's Share of State Legislative Seats." *Free Inquiry in Creative Sociology* 13:165–69.

Almquist, Elizabeth M., and Dana Dunn. 1987. "Women in State Legislatures, 1970–1985." Paper presented at the annual meetings of the American Sociological Association, Chicago.

Almquist, Elizabeth M., and Dana Dunn. Forthcoming. *Gender Inequality in the World of Work*. New York: State University of New York Press.

Andersen, Margaret. 1988. *Thinking About Women*. New York: MacMillan.

Beer, William R. 1983. *Househusbands: Men and Housework in American Families*. New York: Bergin and Garvey.

Blumberg, Rae Lesser. 1978. *Stratification: Socio-economic and Sexual Inequality*. Dubuque, IA: William C. Brown.

———. 1979. "A Paradigm for Predicting the Position of Women: Policy Implications and Problems." Pp. 113–42 in *Sex Roles and Social Policy*, edited by J. Lipman-Blumen and J. Bernard. Beverly Hills, CA: Sage.

———. 1984. "A General Theory of Gender Stratification." Pp. 23–101 in *Sociological Theory, 1984*, edited by Randall Collins. San Francisco: Jossey-Bass.

Bridges, William. 1980. "Industry Marginality and Female Employment." *American Sociological Review* 45:58–75.

Brown, Judith. 1979. "A Note on the Division of Labor by Sex." Pp. 36–47 in *Women and Society*, edited by S. W. Tiffany. Montreal: Eden Press.

Chafetz, Janet Saltzman. 1984. *Sex and Advantage: A Comparative, Macro-structural Theory of Sex Stratification*. Totowa, NJ: Rowman and Allenheld.

———. 1988. *Feminist Sociology: An Overview of Contemporary Theories*. Itasca, IL: Peacock.

———. 1990. *Gender Equity: An Integrated Theory of Stability and Change*. Newbury Park, CA: Sage.

Collins, Randall. 1975. *Conflict Sociology: Toward an Explanatory Science.* New York: Cambridge University Press.

Cowan, Ruth Schwartz. 1983. *More Work for Mother: The Ironies of Household Technology from the Open Hearth to the Microwave.* New York: Basic Books.

Crompton, Rosemary, and Michael Mann (eds.). 1986. *Gender and Stratification.* Cambridge: Polity Press.

Dunn, Dana. 1987. *Sex and Earnings: Examining the Male/Female Earnings Gap Across Metropolitan Labor Markets.* Unpublished Ph.D. dissertation, University of North Texas.

_____. 1988. "Sex and Earnings: Examining the Male/Female Earnings Gap in SMSAs." *National Social Science Journal* 1:1.

England, Paula. 1981. "Assessing Trends in Occupational Sex Segregation, 1900–1976." Pp. 273–295 in *Sociological Perspectives on Labor Markets*, edited by I. Berg. New York: Academic Press.

_____. 1984. "Wage Appreciation and Depreciation: A Test of Neoclassical Explanations of Occupational Sex Segregation." *Social Forces* 62:726–44.

England, Paula, and George Farkas. 1986. *Households, Employment, and Gender.* Hawthorne, NY: Aldine de Gruyter.

England, Paula, and Steven McLaughlin. 1979. "Sex Segregation of Jobs and Male-Female Income Differentials." Pp. 189–213 in *Discrimination in Organizations*, edited by R. Alvarez, K. Lutterman, and Associates. New York: Jossey-Bass.

Etienne, Mona, and Eleanor Leacock. 1980. "Introduction." Pp. 1–24 in *Women and Colonization: Anthropological Perspectives*, edited by M. Etienne and E. Leacock. New York: Praeger.

Friedl, Ernestine. 1975. *Women and Men: An Anthropologist's View.* New York: Holt, Rinehart and Winston.

Guttentag, Marcia, and Paul Secord. 1983. *Too Many Women: Demography, Sex and Family.* Beverly Hills, CA: Sage.

Harris, Marvin. 1974. *Cows, Pigs, Wars, and Witches.* New York: Vintage.

Huber, Joan. 1991. "A Theory of Family, Economy and Gender. Pp. 35–51 in *Gender, Family & Economy: The Triple Overlap*, edited by R. L. Blumberg. Beverly Hills, CA: Sage.

Lenski, Gerhard. 1966. *Power and Privilege: A Theory of Social Stratification.* New York: McGraw-Hill.

Jones, Jo Ann, and Rachel A. Rosenfeld. 1989. "Women's Occupations and Local Labor Markets: 1950 to 1980." *Social Forces* 67:3.

Martin, M., Kay, and Barbara Voorhies. 1975. *Female of the Species.* New York: Columbia University Press.

Murdock, George P. 1936. "Comparative Data on the Division of Labor by Sex." *Social Forces* 15:551–53.

Nerlove, Sara B. 1974. "Women's Workload and Infant Feeding Practices: A Relationship with Demographic Implications." *Ethnology* 13:207–14.

O'Kelly, Charlotte, and G. Carney. 1986. *Women and Men in Society.* 2nd ed. Belmont, CA: Wadsworth.

Parsons, Talcott, and Robert Bales. 1955. *Family, Socialization, and Interaction Process.* Glencoe, IL: Free Press.

Reskin, Barbara, and Heidi Hartman. 1986. *Women's Work: Men's Work*. Washington, DC: National Academy Press.

Rosaldo, Michelle Zimbalist, and Louise Lamphere (eds.). 1974. *Woman, Culture and Society: A Theoretical Overview*. California: Stanford University Press.

Rosenfeld, Rachel. 1983. "Sex Segregation and Sectors." *American Sociological Review* 48:637–55.

Sanday, Peggy Reeves. 1974. "Female Status in the Public Domain." Pp. 189–206 in *Woman, Culture and Society: A Theoretical Overview*, edited by M. Rosaldo and L. Lamphere. California: Stanford University Press.

———. 1981. *Female Power and Male Dominance*. Cambridge: Cambridge University Press.

Schlegel, Alice. 1977. "Toward a Theory of Sexual Stratification." Pp. 1–40 in *Sexual Stratification*, edited by A. Schlegel. New York: Columbia University Press.

Semyonov, Moshe. 1980. "The Social Context of Women's Labor Force Participation: A Comparative Analysis." *American Journal of Sociology* 86(November):534–50.

Semyonov, Moshe, and Richard Ira Scott. 1983. "Industrial Shifts, Female Employment, and Occupational Differentiation: A Dynamic Model for American Cities, 1960–1970." *Demography* 20(2):163–176.

Wallace, Ruth (ed.). 1989. *Feminism and Sociological Theory*. Newbury Park, CA: Sage.

Washburn, Sherwood L., and C. S. Lancaster. 1968. "The Evolution of Hunting. Pp. 293–303 in *Man the Hunter*, edited by Richard Lee and Ira Devore. Chicago: University of Chicago Press.

Youssef, Nadia H., and Shirley Foster Hartley. 1979. "Demographic Indicators of the Status of Women in Various Societies." Pp. 83–112 in *Sex Roles and Social Policy*, edited by Jean Lipman-Blumen and Jessie Bernard. Beverly Hills: Sage.

Chapter 5

Feminism and the Pro- (Rational-) Choice Movement: Rational-Choice Theory, Feminist Critiques, and Gender Inequality

Debra Friedman and Carol Diem

In the early 1970s one could hear the last nails being pounded into the coffin of functionalism, the dominant theoretical perspective of the time. Many types of sociologists vied for the honor of wielding the hammer. Among them were a group of black sociologists—including Nathan Hare, Joyce Ladner, Joseph Scott, and Robert Staples—who protested the theoretical standards by which black communities, achievements, and institutional structures were judged.[1] They considered mainstream sociology unable to break free of its bourgeois, liberal foundations, and therefore unable ever to give a fair accounting of peoples of color. This spawned a call for a black sociology and a corresponding insistence on "the death of white sociology."[2] The basic tenets of black sociology were an emphasis on sociology as a science of liberation, of nationalism, of radicalism, and of ideology. These aims would entail new theories and new methods.

A decade later the call for black sociology is rarely heard, but a new call for feminist sociology resounds. Yet current sociology offers no comparable target to functionalism for the establishment of counter-claims. In our present state of theoretical confusion, or pluralism (depending how one feels about it), there is no stationary target at all. Yet in order to claim out-group status, one must identify an in-group. If there is any target at all that has served as the straw man of feminist theory, it is rational-choice theory.

In its most general form the principal aim of rational-choice theory is to attempt to explain the emergence of social outcomes by the action of purposive agents who are subject to a host of constraints, both external (derived from institutional constraints and opportunity costs) and internal (derived from preferences).[3]

The purposive actor and her preferences rest at the center of these models, for the source of all social action derives from the actor's desire to attain ends that are most consistent with her values. Some rational-choice explanations rest solely on the mechanism of preference.

Other rational-choice explanations rely on two additional mechanisms. The first is the set of constraints that arises from scarcity: The same end can be easy for some to attain while hard for others because of their differential access to resources. Individuals are distinguished, then, by variations in their opportunity costs, or those costs associated with forgoing the next most attractive course of action. On this account, actors will *not* always choose the course of action that satisfies their *most valued* ends.[4]

The second is the set of constraints that derives from given social institutions. Rules, laws, policies, and norms all limit the courses of action—and even our imaginations as to what the true set of actions might be—available to individuals.[5] These limitations have a profound and systematic effect on social outcomes.[6]

Since rational-choice theory has served the role of whipping boy for many feminist theories, we feel it necessary first to address some of the more trenchant criticisms in order to try to win a fair hearing for what rational choice might have to contribute to an understanding of gender inequality. Following that, we will discuss several empirical studies of gender inequality that rely upon theoretical mechanisms drawn from rational choice.[7] These empirical studies include Brinton's (1988) comparative study of the maintenance of gender stratification in Japan and the United States, Luker's (1984) explanation of the variation of pro-choice and pro-life activism among women, and Gerson's (1985) examination of the variation in women's choices about work and homemaking.

A Feminist Critique of Rational-Choice Theory: A Rebuttal

Feminists have launched two broad classes of attacks on rational-choice theory.[8] The first is that, because of its assumptions, rational choice is a theory that excludes women from consideration, or, when it does take women into account, they almost always fail to measure up (i.e., fail to behave as rational-choice theory predicts). In this sense, it is a sexist theory, in the most pejorative sense of that term. This is the claim made most clearly in Paula England's work, particularly in her 1990 essay written with Barbara Stanek Kilbourne, "Feminist Critiques of the Separative Model of the Self: Implications for Rational Choice Theory." In order to address this damning criticism—especially for feminist women practitioners of rational-choice theory—we will speak to each of the principal arguments in their paper.

The second class of attacks, growing out of the first, is that, to the degree that rational-choice theorists do address issues of gender inequality, they do so in a wholly inadequate manner. Although unstated, the implicit claim seems to be that rational-choice theorists—because they rely on individual-level models—are too quick to blame women for their own inferior position in the stratification system.[9] However, we will suggest that rational-choice theory can be helpful in uncovering the *mechanisms* underlying some puzzling empirical outcomes that describe women's place in the world, and are therefore of interest or concern to researchers concerned with gender inequality. We will offer examples of three types of rational-choice explanations that do offer insights into the dynamics of gender inequalities.

England and Kilbourne (1990) criticize rational-choice theory, not for its lack of success in explaining social phenomena, but for the untenability of its assumptions, especially when women are the principal actors.[10] In particular, they argue that these assumptions seem to stem from the use of a separative rather than a connective model of the self. Feminist scholars (see, for example, Keller 1986) have suggested that in Western thought the view of the self that has predominated is one that glorifies individuation and assumes a lack of emotional connection between self and other. That is, the separative rather than the connective model of the self has been used. At the same time, childhood socialization and the structure of our institutions may encourage individuation and separation for males, while females are more likely to find themselves embedded in their social world and emotionally connected to others. As a result, a theory based on the separative model of the self is not only ignoring a vital realm of human experience, but one that is particularly relevant to women.

England and Kilbourne suggest that there are four assumptions of rational-choice theory that are suspect from this perspective: "selfishness; that interpersonal utility comparisons are impossible; that tastes are exogenous and unchanging; and that individuals are rational" (1990, p. 156). We will consider each in turn.

The Assumption of Selfishness

The criticism is that rational-choice theory makes an assumption of selfishness and that this assumption requires the further assumption of a separative self. Relying on a separative-self model, critics argue, leads to an overemphasis on selfishness because empathy and altruism come from emotional connection, a possibility said to be excluded from most rational-choice models. Yet this is a misreading of the behavioral assumption: Rational-choice theorists assume self-interest, *not* selfishness. Selfishness speaks to a choice between something self-concerned and other-concerned, and has a pejorative cast. Self-interest simply means being cognizant (even vaguely) of one's own values and then using them as a guide for action.

Free riding, one of the fundamental insights about social behavior emanating from rational-choice theory, seems, at first glance, to be clear evidence of the kind of selfishness of which this theory is accused. Free riding is said to occur when individuals fail to contribute to the effort to obtain a collective good. Individuals are motivated to free ride either (1) because they will benefit regardless of whether or not they have contributed (e.g., the passage of abortion legislation will benefit all women and men, not just those who gave their time and effort in the fight), or (2) because their particular contribution to the collective good will be so minuscule as to be meaningless (as in the case of one more marcher in a large antinuclear demonstration, or one person who does not use a car so as not to contribute to smog in Los Angeles). England and Kilbourne (1990) claim that these motivations imply selfishness. In doing so, they again confuse self-interest with selfishness. Regardless of the motivation, free riding is self-interested because the individual refuses to expend action that is demonstrably futile: Whether or not the individual joins a collective action has no relevance for whether the collective good is attained or not. *If the individual is persuaded that her action Will make a difference for the outcome, the rational-choice prediction is that she will join.* If she cannot be persuaded that her actions make a difference, the prediction is that she will undertake some other action that speaks efficaciously to her values.

It is true that the very term *free riding* has an amoral cast to it, and may evoke images of selfishness. We wish that the distinction between consequentialist and nonconsequentialist action—or futile and nonfutile action—were more often made explicit in rational-choice research. Believing that one's actions will be futile is sufficient to explain free riding; it is not necessary to invoke an assumption of selfishness. Rational choice is concerned with the estimated consequences of actions for guiding choice, not with the normative evaluation (selfish or not selfish) of those consequences. The point is that even when individuals hold a cherished value they may be unwilling to act if their behavior cannot produce desired consequences.

Further, Schwartz-Shea's and Burrington's (1990) research on the unintended outcomes of feminist organizations seeking to empower their participants through feminist processes (e.g. voluntarism, shared leadership, and consensus decision-making) should not be ignored. In the case of the Seneca "Women's Encampment for a Future of Peace and Justice,"[11] they found that the voluntaristic approach produced—as a direct result of their consciously planned institutional structure—a serious free-rider problem. This happened precisely because the leaders believed that women are naturally cooperative and so assumed that their women members would not free ride.

Self-interest need not be part and parcel of the separative model of the self. Acting on values can as easily lead people to give of themselves and to participate as the disadvantaged party in unequal exchanges as it can lead them toward selfishness.

The reason for the charge of sexism is not difficult to discern: It arises, we think, because economists who are practitioners of rational-choice theory (as against sociologists who are practitioners of rational-choice theory) have often substituted wealth maximization for utility maximization to obviate the problem of tautology. To the extent that this substitution derives from a marketplace in which women are underrepresented among the powerful and becomes a metric by which nonmarket behavior is evaluated, it is problematic.

Nonetheless, a theory must be judged on its own merits, not by how carefully those who employ it in their research utilize its first principles.

Interpersonal Comparisons of Utility

The criticism of rational-choice theory with respect to interpersonal comparisons of utility is twofold:[12] First, it is said, neoclassical economists reject the possibility of such comparisons. They do so because the actors in these models measure their gains and losses in terms of their gains in utility, and utility is purely subjective. Second, since rational choice is a separative-self model, how could it take such comparisons seriously? Interpersonal comparisons take the other into account, by definition. There are two rebuttals. Despite the fact that we use rational-choice theory, we care much less than our critics do what neoclassical economists think is possible or impossible, unless they have compelling reasons for their beliefs. We do not find the neoclassical economists' reasons for rejecting interpersonal comparisons to be convincing. Second, in the section above, we have already made the case that the theory itself is not tied to a separative-self model. Yet, to leave it at that would be to give short shrift to a very interesting—and incredibly complex— theoretical problem.

In fact, interpersonal comparisons have always presented rational-choice theorists with a quandary, and there is no agreement on the possibility of making such comparisons.

Let us first turn to the question of whether women are more likely to make these interpersonal comparisons of utility than are men, as England and Kilbourne (1990) suggest. That may be, but still at least three conceptual and methodological issues still remain: First, even if we all accept the idea that individuals can (somehow) make interpersonal comparisons of utility, it is likely that the degree to which these comparisons are invoked in their decision-making processes varies. How might we be able to observe this variation and then account for it?

Second, within one individual—that is, among multiple selves—how much and what kind of variation is there in the use of "interpersonal" comparisons? (We shall call these *intra*personal comparisons.) How are these intrapersonal comparisons of utility made? If I am balancing a career and a family, which self decides how the next hour of my time is best utilized?

Third, there is a normative issue: Is a person who makes interpersonal comparison of utilities before acting a better, more caring person than one who does not, as England and Kilbourne (1990) seem to imply? What about a monomaniacal wealth maximizer (or, a discriminating monopolist) who has the choice of three potential trading partners? Would he not be best served by making interpersonal comparisons of utility to select among the three, and then setting three different prices for his good or service in consequence? In fact, every person involved in an exchange relation—for whatever end—should seek to make these comparisons. That they do not would seem to suggest that these kinds of comparisons are either too difficult or too costly to make.[13]

Rational-choice theory would be well served by incorporating this dimension. Still, even if we were able to, we would have a no more or less sexist theory than we do now. Interpersonal comparisons of utility are not the same thing as empathy. Nor would including them adequately address the criticism that rational-choice theories pay insufficient attention to power differences. (They have dealt insufficiently with power, although for a major exception, see Coleman 1990.)

The absence of interpersonal comparisons of utility in our model should not be mistaken for theoretical intent rather than for true puzzlement over how to solve the theoretical and methodological quandaries of incorporation. The reason that interpersonal comparisons of utility are not a routine and systematic part of every rational-choice theory—especially every sociological rational-choice theory—is because the problems set out above preclude their inclusion at this time.

Stable and Exogenous Tastes

The assumptions that preferences are stable and that they are taken as given—that is, they are assumed to be exogenous to the model—also raise objections. The first criticism is that tastes do change; therefore, the stability assumption is faulty. The second is that if tastes are assumed to be stable and exogenous, then they cannot be affected by social and economic processes. But this, it is argued, is unrealistic if an individual is connected to others; hence these assumptions are a part of the (sexist) separative-self model. In our view, the assumptions that tastes are stable and exogenous to choice are simplifying assumptions adopted by many rational-choice theorists because no adequate theory of preference formation exists.[14] Although we concede that these assumptions are not ideal, we do not agree that they result from a separative bias. Several points can be made in this regard.

First, the criticism that assails the assumption of stability entails the alternative assumption that tastes *do* indeed change. That tastes change frequently and/or dramatically is, however, open to question. It has been argued that many cases of *apparently* changing tastes may not reflect such instability (Stigler and Becker 1977). Behavior that might at first glance appear to reflect changing preferences may instead reflect changing income or prices. For example, one might conclude that a person who is increasing her consumption of fine wine has a growing taste for fine wine. Such an increase in consumption, however, also might result from something so simple as a decrease in the price of wine or an increase in the person's income. And it is not only such obvious changes in price or income that may be responsible for behavioral changes that might be taken to indicate changes in taste. One would expect that an individual's wine consumption might increase with the development of human capital conducive to the appreciation of fine wine. Training in wine tasting or time spent tasting wine, therefore, might increase the time spent enjoying fine wine because it increases the marginal utility of doing so.

A similar explanation may account for the apparently changing tastes in the example used by England and Kilbourne (1990) of the individual whose preferences for job attributes are affected by the jobs she has held. Changes in desired job attributes may potentially reflect things other than changing preferences. Holding a job may allow a person to develop skills for coping with negative aspects of that job or for exploiting that position in order to obtain all possible benefits (thus increasing the utility derived from the job). There also may be decreasing marginal utility associated with some positive aspects of certain jobs. Initially, it may seem worth the long hours and time away from friends to be a flight attendant, for example, since with such a job comes travel to new and unusual places. But after a flight attendant has been able to enjoy inexpensive travel for a time, the travel may no longer seem worth the long hours and difficulty of dealing with the public. A choice to change jobs in this instance does not reflect changing tastes but rather the decreasing marginal utility of additional travel.

Although Stigler and Becker do not prove that tastes are unchanging, their work does suggest that in many cases behavior that might appear to be a function of changing tastes may instead reflect changing prices, capital stock, or the like. Becker also notes that:

> The preferences that are assumed to be stable do not refer to market goods and services, like oranges, automobiles, or medical care, but to underlying objects of choice that are produced by each household using market goods and services, their own time, and other inputs. These underlying preferences are defined over fundamental aspects of life, such as health, prestige, sensual pleasure, benevolence, or envy, that do not always bear a stable relation to market goods and services. (1986, p. 110).

What may appear to be changes in tastes may appear so because the objects chosen to satisfy those preferences vary according to availability or knowledge rather than as a result of changes in underlying preferences.

But what if preferences, in fact, do change? What can be said of the stability assumption then? In the absence of a theory of preference formation and development, the assumption that preferences are stable is necessary in order to avoid the use of a tautological explanation that traces the cause of inconsistent or changing behavior to inconsistent or changing tastes. As long as we limit ourselves to explaining behavior in a particular situation or in a limited time frame, we can still hope to explain variations in behavior by assuming stable tastes without also making the assumption that preferences never change.[15]

Yet the objection is not only confined to the stability assumption, but to the exogeneity assumption as well. As rational-choice theories are applied to all human behavior and the exogeneity assumption is maintained, it follows that tastes must be viewed as exogenous to all social interaction. "In such a view," England and Kilbourne (1990) write, "tastes cannot be explained by other social sciences' theories since the neoclassical model is seen to replace these theories" (p. 165). It would seem, however, that they overstate the imperialistic impulses of those advocating the value of the rational-choice approach. Becker, a strong advocate of this approach, writes, for example:

> How preferences have become what they are, and their perhaps slow evolution over time, are obviously relevant in predicting and understanding behavior. The value of other social sciences is not diminished even by an enthusiastic and complete acceptance of the economic approach. (1986, p. 119)

If economic theory is to be able to claim to explain all of human behavior, then it is clear that a theory of preference formation needs to be incorporated in the economic model of human behavior. But until the time when such a theory exists, we can still hope to explain behavior in separate realms while assuming exogenous tastes so long as we do not try to take on all of human behavior at once.

Dissatisfaction with the rational-choice assumptions of stable and exogenous tastes is not a uniquely feminist phenomenon. The feminist critique is that these assumptions result from a separative bias. England and Kilbourne (1990) argue that only the individual who is socially isolated might be expected to progress through life with unchanging preferences. The theory, then, reflects a view of humans as being emotionally separated from one another. In response to this we suggest that preferences may change in ways other than through social interaction. It is not difficult to imagine an individual's tastes changing even if she is socially isolated. Tastes may change, for instance, as a result of experience that does not follow from emotional connection. Who is to say that the preferences of an individual who is stranded on a desert island will not change—as a result, say, of experience—even though she is isolated from others? It seem possible, for example, that she might initially long for a return to civilization, but that such longing might disappear as time goes on and as she settles into a peaceful routine.[16]

What is missing from rational-choice theory currently is not simply a consideration of the effects of emotional connectedness on tastes, but rather a consideration of the effects of any number of factors on the formation or determination of tastes. Rational-choice theory is incomplete, but these omissions do not result specifically from lack of consideration of emotional connections among individuals.

The Opposition of Rationality and Emotion

The feminist critique of the separative bias of rational-choice theory can be applied not only to the emphasis on the separation between individuals, but also to the "tendency to *separate human qualities into oppositionally defined dichotomies*" (England and Kilbourne 1990, p. 167; emphasis in original), a tendency that appears in Western thought in the dichotomization of emotion and reason. The conception of rationality in rational-choice theory will be problematic from this perspective if it is conceived as a "radically separate opposite" of emotion. Emotions are subsumed under tastes, according to the critics. Since tastes are assumed to be exogenous, there is thus a separation of reason and emotion.

Although from the rational-choice perspective individuals are expected to use rationality to maximize benefit given their preferences, the separation of preferences and rationality (wherein preferences are not shaped by rational decision-making and vice versa) is entailed in the approach only insofar as the assumption of stable and exogenous tastes applies. To the extent that a separation of tastes and rationality exists then, it is a function of the assumptions regarding tastes. Since we have argued above that the assumptions that tastes are stable and exogenous cannot be said to stem from a separative bias, it follows that the separation of rationality and tastes does not result from a separative bias.

A further question can be asked of the equation of preferences and emotions: Are our preferences emotions because they are our desires? The mere fact that an individual—given her biological makeup and stock of human capital—derives more utility from one good than another does not mean that her emotions are necessarily involved. Moreover, even if we grant that some preferences involve emotion and thus, to the extent that there is a separation of preferences and rationality there exists a separation of emotion and reason, the opposition of emotion and reason is nevertheless not entailed. Separation does not imply opposition any more than interaction implies similarity.

And What of Choice Itself?—A Fifth Critique

One final criticism posed by some feminists concerns the basic issue of choice. Women are often employed in poorly paying occupations. Is their low income a matter of choice? Women take their children and leave their husbands, often with limited resources and low levels of human capital, in order to protect themselves and their children from abuse. Is their resulting poverty a matter of choice? There is a long history of the discussion of such issues.

Aristotle, and many following him, argued that decisions made under duress are still voluntary.[17] The person who robs a bank because someone puts a gun to her child's head and tells her that if she does not rob the bank her child will be killed, is, following such reasoning, making a choice.

Objections to this line of reasoning, such as those that have been offered in some feminist critiques of rational-choice theory, may be based on the belief that if such actions are viewed as choice then those who engage in them should or will be held accountable for the outcome. The assumption seems to be that if women make choices then women must be to blame for their situation. This judgment of responsibility does *not*, however, follow from the assessment of an action as voluntary. The point is that the choices that women make are rational given the constraints that they face. Just as we do not blame the mother for the robbery when she robbed the bank out of fear for her child's life, it does not follow from the rational-choice approach that we would hold women to blame for their position in the socioeconomic structure. The root cause of their position rests with the constraints that they face, not with the choices that they make. Thus the alleged sexist bias rests on the improper confounding of choice and responsibility (by the critics).

Rational-Choice Explanations of Gender Inequality: Three Theoretical Paths

Scrooge as the epitome of the rational-choice decision-maker—atomized, unconcerned with others, a wealth-maximizer above all—is a convenient straw man, but nothing more than that. Maria, the governess in *The Sound of Music*, as the epitome of the connected actor—selfless, devoted to others, aware of their needs and desires even before they are—is a convenient straw woman, but nothing more than that. We are fundamentally uninterested in their psyches. What we are after are explanations of collective outcomes, patterns of inequality, and mosaics of choices.

Can rational-choice theory be at all helpful in providing explanations of the persistence of institutional-level gender inequality?[18] In what follows, we will give a brief example of each of the three mechanisms relied upon by rational-choice theorists to explain variation—institutional constraints, opportunity costs, and preferences—as it is applied to an issue of gender inequality.

The First Source of Variation: Institutional Constraints

If one looks to see what disadvantages women may face in the labor market, one symptom of gender inequality that is immediately striking is the difference in wages received, on average, by women and men. This wage gap in part results from differences in human capital between women and men. To say this, however, is not to say that women are alone determining their level of human capital, that investment in human capital is simply a function of a person's potential, her drive, her family's resources, and other individual factors, or that the human capital of women and men (or of women in different social environments) will be similarly interpreted or rewarded. Instead, it seems that a broad array of institutional constraints shapes the development and evaluation of human capital in a manner that is not immediately apparent.[19] On the basis of her comparison of gender stratification in Japan and the United States, Brinton (1988) argues that an examination of the institutions involved in the formation of human capital can help to explain the extent of gender stratification and the maintenance thereof. In this vein, she suggests that in Japan the organization of the labor market and educational system, the structure of intrafamilial exchange, and strong norms regarding the timing of marriage combine to ensure continued extreme gender inequality.

Although education is crucial for occupational success in both Japan and the United States, education proceeds somewhat differently in these two countries. Tracking in the Japanese educational system occurs by school, with entrance examinations determining where in the hierarchy of schools students find themselves. Personnel are chosen by employers on the basis of the reputation of school attended. Since internal labor markets are strong and there is little interfirm mobility, an individual's first job is crucial in determining her success. Hence, the entrance examinations that determine the school a student attends are of tantamount importance. In recent years, parents have increasingly been providing private education to their children in order to help them do well on such examinations.

Since public support for the aged in Japan is limited, such investment in offspring is encouraged by the fact that parents are likely to need to rely on their children for economic support as they age. Given the real and perceived sex discrimination in the labor market, it is in parents' interests to invest in their sons rather than their daughters in order to ensure future financial security.

Employers also have an incentive to concentrate their attentions on males. As a result of their heavy investment in workers, employers would be wise to invest in workers they believe will remain with their firms. Yet in Japan there are strong norms regarding the time for marriage. The vast majority of women marry between the ages of twenty and twenty-seven. Thus, women are considerably less attractive to employers who want not to lose their investment in workers and expect that they will experience such a loss if they hire women—an expectation due presumably to strong norms not only about timing of marriage but also about women leaving jobs at the time of marriage or childbirth.

According to Brinton then, Japan has a system in which employers, educators, and parents sponsor the development of the human capital of young individuals. Since the returns to the investment of employers and educators (who gain prestige by satisfactorily placing graduates with good firms) from sponsorship are greatest if individuals are committed to the labor force, and given the norms about women's family responsibilities, educators and employers are less likely to sponsor women. Since parents perceive gender discrimination in the labor force, they too may be less likely to sponsor their daughters' human capital development.

Thus the institutions in Japan governing the development and evaluation of human capital combine to maintain a high level of gender inequality. Presumably the development of women's human capital—and thus gender inequality—is affected in all societies by such institutional constraints. It also might be argued that within any given system of human capital development, institutional constraints and opportunity costs, as affected by family composition, may influence parental behavior toward their daughters. Diem (1989) discusses the possible reaction of parents, especially fathers, to having only female offspring, and the resultant consequences of the presence or absence of male siblings for women's human capital and economic attainment. Institutional constraints on socialization, and thus on human capital development, are provided by norms regarding the appropriate behavior of daughters and sons as well as parental behavior toward each. More specifically, within this normative system, fathers may be viewed as having special skills or characteristics to pass on to their sons, they may be expected to serve as role models for their sons, and they may anticipate engaging in certain types of activities with their sons (tossing a football around, to take a rather stereotypical example) from which they derive a certain amount of pleasure. A father may be assumed (by both himself and others) to have less to offer his daughter, and as a result he may tend to leave the raising of his daughters to their mother. Indeed, fathers do tend, perhaps as a result of such norms, to be more involved with their sons than with their daughters (Lamb and Stevenson 1978).

These institutional constraints produce different sets of opportunity costs for parents in different situations. The opportunity costs associated with involvement in the life of his daughter(s), for instance, may decrease when a man has no sons. It may be, then, that fathers involve themselves in the life of a daughter, encourage a daughter to participate in more "masculine" activities, and so on if they have no sons. Women without brothers have higher levels of educational attainment, fewer children, and are more likely to work in male-dominated occupations than women with brothers—a finding suggestive of such an increased involvement in the lives of daughters when men have no sons (Diem 1989).

Other institutional constraints not so obviously connected to human capital may influence both its development and evaluation. Such an effect of institutional constraints would appear to be present in the case of legislation regarding abortion. In the course of her explanation of why abortion has become such a divisive issue, Luker (1984) notes that the majority of activists on both sides are women.[20] In interviews with prochoice and prolife activists in California, Luker (1984, pp. 194–197) found that whereas the few male activists on either side were "virtually indistinguishable," in terms of the extent of their education, their income level, the number of children they had, and their occupation, there were clear differences between prochoice and prolife women in terms of these background variables. The activists on the opposing sides of the debate have disparate worldviews, involving different convictions regarding sexuality, morality, and appropriate roles for men and women. Luker argues that these worldviews are in a sense on trial in the abortion debate. The debate has become a referendum on motherhood, and the differences between these two groups suggest that legislation regarding abortion constitutes an important institutional constraint that differentially affects women who have invested in careers and those who have invested in motherhood.

There were significant educational differences between the two groups, with prochoice activists having higher levels of educational attainment. These educational differences are in turn associated with occupational differences: The prolife activists were much less likely to work in the paid labor force, and when they did, they earned less, reflecting different occupations (the prochoice women tended to be employed in the professions, as executives, and the like, whereas the prolife women, if employed, were employed in jobs that women have traditionally filled, e.g., teaching or nursing). These differences in education and occupation are also tied to these women's different involvement in marriage and family roles. The prochoice activists were less likely to be married, were more likely to be divorced, and tended to have fewer children than the prolife activists. The different life-styles of prochoice and prolife activists are associated with a different need for abortion or, put another way, different costs associated with a lack of control over fertility. For example, the person who has already committed herself to a large family and who is not employed in the paid labor force will be less dramatically affected by an unplanned pregnancy than will an individual who is employed full time and who has an affluent life-style that is dependent on her income.

Since prolife women have invested in the traditional female role, something that supports the traditional division of life into distinct male and female roles supports their interests (but opposes the interests of prochoice women). A restriction on the availability of abortion supports traditional gender roles. "Women who oppose abortion and seek to make it officially unavailable," Luker writes, "are declaring, both practically and symbolically, that women's reproductive roles should be given social primacy" (1984, p. 200). Restrictions on abortion mean that nonreproductive roles may have to be subordinated to pregnancy, and the ("male") resources of women who have committed themselves to nonreproductive roles are subsequently devalued along with those nonreproductive roles. In this way, such restrictions are an institutional constraint that limits women's ability to succeed in the labor market. If employers know that reproduction is not completely under the control of sexually active women, then they may be less willing to hire them, invest in their human capital, and promote them, and women's investment in their own human capital also becomes less profitable. In these ways, then, the legal restriction of abortion is an institutional constraint that is expected to contribute to gender inequality in the labor market.

Officially legitimated access to abortion, in contrast, seems to downgrade the status of women who have devoted themselves to family roles, and to threaten the set of social relations between men and women that provided some protection to themselves and their children. By making pregnancy discretionary, abortion de-emphasizes the differences between men and women, differences that support the traditional division of labor in which prolife women have invested and on which they depend. Thus the easy availability of abortion provides a constraint on women's decision-making, since it makes investment in family roles less stable.

A view of abortion laws as providing institutional constraints does two things: It provides a theoretical mechanism by which it is possible to understand the emotion stirred by this debate. In addition, it points to how a lack of control by women over their reproduction may be a contributing factor to their inequality in the workplace.

These three empirical applications of rational-choice theory serve to explicate one way in which—through the examination of institutional constraints—it may contribute to the explanation of gender inequality.

The Second Source of Variation: Opportunity Costs

Suppose that we wished to explain the full range of the distribution of women's and men's career and domestic lives. How might we produce an explanation that would give meaning to a twelve-celled table crosstabulating employment status (full-time, part-time, none) by family status (married with children, married without children, unmarried without children, unmarried with children)? What social or background characteristics would explain the considerable variation among women as well as between women and men? Must we rely only upon prior empirical knowledge?

Rational-choice theory offers a mechanism by which these variations might be understood. Opportunity costs are a feature of all situations in which actors make choices. They are defined as those costs that consist of forgoing the next best alternative. Consider two available alternatives that an actor deems most valuable (using pecuniary and/or nonpecuniary criteria). The opportunity cost of choosing A is the (forgone) value of B; similarly, the opportunity cost of choosing B is the (forgone) value of A. When actors maximize their utility by choosing the alternative that is valued most highly, that choice entails costs, one of which is the opportunity cost.

One general implication that can be drawn from a consideration of opportunity costs is that when the difference between the value of the two alternatives, A and B, is very small, the choice becomes a more difficult one (in the absence of perfect information) because it involves forgoing a highly valued alternative course of action. Hence, individuals who have alternatives that are close in value bear greater opportunity costs than those whose choices include alternatives of clearly unequal value. Any factor that systematically affects the number of available choices close in value may be an important one, according to this line of reasoning. Gender is one such factor.

There are several implications of opportunity cost arguments for the explanation of gender differences, as well as for the explanation of differences in choices within gender groups. For example, consider the alternatives of full-time employment and full-time homemaking. Choosing homemaking is an option much more available to women than it is to men, for many social and historical reasons. As women and men consider the choice between employment and homemaking, this means that women who choose employment bear greater opportunity costs of deciding to be employed than men do, precisely because homemaking is a more valued (and viable) option for (most) women than it is for (most) men. Thus, even if women and men were to have identical employment opportunities and wages, women still would bear more cost than men in entering the labor market on account of this difference in opportunity costs.

Hence, whereas most (non-rational-choice) studies of gender inequality have focused almost exclusively on poorer wages and benefits associated with most jobs available to women (the macroeconomic realities of the labor market), a theoretical model of gender inequality emanating from a rational-choice model suggests that this *under*estimates the total costs to women in the labor market: Not only do women have to suffer financially when they do engage in paid labor, but they also bear opportunity costs that men in the labor market do not, at least not to the same degree.

It is also possible to draw upon this sort of reasoning to understand the variation in decisions about paid employment and homemaking among women. In her book *Hard Choices*, Kathleen Gerson (1985) chronicles a sample of women who seek to make choices that simultaneously enhance their work and home lives, and that entail as few costs as possible.[21] Thus, the choice to have one child (as against none, or more than one), for instance, is a decision born of rational calculation. For nondomestic women who do not wish to remain childless, this is the path of least resistance; it simultaneously reduces the costs of children to careers as well as the long-term costs of childlessness. This is because the opportunity cost of employment measured in the value of children suggests that, for most women, forgoing two children as against one entails a lower opportunity cost than forgoing one child (i.e., remaining childless).

Gerson offers an analysis of why it is that some of her sample opted for full-time homemaking, some for interrupted or part-time work combined with homemaking, some for combining work and motherhood, and some for work and childlessness. Gerson demonstrates that while socialization is an inadequate explanation for these variations, the interplay of two factors—relationship status and occupational opportunities—prove powerful in accounting for choices across the array of alternatives.

Stable relationships (and their absence) shape these choices. Of the thirty-three women who set out to have a predominantly domestic life, only eleven managed to do so.[22] Unstable relationships—which undermined child rearing, the mainstay of the domestic alternative—thwarted these women in their plans to become mothers and homemakers. Of the thirty women who had planned to be nondomestic, twenty-two found themselves primarily in domestic situations. Here a stable marriage—one that provided the basis for child rearing as an alternative occupation, thereby lowering its opportunity cost—made the domestic option more attractive than originally had been anticipated.[23] Childlessness was also largely explicable in terms of the stability or instability of relationships. Roughly half of the sample were childless at the time of interview; 22 percent intended to remain so. A significant number of this latter group lacked partners altogether, or lacked partners who wanted to participate in rearing children. In contrast, those who decided to combine paid work and motherhood had stable relationships where partners could be counted on to participate in child rearing.[24]

Second, workplace opportunities (and the lack thereof) are also instrumental in decision-making. The women who began with a domestic orientation and ended up with a nondomestic life in large part were seduced by the attractions of work. Some originally pursued traditional female jobs but fortuitously ended up in firms with affirmative action employment policies. These jobs gave them advancement possibilities they had not expected but were nonetheless delighted to receive. Others, either by design or happenstance, found rewarding work in nontraditional occupations that made the domestic alternative pale by comparison. The lure of the workplace also contributed to the decision to remain childless by increasing the opportunity costs of childbearing. For still others, the ghettoization of women's jobs and blocked mobility paths lowered the opportunity costs of following the domestic path, as well as highlighted, by contrast, the pleasure of domestic autonomy and child rearing.

Although the comparative case for men is not presented, it is not difficult to imagine that their dilemma would not be nearly so omnipresent or poignant. One effect of structural inequalities is simply to make the choices that women face much more difficult *on account of the opportunity costs that they face*. To the degree that women in a given social class have a choice about whether or how much to work for pay, their opportunity costs will be considerably greater than those borne by their male counterparts in that same social class. The very fact that relatively privileged women have a choice at present that does not realistically exist for men creates opportunity costs that women alone bear.

The Third Source of Variation: Preferences

There are various possible motivations for discriminatory outcomes; and if the extensive and profound work on this subject in the area of race relations is any indication, all of them—personal, institutional, covert, overt, legal, and illegal—operate simultaneously to some degree. The primacy of structuralist models in general has meant that preferences as expressed, say, in attitudes, have been de-emphasized. Some of the work of rational-choice scholars suggests, however, that there is a very important link to be understood between individual preferences and social outcomes. In general, the lesson is that the intensity of individual preferences cannot be inferred from the degree of inequality apparent in social outcomes.

Thomas Schelling (1978) has presented an intriguing model for the case of residential segregation. Suppose that an individual wishes to live in a neighborhood in which at least half (but not necessarily more than 50 percent plus one) of her neighbors are of the same race. Fewer than 50 percent will cause her to move. Let us add to her neighborhood someone who requires only that 30 percent of her neighbors be of her same race. Even the first individual has a relatively weak preference for living among "her own kind." Both have a preference for living with others, provided the minimum condition of a slight majority (in the first case) or some (in the second case) people of the same race also live in the neighborhood. These weak preferences, Schelling demonstrates, are likely to lead—quickly or slowly, depending on the initial composition and the rate of entry and exit by others—to a situation of extreme segregation. Integration, although preferred, will not be achieved without collective sanctions. Nonetheless, it would be in error to infer from the strikingly segregated outcome that individuals prefer extreme segregation.

This is because of what Schelling calls an "unraveling" process: A chain reaction may take place because each person's actions (in the residential example, each person's choice to move or to stay) affects the calculus of the others involved (in the example of the person moving out of the neighborhood, by affecting the environment of the neighborhood left behind and the environment moved to). If everyone in a neighborhood wants at least half of her adjacent neighbors to be of the same race, and if this neighborhood is almost evenly composed of blacks and whites so that all but one of the many people in the neighborhood have the desired mix of adjacent neighbors, the fairly well integrated neighborhood will "unravel" into a segregated one because the one discontented individual will move, causing one of more of her immediate neighbors to lose the desired mix of neighbors and to move, causing their neighbors to become discontented and move, and so on.

There are important lessons here for the study of gender inequality. Men and women might each prefer to work with (or hire) other individuals of their own gender. This may well be a weak preference in both cases. But if a similar kind of mechanism as that operating in the case of residential segregation can be observed, extreme sex-typing of occupations might be the observed outcome, even though it is preferred by no one.

If this is a plausible mechanism, it provides a powerful reason—a much more powerful rationale than those currently in vogue—for public policies upholding gender equality in the workplace. The reason is this: Such policies enforce a reality closer to the true preferences of individuals than obtains if the government fails to intervene. Without such intervention, individuals are unable to produce the collective outcome their preferences would lead them to desire.

Conclusion

Feminist scholars and others have typically assumed that rational-choice theory is a fundamentally sexist theory. In the first part of our paper we have tried to refute that claim, showing that, while it has its biases, they are not sexist ones. We argued that self-interest cannot be equated with selfishness and that women and men alike are interested in avoiding futile, nonconsequentialist action. We suggested that rational-choice theory is not at all inconsistent with interpersonal comparisons of utility, even thought the task of incorporating them has not yet been undertaken. We have argued that the stability of tastes is an open question for rational-choice theory, but that when stable tastes are assumed, this assumption is not one borne of any alleged male separative basis. Finally, we question the opposition of rationality and emotion as suggested by our critics.

The wholesale rejection of rational choice has, we believe, impeded general theoretical progress. Like any theory, rational choice is incomplete. We join with feminist critics—like England and Kilbourne—in calling for work that includes selfishness/altruism as a variable, that explicitly brings in interpersonal preferences within the model, and that resolves the role of emotions. Like most good theories, rational choice elucidates issues that others fail to see.

In the second section of this paper we have suggested that rational choice is particularly well suited to casting light on some of the mechanisms by which gender inequality is perpetuated. We have discussed empirical studies that illustrate each of these mechanisms, and in each we have identified at least one nonintuitive conclusion.

Thus, if one wishes to judge theories on their degree of contribution to debate about substantively important problems such as gender inequality, then we think that rational choice has passed muster by yielding nonintuitive implications that have not been produced by any other theory. If one wishes to judge theories on the degree of sexism of their fundamental principles, then we think that we have made a case that the first principles and assumptions of rational choice do not suffer from inherent male bias. If one wishes to judge theories on their degree of completeness—that is, how much more work there is to be done to deepen and broaden the theory—then rational choice would not win the day. Yet we regard work on issues such as the interpersonal comparison of utilities and the understanding of preferences as a challenge. Where theories are concerned, we would rather be creators than merely users. If to do so we must swim upstream in a river of sexism, so be it; this is hardly something that any feminist scholar we know would shy away from.

Acknowledgments

We are grateful to Paula England for her exceptional editorial guidance: her repeated challenges to us to clarify our position and her many suggestions for improvement made this a better paper than it otherwise would have been. We are also grateful to Michael Hechter for his comments on earlier drafts of this paper.

Notes

1.   There was plenty of evidence that the most prominent sociologists for a long time had perpetrated a view of blacks that was quite pejorative. Robert Park's and Ernest Burgess's 1924 introductory text included the following passage: "The temperament of the Negro as I conceive of it consists in a few elementary but distinctive characteristics, determined by physical organizations and transmitted biologically. These characteristics manifest themselves in a genial, sunny, and social disposition, in an interest in and attachment to external physical things rather than to subjective states and objects of introspection, in a disposition for expression rather than enterprise and action (pp. 138–39)." More than forty years later, in 1970, Daniel Moynihan and Nathan Glazer would write, "It is not possible for Negros to view themselves as other ethnic groups viewed themselves because—and this is the key to much in the Negro world— the Negro is only an American, and nothing else. He has no values and culture to guard and protect" (1965, p. 53).

2.   This is the title of a collection of papers edited by Joyce Ladner in 1973.

3.   A detailed discussion of the form of rational-choice models can be found in Friedman and Hechter (1988).

4.   This is a very important point and one that is hard to reconcile with the strawman view of rational choice.

5.   Rational-choice theories differ considerably in what they leave exogenous and what they attempt to endogenize. The status (endogenous or exogenous) of laws, norms, and values across these theories is especially inconsistent.

6.   Two additional assumptions are found in every rational-choice explanation: first, those about the information that agents have about the future consequences of their present action; and second, those about the mechanisms by which individual preferences and actions are aggregated to arrive at the relevant social outcome.

7.   These studies use rational-choice principles to guide their analysis. Those mechanisms sometimes are explicitly stated and linked to the rational-choice literature, but at other times are implicit.

8.   We deal here only with frontal attacks on rational-choice theory itself. Often it is caught in the barrage of a broad-based attack on all positive theories.

9.   Human capital theory, for example, emphasizes the role played by an individual's training and experience in determining her occupational position. This emphasis on individual characteristics has led some critics to believe that the theory implies that the individual is responsible for her eventual situation. (This implication holds only if the sole force determining the development of human capital is the individual, however.)

10.   England and Kilbourne are to be commended for their explicit theoretical attack. Much of the feminist critique of rational choice theory is carried out in the shadows of journals and professional meetings.

11.   A radical feminist organization, inspired by a peace camp at Greenham Common in England and growing out of a meeting in New York City at the Conference for Global Feminism and Disarmament.

12.   Interpersonal comparisons of utility occur when an individual attempts to assess the utilities that other individuals would derive from alternative social situations and tries to compare these utilities with the utilities that she herself will derive from these alternative social situations (Harsanyl 1977, p. 51).

13.   There are other complex relations to sort out on the way toward incorporating interpersonal comparisons into our models. What about the relationship between agents and the principals they serve? Can doctors be relied on to make the right choices for comatose patients? Can parents be trusted to put themselves in the bassinets of their premature (and seriously comprised) infants? Furthermore, what about agents who make decisions that have serious future consequences for other individuals? Mothers and fathers routinely deny immediate pleasure to their children (a candy bar, another television show) in favor of anticipated future payoff. Yet in so doing they ignore the probabilities of the future outcomes that they seek to produce (or avoid)—for instance, it is unlikely that a candy bar will lead to a cavity or one more television show will be responsible for later poor school performance—and they ignore the discount rate of pleasure, as well.

14.   The importance of this omission in social theory grows ever more apparent. Concentrated collective work by theorists of many persuasions seems to be critical at this time. Some preliminary interdisciplinary work on the subject is available (Hechter et al. 1993).

15.   This would not be so terribly problematic if one believed that measured attitudes accurately reflected internal states. Though this would be a convenient solution, we cannot convince ourselves that such a correspondence really does exist.

16.   Elster (1983) terms this "adaptive preference formation."

17.   Aristotle writes: "What comes about by force or because of ignorance seems to be involuntary. What is forced has an external origin, the sort of origin in which the agent or victim contributes nothing—if, e.g., a wind or human beings who control him were to carry him off. . . . But now consider actions done because of fear of greater evils or because of something fine. Suppose, e.g., a tyrant tells you to do something shameful, when he has control over your parents and children, and you do it, they will live, but if not, they will die . . . [These sorts of actions] would seem to be more like voluntary actions . . . in fact [the actor takes such actions] willingly; for in these sorts of actions he has within him the origin of the movement of limbs that are the instruments [of the action], and when the origin of the action is in him, it is also up to him to do them or not to do them. Hence actions of this sort are voluntary (1985, p. 1110a5).

18.   What we would most like is an explanation of the origins of these persistent inequalities. Yet most theories, like those emanating from a rational-choice perspective, are mute on the issue of origins.

19.   Following the usual sociological definition of institutions, of course, norms are institutions. Indeed, most institutional constraints *are* normative in this sense.

20.   Many would like to claim an alliance with this excellent work, and we are no exception. Note that her book was published in the University of California Press series Social Choice and Political Economy, edited by Brian Barry and Samuel L. Popkin. No doubt Luker had alternatives.

21.   Gerson's book is published in the same series as Luker's. She too undoubtedly had alternatives.

22.   One possible objection to Gerson's reasoning should be noted. A critic of Gerson might argue that what really explained variation in women's choices was

their different initial preferences about whether to be married, to have children, and to be employed. (This would be a rational-choice explanation, but one that relied on the mechanism of preferences, rather than opportunity costs.) However, by gauging their intent (albeit retrospectively), Gerson manages to control, to some extent, for preference over these alternatives. For example, when she shows that the opportunities offered by women's jobs were correlated with choices to remain employed or not, she controls for preferences by making comparisons with a group of women all of whom started with a preference for domestic life. Thus, it is not preferences about domesticity that explain the different choices of jobs among these women; it is more plausible that the differences in the opportunity costs of choosing homemaking explain this variation.

23.   Gerson's language is not cast in explicitly rational-choice terms, but her interpretation of the choices the women made unambiguously draws upon a rational-choice line of reasoning.

24.   Paula England has pointed out to us that it may constitute a departure from neoclassical economics to discuss opportunity costs in this way. She notes—as we do—that economists talk about opportunity costs both in terms of fixed metrics (usually money) as well as in terms of preferences and utility. In either case, however, it would be problematic, England claims, to make cross-sectional comparisons, unless we are willing to make the assumption that tastes are randomly distributed among groups of people (like the women in Gerson's study) who may well have different initial endowments.

We are more than willing to make this assumption. One of the strengths of rational-choice theory is precisely that theorists do not assume differences in character—and tastes—between the rich and poor (or other social groups). Further, without a theory of tastes, as we have noted before, we are hardly in a position to make pronouncements about how tastes across individuals or across groups of individuals differ in any systematic fashion. We are willing to make the assumption because we think that initial endowments change the array of choices available, not the tastes that individuals have. Thus, we assume that women in different structural positions have the same set of tastes, but differ in the opportunities available to them. Furthermore, in Gerson's study, as noted above, women were grouped by their initial tastes for domesticity.

References

Aristotle. (1985). *Nichomachean Ethics*. Tr. Terence Irwin. Indianapolis, IN: Hackett. Written approximately 384–322 B.C.

Becker, Gary. 1986. "The Economic Approach to Human Behavior." pp. 108–122 in *Rational Choice*, edited by Jon Elster. Oxford: Basil Blackwell.

Brinton, Mary C. 1988. "The Social-Institutional Bases of Gender Stratification: Japan as an Illustrative Case." *American Journal of Sociology*, (2)94; September:300–34.

Coleman, James S. 1990. "The Emergence of Norms." pp. 35–39 in *Social Institutions: Their Emergence, Maintenance, and Effects*, edited by Michael Hechter, Karl-Dieter Opp, and Reinhard Wippler. Hawthorne, NY: Aldine de Gruyter.

Diem, Carol. 1989. "Is He Heavy?" He's My Brother: The Impact of Brothers on the Status Attainments of Women." Unpublished manuscript, University of Arizona.

Elster, Jon. 1983. *Sour Grapes*. Cambridge: Cambridge University Press.

England, Paula, and Barbara S. Kilbourne. 1990. "Feminist Critique of the Separative Model of the Self: Implications for Rational Choice Theory." *Rationality and Society* 2(2):156–71.

Friedman, Debra, and Carol Diem. 1990. "Comment on England and Kilbourne." *Rationality and Society* 2(4):522–525.

Friedman, Debra and Michael Hechter. 1988. "The Contribution of Rational Choice Theory to Macrosociological Research." *Sociological Theory* 6:201–218.

Gerson, Kathleen. 1985. *Hard Choices: How Women Decide about Work, Career, and Motherhood*. Berkeley: University of California Press.

Glazer, Nathan, and Daniel P. Moynihan. 1970. *Beyond the Melting Pot: The Negroes, Puerto Ricans, Jews, Italians, and Irish of New York City*. 2nd ed. Cambridge, MA: MIT Press.

Harsanyl, John C. 1977. *Rational Behavior and Bargaining Equilibrium in Games and Social Situations*. Cambridge: Cambridge University Press.

Hechter, Michael, Lynn Nadel, and Richard Michod editors. *The Origin of Values*. Hawthorne, NY: Aldine de Gruyter.

Keller, Catherine. 1986. *From a Broken Web*. Boston: Beacon Press.

Ladner, Joyce A. 1973. *The Death of White Sociology*, New York: Random House.

Lamb, Michael E., and Marguerite B. Stevenson. 1978. "Father–Infant Relationships: Their Nature and Importance." *Youth and Society* (3) 9, March:277.

Luker, Kristen, 1984. *Abortion and the Politics of Motherhood*. Berkeley: University of California Press.

Park, Robert E., and Ernest W. Burgess. 1924. *Introduction to the Science of Sociology*. Chicago: University of Chicago Press.

Schelling, Thomas. 1978. *Micromotives and Macrobehavior*. New York: Norton.

Schwartz-Shea, Peregrine, and Debra D. Burrington. 1990. "Free Riding, Alternative Organization and Cultural Feminism: The Case of Seneca Women's Peace Camp." *Women and Politics* 10(3), 1–87.

Stigler, George J., and Gary S. Becker 1977. "De Gustibus Non Est Disputandum." *American Economic Review* 67(2):76–90.

Chapter 6

Functionalism and Feminism: Is Estrangement Necessary?

Miriam M. Johnson

Few sociologists today, regardless of their actual practice, would relish being labeled a "functionalist" because of the bad reputation functionalism acquired in the 1960s and 1970s when, as the reigning paradigm in sociology, it was attacked from all sides by competing theories. These attacks came from Marxists and conflict theorists of other sorts. They also came from symbolic interactionism and ethnomethodology, both of which focused on face-to-face, microlevel interaction. Functionalism was also attacked by feminists, who took it to task for its conservatism about gender arrangements.

The functionalism that was being attacked was usually associated with Talcott Parsons, whose theory of social action employed a functionalist model. Specifically he was accused by feminists of trying to justify male dominance by describing an instrumental (occupational) role for men and an expressive (domestic) role for women as a division of labor that was functional for family solidarity, and for implying that the nuclear family ideal of the 1950s was a fixed and desirable reality.

During the 1980s the critiques of Parsons and functionalism diminished in the light of critiques of the critiques and as competing theories began to have their own troubles. Now we have "neofunctionalism," so labeled by Jeffrey Alexander (1985), to describe the views of a loosely connected group of Europeans and Americans who have taken functionalism more to the left and who have demonstrated how the multidimensional aspect of Parsons's model allows competing theories to be incorporated in its own wider framework. In his introduction to the volume of neofunctionalist writings that he edited, Alexander lamented the term *functionalism* and noted that even Parsons himself tried to escape the label in later years but to no avail. Functionalism remains in the public vocabulary to such an extent, however, that the only solution to the labeling problem is to adopt the term *neofunctionalist* to create a better image and signal a more critical stance.

I begin with a brief overview of Parsons's position, what his model claims and does not claim, and in so doing examine the major criticisms of functionalism itself from feminists and others. I then turn to some features of his work that I feel are positive from a feminist standpoint compared to selected other theories. Next I address specific feminist criticisms of Parsons that I feel are justified in some ways and unjustified in others. In so doing I bring in examples from my own work to show how one might build upon some aspects of Parsons's work while rejecting others.

Parsons and the Problem of Order

For Parsons, the basic question to be explained by sociology was what he called "the problem of order." This phrase has often been misinterpreted to mean that disorder was deviant or abnormal and that the problem was to keep control over the populace to maintain equilibrium or the status quo in a society. The real issue for Parsons, however, was the deeper question of how, if individuals were really separate entities pursuing their self-interest, there could be any order at all: How could there be anything but disorder? Parsons was asking how individuals could interact cooperatively at all, or how there could be any social integration at all. Dissatisfied with simplistic utilitarian answers and theories of social contract, and equally dissatisfied with Marxist views of social order (under capitalism) as being created by class domination and sustained by a false consciousness, Parsons answered that social order could be accounted for by the fact that individuals shared values and norms and that these were internalized in the motivational systems of individuals. In my view, Parsons and Marxists are talking past each other since their initial question differs. In a sense, Parsons begins with the problem of social integration (getting along with one another) and Marxists begin with the problem of adaptation (making a living or surviving in the environment). But each analysis in the end must deal with both issues.

It is now generally agreed that Parsons overemphasized the degree to which values were held in common and underemphasized the degree to which ruling groups controlled others. Nonetheless, his answer to the problem of order, which finally came to include four levels of analysis—the biological, psychological, social, and cultural systems, which interpenetrated one another—provided an answer concerning the relationship of the individual to larger collectivities that goes considerably beyond the theorists who preceded him.

For Parsons, the earliest and most basic internalizations took place within primary groups, most notably families of one sort or another. Drawing on both Freud and G.H. Mead, he saw the child as internalizing basic cultural values along with the structure of the family itself and the child's own place within it. While tending to take the nuclear family unit as his point of reference, Parsons understood that age, sex, and kinship were socially constructed and did not mean the same thing from one culture to another.

Fairly early in his career, but sometime after he had written his first major work, *The Structure of Social Action*, Parsons borrowed the idea of function from anthropology as a way of talking about the consequences of any given pattern or patterns of social interaction for the stability and ongoingness of systems of interaction. For Parsons, these systems may be as large as the society as a whole, or as small as a two-person group. One may also refer to the personality of an individual as forming a system. Later on he developed the so-called fourfold functional paradigm AGIL, referring to Adaptation (making a living), Goal attainment (organizing in terms of a common goal), Integration (solidary, expressive interaction), and Latency or value maintenance (preserving and passing on the cultural values and knowledge store). These are functions that must be fulfilled at least minimally if a social group is to survive.

Common Misunderstandings About Functionalism

The three most common accusations that have been leveled at functionalism are that it is circular, teleological, and supportive of the status quo. While it would be hard to claim that functionalism is a radical doctrine, I would maintain that the three perceptions of functionalism discussed below—all related to the view that it is conservative—are inaccurate.

Functionalism as Circular

It is not true, as is often claimed, that Parsons believed that "whatever is, is functional." For Parsons, the degree to which a given pattern or fit between patterns is functional was an empirical question to be investigated. As Alexander (1985, p. 9) puts it, "Functionalism is concerned with integration as a possibility and with deviance and processes of social control as social facts." Moreover, functionalism allows one to talk about strain and dysfunction as well as positive functions. Parsons explicitly pointed to patterns that were dysfunctional or points of strain in a given system. Indeed, in his early essays, he was far more concerned with conflict and strain than with integration, and argued that the functional fit between the nuclear family and the occupational system created a major point of strain in the "feminine role." This strain resulted from the wife's being deprived of her role in a common enterprise with her husband and being given the "pseudo role" of housewife.

Functionalism, Teleology, and Change

It has also been said (often in connection with the erroneous claim that Parsons believed that "everything is functional") that Parsons could not or did not deal with change. Parsons did indeed deal with change, and in 1966 he wrote a book on societal evolution. Here he posited four evolutionary processes, the most important of which was structural differentiation, whereby increasingly specialized agencies took over functions previously performed by a single agency. An example of this process would be the separation of the educational system from the family, which allowed for a general upgrading of standards and the inclusion of more children, including female children, in higher levels of learning. In this generally progressive trajectory, Parsons did not preclude the possibility of major areas of dysfunction, but in his discussions of evolution, he did not elaborate on what these might be.

As for the criticism that Parsons gave a teleological account of change, he did imply that the changes resulting from increasing structural differentiation were on the whole functional, but this does not say they came about because of some functional zeitgeist, or *because* they were functional. The argument was more that once a functional process began it was likely *to be retained* because it worked, i.e., because it was functional for a given system.

While Parsons did posit an evolutionary trend toward increasing structural differentiation, he left open the question of what factors caused any given change. Indeed many of the specific critiques of Parsons coming from historians are really more specifications of detail rather than fundamental refutations of his basic contentions about the structural differentiation that accompanied the shift from an agrarian to an industrial society and about the kind of family system that became institutionalized with industrial society.

System Analysis as Conservative

The element of truth in all of the above perceptions is that Parsonian functionalism is not likely in itself to lead to radical thinking or emancipatory insights. For example, functionalism did not lead me to become a feminist. My experience as a woman and the temper of times accomplished this. Yet, once converted, I did not totally abandon functionalism, even though I recognized that its social system reference could obscure women's situation.

In general, my own position is that functional analyses are not inherently conservative if one specifies, functional for whom or what? If one asks this question, there is nothing to prevent one from using a functional analysis in connection with an explicitly emancipatory aim. Parsons, however, in developing his theory generally focused on the social system as a whole and failed to consider explicitly who profited most and least from the system. This does make him vulnerable to the conservative label, since in taking the larger system as his point of reference, he ignored the power relationships within that system that privileged some groups other others. I will return to the issue of power again in a discussion of specifically feminist critiques.

Parsonian Functionalism Versus Other Approaches

In analyzing the possible compatibilities between Parsons's functionalism and feminism, compared with other approaches, two major factors stand out: (1) Parsonsian functionalism has explicitly taken gender into account more than have other perspectives, and (2) Parsonsian functionalism offers a broader and more multidimensional approach than other perspectives.

Concern with Gender in Functionalism

Parsons had more to say about gender, the family, socialization, and evolutionary change in the family and gender relations than have other approaches, either macro or micro. Parsons also had much to say about the relationships between the family and the occupational system, and himself did not contribute to the notion that the private sphere has no functional connection with the public sphere. Moreover, as mentioned, Parsons was aware that this sharp differentiation between "work" and home produces strain in the "feminine role."

Marxists and conflict theorists concerned with gender have had a particularly hard time to the extent that they have attempted to explain gender oppression as a side effect of the class system. Indeed many Marxists who are feminists have found it necessary to add the independent category of patriarchy to their analyses. Thus most Marxist-oriented feminists now call themselves socialist feminists and grant that classical Marxism must be combined with radical feminist analyses to explain (and change) women's disadvantage. (See Shelton and Agger in this volume for a discussion of Marxist and socialist-feminist views.)

The more microlevel theories that stress the socially constructed and highly contingent nature of social interaction are not especially oriented to studying power, class, or gender. But ethnomethodologists and variants thereof have shown how gender is "displayed," "accomplished," or "done" in interaction. (See West and Fenstermaker in this volume.) Such a focus does have the potential for encouraging change by showing that things do not have to be the way they are. Even so, these microapproaches are not particularly useful in explaining the ubiquitous and intractable nature of gender inequality, that is, the way that specific interaction patterns can change and yet inequality can reassert itself in a new guise.

In contrast to both Marxist and interactionist theories, functionalism can at least potentially analyze patterns that are functional and dysfunctional for women in certain structural positions in a manner that treats women as neither a residual category of worker, nor as equally privileged "members" in an interaction. A major reason this is possible is the multidimensional nature of neofunctionalism.

Multidimensionality

To the extent that Marxist and interactionist theories claim they have *the* explanation that renders others useless, functionalism, which makes no such claims, seems more realistic and flexible. Neofunctionalists have particularly stressed the multidimensional aspect of the perspective and have attempted to incorporate insights from both Marxism and microlevel theories into a new approach containing multiple levels of analysis (see especially Alexander 1985, 1987). Neofunctionalism does not require that one use all levels for all problems. Depending on the problem at hand, one approach or several different approaches may be more appropriate to the question, but always with an awareness that this is not the whole picture.

In spite of Parsons's overall tendency to privilege the level of values and norms, to stress stability over instability and predictability over contingency, he was leary of single-factor explanations and partial explanations that purported to explain the whole. Neofunctionalism, then, seeks to retain Parsons's emphasis on multicausal, multilevel analysis while giving greater play to dysfunctional and problematic aspects of society.

A multidimensional approach seems especially essential for rethinking gender, whose manifestations can appropriately be analyzed at the biological, psychological, social, and cultural levels. After all, males and females have bodies and, in my view, we ignore biological differences at our peril. At the same time we need to study gender at the level of interaction and also at the more general level of social organization. My recent book, *Strong Mothers, Weak Wives* (Johnson 1988), although coming to more critical conclusions than Parsons, is within a Parsonian functionalist framework in that I combine varying levels of analysis and link male-dominant family structure with interaction processes through which fathers "teach" daughters to be subordinate wives. It is not socialization as it is usually understood, but nuclear family structure itself, along with specific interactional sequences, that contribute to the reproduction of female subordination and male superiority in this society.

Specifically I argue that male dominance in heterosexual interaction is transmitted to the child through interaction with the father, while mother-son interaction works against male dominance. This view is contrary to that of Chodorow (1978, 1979). (Chodorow's view is discussed in Williams's paper in this volume.) In my view, the primary significance of females being the first socializers of children, is that, in the mother-child dyad, children of both sexes acquire the basic learnings that make them human. Infants of both sexes in this early interaction with a mother figure learn to love and be loved and internalize a nurturant as well as a nurtured self. Thus the maternal identification represents the common humanity that both genders share and lays down basic capacities for love and caring in both genders.

While Chodorow (1978, 1979) emphasizes the boy's tendency to differentiate himself from the mother by adopting a superior attitude toward women, and the girl's tendency to overidentify with the mother, I emphasize that these tendencies only develop when children become aware of male-dominant family structure, that is, when they become aware that their mother is father's wife and as such is the lesser member of the partnership. The tendency of males to differentiate and dominate is only indirectly related to women's mothering, and tends to be established in interaction within male peer groups.

In my work I bring together considerable evidence that fathers respond to girls and boys more differently than mothers do. Generally this gender-differentiating behavior of fathers takes two forms: withdrawal from girls (or preference for boys) and a different style of interacting with girls than with boys. This differentiated style of the father's seems closely related to a specifically sexual awareness, as opposed to the mother's more caretaking awareness that is less differentiated according to the sex of the child. The father is more likely to approach the daughter as a sexually interested male than the mother is to approach her son as a sexually interested female. Moreover, socially approved adult hetero-sexual relationships are more similar to the father-daughter relationship than to the mother-son relationship. This is a radical feminist analysis in that it breaks with the tendency to blame male dominance on mothers, and instead indicts male peer groups, who make women into sex ob-jects, and fathers, who dominate mothers and bring up daughters to be wives. (See Tuana's critique of Chodorow in her comments on Williams in this volume.)

In other sections of my book (Johnson 1988) I analyze gender roles in the economy and polity and the wider culture and show how these depend upon expectations that women are, will be, or should be wives, whether "real" wives or office wives. My approach is multileveled and interdisciplinary in that I try to analyze male dominance as it operates on many different levels, and also to show how the levels interpenetrate.

Was Parsons Conservative and Biased Against Women?

While often depicted as a conservative by his earlier critics, including feminists in the 1960s and 1970s, most theorists today would understand Parsons to be a liberal—a believer in the virtues of individual freedom, democracy, and pluralism. He tended to see capitalism and socialism as *not* being mutually exclusive alternatives within advanced industrial societies. He had problems with unbridled capitalism and problems with the totalitarian tendencies manifested by socialist regimes. His evolutionary trajectory might well predict some sort of merger between the two.

With regard to gender, Parsons, as a person, was more liberal than most, encouraging women to enter Harvard as graduate students and assuming their intellectual equality with men—a stance that was far from typical at midcentury. In my view, his earlier works on women show him to be more sensitive than his contemporaries to women's disadvantaged situation. (For a discussion of gender and social science in the 1950s, see Breines 1986.) For example, Parsons pointed to the contradiction that males' and females' educations, even at higher levels, were converging more and more, while at the same time sex roles, in some respects, were becoming more, rather than less, differentiated. He analyzed in some detail how the alternatives to domesticity in the middle class (short of a full-fledged career), such as the pursuit of glamour or "culture," were less than satisfactory solutions for well-educated married women (1954, pp. 96–97). Moreover Parsons was keenly aware of the unfairness of a woman's status depending to so great an extent on the man she married (1954, p. 308).

In a previous paper (Johnson 1989), I argued that Parsons's evolutionary schema for understanding social change can readily be applied to the aims of the feminist movement, which has evidenced all four of the basic evolutionary processes of structural differentiation, inclusion, upgrading, and value generalization. Parsons used the term *structural differentiation* not only to refer to more specialized agencies taking over functions previously performed by a single agency, but he also used differentiation to refer to an increasing distinction between culture, social organization, personality, and the biological organism. With increasing modernization, a clearer differentiation between personality and society occurs which is related to the increasing autonomy of individuals (Parsons 1966, p. 24), that is, individuals come to see themselves as being increasingly separable from the social matrix. Thus it became possible to problematize gender itself and to ask how it had been socially created and how its definition worked against women. This change of consciousness was most fully developed among middle-class white feminists, who were privileged in terms of race and class and therefore were more able to see their disadvantaged position as women.

The feminism that developed in the 1960s represented a push by women for *inclusion* in the mainstream of society. Women sought occupational opportunities commensurate with men of their class and in the political arena sought elective office. The so-called sexual revolution could also be considered an example of inclusion; in this case women wanted inclusion in the sexual freedoms taken for granted by men.

Adaptive upgrading refers to the increased efficiency and effectiveness expected to result from differentiation and inclusion. Indeed, in their arguments for inclusion, feminists specifically pointed to the adaptive upgrading that would occur if their talents were no longer wasted by exclusionary practices. Nowadays, most would surely agree that the inclusion of educated women into the occupational world outside the home constitutes a more rational utilization of time and talent.

The last change process that Parsons posited, *value generalization*, refers to the fact that all of the foregoing processes necessitate changes in the overall values of society—value changes that can incorporate a wider variety of goals, activities, and types of people. It does seem that overall societal values are changing in ways that give more emphasis to perspectives that have been more typical of women than men. Certainly much feminist writing can be seen as an effort to bring about such a redefinition. For example, Carol Gilligan's (1982) description of gender differences in the moral sphere is significant as an effort to integrate women's greater orientation toward care and responsibility, in addition to the male emphasis on rights, into the general definition of morality.

In sum then, while Parsons himself did not call for change, his outline of directions of evolutionary change fits the feminist agenda and I would contend, the post-1950s wave of feminism could have been anticipated by his own analysis of the conflict and strain under which middle-class women lived.

The Question of Power

One of the most persistent criticisms of Parsons by feminists has been his failure to adequately analyze power. While one may think of Marxism as being all about power and how economic power maintains inequality, Parsons does not make power, per se, a central concern. He defined power as the capacity to make decisions that are binding on some or all members of society. Yet, while he recognized that power was ultimately backed up by force, he saw power as depending heavily on a consensus of the governed that gave it legitimacy. In his later period in which he had developed his fourfold functional paradigm, power was seen as a facility for the attainment of group goals ("goal attainment").

When describing the family, Parsons tended to see the generational axis, not the husband-wife axis, as the power axis. Thus parents had more power than children "for the children's own good" as it were. Parsons depicted the father as being head of the family only in the sense that he represents the family as a unit. He did not depict the father as dominating his wife and children but only as having power by virtue of being their representative.

Feminists, of course, have rightly criticized Parsons's failure to see the power husbands have over wives and men have over women. They have also argued that the terms he used to describe a division of labor, such as *instrumental* and *expressive*, and the term *role* itself, appeared to be value neutral and thereby masked unequal power while legitimating the gender status quo. I agree that Parsons failed to recognize the extent of husbands' power (both economic and psychological) over wives, but I disagree that the terms *instrumental*, and *expressive*, and *role* are necessarily obfuscatory. I explain below.

The Instrumental Expressive Distinction and Power

In order for the instrumental/expressive distinction to make sense for systems of varying types and sizes, Parsons defined it very abstractly. He defined instrumental action as action directed toward moving a system in its environment and expressive action as action directed toward the internal integration of the system. Applying this abstract definition to the family, Parsons claimed that the family depended on the husband/father's occupation to survive in the environment (i.e., outside the home), while it depended on the mother/wife's expressive or integrative activity (responding to the psychic needs of husband and children, nurturance, warmth, and general caretaking activities within the family) to hold the family together internally. He saw a gender division of labor along these lines as being generally functional for martial solidarity because it prevented potentially divisive competition between husband and wife.

At the time feminists interpreted this as an attempt to justify a division of labor that kept women out of the labor market altogether or consigned them to inferior jobs. This was not Parsons's intention, but clearly he must be faulted for not seeing the degree to which the instrumental/expressive division of labor, as it related to the husband's connection with the occupational world, gave husbands power over wives. While Parsons was empirically correct when he noted that marital instability tended to be associated with a relatively equal occupational status between husband and wife, he did not see the extent to which marital *stability* may have resulted from the woman's financial dependency rather than role differentiation per se. Husbands and wives may have been staying together in a marriage because the wife literally could not afford to leave, rather than because the lack of competition provided by the sex-based division of labor created emotional solidarity.

While Parsons missed the power attaching to the instrumental or provider role, he was, I believe, correct to keep the concepts instrumental and expressive separate from the question of power. Indeed research on small decision-making groups (Bales and Slater 1955) found instrumental leaders and expressive leaders, sometimes combined in a single person, and considered both types of action as carrying power, albeit of different sorts. In the all-male experimental groups they used, instrumental leaders were the "idea" people who made suggestions concerning the imposed experimental task (such as where to locate the railroad in a city). These leaders received respect from others in the group while at the same time generating hostility. Expressive leaders specialized in tension-releasing responses, which made for group solidarity and were accorded the power of being well-liked, of being "sociometric stars."

Parsons's use of the instrumental/expressive distinction as a marker for two different types of action, equally functional for a social system's survival, is not inherently sexist. In a society that is so instrumentally oriented, an emphasis on the importance of expressiveness is potentially progressive, so long as any connotations of dependence, lack of emotional control, and lack of instrumental competence are removed. (For reports of research using a nonpejorative definition of expressiveness (see Johnson et al. 1975; Gill, Stockard, Johnson, and Williams 1987; Rossi and Rossi 1990.) The reason for the pejorative connotations becoming attached in the first place is both sexism itself (that is, the devaluing of women) and the devaluing of anything that does not fit ordinary (male) conceptions of what constitutes work.

While feminists shared this instrumental bias in the early days of the women's movement, by the late 1970s many feminists began to view expressiveness or women's more relational concerns more positively. These feminists have criticized the instrumental emphasis of our society and the male paradigm it represents. In addition to Carol Gilligan (1982), whom I mentioned earlier, other feminists of this genre would include Jean Baker Miller (1976, 1986), Nel Noddings (1984), Jessie Bernard (1981), and Nancy Chodorow (esp. 1979). Feminists who continue to maintain that this focus on women's expressivity is dangerously traditional (e.g., Segal 1987) need to understand that valuing expressiveness need not imply advocacy of women continuing to do more than their share of the expressive work, or locking women into expressive roles to the exclusion of instrumental roles. Rather it is meant to advocate greater recognition of the expressive work women (and sometimes men) do. So-called cultural feminists, network feminists, or maternal feminists are seeing that these expressive activities have value and perhaps represent a more unalienated form of work than the kinds of work men do (Di Leonardo 1987).

In my view then, there is nothing inherently wrong with the functionalist use of the very general terms *instrumental* and *expressive*. Indeed, keeping the terms allows one to utilize expressivity as a positive concept to describe one aspect of women's work, and keeping both terms separate from power allows us to analyze the structural conditions under which expressivity is debilitating for women and those in which it may be empowering. I have argued (Johnson 1988) that the male-headed, privatized, nuclear family isolates women and puts expressiveness in the service of their husbands, which is debilitating for women. Yet in matrifocal societies that do not emphasize the wife role for women, women have higher status vis-à-vis men in the household and hold important roles in the community. African-American women, unlike white women, have always tended to define themselves more as mothers than as wives, and their mothering and expressivness is less privatized and more integrated into a network or community. Their overall status in the community is enhanced by mothering and is less dependent upon their husbands' position than is true for white women. This is not matriarchy but matrifocality, which involves women as what Bernice Reagon (1986) calls "cultural workers."

The Concept of Role and the Question of Power

The concept of role, defined as the set of expectations for the behavior of a person occupying a given position, has been criticized from many different standpoints, many of which in one way or another see role as "mystifying" (and thus leaving uncriticized) unequal power relationships. For example, Stacey and Thorne (1985) have suggested that the functionalist use of sex roles depoliticizes gender. They point out that we do not speak of race roles or class roles. Yet, in a situation in which men clearly dominate, we speak of sex roles or, more recently, of gender roles.

I agree with Stacey and Thorne that it is misleading to speak of there being a *single* role attached to the status of being female, as the terms *gender role* or *sex role* seem to imply. I also acknowledge that role definitions themselves contain rules of interaction that have implications for superior and inferior power. Yet, I believe that the term *role* has too many conceptual advantages to abandon it altogether. Instead I suggest we retain the concept of role for certain structural analyses and make the question of how much or how little, and what kind of, power it carries an empirical issue. Women and men play many different roles in their lives and the amount of power attaching to these roles differs; moreover, a role that in one cultural context denotes inferiority may denote superiority in another.[1]

In *Strong Mothers, Weak Wives*, I argue that if one breaks the mother-wife role into two analytically separable roles, it is easier to see that the power potential of the two roles is not identical. Women as wives tend to be relatively powerless compared to women as mothers. The mystification comes in thinking of the two roles together, not in the term *role* itself. I argue that marriage is the mechanism by which women's power as mother is coopted and controlled by men. *Mother* implies women's power over children, *wife* implies men's power over women. This is true at both the level of cultural expectations (wives should not be better than their husbands) and at the social structural level, which includes the wife's relative economic dependency. As the political scientist Carole Pateman (1988) has argued, the unspoken contract that underlies the literally man-made social contract is the marriage contract, which makes women into subordinate "wives."[2]

While it is true that Parsons did not give sufficient weight to the power husbands held over wives by virtue of their control over money and its distribution, and while it is also true that he did not give sufficient weight to the use of power and force in societies in general, there is a progressive potential in Parsons's conception of power as a "facility" for accomplishing group goals. Indeed, feminists have begun to criticize those male theorists who see power as a matter of making someone do something against their will, while ignoring those conceptions of power that entail empowerment for both self and others. While there are problems with Parsons's treatment of power as generally benign (because it overlooks domination and exploitation), in the last analysis it is a conception of power that fits with a humane and women-centered society in which power is used to facilitate rather than obstruct collective goals.

In sum, then, I would argue for retaining the concept of role, but for also giving careful attention to each role's implication for the power it bestows on the incumbent. Parsonsian functionalism suggests the importance of combining other levels of analysis with a role analysis. It is true that Parsons tended to assume a too smooth integration between levels, but conceptually there is nothing inherent in the general scheme to prevent a more dynamic analysis.

Conclusion

The most recent wave of feminism has generated many apparently competing analyses and has weathered its share of disagreements. The current temper among feminists now seems to be to recognize increasing diversity—among analyses and among themselves. As middle-class white feminists have become more sensitized to class and race differences in perspective, we have all become far less sure that there is a single root cause of male dominance, or that there is a single male dominance, for that matter. I do not suggest that feminists return to Parsonsian analysis a la Parsons himself. However, it is appropriate in the current climate to see the value in a larger, more integrative theory that recognizes the validity of various levels and kinds of analyses, and allows for productive combinations of approaches.

Finally, I do not suggest that feminism and Talcott Parsons's functionalist approach can ever have a total rapprochement. His use of functionalism did not encourage a critical attitude toward society, much less a radical response. My aim has been merely to show, however, that his rather abstract scheme is not antithetical to feminist thinking and can be put to more critical and emancipatory uses. Indeed this abstract quality is precisely what allows for analyses that are dissimilar to his and more critical. The neofunctionalists have taken Parsons's abstractness, which appears at first to be a vice, and have made it into a virtue, stressing that functionalism is not so much a theory as a broad intellectual tendency (Alexander 1985, p. 11) that by virtue of its generality can encompass more critical and conflict-oriented approaches.

Notes

1. Marriage is a cultural universal and generally husbands hold domestic power, but this power can be and is counteracted by other features of a given kinship system, such as the residence system or lineage system. In the isolated nuclear family, husband power is particularly prominent because it is not counteracted by that of other relatives and because of the husband's stronger link in industrialized countries with the public sphere.

2. The term *role* has also been criticized for its static quality. This is quite true, but for certain analytical purposes one need not focus directly on process. Again, within a multidimensional scheme, one uses what is useful for the analytical purpose at hand, as opposed to claiming that only one approach or scheme is correct.

References

Alexander, Jeffrey. 1985. "Introduction." Pp. 7–18 in *Neofunctionalism*, edited by Jeffrey C. Alexander. Beverly Hills, CA: Sage.

———. 1987. "Action and Its Environments." Pp. 289–318 in *The Micro-Macro Link*, edited by Jeffrey C. Alexander, Bernhard Giesen, Richard Munch, and Neil J. Smelser. Berkeley: University of California Press.

Bales, Robert F. and Philip E. Slater. 1955. "Role Differentiation in Small Decision-Making Groups." Pp. 259–306 in *Family Socialization and Interaction Process*, edited by Talcott Parsons and Robert F. Bales. Glencoe, IL: Free Press.

Bernard, Jessie. 1981. *The Female World*. New York: Free Press.

Breines, Wini. 1986. "The 1950s: Gender and Some Social Science." *Sociological Inquiry* 56:69–92.

Chodorow, Nancy. 1978. *The Reproduction of Mothering*. Berkeley: University of California Press.

———. 1979. "Feminism and Difference: Gender, Relation, and Difference in Psychoanalytic Perspective." *Socialist Review* 46:51–69.

Di Leonardo, Micaela. 1987. "The Female World of Cards and Holidays: Women, Families and the Work of Kinship." *Signs: Journal of Women in Cultural and Society* 12:440–53.

Gill, Sandra, Jean Stockard, Miriam M. Johnson, and Suzanne Williams. 1987. Measuring Gender Differences: The Expressive Dimension and Critique of Androgyny Scales." *Sex Roles* 17:375–400.

Gilligan, Carol. 1982. *In A Different Voice*. Cambridge, MA: Harvard University Press.

Johnson, Miriam M. 1988. *Strong Mothers, Weak Wives: The Search for Gender Equality*. Berkeley: University of California Press.

———. 1989. "Feminism and the Theories of Talcott Parsons." Pp. 101–118 in *Feminism and Sociological Theory*, edited by Ruth A. Wallace, Newbury Park, CA: Sage.

Johnson, Miriam M., Jean Stockard, Joan Acker, and Claudeen Naffziger. 1975. "Expressiveness Re-evaluated." *School Review* 83:617–644

Miller, Jean Baker. 1986. Toward a New Psychology of Women. (Second ed.) Boston: Beacon.

Noddings, Nel. 1984. *Caring: A Feminine Approach to Ethics and Moral Education*. Berkeley: University of California Press.

Parsons, Talcott. 1954. *Essays in Sociological Theory*. Rev. ed. Glencoe, IL: Free Press.

Parsons, Talcott, 1966. *Societies: Evolutionary and Comparative Perspectives*. Englewood Cliffs, NJ: Prentice-Hall.

Pateman, Carole. 1988. *The Sexual Contract*. Stanford, CA: Stanford University Press.

Reagon, Bernice Johnson. 1986. "African Diaspora Women: The Making of Cultural Workers." *Feminist Studies* 12:79–90.

Rossi, Alice S., and Peter H. Rossi. 1990. *Of Human Bonding: Parent-Child Relations Across the Life Course*. Hawthorne, NY: Aldine de Gruyter.

Segal, Lynne. 1987. *Is the Future Female? Troubled Thoughts on Contemporary Feminism*. New York: Peter Bedrick Books.

Stacey, Judith, and Barrie Thorne. 1985. "The Missing Feminist Revolution in Sociology." *Social Problems* 32:301–16.

Chapter 7

Psychoanalytic Theory and the Sociology of Gender

Christine L. Williams

The writings of Sigmund Freud have had a rather stormy relationship with feminist social scientists. In the 1960s, Freud was condemned for holding misogynist beliefs, and his writings were blamed for perpetuating women's oppression in society (Mitchell 1974). After all, it was Freud who argued that all girls are overcome with "penis envy" the instant they first see a naked male because they immediately recognize the inherent inferiority of their female genitals. Even though penis envy and other misogynist ideas in the theory have long been discredited, Freud's notorious sexism understandably has led many feminist social scientists to reject the theory. Even today, many of my social science colleagues question my embrace of both Freud and feminism.

But not all feminist sociologists have rejected the theory. In the 1970s, some scholars began to appropriate the psychoanalytic framework, reinterpreting its major insights to shed light on the origins of gender inequality. This paper examines some of those efforts. I first review the uses of psychoanalytic theory by sociologists, focusing specifically on feminist theoretical and empirical studies utilizing this framework. Second, I review the criticisms most commonly directed against the theory by other feminist sociologists. Finally, I respond to these objections, arguing in favor of more open reception of Freudian ideas. Freud may have been a sexist, but the theory he began can provide feminist sociologists with valuable tools for understanding the links between gender identity and male domination.

Psychoanalysis and the Sociology of Gender

The theoretical tradition initiated by Sigmund Freud, although known under the general rubric of psychoanalysis, splintered into competing theoretical and clinical schools even before his death in 1939. The particular school of thought that has been most closely allied with sociology is object relations theory. This perspective, initiated by W. Ronald Fairbairn and D. W. Winnicott, emphasizes the importance of real experiences with other people (unfortunately termed objects) in the formation, organization, and repression of desire.

Like the other schools of psychoanalysis, the object relations approach posits the existence of the unconscious, as well as innate erotic and aggressive urges. But unlike other traditions in psychoanalysis (such as drive theory or ego psychology), the objects relations approach assumes that these innate dispositions are not at all focused or directed until society "shapes" them. That is, the individual does not innately hate or desire anything in particular. Experience in social interaction teaches individuals how to "direct" their desires in socially appropriate ways.

Object relations theory is not identical to simple socialization models of human behavior and development, however. There is never a simple one-to-one correspondence between society's demands and the outcome of the socialization process. The individual does not passively receive social stimuli from the environment: fantasy, projection, and repression constantly intervene and distort reality. The individual is constantly forced to mediate between social demands and unconscious, internal drives.

This particular tradition within psychoanalytic theory was first introduced into American sociology by Talcott Parsons. According to Parsons, object relations theory was "the most important area of articulation between the psychoanalytic theory of the personality and the sociological theory of the structure and functioning of social systems" ([1954] 1970, p. 79). In several essays, Parsons showed how psychoanalysis provides the key to understanding the process whereby cultural norms and values are internalized, thus (in his view) "filling in" where Durkheim's analysis of the individual and society left off.

Many of Parsons' psychoanalytic writings focus specifically on the socialization of girls and boys into appropriate sex role characteristics. Parsons believed that girls had to be socialized to fit "expressive" roles and boys, "instrumental" ones, and he used object relations theory to describe how these personality patterns were reproduced by the nuclear family structure. In an argument that would be repeated twenty years later by Nancy Chodorow, Parsons demonstrated that the traditional division of labor in middle-class families between "breadwinning" husbands and "homemaker" wives produced nurturing, empathetic daughters, and industrious, analytic sons.

In the nuclear families characteristic of the 1950s in which Parsons was writing, early child care was almost exclusively the mother's responsibility. Because of this allocation of work, Parsons argued that all infants originally "identify" with the female parent. The infant first develops a sense of his/her own selfhood in a close, one-on-one relationship with the mother, and qualities possessed by the mother are internalized by the infant to form the beginnings of the child's personality. Thus, the "feminine" qualities adult women exhibit in their relationships with their newborns form the core of the infant's identity.

During this early pre-oedipal phase, the mother also becomes the object of the child's erotic longing. Because the mother satisfies the baby's desires (she feeds, clothes, and nurtures the baby), the child learns to associate all gratification with her presence. Thus, Parsons writes, "for childhood eroticism regardless of the sex of the child the original object is the mother" (Parsons [1954] 1970, p. 74).

This erotic attachment to females persists in heterosexual adult men (although in more generalized form, directed to all women and not to mother in particular). But in the course of their socialization, boys are forced to replace their identification with the mother with a "masculine" identification. That is, boys must learn the male role in society, and incorporate personality attributes associated with that role.

Learning the masculine role is problematic for males since adult men are typically absent during most of young children's waking hours. Consequently, boys come to define masculinity as whatever is not feminine. They condemn anything associated with the female role as inferior to compensate themselves for the loss of their original, fulfilling attachment to their mothers (Parsons 1954, p. 305). Girls, on the other hand, are encouraged to retain their original feminine identification (and it is backed up by play emphasizing future homemaking functions), but eventually must change their erotic attachment to their fathers. Parsons recognized heterosexuality as a problematic achievement for girls since fathers are rarely available for the kind of intimate contact and erotic gratification mothers provide. Femininity and heterosexuality also pose problems for girls because they require girls to accept men's negative assessment of their feminine identification, and accede to financial dependency on men (Parsons 1954, p. 308).

Thus, following Freud, Parsons stressed that the acquisition of the appropriate sex role is a psychological achievement, by no means guaranteed by the individual's biological endowment. In fact, he believed that sex role socialization could be derailed at various stages. For example, Parsons describes "exaggerated and distorted masculinity," a character flaw of men who fail to sever entirely their original feminine identifications:

> The attitude toward women typical of the so-called "wolf" is one of fundamental ambivalence with respect to masculinity. . . . The positive side is expressed in the need to impress and gain control over women; the

negative side in the inability to accept the normal responsibilities which a socially integrated sexual relationship should involve, and often in the unconscious desire to injure women, by making them commit themselves and then deserting them. ([1954] 1970, p. 53)

But despite Parsons's recognition of strains associated with the proper acquisition and performance of adult sex roles, he nonetheless stressed the importance of sex role compliance for promoting the smooth functioning of the social system. This discussion of "distorted masculinity" (which Parsons calls a "familiar American example") is one of the few passages where Parsons acknowledges the existence of male domination and oppression of women—although he clearly dismisses such behavior as abnormal. In his view, the normal products of successful socialization are women with the capacity and desire to nurture children, and men with the achievement orientation required for success in the occupational sphere.

This conservative bias no doubt hindered the acceptance of Parsons's appropriation of psychoanalysis by feminist sociologists. Miriam Johnson (1989) has shown that feminists in the 1960s and 1970s angrily dismissed Parsons as an apologist for the oppression of women. His use of psychoanalytic theory seemed to lock women ever more resolutely to their sex role, offering little hope for transformation or change (see Morgan 1975, pp. 42–47).

It was not until Nancy Chodorow resurrected object relations theory in the 1970s—injecting into it a strong dose of critical theory—that some feminist social scientists were moved to reconsider Freud's potential contribution to the sociology of gender. Chodorow has been heralded as doing more than any other theorist to "convince American sociologists and (nonpsychoanalytic) feminists that psychoanalysis is not analogous to the plague" (Kurzweil 1989, p. 95).

Chodorow turned to psychoanalytic theory for one of the same reasons that earlier feminists had rejected Freud (and Parsons): This theory provided a compelling account of the resiliency of our gender roles. In Chodorow's view, over ten years of feminist theory, research, and practice had failed to come to terms with the persistence of gender roles despite compelling efforts to alter or eliminate them. The popular "role learning" theorists, for example, had argued that gender roles persist because parents (and other socializers) actively train girls and boys to conform to their appropriate sex roles by dressing girls in pink and giving them dolls, and dressing boys in blue and giving them trucks. Presumably, these patterns could be eliminated by consciously refusing to participate in this sex-typing. Chodorow criticized this perspective because in her view, a theory was needed to explain how—and why— oppressive gender relationships were reproduced independent of our conscious intentions (Chodorow 1978, p. 34).

Chodorow acknowledged her debt to Parsonian sociology at the outset of her seminal work, *The Reproduction of Mothering* (1978). In her view, Parsons's psychoanalytic approach had successfully linked the structure of the nuclear family to the generation of masculine and feminine personalities that unconsciously reproduced similar family forms. However, she was quite critical of Parsons's apparent acceptance of this cycle of reproduction; Parsons, as she put it, "always sounds as though he wants to understand order to contribute toward its maintenance" (1978, p. 38).

Chodorow turned to a second tradition in psychoanalytic sociology for the critical edge for her study of gender roles: the theorists of the Frankfurt School. Horkheimer, Adorno, and Marcuse had used Freudian theory to show how changes in family structure brought about by postindustrial capitalism produced personality types that compliantly acquiesced to authority on the job and in public life. These critical theorists provided a model for integrating a critique of domination into the psychoanalytic approach. In their view, strains produced in the individual by the socialization process, which Parsons had barely acknowledged—became the wedge for challenging oppressive social relations.

Thus in Chodorow's hands, the "strains" Parsons had identified in the sex role socialization process are the focus of the analysis, and ultimately they provide the rationale for radically reorganizing society. In contrast to Parsons's image of modern nuclear families as "factories" producing well-adjusted human personalities (1955, p. 16), in Chodorow's view, "the processes through which mothering is reproduced generate tensions and strains that undermine the sex-gender system even while reproducing it" (1978, p. 211).

One of the central strains she describes is the masculine urge to dominate and oppress women. Far from being a pathological exception, Chodorow argues that what Parsons called "distorted masculinity" is the *normal* by-product of nuclear families in which men rarely engage in child care. Boys who are raised exclusively by mothers learn to devalue and reject whatever is associated with femininity, developing what Freud called "the normal male contempt for women" (quoted in Chodorow 1978, p. 182). This devaluation is both a way to assuage the pain of renouncing identification with the mother and an incentive to identify instead with the male role. This contempt is then institutionalized in the public sphere, where men have the power to realize and enforce these unconscious needs, resulting in sex segregation in the labor force, a general cultural devaluation of women as well as their domestic and paid work, and laws and customs that give men control over women in families.

Chodorow thus views male domination as a fundamental feature of

our social relationships. However, at the same time, she rejects the
radical feminist claim that women are simply coerced into their primary
parenting role (1978, pp. 31–36). She argues that the dynamics of female
psychosexual development result in a particular configuration of emotional needs and relational capacities in women that can only be satisfied
in the mothering role, given our society's present social and economic
arrangements. Because adult women were reared by a woman, they
were never forced to give up their first connection and identification, as
males were. As a consequence, they experience themselves more "rela-
tionally"; that is, women maintain affective connections to others more
easily and possess greater needs for emotional closeness and intimacy
than men. But granted that "deep affective relationships to women are
hard to come by on a routine, daily, ongoing basis for many women"
(1978, p. 200)—due in part to the persecution of lesbianism and, in part,
to women's economic dependence on men—women are forced to turn
to men to fulfill their emotional needs. Unfortunately, adult men are
typically threatened by such relational demands: Their early childhood
experiences have taught them to deny their needs for emotional connection to others, and to develop a stronger sense of being separate,
independent, autonomous selves. Men's emotional distance then draws
the woman to motherhood, her only alternative for recreating the intense emotional bonds she unconsciously desires. Chodorow notes that
when motherhood is women's only source of emotional fulfillment
(which is typically the case in white, middle-class, suburban homes), the
result can be pathological:

> That women turn to children to fulfill emotional and even erotic desires
> unmet by men or other women means that a mother expects from infants
> what only another adult should be expected to give. . . . In a society where
> women do meaningful productive work, have on-going adult companion-
> ship while they are parenting, and have satisfying emotional relationships
> with other adults, they are less likely to overinvest in children. But these
> are precisely the conditions that capitalist industrial development has
> limited. (1978, p. 212)

Thus, Chodorow characterizes the reproduction of gender roles in the
family, as well as in the labor force, as a pathological cycle of oppression,
denial, and dependency. Her only hope for change is a radical reorganization of society to enable coparenting to take place in the family:

> Children could be dependent from the outset on people of both genders
> and establish an individuated sense of self in relation to both. In this way,
> masculinity would not become tied to denial of dependence and devalua-
> tion of women. . . . This would reduce men's needs to guard their mas-
> culinity and their control of social and cultural spheres which treat and

define women as secondary and powerless, and would help women to develop the autonomy which too much embeddedness in relationships has often taken from them. (1978, p. 218)

Chodorow's work has inspired several studies that attempt to document the social consequences of these inner psychic dynamics. Three examples are the works of Lillian Rubin, Evelyn Fox Keller, and my own research. Lillian Rubin's *Intimate Strangers* (1982) illustrates men's and women's different emotional needs and relational capacities with in-depth interviews with middle-class couples in marriage counseling. She describes differences in men's and women's experiences of intimacy, friendship, and sexuality, which neatly corroborate the theory that men possess more rigid ego boundaries than women. For example, she claims that women tend to crave intimacy while men tend to want to avoid it, demonstrating women's greater need and capacity for connection to others, and men's repression of such affect. These differences, she argues, set the stage for miscommunication and conflict in heterosexual relationships.

In *Reflections on Gender and Science* (1985), Evelyn Fox Keller uses Chodorow's version of object relations theory to explain the cultural connection in our society between science and masculinity. In her view, the dominant scientific paradigm in the West is focused on objectivity, seen as the separation between a scientist and what is being studied, and domination over nature. This way of doing science reflects characteristically masculine concerns with separation, autonomy, and control over women. This orientation, she argues, draws personalities to science that are obsessively concerned with these issues (who are typically, but not always men), thus reproducing and promoting a singular vision and approach to science. Her biography of Barbara McClintock, a Nobel prize–winning geneticist whose research on corn was unrecognized for most of her career, sought to demonstrate that taking a "maternal" attitude of caring, emotional connection toward one's subject matter, may allow for new discoveries less likely under the rigidly masculine notions of objectivity current in the scientific establishment.

In *Gender Differences at Work* (1989) I used Chodorow's object relations approach to help understand the asymmetrical experiences of men and women who enter nontraditional occupations. For this book, I examined two token groups: male nurses and female marines. I found that these two groups—although formally similar in terms of proportional representation and popular stereotypes—encounter vastly different work environments. Female marines are restricted from the most prestigious specialties and highest commands due to combat exclusionary rules, they are segregated in basic training, where they are given special training in poise and makeup (in addition to the regular regimen given to male marines), and they are subject to all sorts of rules governing their dress and comportment to ensure that they present an adequately feminine image. Male nurses, on the other hand, encounter no legal barriers to their practice of nursing, they tend to be concentrated in the most prestigious and better paying specialties, and they receive special treatment from physicians, female nurses, and educators, which enhances their status. Furthermore, I found that whereas female marines struggle to be accepted as legitimate, full-fledged members of the Corps, the male nurses actively strive to set themselves apart from their female colleagues. They do this by referring to their special "masculine" attributes—such as physical strength, decisiveness, and technical prowess—which, they believe, suit them to "unfeminine" types of practice. They also devalue the traditionally female personality traits they perceive their female colleagues to have.

To some degree, the difference in the experience of male nurses and female marines can be explained by the status difference of the two groups. Because our society defines maleness and men's jobs as more prestigious than female jobs, women have a built-in incentive to enter male arenas, and men to avoid female ones. Psychoanalytic theory is useful in helping to explain the origin of that status difference, and the intensity with which the men pursue the differentiation between themselves and their female colleagues. The psychological dramas described by Chodorow are played out in both the military and nursing: Men make greater efforts in these settings to distinguish their roles from those performed by women, and to devalue women in the process. Thus, male nurses contend that although they care for their patients, their caring is provided in a characteristically "masculine" sort of way. One male nurse told me:

> I think men demonstrate nurturance and caring to the same degree as a female would, but the demonstration of it is different. I don't think we always touch as frequently, and say soft, kind words. I think my caring is of the same depth and degree, but it's more overt than covert. It's not warm fluffy, it's different. Some might say that's not caring or nurturing.

Likewise, male soldiers distance themselves from their female counterparts, insisting that women are incapable of achieving full-fledged membership in the Marine Corps. Former Marine Corps Commandant William Barrows recently told a reporter,

> War is man's work. Biological convergence on the battlefield would not only be dissatisfying in terms of what women could do, but it would be an enormous psychological distraction for the male who wants to think that he's fighting for that woman somewhere behind, not up there in the same

foxhole with him. It tramples the male ego. When you get right down to it, you have to protect the manliness of war. (Quoted in Williams 1989, pp. 9–10)

Of course, the important difference in the two occupations is that men in the military monopolize positions of authority. They have the power to deny women full active participation in the military, and they do.

Women, in contrast, do not seem to be threatened by the same fundamental psychological way as men by the entrance of men into a female-dominated occupation. Men's experiences in nursing suggest that women are supportive colleagues. Clearly, there are economic reasons for this: Encouraging more men to enter nursing may result in increasing pay and prestige for the profession. But the women do not fear that their femininity is at stake when they participate in "male" activities, or when men participate in "their" activities. Compare these comments of a female Marine Corps recruit that I interviewed:

I chose the Marine Crops because I respect them the most.
[Did you consider the masculine stereotype about the marines?]
That may have been one of the reasons I chose the marines—because it seemed like it was so tough and high-charged.

Far from distancing themselves from the men, female marines expressed the desire to join them in basic training, on the rifle range, and in combat. And, significantly, they saw nothing incompatible with doing this work and maintaining a feminine identification. As one drill instructor told me, "You're a marine twenty-four hours a day, but you're a woman always."

The women generally agreed why they were not permitted to participate on equal footing with the men: because the men—not the women— couldn't handle it. A Marine Corps lieutenant colonel told me: "Gender is an issue for the males, not the females. Males are threatened by women marines and gays; women are not." A similar sentiment was expressed in an interview with a female nurse, who related this story:

It takes a special kind of man to go into nursing. . . . I remember being at a party . . . with mostly male attorneys. Three of them said, "I'll dig ditches before I do that kind of stuff" [referring to nursing]. And these are people who pride themselves on being liberal. First of all, it's insulting to me. But they only think that it's insulting when you're talking about their own sex doing it. Because of the nurturing part of it, because you're dealing with people's bodily excrement. They made comments like, "Not only do you have to shovel shit, you have to smile when you do it." . . . We're never going to have to worry about having a lot of men in nursing.

The women I interviewed did not dissociate their work from the more "feminine" nurturing aspects as they would have been expected to do if status were all that mattered to them. For these women, gender identity was not threatened by engaging in "masculine" jobs or by having men enter their profession, as was the case with the men.

Occupational sex segregation fulfills a powerful psychological need for men. The occupational world is an arena in which men have traditionally proven their masculinity, actively distancing themselves from femininity. The entrance of women into male-only fields threatens men's ability to achieve this psychological sense of distance from femininity through their jobs. Thus women are excluded, or their participation is greatly constrained in order to preserve this arena as a "masculinity proving ground." The theory of object relations can therefore inform the underlying reasons for the persistence of segregation in the labor force.

Chodorow's feminist rereading of psychoanalysis has also informed studies of moral development (Gilligan 1982), men's involvement with sports (Messner 1987, 1989), and women's consumption of mass culture (Radway 1983). However, the theory has by no means enjoyed universal acceptance by feminist sociologists. In the next section of the paper, I will review some of the major criticisms feminists have directed against the use of psychoanalysis to study gender roles.

Feminist Critiques of Feminist Psychoanalytic Theory

Judith Lorber's 1981 review of Chodorow's work begins, "When I read *The Reproduction of Mothering* I found to my disappointment that it is primarily an exegesis of psychoanalytic theory (p. 482). Similarly, a review of the book by Pauline Bart concludes: "The rehabilitation of psychoanalytic theories in the women's movement here and in Britain and France makes my blood run cold" (1983, p. 152). Several other feminist sociologists have sharply criticized the use of psychoanalytic theory in the study of gender. I will review and discuss three sets of these criticisms: first, a methodological critique concerning the nature of sociological evidence; second, a theoretical critique of psychological reductionism; and third, a political critique about the possibilities for change implicit in the model.

Methodological Critique

Psychoanalytic theory has been slow to gain acceptance by many sociologists trained in positivistic and quantitative methodologies. Feminists have been among those sociologists raising questions about the nature of psychoanalytic "data," the reliability of its methodology, and its usefulness for causal explanation.

Alice Rossi criticized Chodorow's (and other psychoanalytic theorists') overreliance on clinical case studies to provide evidence for patterns of normal human development. She notes that many of psychoanalytic theory's insights about the general human condition are inferred from clinical observations of disturbed adults and children. In Rossi's view, pathology does not simply exaggerate the normal processes found in healthy adults; rather, in many cases, it reverses normal tendencies. Therefore she is skeptical about the theory's applicability to the general population, and exhorts "those of us with research inclinations" to take the initiative to convert the theory into "testable hypotheses" to be confirmed or disproved by empirical research (Rossi, 1981, p. 493–94).

In this same vein, Judith Lorber has criticized the methodology of psychoanalytic research for its lack of reliability. She notes that for the most part, the theory is based on psychoanalysts' reports and interpretations of their patients' personal accounts during analysis (Lorber 1981, p. 483). By the theory's own admission, hidden desires and unconscious motives characterize the analyst's relationship to the patient (countertransference), bringing into question the replicability of findings from one analyst to another. Such an unreliable data collection procedure, she argues, is too narrow to meet sociological standards of evidence.

Finally, the approach has been challenged regarding its usefulness for making causal inferences about human behavior. Chodorow asserts in her book that she intends to explain a universal fact of human experience: the primary mothering of all infants. Her argument is that the evidently universal practice of assigning primary infant care to women can be explained by the psychological patterns reproduced in family settings where women are the primary caretakers of infants. The circularity of this position has been noted and criticized by several feminist sociologists (Chafetz 1988, p. 60). But the theory has also come under fire on empirical grounds: Not all mothers were primarily mothered themselves, and not all women who were mothered as infants want to mother as adults. Cynthia Fuchs Epstein, for example, marshals sociological research findings to argue that "in the United States as well as elsewhere, there is no evidence to indicate consistent socialization patterns and consistent orientations toward motherhood for all women" (1988, p. 199).

All of these objections reflect the positivistic orientation of mainstream American sociology rather than any uniquely feminist viewpoint. I would argue that the dominance of this particular epistemological tradition within sociology has made psychoanalysis less acceptable than in the more interpretive disciplines such as anthropology, literature, and

history, where psychoanalytic inquiry is flourishing among feminist
scholars. Without wishing to dismiss the objections raised by Rossi,
Lorber, and others, I encourage further dialogue along the lines proposed by Stacey and Thorne in "The Missing Feminist Revolution in
Sociology" (1985). There the authors argue that the *exclusive* focus on
quantitative variable analysis and hypothesis testing militates against
the discovery of women's lived experience, in many instances denying
women their own voices. Psychoanalytic theory, in contrast, is based on
the subjective expression of individual meaning. While the data gained
from psychoanalytic research may not easily fit into quantifiable categories for analysis, and perfect reliability is often sacrificed, to deny the
project altogether is to prematurely cut off inquiry into crucial layers of
social life.

For example, Epstein is correct in noting that increasing numbers of
American women are choosing not to become mothers. But does this
mean that women have discarded the emotional needs and lost the
relational capacities that Chodorow and others attribute to women who
were primarily mothered as children? To amply address this question, a
different type of data-gathering procedure may be needed, one that
focuses on "subjective" meaning instead of "objective" behaviors. Qualitative methods—including the individual case study approach favored
by psychoanalytic theorists—are appropriate ways to approach these
issues. Rather than dismissing these alternative methodologies for their
failure to comply with positivistic standards of evidence and reliability,
they should be recognized for the potential contributions they uniquely
can bring to the study of gender. (See also Miller, Mauksch, and
Statham 1988; Williams 1991.)

Psychological Reductionism

A second critique commonly made by feminist sociologists against
using psychoanalytic theory is that the approach emphasizes psychological processes over structural or social ones. Lorber, for example,
writes in her review of *The Reproduction of Mothering*,

> Although Chodorow does discuss structural factors that affect parenting
> throughout the book, she ultimately opts for psychoanalytic interpreta-
> tions over social structural and behavioral analyses. Chodorow argues that
> personality is the crucial link between the individual and social institu-
> tions. . . . I would argue that social structures are the crucial variable.
> (1981, p. 483)

Mary Frank Fox raises a similar criticism about the work of Evelyn Fox
Keller when she writes that "Any connection between early experience

and outcomes for scientific practice and orientation is mediated by political and social structures that are simply overlooked in these psychoanalytic essays" (1986, p. 198). Finally, Iris Young is critical of psychoanalytic feminists who "think that psychological dispositions associated with gender can themselves explain social structural phenomena, such as a distinction between public and private spheres, or relations of hierarchy in institutions" (1983, p. 135).

At the heart of all of these criticisms is a presumed dichotomy between structural approaches to explaining gender inequality and psychological ones, probably stemming from Durkheim's original insistence that sociological explanation not "reduce" social facts to outcomes of psychological processes.

While it is certainly true that some—perhaps even most—perspectives in psychology lack viable notions of social structure, this is not the case with psychoanalytic theory. Theorists in the objects relations tradition, in particular, explore how society structures the individual psyche, and in turn how the needs and dispositions of the individual structure interactions in our social institutions. Unfortunately psychoanalysis is often grouped with other psychological theories inconsistent with this sociological approach, and dismissed accordingly.

Part of the problem might also stem from ambiguity in the word *structure*. Neil Smelser (1988) has recently added conceptual clarity to the term, defining it as patterns of interaction produced by social forces. In his view, which I share, these patterns occur on varying levels—among individuals, groups, or institutions. Social structure, in other words, can characterize both micro- and macrolevels of analysis. Thus, when we discuss "patterned interaction" occurring among family members or male and female coworkers, we are referring to social structure just as when we speak of relationships occurring among political parties, religious organizations, or social classes. The fact that women do the primary infant care in most families can, by this definition, be considered a structural phenomenon. Nancy Chodorow made this point in a response to her feminist critics: "A main argument of [*The Reproduction of Mothering*] is that women's mothering *is* a social structure, which affects other structures; it is not something apart from social structure or society" (1981, p. 501).

Confusion arises when social structure is used to refer only to macrolevel or public forms of social organization (e.g., politics, the economy) as opposed to private or domestic forms. This selective use of the expression promotes a false dichotomy within sociology, perpetuating the notion that interpersonal relationships are somehow less affected by social forces than more public, impersonal ones. Clearly, we do tend to view our friendships, family ties, and intimate relationships as products of personal choice rather than social structure. It may be more threatening to think that these types of relationships are as constrained as, say, our voting behavior or occupational status. Nevertheless, it behooves us as sociologists to explore the possibility that such constraints do exist and have effects that extend even into the unconscious.

The issue of choice may be linked to this rejection of psychoanalysis in another way, although this is more speculative. Because the focus of psychoanalysis is the internalization of social demands and cultural patterns—including patterns that are clearly oppressive to women—feminists may interpret the approach as claiming that women are choosing motherhood (for example), when, in fact, discrimination in institutions such as employment and the law make few alternatives really available to most women. If the desire to mother is indeed as deeply internalized as Chodorow and others suggest, the issue of women's complicity in sustaining patterns of domination in the family arises. The theory begins to sound like the biological determinism that sociologists of gender have worked so hard to debunk.

Although I share the concern that psychoanalytic theory can be used to justify the status quo by appealing to women's ingrained needs and desires, there are other, more emancipatory moments in the theory that should not be overlooked. One of the most powerful insights in psychoanalysis is that conformity is never achieved without substantial psychical costs. Our relationships with others are always characterized by ambivalence; the theory does not recognize any social relationship as "given" or "natural"—including the mother-child relationship. Thus, the observation that mothering fulfills some inner psychic needs does not preclude the possibility that mothering fails to completely satisfy these needs, nor that it stultifies others. Psychoanalysis, unlike other theories of socialization, provides us with a concept of internalization that does not ignore individuals' resistance to conformity, and the sacrifices our relationships demand of us. The theory holds open the possibility that other relationships might fulfill our needs and desires without exacting the high psychological and social costs of our present arrangements. Feminist psychoanalytic theorists' call for coparenting is premised on precisely this possibility.

However, the coparenting strategy itself has come under fire from many feminist sociologists. Because this strategy for changing our current gender arrangements is so controversial, I will consider it as a separate feminist critique in the next section.

Psychoanalytic theory is complementary rather than incompatible with feminist insights about the existence of discrimination in our social institutions. In a sense, psychoanalytic theory examines the flipside of discrimination: Instead of looking at discrimination as causing women's primary child care responsibility in the home by constraining women's participation in the public world, psychoanalytic theory looks at women's primary child care responsibility as a cause of discrimination in the public sphere. The structured inequality in the family, which absolves men of the duty to participate equally in child care, produces men who have the desire to differentiate from and debase women. Because these men monopolize positions of power and authority in our society, these desires are institutionalized in discriminatory policies and practices. Surely the causal effects operate in both directions between gender inequality in the household and gender inequality in public roles.

Strategies for Change

Because psychoanalysis focuses on the family as the site of the reproduction of gender and gender domination, psychoanalytic feminists' strategies for change have centered on transforming familial roles. Chodorow and others argue that men must be as involved as women in early child rearing so that children will identify with members of both sexes, thus breaking the cycle of masculine and feminine gender identity formation. This approach to social change has been criticized by feminist sociologists for a number of reasons.

Several feminist sociologists have noted the logical contradiction posed by this solution in the context of the theory's own propositions. If it is the case that men lack the relational capacities and emotional needs that draw women to mothering, can they be forced to nurture infants? Andrea Nye questions how successful efforts have been to force men to participate in child care:

> In liberated families eager to try shared parenting . . . the father participates in child-care and housework, but only while maintaining at the same time a stubborn and often unconscious resistance which shows that the structure of the family remains intact. (1988, pp. 132–33)

In addition, some argue that it may not be in the best interests of children to subject them to caregiving by men who lack the orientation needed to do the job properly. Miriam Johnson, for example, argues that since men are more concerned with establishing and maintaining gender differences than women are, allowing them to participate equally in child care could possibly exacerbate gender stereotyping and promote gender role conformity in girls and boys (Johnson 1988, pp. 85–86). Rose Laub Coser argues that it may not even be in the best interests of *women* to increase men's roles in child care: "In an authoritarian relationship," she writes, "the one thing that is worse than a nonparticipating husband is a meddling husband" (1981, p. 490).

A second objection raised by feminists against the coparenting strategy is that it ignores or, at best, deflects attention from public forms of protest. The solution to gender inequality—which affects all layers of society—should not depend on the outcome of private struggles between individual women and men over the allocation of household labor. Economic and political struggles are seen as far more essential. (See Housman 1982; Sayers 1982; Wilson 1981.)

Finally, the coparenting strategy has been criticized for its heterosexist bias. Coparenting designates the heterosexual couple as the ideal child-rearing unit, implicitly denigrating alternative family forms, including lesbian and single-parent households. In terms of a practical politics for feminism, the strategy thus ignores an essential feminist constituency.

Psychoanalytic feminists have not persuasively countered these theoretical and political objections to the coparenting strategy. As a practical solution to gender inequality, it *is* optimistic, if not unrealistic. Coparenting is unlikely to be a widespread practice as long as economic and political control continues to be monopolized by men. Indeed, the theory itself helps us to understand the depth and tenacity of men's resistance to sharing *any* roles with women. Affirmative action policies and other antidiscrimination legislation that "force" men to accept women into "their" occupations or public offices may be the only means available to counter those deep psychological resistances that have been institutionalized throughout our society.

Clearly, transformations of both the public and private arenas are needed to adequately address the problem of gender inequality. Men will not accept women as equals in the public sphere as long as structured inequality within the family continues to produce sexist men. Thus, the goal of transforming intimate relationships so that women are not forced to shoulder the entire burden of child care alone should be a part of any feminist agenda, but it should be combined with strategies designed to enhance women's economic, political, and cultural equality as well.

Conclusion

In this essay, I have described the uses of psychoanalysis by feminist sociologists. I have tried to show that the theory of object relations enhances our understanding of the links between gender socialization and the institutionalization of male domination in both the private and the public spheres. The structure of the traditional, Western nuclear family creates asymmetrical needs and dispositions in men and women that contribute to the reproduction of unequal and essentially oppressive relationships. Psychoanalytic feminist theory helps to explain this reproduction while managing to steer clear of both essentialist arguments and purely voluntaristic ones.

It is true that many questions raised by the theory have been left unexplored, or are only partially addressed by psychoanalytic feminists. More attention needs to be paid to the linkages between ideology and gender identity (as in the work of Connell 1987); alternative family structures and the resulting variations in gender identity (see Spelman 1988); and avenues for challenging the cycle of gender reproduction (see Johnson 1988). But there is no question that psychoanalytic theory and methods can continue to contribute to research in these areas.

Feminist theory and psychoanalysis have mutually benefited from their nearly century-long history of critical exchange. I hope that this paper will continue that dialogue to further enrich feminist sociology.

Acknowledgments

I would like to thank Paula England and Debra Umberson for their comments and criticisms of earlier versions of this paper.

References

Bart, Pauline. 1983. "Review of Chodorow's *Reproduction of Mothering*." pp. 147–152 in *Mothering: Essays in Feminist Theory*, edited by Joyce Trebilcot, Totowa, NJ: Rowman & Allenheld.

Chafetz, Janet Saltzman. 1988. *Feminist Sociology*. Itasca, IL: Peacock.

Chodorow, Nancy. 1978. *The Reproduction of Mothering*. Berkeley: University of California Press.

———. 1981. "On *The Reproduction of Mothering*: A Methodological Debate." *Signs* 6(3, Spring):500–14.

Connell, R. W. 1987. *Gender and Power*. Stanford, CA: Stanford University Press.

Coser, Rose Laub. 1981. "On *The Reproduction of Mothering*: A Methodological Debate." *Signs* 6(3 Spring):487–92.

Epstein, Cynthia Fuchs. 1988. *Deceptive Distinctions*. New Haven, CT: Yale University Press.

Fox, Mary Frank. 1986. "Mind, Nature and Masculinity." *Contemporary Sociology* 15(March):197–99.

Gilligan, Carol. 1982. *In a Different Voice*. Cambridge, MA: Harvard University Press.

Housman, Judy. 1982. "Mothering, the Unconscious, and Feminism." *Radical America* 16(6, Nov.–Dec.):47–61.

Johnson, Miriam. 1988. *Strong Mothers, Weak Wives*. Berkeley: University of California Press.

―――. 1989. "Feminism and the Theories of Talcott Parsons." Pp. 101–118 of *Feminism and Sociological Theory*, edited by Ruth Wallace, Newbury Park, CA: Sage Publications.

Keller, Evelyn Fox. 1985. *Reflections on Gender and Science*. New Haven, CT: Yale University Press.

Kurzweil, Edith. 1989. "Psychoanalytic Feminism: Implications for Sociological Theory." Pp. 82–97 of *Feminism and Sociological Theory*, edited by Ruth Wallace. Newbury Park, CA: Sage Publications.

Lorber, Judith. 1981. "On *The Reproduction of Mothering*: A Methodological Debate." *Signs* 6(3, Spring): 482–86.

Messner, Michael. 1987. "The Meaning of Success: The Athletic Experience and the Development of Male Identity." Pp. 193–209 in *The Making of Masculinities*, edited by Harry Brod. Boston: Allen & Unwin.

―――. 1989. "Masculinities and Athletic Careers." *Gender & Society* 3(1, March):71–88.

Miller, Eleanor M., Hans O. Mauksch, and Anne Statham. 1988. "The Qualitative Approach to the Study of Women's Work: Different Method/Different Knowledge." Pp. 309–315 in *The Worth of Women's Work*, edited by Anne Statham, Eleanor M. Miller, and Hans O. Mauksch. Albany: State University of New York Press.

Mitchell, Juliet. 1974. *Psychoanalysis and Feminism*. New York: Random House.

Morgan, D. H. J. 1975. *Social Theory and the Family*. London: Routledge & Kegan Paul.

Nye, Andrea. 1988. *Feminist Theory and the Philosophies of Man*. New York: Routledge.

Parsons, Talcott. 1954. *Essays in Sociological Theory*. New York: Free Press.

―――. 1955. *Family: Socialization and Interaction Process*. Glencoe, IL: Free Press.

―――. [1954] 1970. *Social Structure and Personality*. New York: Free Press.

Radway, Janice. 1983. "Women Read the Romance: The Interaction of Text and Context." *Feminist Studies* 9(1, Spring):53–78.

Rossi, Alice, S. 1981. "On *The Reproduction of Mothering*: A Methodological Debate." *Signs* 6(3, Spring):492–500.

Rubin, Lillian. 1982. *Intimate Strangers*. New York: Harper & Row.

Sayers, Janet. 1982. "Psychoanalysis and Personal Politics." *Feminist Review* 10(February):91–95.

Smelser, Neil. 1988. "Social Structure." Pp. 103–129 in *Handbook of Sociology*, edited by Neil Smelser. Newbury Park, CA: Sage.

Spelman, Elizabeth V. 1988. *Inessential Woman: Problems of Exclusion in Feminist Thought*. Boston: Beacon Press.

Stacey, Judith, and Barrie Thorne. 1985. "The Missing Feminist Revolution in Sociology." *Social Problems* 32(4, April):301–16.

Williams, Christine. 1989. *Gender Differences at Work*. Berkeley: University of California Press.

―――. 1991. "Case Studies and the Sociology of Gender." Pp. 224–243 in *A*

Case for the Case Study, edited by Joe Feagin, Anthony Orum, and Gideon Sjoberg. Chapel Hill: University of North Carolina Press.

Wilson, Elizabeth. 1981. "Psychoanalysis: Psychic Law and Order?" *Feminist Review* 8(Summer):63–78.

Young, Iris Marion. 1983. "Is Male Gender Identity the Cause of Male Domination?" Pp. 129–146 in *Mothering: Essays in Feminist Theory*, edited by Joyce Trebilcot. Totowa, NJ: Rowman & Allenheld.

Chapter 8

Power, Inequality, and the Accomplishment of Gender: An Ethnomethodological View

Candace West and Sarah Fenstermaker

Introduction

As Connell (1985, p. 260) has observed, "We are in the middle of the most important change in the social sciences, and Western social thought generally, since the impact of socialist class analysis in the mid-nineteenth century." What is involved is a thoroughgoing rethinking of gender relations: the division of labor, the formation of gender identities, and the social subordination of women by men. The impact of such thinking has been profound, resulting in new conceptualizations of the very foundations of gender inequality (for example, women's relationship to the means of production, the relationship between work and family, and the politics of sexual object choices). Despite these advances, we have yet to see a feminist revolution in our field (Stacey and Thorne 1985). In sociology, as in psychology and economics, new conceptualizations of the foundations of gender inequality have relied on old conceptualizations of gender.

Elsewhere (Fenstermaker Berk 1985; West and Zimmerman 1987; Fenstermaker, West, and Zimmerman 1991), we offer a critical analysis of conventional sociological understandings of gender, including its interpretation as an individual attribute and as a role. We argue that the bifurcation of gender into femininity and masculinity effectively reduces gender to sex (cf. Gerson 1985), while the treatment of gender as a role obscures the work involved in producing gender in everyday activities. By contrast, we offer an ethnomethodological understanding of gender as an *accomplishment*: an emergent feature of social situations that is both an outcome of and a rationale for the most fundamental division of society.

151

In this chapter, we extend our analysis to an explicit consideration of questions of power and inequality. First, we reiterate our view of gender as an interactional accomplishment, contrasting it with traditional perspectives on sex roles and on masculinity and femininity as internalized attributes. In so doing, we stress the limitations of role theory and conventional understandings of masculinity and femininity in relation to questions of power and social control (cf. Connell 1985, 1987; Stacey and Thorne 1985; Thorne 1980). We also emphasize the theoretical necessity for distinctions among *sex* (biological classification as female or male), *sex category* (social identification as a woman or a man), and *gender* (conduct that is accountable to normative conceptions of womanly or manly natures).

Second, we review empirical evidence that indicates the utility of our perspective to address widely acknowledged aspects of gender inequality. Here, we cast a broad net over a number of diverse problems, ranging from the subordination of women in the family and in the economy to the domination of women in face-to-face interaction. Through these examples, we attempt to show that a wide variety of activities may be implicated in the accomplishment of gender. And, just as individuals are accountable to normative conceptions of their womanly or manly natures, so may institutional arrangements be accountable to normative conceptions of gender (cf. Goffman 1977).

Third, and perhaps most important, we suggest that an ethnomethodological perspective on gender can advance our understanding of less widely acknowledged—but increasingly significant—areas of sociological concern, such as those that lie in the interstices of gender, race, and class (cf. Hurtado 1989).

Basic Assumptions of Ethnomethodology

Zimmerman (1978) offers a succinct description of ethnomethodology that is useful to our purposes here. As he notes, "Ethnomethodology proposes that the properties of social life which seem objective, factual and transsituational, are actually managed accomplishments or achievements of local processes" (p. 11). In other words, "objective" and "factual" properties of social life acquire their status as such through the situated conduct of societal members. The aim of ethnomethodological inquiry is to analyze the situated conduct of societal members in order to see how "objective" properties of social life are achieved.

For example, within Western societies, people in everyday life take for granted that there are two and only two sexes (Garfinkel 1967, pp. 122–128). This state of affairs is perceived as "only natural" insofar as persons are seen to be "essentially, originally [and] in the final analysis,

either 'male' or 'female' " (Garfinkel 1967, p. 122). When persons interact with one another, they take for granted that each has an essential
manly or womanly nature—one that derives from their sex and one that
can be detected from the "natural signs" they give off (Goffman 1977,
p. 75).

These then are the *normative conceptions* of our culture regarding the
properties of normally sexed persons. Such conceptions underlie the
seemingly "objective," "factual," and "transsituational" character of
gender in social life and, in this sense, are experienced as exogenous—
outside the particular situation and particular individual. However, at
the same time, the "meaning" of these conceptions is dependent on the
context in which they are invoked—rather than transsituational, as
suggested by the popular notion of "cognitive consensus" (Zimmerman
1978, pp. 8–9). Moreover, because these conceptions are held to be only
natural, to question them is tantamount to calling oneself into question
as a competent cultural member. Thus, it is not surprising that traditional perspectives of gender have also relied on these conceptions.

Sex Differences and Sex Roles

Conventionally, the distinction between sex and gender has rested on
the ascribed status of the former and the achieved status of the latter.
Since the early 1970s, social scientists have taken pains to point out this
distinction in the texts they produce for classroom use. *Sex* is typically
described as a biological given, determined by anatomical, hormonal,
and chromosomal factors. *Gender* is conceptualized as a social identity,
constructed by culture and society. Distinguishing sex from gender in
this way has made for clarity in classroom discussions—at least, for the
first few weeks of every term.

However, in later weeks, and in the social science literature more
generally, considerable confusion prevails. Despite their acknowledg-
ment that gender is socially constructed, many theories and empirical
studies treat it as an individual attribute: the masculinity or femininity
inherent in a person. While the "sex differences approach" (Hochschild
1973; Thorne 1980) is perhaps most widely employed by psychologists,
sociological journals and conferences are rife with examples of its use.
One problem with this approach is that conceptualizing gender as an
individual characteristic obscures our understanding of how it structures distinct domains of social experience (Stacey and Thorne 1985, pp.
307–308). Sex differences become the explanation, rather than the analytic starting point. To be sure, many scholars who take this perspective
invoke socialization to account for how masculinity and femininity are

"internalized." But while these accounts acknowledge that sex differences may be learned, they suggest that by approximately five years of age, such differences have become fixed and immutable characteristics of individuals—like sex (West and Zimmerman, 1987, p. 126). With that, the distinction that was so carefully drawn is obliterated, as gender reduces effectively to sex (Gerson 1985, p. 1). It thus becomes difficult to account for variation in gender relations because the social meanings of sex are rerooted in its biological underpinnings.

A complementary approach is to treat gender as a role or status, focusing on how it is learned and displayed. Originating in a formal theory of social action (Linton 1936; Parsons 1951; Parsons and Bales 1955), the sex roles approach has stressed the specific social locations that yield particular expectations and actions (e.g., Komarovsky 1946, 1950). From this perspective, the actual enactment of one's sex role (or more recently, one's gender role) depends on one's position in the social structure and the expectations that are associated with that position. One problem with this perspective is that the concept of sex roles cannot specify actions appropriate to those roles in advance of their occurrence (Fenstermaker et al. 1991). Since gender is potentially omnirelevant to the organization of social life, virtually any action can count as an example of its role performance.[1] Another problem with this view is that sex roles (unlike most roles, such as physician and patient, or teacher and student) are not located in a particular site or organizational context. In practice, they often serve as "master statuses" (Hughes, 1945), cutting across a variety of social situations. This limits any effort to articulate how variations in *situation* determine variation in the enactment of such roles. Similarly, when gender itself is conceptualized as a role, it is hard to evaluate its impact on other, more situation-specific roles—especially those which are usually restricted to women or to men (Lopata and Thorne 1978; Thorne 1980).[2]

The most serious problem with the sex roles approach is its inadequacy in relation to questions of power and inequality (Connell 1985; Lopata and Thorne 1978; Thorne 1980). Conceptions of the male role and female role suggest a separate but equal arrangement between the two—an arrangement characterized by complementarity rather than conflict. As Thorne and her colleagues observe (Lopata and Thorne 1978; Stacey and Thorne 1985; Thorne 1980), it is telling that social scientists (with the exception of Pettigrew 1964) have not employed role theory in their analyses of race and classic relations; concepts like *race roles* and *class roles* are obviously inadequate to account for the dynamics of power and inequality in these areas.[3]

Nonetheless, assumptions about race and class relations permeate applications of role theory to gender. As many critics have noted, empirical descriptions of the "male role" and "female role" have tended to treat white middle-class persons' experiences as prototypical, relegating departures from these prototypes to the status of deviant cases. Such treatment has not only stimulated widespread charges of racism and class bias, but has also reduced the explanatory utility of this approach in accounting for the diversity of gender relations across different groups (e.g., reducing the study of African American family relations to the "matriarchal" tendencies of women, and the study of Chicano gender relations to the "patriarchal" inclinations of men—see Bridenthal 1981, p. 85; Zinn 1990, pp. 72–73).

Elsewhere (Fenstermaker Berk 1985; Fenstermaker et al. 1991; West and Zimmerman 1987) we return to the conventional distinction between sex and gender to advance a new understanding of gender as an accomplishment. In reconceptualizing the work such accomplishment entails, we stress some theoretical distinctions that have been obscured in traditional perspectives of gender.

"Doing" Gender

We begin with the claim that gender is not merely an individual attribute but something that is accomplished through interaction with others. When we look at it this way, our focus shifts from characteristics of individuals to interactional and, ultimately, institutional doings. For example, consider the process of sex assignment: the initial classification of individuals as female or male. This process is generally regarded as a biological determination, requiring of onlookers only a straightforward examination of the "facts of the matter" (hence, the description of sex as an ascribed status in our introductory texts). However, the *criteria* for sex assignment may vary from case to case (e.g., chromosome type before birth or genitalia after birth); they may or may not agree with one another (as in the case of hermaphrodites); and they may differ considerably across cultures (Kessler and McKenna 1978). It is the firmly held belief that there are two and only two sexes (Garfinkel 1967, pp. 116–18) that explains the relative ease with which initial sex assignment is achieved. This belief accords females and males the status of natural and unequivocal entities, whose social and psychological tendencies apparently follow from their reproductive functions. Thus, from an ethnomethodological perspective, *sex* is a social and cultural construction, rather than a simple statement of the biological facts.

Next, consider the process of sex categorization: the ongoing identification of individuals as girls or boys and women or men in everyday life. Here, there is no well-defined set of criteria that must be met in order to make an identification. Instead, we treat appearances (e.g., deportment, dress, and bearing) as indicative of underlying states of affairs. The point to be noted here is that sex category serves as an emblem of sex, but does not depend on it. For example, preoperative transsexuals can pass as members of the sex category they aspire to, even though the requisite biological criteria are absent. Moreover, members of society can "see" a world populated by two and only two sexes, even in those public situations that prevent examination of the physiological evidence. Thus, from an ethnomethodological perspective, *sex category* must be analytically distinguished from sex assignment—but both must be analytically distinguished from the doing of gender.

Gender, we contend, is a situated accomplishment: the local management of conduct in relation to normative conceptions of appropriate attitudes and activities for particular sex categories. Here, as in our earlier work, we draw on Heritage's (1984, pp. 136–37) discussion of *accountability*: the possibility of describing actions, circumstances, and even descriptions themselves in serious and consequential fashion (e.g., as unwomanly or unmanly). Heritage observes that societal members routinely describe activities in ways that take notice of those activities (e.g., naming, characterizing, blaming, excusing, or simply acknowledging them), placing them in a social framework (i.e., locating them in relation to other activities that are similar or different). The fact that activities can be described in these ways leads to the possibility of designing them with an eye to how they might be evaluated (e.g., as womanly or manly behaviors). Two subtle but important points are worth stressing here. First, from an ethnomethodological perspective, the notion of accountability pertains not only to those activities that *conform* to prevailing normative conceptions (e.g., activities that are conducted in ways that are specifically unremarkable and therefore not deserving of more than passing notice) but also to those activities that deviate. Deviance or conformity is not the issue; rather, it is the possible *assessment* of action on the basis of normative conceptions. Second, the process of rendering something accountable is an *interactional* accomplishment. As Heritage (1984, p. 179) puts it, accountability allows persons to conduct their activities in relation to their circumstances—in ways that allow others to systematically take those circumstances into account and recognize the activities for what they are. Thus, "the intersubjective intelligibility of actions ultimately rests on a symmetry between the *production* of actions on the one hand and their *recognition* on the other" (Heritage 1984, p. 179).

We do not contend that individuals regularly fail to comply with normative prescriptions for gendered behaviors and then account for their failures in normatively appropriate ways. Rather the core of our argument is as follows: To the extent that members of society know their actions are accountable, they will design their actions in relation to how they might be seen and described by others. And to the extent that sex categories are omnirelevant circumstances of action (Garfinkel 1967, p. 118), they provide others with an ever-available resource for interpreting those actions. In short, persons engaged in virtually *any* activity can hold themselves accountable and be held accountable for their performance of that activity *as women* or *as men*. Their membership in one or the other sex category can be invoked to legitimate or discredit their performance. Moreover, virtually any course of action can be assessed according to its womanly or manly nature. To reiterate, doing gender does not always mean living up to normative conceptions of femininity or masculinity; what it means is rendering action *accountable* in these terms. So, while individuals are the ones who do gender, accountability is interactional in character, its idiom drawn from the institutional arenas in which social relationships are brought to life.

What are the implications of this ethnomethodological perspective? First, and perhaps most important, conceiving of gender as an ongoing accomplishment, accountable to interaction, implies that we must locate its emergence in *social situations*, rather than within the individual or some ill-defined set of role expectations. The task of rendering actions accountable arises recurrently across different situations and different particulars of conduct. What it involves is crafting conduct that can be evaluated in relation to normative conceptions of manly and womanly natures (Fenstermaker Berk 1985, p. 203), and assessing conduct in light of those conceptions—given the situation at hand (West and Zimmerman 1987, pp. 139–140).

A second and related implication of our perspective is that we cannot determine the relevance of gender to social action apart from the context in which it is accomplished (Fenstermaker et al. 1991). While sex category is potentially omnirelevant to social life, individuals inhabit many different social identities that may be stressed or muted, depending on the situation. To be sure, some standardized social occasions (e.g., organized sporting events) seem specifically designed to pay homage to "essential" and "natural" differences between women and men (Goffman 1977). Other occasions (e.g., those involving the manipulation of heavy objects or the changing of flat tires) seem conventionally expressive in themselves—virtual prototypes of situations in which masculine and feminine virtues can be compared. But as Goffman (1977, p. 324) points out, heavy, messy, and threatening concerns can be constructed from (and thus "discovered" in) *any* social situation, however light, clean, or safe these may appear in another context. Thus, any social situation can be adapted to the doing of gender—*and that adaptation* makes gender relevant to social interaction and the workings of social institutions.

A third implication of this view is that doing gender does not require heterosocial situations (Fenstermaker et al. 1991). Social situations "do not so much allow for the expression of natural differences as for the production of that difference itself" (Goffman 1977, p. 324). Hence, we may find some of the most extreme versions of essential womanly and manly natures in those settings that are reserved for members of a single sex category, for example, locker rooms or beauty salons (Gerson 1985). Heterosocial situations may highlight categorical membership and make gender's accomplishment more noticeable, but they are not necessary for doing gender in the first instance. This point bears emphasizing, particularly insofar as role theory's assumptions of complementary role relations might lead one to believe that members of both sex categories must be present for gender to get done.

A fourth implication of our reconceptualization is that institutions as well as individuals may be held accountable to normative conceptions of gender. For example, here in the United States, when the activities of children or teenagers have become foci of public concern, both mother-hood and the family have been held accountable to normative concep-tions of essential femininity (including virtues such as nurturance, pro-tectiveness, and caring). In such cases, gender is clearly much more than an individual attribute or role: it is central to our understanding of how situated social action contributes to the reproduction of social structure.

Fifth and finally, we suggest that doing gender is so central to the organization of human conduct that it should not be conceptualized as an intrusion on—or "intervening variable" in—such conduct (as ap-proaches predicated on sex differences often imply). Indeed, in the case of some social arrangements, gender's achievement may be the central work accomplished (Fenstermaker et al. 1991). For example, throughout North America, public bathrooms conventionally separate girls from boys and women from men, despite their functional equivalence with respect to "waste products and their elimination" (Goffman 1977, p. 315). Boys' and men's bathrooms are equipped with urinals, girls' and women's with lavish grooming facilities—even though both sexes use the same means to the same ends in the privacy of their own homes. As Goffman observes, toilet segregation involves the *functioning* of sex-differentiated organs, but nothing in that functioning requires segregation.

[W]hat one has is a case of institutional reflexivity: toilet segregation is presented as a natural consequence of the difference between the sex-classes, when in fact it is rather a means of honoring, if not producing, this difference. (1977, p. 317)

In summary, doing gender consists of creating differences between girls and boys and between women and men—differences that are neither natural nor biological (West and Zimmerman 1987, p. 137). Once created, these differences are used to maintain the essential distinctiveness of feminine and masculine natures. From this perspective, femininity and masculinity are not invariant idealizations of our human natures that are uniformly distributed in society. Nor are normative conceptions of attitudes and activities appropriate for one's sex category templates for manly or womanly behaviors. Rather, what is invariant is the notion that women and men *possess* essentially different natures, for which they will be held accountable in human affairs.

Below, we consider empirical evidence that illustrates the utility of this perspective in addressing many diverse aspects of gender inequality.

Power, Inequality, and the Accomplishment of Gender

To evaluate the empirical evidence that might be relevant to our ethnomethodological view, we begin by considering the conditions under which concerns for *accountably* gendered conduct are likely to emerge. In Western societies, whenever people confront issues of *allocation* (e.g., who will do what, get what, plan or execute some activity, give directions or take them), sex category becomes especially salient (West and Zimmerman 1987, p. 143). Because our existing institutional arrangements are predicated on the belief that women are not only essentially different from—but essentially inferior to—men, the resolution of such issues shapes the exercise of power and manifestation of inequality between women and men through the enactment of our essential natures.

Conversational Shift Work

Questions of allocation can arise even in something so mundane as casual conversation. There, the activities that must be coordinated include opening and closing a state of talk, maintaining an orderly exchange of turns at talk, and providing for a steady stream of conversational topics. Empirical research on the allocation of work involved (e.g., Fishman 1978; West and Zimmerman 1983; West and Garcia 1988) indicates that such activities afford the resources for doing gender. For example, in a recent study of conversations between white, middle-class women and men (West and Garcia 1988), we examined the allocation of "shift work"—the procedures speakers use to effect topical transitions.

Our examination of exchanges among unacquainted persons showed
that most topic transitions were the products of speakers' collaborative
activities, or a means of coping with topics that had "died." But some
transitions were the result of unilateral topic changes—and all of these
were initiated by men. Detailed analysis of these changes showed
how sex category membership became relevant to particular conversational trajectories and thereby provided for men's control over topics
in progress.

Below are three examples of a man's unilateral topic changes in the
vicinity of a woman's potential "tellables," that is, things about which
more might have been said if only they had been pursued. (Here,
verbatim transcripts have been simplified for ease of presentation. The
brackets are used to indicate portions of speakers' utterances that are
simultaneous; capital letters are used to designate stressed utterances or
portions of utterances.)

(1) (West and Garcia 1988, pp. 569–570)

   Beth: If I didn't live in VenTURa I'd really like it on the beach. It's just so
            close, my Mom comes up to see me all the time ya' know. My sister
            comes up to see me all the time.

   Andy: (softly) Ah. (inhales, then exhales) Have you ever participated in
            something like this before?

(2) (West and Garcia 1988, p. 563)

   Andy: I'm in Soc. Soc One, but I find it's so much

            Be⌈e Es⌉that—⌈I'm ⌉
   Beth: ⌊Oh ⌋   ⌊Well,⌋this is my major
   Andy: (softly) Oh!
   Beth: (laughter,⌈more laughter)⌉
   Andy: ⌊My goodness! ⌋(intake of breath)
   Beth: But I'm gonna do it, like I wanna go to law school.
   Andy: Oh I follow.
   Beth: So it's a good⌈major for that ⌉
   Andy: ⌊Did ju   ⌋take this for—did you sign up for
            this test to impress?

(3) (West and Garcia 1988, p. 570)

   Beth: Yeah, I'd like to take uh—⌈something like⌉History
   Andy: ⌊(breathing)   ⌋
   Beth: of Philosophy or something where you don't have to do any of that
            kind of—I don't thINK that way, I'm not that logical. Yuh know they
            go step by step. An' I just—I'm REally an irRAtional person some-
            times. So
   Andy: Where do you live in IV?

Here, Beth's turns at talk *prior* to Andy's topic changes offer strong
evidence that she had something more to say. For example, her com-

plaints about family members' visits, her statement of her future plans, and her successive self-deprecations suggest that there were additional tellables that might have been told. But note further the *nature* of the tellables that were curtailed by Andy's unilateral shifts: In the first excerpt, Beth's feelings about being too close to her home and family; in the second, her hopes for law school; and in the third, any grounds for disagreeing with her negative self-assessment.

The point here is not merely that Beth pursued certain conversational activities (such as description of her personal feelings) that Andy wanted to avoid. Rather, we argue that Beth's pursuit of these activities—and Andy's curtailment of them—both drew on and demonstrated what it was *to be a woman—or a man*—in these contexts (West and Garcia 1988). Thus, explanation of the relationship between Beth's major and her plans for law school (arguably, an unwomanly aspiration) was aborted midstream; exploration of her feelings about being too close to family members (perhaps an unmanly course of topical talk) never took place; and her assessment of herself as "REally an irRAtional person sometimes" received no disagreement. Simultaneously, Andy demonstrated his essential nature as a man through his exercise of control over topics in progress.

The conclusion we draw from such findings is not that men always (or even usually) change topics unilaterally (West and Garcia 1988). Instead, it is that *when* unilateral changes occurred, they were initiated by men—in ways that curtailed the development of women's activities and tellables. Hence, the enactment of women's and men's essential natures conditions what gets talked about (and by whom).

Household Labor

Next, we turn to what might be characterized as a more "scripted" set of allocation issues, namely, those involved in household labor. We use *scripted* to underscore the following facts. First, the division of labor within U.S. households is grossly asymmetrical, with women doing the vast majority of household work (Berheide, Fenstermaker Berk, and Berk 1976; Berk and Fenstermaker Berk 1979; Fenstermaker Berk 1985; Hochschild 1989; Zavella 1987; Zinn 1980). Second, despite the lopsidedness of this arrangement, most household members perceive it as "fair" (Berheide et al. 1976; Fenstermaker Berk 1985). Third, although work imperatives (such as the presence or absence of children and the nature of one's employment outside the home) determine the extent of *women's* contributions to household labor, they do not have a significant effect on men's (Bahr 1974; Berk and Fenstermaker Berk 1979; Farkas 1976; Fenstermaker Berk 1985; Meissner, Humphreys, Meiss, and Sheu 1975; Pleck 1977). And fourth, while women's participation in the paid labor

force has increased dramatically in the past fifteen years, men's participation in the unpaid work of the household has remained virtually
unchanged (cf. Bahr 1974; Hochschild 1989). These are among the most
thoroughly documented dynamics of social life, yet existing theories
have been hard-pressed to account for them. From a sex roles perspective, one might seek to explain these facts through reference to internalized norms for behavior (e.g., suggesting that both women and men
internalize the expectation that household labor is wives' responsibility
and economic provision for the family is husbands' responsibility). But
this approach fails to account for why wives do the majority of household tasks even when they are employed outside the home, and why
this is perceived as a fair arrangement by both husbands and wives.

Elsewhere (Fenstermaker Berk 1985), we suggest that the "missing
link" in our understanding of these facts is the accomplishment of
gender. We note that it is hard to see how people could rationally
arrange things as they have, *solely* for the "rational" or "efficient"
production of household goods and services. The evidence indicates
that the determination of who does what in the household is not merely
a question of who has more time, whose time is worth more, or whose
skills are superior for the task at hand. Rather, it is determined by a
complex relationship between the structure of work imperatives and the
structure of normative conceptions of that work as *gendered* (i.e., only
natural for a woman and not natural for a man).

There are actually *two* processes involved here: the generation of
household goods and services, *and* the accomplishment of gender (Fenstermaker Berk 1985). In everyday synchrony with one another, they
result in a fusion—interactionally speaking—of household work and
gender. The naturalness of each is reflexively defined by the other, and
as a result of their accomplishment in concert, the equity of the arrangements they sustain is virtually impossible to question. For example, the
doing of laundry provides the occasion for producing commodities
(e.g., clean, dry, and folded clothes), but it also affords the opportunity
to affirm one's *gendered* relationship to the work itself. As one woman
put it (in response to the question, What household work does your
husband do?):

> He never helps me. I suppose I should say "rarely." That's a better word
> to describe it. He hangs up his clothes once in a while. He puts his dirty
> socks down the laundry chute. In extreme circumstances, he makes the
> bed. He does nothing. He doesn't have to. It's not his job. (Fenstermaker
> Berk 1985, p. 205)

Our claim is not simply that household labor is *regarded* as women's
work, but that for a woman to do it and a man not to do it draws on and

affirms what people conceive to be the essential nature of each. From this perspective, the seeming irrationality and inefficiency of household task allocation becomes intelligible—as does the perceived fairness of resulting arrangements, and the structured inequality of social life (cf. Goffman 1977).

To be sure, the specific situations in which work and gender are fused may vary considerably from one another, and thus the manifestations of gender inequality may look very different across household work sites. In one household, the task of drying the clothes may involve hanging them up on a line outdoors; in another, it may only involve moving them from a washer to a dryer. Such variation in situational particulars does not *determine* who will do what in the household or the essentially gendered nature of the work to be done. What such variation shows are the many and diverse situations in which sex category can be made to matter in the determination of who will perform such tasks and how they will be carried out:

> Simultaneously, members "do" gender as they "do" housework . . . and what has been called the division of labor provides for the joint production of household labor and gender; it is the mechanism by which both the material and symbolic products of the household are realized. (Fenstermaker Berk 1985, p. 201)

Parenting

Consider now the issues of allocation involved in parenting. As Coltrane (1989, p. 473) observes, mothering is often seen as "the quintessence of womanhood." The tasks it involves, especially those associated with caring, offer countless occasions for the expression of essential femininity. By contrast, fathering is generally regarded as a more limited vehicle for the expression of manhood, restricted as it is to the tasks of "begetting, protecting and providing" (p. 473). To assess the nature of relations between sex category and the allocation of caring tasks, Coltrane conducted intensive interviews with white, dual-earner couples in which fathers assumed significant responsibility for child care.

Like participants in our own studies of household labor (Berk and Berk 1979; Fenstermaker Berk 1985), Coltrane's (1989) dual-earner couples perceived their parenting arrangements as fair. Moreover, these couples also cited work imperatives (such as outside employment schedules) as central to their allocation of tasks. But in this case (admittedly, an atypical sample), over half the couples reported that they took *equal* responsibility for child care. And among all the couples, the allocation of parenting tasks varied with perceptions of the essentially gendered character of the work involved.

For example, mothers and fathers who shared tasks most successfully also believed that men could nurture children as well as women could. One mother explained:

> I don't necessarily think that skill comes with a sex-type. Some women nurture better than others, some men nurture better than other men. I think that those skills can come when either person is willing to have the confidence and commitment to prioritize them. (Coltrane 1989, p. 485)

Parents who shared equally in child care also reported that their children were emotionally "close" to both of them, and that they often called their mothers "Daddy" or fathers "Mommy," when turning to someone for comfort.

Conversely, parents who shared parenting tasks less equally (i.e., those with "manager-helper" arrangements) legitimated their arrangements by citing essential differences between women and men. For example:

> Anybody can slap together a cream cheese and cucumber sandwich and a glass of milk and a few chips and call it lunch, but the ability to see your child is troubled about something or to be able to help them work through a conflict with a friend, that is really much different. (Coltrane 1989, p. 484)

Another mother claimed that "the woman has it more in her genes to be more equipped for nurturing" (p. 485).

But no matter how mothers and fathers legitimated their arrangements to themselves and to their interviewer, they were still held accountable for those arrangements by others with whom they interacted. One mother observed:

> I think I get less praise because people automatically assume that, you know, the mother's *supposed* to do the child care. . . . I can bust my butt at that school and all he has to do is show up at the parking lot and everybody's all *gah gah* over him. (Coltrane 1989, p. 486)

And one father complained of

> constantly going shopping and having women stop me and say "Oh it's so good to see you fathers." I was no longer an individual; I was this generic father who was now a liberated father who could take care of his child. (Coltrane 1989, p. 486)

Another father spoke of being "in the closet" with respect to his execution of child care tasks, lest his business associates interpret his commitment to parenting as fundamentally equivalent to a *lack* of commitment to his job (cf. Bourne and Wikler 1978). Thus, their own arrangements and their own perceptions of those arrangements notwithstanding, these couples were accountable to normative conceptions regarding the essential womanly nature of child care.

Paid Labor

Finally, we turn to questions of allocation that arise in the paid labor force. Here, as in our earlier work (Fenstermaker et al. 1991; West and Zimmerman 1987), we draw on Hochschild's 1983a, 1983b) study of airline flight attendants—some of the most detailed evidence we have seen of what it means to do gender on the job. Hochschild's interviews and observations indicate that the job of flight attendant is something quite different for a woman that it is for a man. She found that women flight attendants served as airline "shock absorbers," placating and soothing mishandled passengers in ways that insulated the company from potential complaints. By contrast, men flight attendants were used as authority figures, charged with tasks such as managing "uncontrolled" passengers or settling differences between occupants of different seats.

Hochschild's (1983b) observations at a training center for flight attendants show that preparation for the job drew explicitly on white, middle-class ideals of essential femininity and masculinity. For example, women trainees were told to treat their passengers as they would treat guests in their living room—thus invoking the duties of hostess as an essentially feminine set of activities. Through such instructions, the job of flight attendant was portrayed to them as a natural extension of women's nature, and doing gender was fused with doing the work itself:

> [I]n this case, they are not simply women in the biological sense. They are also a highly visible distillation of middle-class American notions of femininity. They symbolize Woman. Insofar as the category "female" is mentally associated with having less status and authority, female flight attendants are more readily classified as "really" females than other females are. (Hochschild 1983a, p. 175)

Thus, while performing the emotional labor needed to generate profits for the airline, Hochschild's women flight attendants simultaneously produced enactments of their essential feminine natures.

Here, we can see accountability operating not only at the interactional level, but also at the level of corporate doings. For example, consider the advertising campaigns, waged by competing airline companies, that invite customers to "catch our smile," offer to "move our tails for you," or feature "The Singapore Girl—she's a great way to fly." That such campaigns are sexist and racist is indisputable (Hochschild 1983a, pp. 93–95), but beyond that, they reformulate the *business* of this business as, in part, the production of essential femininity (Fenstermaker et al. 1991). They invite customers to select an airline and evaluate its performance in relation to idealized notions of feminine nature; in fact, they imply that living up to such notions is the primary work of the airlines.

Gender, Race, and Class

To this point, we have focused on white, middle-class enactments of womanly and manly natures because these have dominated scholarly discourse on sex differences and sex roles. Indeed, to the extent that existing theories of gender relations are predicated on femininity and masculinity as individual attributes—or on white middle-class prototypes of the female role and the male role—they are incapable of accounting for the considerable diversity of human conduct across class and color lines.[4] We suggest that by reconceptualizing gender as a situated accomplishment, further theoretical and empirical gains can be made.

Feeding the Family

DeVault (1991) employs our perspective in an effort to understand what is involved in "feeding the family." Her interviews and observations in poor, working-class, and middle-class households reveal remarkable diversity in the content and experience of the work itself. As she observes (DeVault 1991, p. 191), both middle-class and poor women may see feeding the family as a way of showing love and caring to family members, but poor women are also conscious of the work as a matter of survival. Middle-class women may see provisioning, cooking, and serving food as restrictions on their personal autonomy, but less affluent women are more likely to see these activities as essential contributions to group survival—contributions that they are not always able to provide. And while some women see the work of feeding as a fundamental aspect of their identity and family relations, others simply get it done as best they can.

In light of this diversity, DeVault (1991) argues that women's responsibility for feeding the family involves something far more complex than the reflection of sex differences or execution of sex roles. It is not only that women *do* more of the work, but that the work affords the resources for doing gender. For example, in one working-class household,

> [Teresa] talks quite straightforwardly about the fact that she does not enjoy cooking, but she does not complain about doing it; instead she cooks simple meals so that she can "get it over with." Her husband does the shopping for meats, and Teresa explains that he does so *because* he knows more about meat and can negotiate more successfully with the neighborhood butcher . . . he also helps more with the shopping when she is pregnant. (DeVault 1991, p. 99, emphasis added)

Here, a woman's cooking is described as something she simply does (without complaint and despite her obvious dislike for it), while a man's small contribution to provisioning is something that must be explained (citing his knowledge and ability to negotiate with the butcher). Through these means, the tasks involved in feeding the family are constituted as activities that are *only* natural for a woman (her departure from their full expression must be accounted for), and *not* natural for a man. In this context, it is interesting to note that Teresa's husband "also helps more with the shopping when she is pregnant." Insofar as being pregnant can be seen as the ultimate expression of essential womanliness, perhaps it serves to rationalize the reorganization of a previously established gendered division of labor.

Certainly, pregnancy itself is invoked as the basis for women's "natural" responsibility for feeding. As one woman put it:

> Now that I'm pregnant I'm trying to have a pretty decent lunch. Before, if I felt like peanut butter and jelly I would have it, not worrying about getting enough vitamins and stuff. Now I'm more conscious about it. (DeVault 1991, p. 112)

Of course, females are, by virtue of their *sex*, the ones who nourish fetuses. However, subsequent to birth, this biological fact is put forward to explain a variety of social practices. As DeVault (1991) observes, women are held accountable as women for the nutrition of infants and children, and they "learn from public sources all around them about their responsibility for another life" (pp. 113–114). On these grounds, poor women's inability to fulfill such responsibility may mark them as "unfit mothers" (even before childbirth), and it can be used to legitimize a variety of interventions in their lives by medical and social welfare workers (pp. 183–184, 195–196).

Thus, DeVault's analysis shows how normative conceptions of essential womanliness are easily brought to bear on the activities of women in vastly different material circumstances:

The category "woman" obscures these differences, however, by calling for a particular kind of activity . . . that assumes particular features of material settings—not just money, but also time, space, equipment, the security of an adequate home and safe neighborhood, and so on. Discourses of "family life," instructions for being a "wife" and especially for "mothering," suggest that those for whom the models are often inappropriate should be held to the same standards as others, and if they do not measure up, should be blamed, *as inadequate women*, for their families' difficulties. (p. 230 emphasis added)

Relating to Privilege

Hurtado (1989) also draws on our notion of gender as an accomplishment in her analysis of relationships of white women and women of color to white men. In launching this analysis, she characterizes much of what passes for feminist theory as "white feminist theory," noting its inability to account for the experiences of women of color. The primary problem, she suggests, is uncritical reliance on *women* and *men* as self-evident categories (cf. Connell 1987):

When Sojourner Truth, baring her muscular arm asked "ain't I a woman," the reply might not have been obvious, even though she had borne thirteen children. The answer to her question involves defining *woman*. The white women in the room [when she posed the question] did not have to plough the fields, side by side with Black men, and see their offspring sold into slavery, yet they were clearly women. Sojourner Truth had worked the fields, and she had borne children, but she was not a woman in the sense of having the same experiences as the white women at the meeting. (Hurtado 1989, pp. 844–45)

Hurtado (1989) argues that white men's subordination of white women and women of color involves holding them accountable to normative conceptions of essential womanly nature in different ways. By virtue of the fact that white men need white women to produce racially pure offspring, they are subordinated through *seduction*: wooed into joining white men with the expectation of sharing privilege with them (p. 845). Hence, for white women, received notions of essential femininity include qualities of docility, passivity, and subservience. In the daily doing of gender between white women and white men, the distinction between public and private spheres of activity looms large, enactments of essential femininity serving to legitimate white women's proper place as a sheltered one. Thus, white women's concerns for liberation from their subordination involve recasting the personal as political (e.g., their domination by white men in conversation, their exploitation by white men in household labor, and their use as emotional shock absorbers by white men on the job)—freedom from the continuing consequences of seduction.

By contrast, Hurtado (1989) argues, women of color cannot meet white men's need for racially pure offspring. As a result of this difference in their circumstances, women of color are subordinated through *rejection*: denied the patriarchal invitation to privilege, and seen primarily as workers and objects of sexual aggression (pp. 845–46). Hurtado notes that white men's sexual objectification of women of color allows them to display power and aggression sexually, minus the intimate rituals and emotional involvements that are requisite to their relations with white women:

> In many ways the dual conception of woman based on race—"white goddess/black she-devil, chaste virgin/nigger whore, the blond blue-eyed doll/the exotic 'mulatto' object of sexual craving"—has freed women of color from the distraction of the rewards of seduction. Women of Color "do not receive the respect and treatment—mollycoddling and condescending as it sometimes is—afforded to white women." (Hurtado 1989, p. 846, including the quote from Joseph 1981, p. 27)

And here, the distinction between public and private dissolves, as normative conceptions of essential femininity are employed to legitimate welfare programs that militate against family life and sterilization programs that have restricted reproductive rights. Thus, the concerns of women of color for liberation involve acute recognition of the ways in which the public is *personally* political (p. 849).

Hurtado's analysis is a compelling one. It shows how gender is accomplished differently for white women and women of color, due to differences in their circumstances. In relation to white men, white women are held accountable as subservients—dependent, fragile, and somewhat childlike. But women of color are held accountable as drones and as sexual objects—willful, resilient, and bawdy. Hence, the doing of gender may involve something very different for white women and women of color, given the difference in their *relational position* to white men (Hurtado 1989).

Conclusions

Of course, this is only the tip of the iceberg. We have indicated the utility of our ethnomethodological perspective to address widely recognized aspects of social inequality, but we have not yet tested it empirically. And while works such as DeVault's (1991) and Hurtado's (1989) further our understanding of specific aspects of the relations among gender, race, and class, full-fledged integration of these concerns remains to be achieved. For example, how might the notion of gender as a situated accomplishment contribute to our understanding of relationships between women of color and men of color in everyday life (cf. Hurtado 1992)? If the ways gender is accomplished may vary with relational positions between groups, what are the mechanisms that distinguish the subordination of, for example, African American women by African American men from the subordination of Chicanas by Chicanos? And, how may the doing of gender be affected by differing material circumstances? These are but a few of the questions that are stimulated—rather than stifled—by a shift from conventional conceptions of gender to an ethnomethodological view.

In closing, we wish to address one question that often arises in conjunction with theories of gender relations, namely, the question of *why* these relations demonstrate such persistence and ubiquity. For theories predicated on sex differences, the why question is a moot one: Insofar as gender is conflated with sex, the answer is biological determinism (albeit usually dressed up in more lavish attire). But for theories based on some notion of sex roles, the why question is a serious and troubling one: Why would people persist in socialization practices that restrict the activities of their children, and why would girls and women internalize expectations that disadvantage them in relation to power, freedom, and other resources? And given that, what explains obvious variation among women in their preferences, demands for opportunity, and ultimate life choices? As Connell (1987) observes, these questions do not admit to answers within the formal parameters of role theory— unless we track them through some variant of infinite regress (e.g., parents socialize their children in accord with their own internalized expectations, because they were socialized as children in accord with their parents' internalized expectations, etc.).

With respect to our reconceptualization of gender, the same why question is often posed as follows: Why would people attempt to render actions accountable in terms of normative conceptions of manly and womanly natures? By this point, we hope the answer will be obvious: because they cannot avoid it. Since sex category and the demonstration of essential difference are potentially omnirelevant to social life, and since gender is an *interactional* accomplishment, we can be held accountable for our essential nature as women or men even when we wish it otherwise. This is not to say that individual resistance and collective social change are impossible. Indeed, the accomplishment of gender is what gives existing social arrangements that are predicated on sex category their legitimacy (i.e., as "only natural" ways of organizing social life). So, even as we as individuals may be held accountable (in relation to our character and motives) for our failure to live up to normative conceptions of gender, the accountability of *particular* conduct to sex category may thereby be weakened. What is more, collective social movements may, by calling into question *particular* institutional practices based on sex category, promote alternatives to those practices. Thus, while accountability is invariant and hence doing gender is unavoidable (West and Zimmerman 1987, pp. 145–47), there is no necessary or inherent link between particular classes of behaviors or specific institutional practices and "essential" manly or womanly natures.

Acknowledgments

For their helpful comments on earlier versions of these ideas, we thank Scott Coltrane, Marjorie DeVault, Paula England, Aída Hurtado, and Don Zimmerman.

Notes

1. For example, from this perspective, we might all agree that at a Thanksgiving gathering of kin, it would be more consistent with conventional notions of sex roles in our society if women—rather than men—were the ones to clean up and wash dishes. We might also agree that as a man and a woman approach a door together, it would be more consistent with these roles for the man to open the door (Paula England, personal communication). But in order to see such agreements as evidence of the *predictive power* of this approach, we would have to assume that sex roles consist merely of plugging discrete, well-defined bundles of behavior into interactional situations to produce identifiable enactments of masculinity and femininity. The man enacts his male role by, for instance, opening the door for the woman, and she enacts her female role by standing aside and refraining from opening it herself. We could think of many more behaviors that are generally regarded as enactments of sex roles, but any list we might compile would be necessarily incomplete (Garfinkel 1967, pp. 66–75; West and Zimmerman 1987, p. 135). Moreover, such enactments must be finely fitted to the situation (e.g., when the man is the woman's business superior) and adapted to the demands of the occasion (e.g., when the woman is able-bodied and the man is disabled).

2. For example, Lorber (1975) notes that sex roles have traditionally been invoked to explain the historical absence of women in medicine and their concentration within a few selected specialties. Thus, pediatrics has been seen as consistent with the female role insofar as it is devoted to infants and children. However, as Lorber points out, the demands of pediatrics (including long hours, an irregular schedule, and extended absences from one's own family) are far less

compatible with the roles of wife and mother than specialties such as dermatology or ophthamology.

3. Of course, there are accounts that accord power a central place in their analyses of gender relations. For example, those radical feminist analyses that focus on women as a class begin with a systematic description of their structural location in relation to men. However, as Connell (1987, pp. 55–59) observes, work in this tradition generally treats women and men as internally undifferentiated groups—and its interest in the construction of gender is largely limited to changing societal definitions.

4. To be fair, we should point out that there is nothing inherent in role theory that would preclude such explanation—*if* it could provide an understanding of the mechanism by which people achieve diversity of human conduct in the first instance.

References

Bahr, Stephen J. 1974. "Effect on Power and Division of Labor." Pp. 167–185 in *Working Mothers*, edited by Lois Hoffman and Felix I. Nye. San Francisco: Jossey-Bass.

Berheide, Catherine W., Sarah Fenstermaker Berk, and Richard A. Berk. 1976. "Household Work in the Suburbs: The Job and Its Participants." *Pacific Sociological Review* 14:491–518.

Berk, Richard A., and Sarah Fenstermaker Berk. 1979. *Labor and Leisure at Home: Content and Organization of the Household Day*. Beverly Hills: Sage.

Bourne, Patricia G., and Norma J. Wikler. 1978. "Commitment and the Cultural Mandate: Women in Medicine." *Social Problems* 25:430–40.

Bridenthal, Renate. 1981. "The Family Tree: Contemporary Patterns in the United States." Pp. 47–105 in *Household and Kin*, edited by Amy Swerdlow, Renate Bridenthal, Joan Kelly, and Phyllis Vine. Old Westbury, NY: Feminist Press.

Coltrane, Scott. 1989. "Household Labor and the Routine Production of Gender." *Social Problems* 36:473–91.

Connell, R. W. 1985. "Theorizing Gender." *Sociology* 19:260–72.

———. 1987. *Gender and Power: Society, the Person and Sexual Politics*. Stanford, CA: Stanford University Press.

DeVault, Marjorie. 1991. *Feeding the Family: The Social Construction of Caring as Gendered Work*. Chicago: University of Chicago Press.

Farkas, George. 1976. "Education, Wage Rates, and the Division of Labor between Husband and Wife." *Journal of Marriage and the Family* 38:473–83.

Fenstermaker Berk, Sarah. 1985. *The Gender Factory: The Apportionment of Work in American Households*. New York: Plenum.

Fenstermaker, Sarah, Candace West, and Don H. Zimmerman. 1991. "Gender Inequality: New Conceptual Terrain." Pp. 298–307 in *Gender, Family, and Economy: The Triple Overlap*, edited by Rae Lesser-Blumberg. Newbury Park, CA: Sage.

Fishman, Pamela. 1978. "Interaction: The Work Women Do." *Social Problems* 25:397–406.

Garfinkel, Harold. 1967. *Studies in Ethnomethodology.* Englewood Cliffs, NJ: Prentice-Hall.

Gerson, Judith M. 1985. "The Variability and Salience of Gender: Issues of Conceptualization and Measurement." Paper presented at annual meeting of the American Sociological Association, Washington, D.C., August.

Goffman, Erving. 1977. "The Arrangement between the Sexes." *Theory and Society* 4:301–31.

Heritage, John. 1984. *Garfinkel and Ethnomethodology.* Cambridge: Polity Press.

Hochschild, Arlie Russell. 1973. "A Review of Sex Roles Research." *American Journal of Sociology* 78:1011–29.

———. 1983a. *The Managed Heart: Commercialization of Human Feeling.* Berkeley: University of California Press.

———. 1983b. "Smile Wars: Counting the Casualties of Emotional Labor." *Mother Jones* (December):35–43.

———. 1989. *The Second Shift: Working Parents and the Revolution at Home.* New York: Viking.

Hughes, Everett C. 1945. "Dilemmas and Contradictions of Status." *American Journal of Sociology* 50:353–59.

Hurtado, Aída. 1989. "Relating to Privilege: Seduction and Rejection in the Subordination of White Women and Women of Color." *Signs* 14:833–55.

———. 1992. "The Politics of Sexuality in the Gender Subordination of Chicanas." Unpublished manuscript, Psychology Board, University of California, Santa Cruz.

Joseph, Gloria I. 1981. "White Promotion, Black Survival." Pp. 19–42 in *Common Differences: Conflicts in Black and White Feminist Perspectives,* edited by Gloria I. Joseph and Jill Lewis. Garden City, NY: Anchor Press/Doubleday.

Kessler, Suzanne J., and Wendy McKenna. 1978. *Gender: An Ethnomethodological Approach.* New York: Wiley.

Komarovsky, Mirra. 1946. "Cultural Contradictions and Sex Roles." *American Journal of Sociology* 52:184–89.

———. 1950. "Functional Analysis of Sex Roles." *American Sociological Review* 15:508–16.

Linton, Ralph. 1936. *The Study of Man.* New York: Appleton-Century.

Lopata, Helen Z., and Barrie Thorne 1978. "On the Term 'Sex Roles.' " *Signs* 3:718–21.

Lorber, Judith. 1975. "Women and Medical Sociology: Invisible Professionals and Ubiquitous Patients." Pp. 75–105 in *Another Voice: Feminist Perspectives on Social Life and Social Science,* edited by Marcia Millman and Rosabeth Moss Kanter. Garden City, NY: Anchor Press/Doubleday.

Meissner, Martin, Elizabeth W. Humphreys, Scott M. Meiss, and J. William Sheu. 1975. "No Exit for Wives: Sexual Division of Labor and the Cumulation of Household Demands." *Canadian Review of Sociology and Anthropology* 12:424–39.

Parsons, Talcott. 1951. *The Social System.* New York: Free Press.

Parsons, Talcott, and Robert F. Bales. 1955. *Family, Socialization and Interaction Process*. New York: Free Press.

Pettigrew, Thomas F. 1964. *A Profile of the Negro American*. Princeton, NJ: Van Nostrand.

Pleck, Joseph H. 1977. "The Work-Family Role System." *Social Problems* 24: 417–27.

Stacey, Judith, and Barrie Thorne. 1985. "The Missing Feminist Revolution in Sociology." *Social Problems* 32:301–16.

Thorne, Barrie. 1980. "Gender . . . How Is It Best Conceptualized?" Unpublished manuscript. Department of Sociology, Michigan State University, East Lansing.

West, Candace, and Angela Garcia. 1988. "Conversational Shift Work: A Study of Topical Transitions between Women and Men." *Social Problems* 35:551–75.

West, Candace, and Don H. Zimmerman. 1983. "Small Insults: A Study of Interruptions in Conversations between Unacquainted Persons." Pp. 102–117 in *Language, Gender and Society*, edited by Barrie Thorne, Cheris Kramarae, and Nancy Henley. Rowley, MA: Newbury House.

———. 1987. "Doing Gender." *Gender & Society* 1:125–51.

Zavella, Patricia. 1987. *Work and Chicano Families: Cannery Workers of the Santa Clara Valley*. Ithaca, NY: Cornell University Press.

Zimmerman, Don H. 1978. "Ethnomethodology." *American Sociologist* 13:6–15.

Zinn, Maxine Baca. 1980. "Employment and Education of Mexican-American Women: The Interplay of Modernity and Ethnicity in Eight Families." *Harvard Educational Review* 50:47–62.

———. 1990. "Family, Feminism and Race in America." *Gender & Society* 4: 68–82.

Chapter 9

Gender, Status, and the Social Psychology of Expectations

Cecilia L. Ridgeway

Gender inequality has many iniquitous effects, but some of the most powerful and subtle of these occur in interaction. When women find, as they often do, that what they say in interaction is not listened to or taken as seriously as what men say, the consequences are varied and serious. Much of what happens in human society occurs through the medium of interaction. In our own society, the processes by which people are given access to rewards, evaluated, and directed toward or away from positions of power and wealth occur largely through goal-oriented interaction. When women are systematically disadvantaged in such interaction, they end up disadvantaged in power and wealth as well. They also end up disadvantaged in the struggle for identities of competence and self-worth, since interaction is the arena in which these are formed and affirmed.

Despite its importance, the interactional level of analysis is a relatively neglected component of the production of gender inequality. Most sociological theories of gender focus on either the individual level of self and identity or on the societal level of socioeconomic organization. An adequate theory of gender requires that we incorporate an account of gender and interaction. Expectation states theory uses the social psychology of expectations and the concept of status characteristics to account for the way women are disadvantaged in goal-oriented interaction (Berger, Conner, and Fisek 1974; Berger, Fisek, Norman, and Zelditch 1977; Berger and Zelditch 1985; Webster and Foschi 1988). While not a theory of gender per se, its value to gender theorists is that it offers a systematic account of the interactional inequalities of power and influence produced by gender.

In this chapter, I will describe the contribution expectation states theory can make to an account of gender inequality. I begin with interactional inequalities, traditional explanations for gender's role in them, and the distinctiveness of expectation states theory's approach to explaining them. In the core of the chapter, I describe the theory itself and its account of interactional inequalities and gender. I also consider evidence for this explanation and way it has been used to intervene against women's disadvantages in interaction with men. Then I step back from the theory to consider it from a feminist standpoint and analyze its strengths and weaknesses in that regard. Finally, I draw some conclusions about what the theory can offer to an understanding of gender inequality.

Interactional Inequalities

A long tradition of research shows that when people interact in regard to a collective goal or task, they quickly develop stable inequalities in how much they participate, how much attention they receive, and how influential they are over group events (e.g., Bales 1950, 1953; Torrance, 1954; Strodtbeck, James, and Hawkins 1957). Expectation states theory views such interaction inequalities as behavioral indicators of an informal "power and prestige" order or status hierarchy that effectively directs the group's goal-related activities and distribution of rewards (Berger, Comer, and McKeown 1974; Meeker 1981). Research dating back to the 1950s has shown that women generally rank lower in these informal hierarchies of power and prestige than do men of similar background (Strodtbeck and Mann 1956). The question for gender theorists is why.

Early explanations drew on Parsons, arguing that men are socialized to be "instrumental" (i.e., goal or task directed) and women to be "social" or "expressive" (i.e., oriented to interpersonal relations) because this division of labor is functional for the group (Parson and Bales 1955; see Meeker and Weitzel-O'Neill 1977 for a review). The claim that such a role division by sex is functional for the group or society is now rejected by most sociologists (Meeker and Weitzel-O'Neill 1977). However, explanations in terms of socialized dispositions persist (for a review, see Eagly 1987). They explain behavior by means of dispositions that women and men internalize and carry with them from one situation to the next. These dispositions make people prefer to act in gender-stereotypic ways across a variety of situations. Such arguments suggest that women have learned to be less interested in instrumental activities than men, despite their importance in our society, and that this accounts for women's disadvantage in behavioral status orders.

A related explanation argues that men and women learn different subcultural rules for interaction in childhood (Maltz and Borker 1982). The rules of women's subculture neither value nor teach the tricks of instrumental accomplishment and power in the way that those of men's subculture do. Although interesting, this argument has yet to be formulated in a fashion specific enough to explain how gender subcultures could be powerfully different when adult men and women interact so frequently. Also, it must explain that substantive content of women's subculture without falling back on essentialist views of sex differences.

A problem that both socialized dispositions and subcultural explanations face is the variety of women's and men's behavior over differing interactional contexts. No woman's societal standing is so low that there is not some goal-oriented interactional context where she acts high in situational power and prestige (with her children, for instance). Men similarly enact low interactional power and prestige in some settings. In fact, as Wagner, Ford, and Ford (1986) note, all men and women learn the behavioral repertoires of both high and low positions in interactional status hierarchies. It is just that men have more opportunities to enact the high status repertoire than do women.

Because of this behavioral variability, expectation states theory takes a radically *situational* and social structural approach to gender's role in interactional status hierarchies. This situational approach contrasts with the transsituational view of socialized dispositions and subcultural explanations, but it is not necessarily opposed to it. In my view, if formulated more systematically, the subcultural and socialized dispositions arguments may yet contribute valuable insights into gender and interaction. However, the situational approach is a different level of analysis that looks to process in interaction itself, rather than to the individual level of women's and men's traits, to explain how women are disadvantaged in power and prestige orders.

Expectation states theory argues that women are disadvantaged in interaction not because of their preferences or knowledge, but because women have lower status value in our society than men. That is, widely held beliefs in our society say that men are more valuable, worthy of respect, and competent than women. This makes gender an external *status characteristic* in the theory's terms (Lockheed and Hall 1976; Berger, Rosenholtz, and Zelditch 1980; Pugh and Wahrman 1983; Wagner 1988). Under specified situational circumstances, the normal processes of organizing goal-oriented interaction make these gender status beliefs salient, assuming the participants hold them. The theory explains how, through a series of interaction processes, these beliefs affect behaviors and reactions in a way that becomes self-fullfilling, shaping the resulting power and prestige order. Thus the social structural fact of women's

lesser status value joins with interactional processes to produce women's disadvantage in group hierarchies without any assumption about
the individual dispositions or abilities of men and women.

To understand how beliefs about the status value of gender become
implicated in the formation of power and prestige orders, it is first
necessary to understand how these orders are created in interaction.
Consequently, I begin with expectation states theory's explanation for
the way inequalities of influence and prestige come about in goal-
oriented interaction. Then I turn to the role of status characteristics such
as gender in shaping interactional inequality.

The Formation of Behavioral Status Orders

Expectations and Behavior

Expectation states theory limits its scope to interaction where participants are interested in accomplishing a collective goal. Since much
interaction, particularly that with significant consequences for social
inequality, is goal oriented, this is a fairly broad scope. The theory
begins with the observation that when interaction is goal oriented,
participants look for a way to anticipate the likely usefulness of their
own and their fellow interactants' suggestions. They do this in order to
decide how to act in the situation, whether to speak up, who to listen to,
and who to agree with when choices or conflicts emerge. In the theory's
terms, interactants form *performance expectations*, which are anticipations
about how useful their own contributions to the group goal are likely to
be compared to those of each other group member. These expectations
for self and others are usually implicit, out-of-awareness hunches or
guesses rather than conscious judgments. Since interactants follow similar cognitive principles in forming performance expectations, as long as
they have roughly similar cultural beliefs and information about one
another, the expectations they develop are shared.

Self-other performance expectations are important because they not
only guide the way you act in relation to another, they also guide the
other's reactions to you. In so doing, they tend to become self-fulfilling.
The higher your expectations for your own contributions compared to
another, the more likely you are to speak up with your own suggestions
and stick to them in the face of disagreement, and the less likely you are
to ask others for their opinions. On the other hand, if your expectations
for yourself are lower than for the other, you will hesitate before offering
your own ideas. If the other disagrees with you, you may feel that s/he

must be right. In addition, you are likely to ask the other for her or his ideas, listen attentively when they are offered, and be inclined to evaluate them positively. Following this logic, the theory argues that the higher the expectations held for one actor compared to another: (1) the more opportunities the actor will be given to participate, (2) the more task suggestions s/he will make, (3) the greater the likelihood that these suggestions will be positively evaluated by others and, (4) the more influential s/he will be over group decisions. These behaviors together constitute the behavioral status or power and prestige order, as defined by the theory.

According to the theory then, the behavioral status order is determined by the order of performance expectations that group members develop for one another. The question then becomes, What determines the performance expectations held for one member over another? The theory asserts that people form performance expectations on the basis of information available to them about one another's external status characteristics, reward levels, specific abilities, and behavior in the situation. Gender affects performance expectations because it is a status characteristic in our society.

Status Characteristics and Expectations

A status characteristic is an attribute on which individuals vary that is associated in a society with widely held beliefs according greater esteem and worthiness to some states of the attribute (e.g., being male) than others (being female). Since it is based in consensual beliefs, the status value of an attribute can change over time and vary among populations.

Perhaps expectation states theory's most important insight is that the beliefs that give a characteristic status value (i.e., associate it with worthiness) also associate it with implicit expectations for competence. Race, gender, class, educational attainment, occupation, and age, among others, are status characteristics in our society. For each, those with more valued states of the characteristic are implicitly assumed by general beliefs to be somehow more able. It is these unstated assumptions that women are less capable than men that subtly but persistently disadvantage them in interaction.

Status characteristics range from diffuse to specific, depending on the specificity of the competence associations they carry. Gender, however, is a diffuse status characteristic. While beliefs do associate gender with specific skills (e.g., stereotypically masculine and feminine abilities), they also link it with diffuse expectations that men will be generally more able than women in most situations.

When a status characteristic is *activated*, or salient, in a goal-oriented encounter, interactants use the diffuse and/or specific competence expectations associated with it to form performance expectations for one another in the encounter. Research has shown that this occurs even when the characteristic is completely irrelevant to the collective task or goal unless something explicitly happens to stop it (Berger, Cohen, and Zelditch 1972; Berger et al. 1977). This means that once gender is activated in a situation, interactants use the culture's general assumption that men are more capable than women to form expectations about the likely value of particular men's and women's contributions in this specific situation. Depending on other factors present in the situation, this usually means that both men and women assume that what the women have to offer will not be quite as useful as what the men offer and so need not be taken as seriously.

Since status characteristics are attributes of individuals, they are carried from situation to situation. However, whether these characteristics are activated and, if they are, what their status implications are varies depending on the nature of the situation and the other people in it. This is what makes the status expectancy account of gender and interactional inequality a situational and contextually specific one. Although the theory argues that people follow general principles in organizing their interactional status relations, people apply these principles to the specific details of each goal-oriented context. As a result the particular order of influence and status that emerges is specific to that context.

The theory assumes that the status characteristic of gender is activated (and affects the influence hierarchy) whenever the interactants include both men and women or whenever gender is believed to be relevant to their collective task. This means that gender will be activated and influence the status hierarchies of mixed-sex groups but not always those of same-sex groups. In mixed-sex groups gender will advantage men over women except when the collective task is a stereotypically female one. In that condition, women will have a moderate advantage over the men. In same-sex groups a gender-stereotypic task or goal activates the status implications of gender as well, but these equate the members rather than differentiate them. A task stereotypic for the other sex activates assumptions of low competence and status worthiness for all members of a same-sex group. A task stereotypic for the group members' own sex activates assumptions of shared high competence and status worthiness. In addition to these well-documented means of activation, Fennell, Barchas, Cohen, McMahon, and Hildebrand (1978) and I (Ridgeway 1988) argue that, when a group is delegated its task by an organization whose authority structure is disproportionately one sex, and the members of the group are the other sex, gender will be activated in that group. This means that in a male-run organization, women will struggle with the low-status implications of being female even in an all-female work group.

As these conditions of activation indicate, society's status valuing of men over women has complex and varying effects on the influence hierarchies of encounters. First, the status value of gender is salient in most goal-oriented encounters, particularly those with women members, but there are some where the theory predicts it will not be salient. The status value of gender should not be salient, for instance, in an all-male group working on a gender-neutral task. Second, when it is salient, it can advantage men over women, occasionally advantage women over men, or equate all group members with high or low status.

Thus far, I have talked about gender's effects in the abstract, as if it were people's only distinguishing trait. The fact is that people have many attributes that carry status value in the society. A woman on a school board may be distinguished not only by being a woman, but also by being black, a physician, and older or younger than the other members. These other status characteristics are activated according to the same principles as is gender.

Expectation states theory argues that people *combine* the competence implications of all of a person's salient status characteristics to form an aggregate performance expectation for that person relative to others in the group. This includes characteristics that have positive (e.g., physician) as well as negative (e.g., woman or black) implications for the person's anticipated competence in the situation. The impact of each characteristic is weighted by its relevance to the group's goal. Thus, for a woman surgeon in an otherwise male medical term, being a surgeon will have a stronger impact than being a woman, but being a woman will still have an effect (Webster and Driskell 1978).

The theory proposes a formula for the way people combine information from status characteristics and other factors to create aggregate performance expectations (Berger et al. 1977). The impacts of all positive factors are combined, weighted by their relevance and subject to a diminishing marginal effect, and the similarly combined negative factors are subtracted from them. One effect of this formula is that inconsistent status information has a larger impact than additional consistent information of equal relevance, as evidence indicates (Norman, Smith, and Berger 1988). Importantly, the theory does *not* assume that people necessarily make such calculations but that they *act as if* they made them. The formula is a heuristic to predict behavior rather than necessarily a model of cognition.

Other Factors

In addition to external status characteristics, reward levels assigned to the interactants, their actual behavior in the situation, and outside feedback also combine to affect aggregate performance expectations and so status in interaction. The effects of these factors interact with status characteristics like gender in complex ways that I will discuss shortly. First, I will briefly describe the basic effects of each.

When interactants receive differential rewards, they tend to assume unless there is clear evidence to the contrary that there are also differences in competence. As a result, differences in rewards cause corresponding differences in performance expectations and status in the group (Cook 1975; Harrod 1980; Berger, Fisek, Norman, and Wagner 1985; Stewart 1988). The rewards can be almost anything of value, but the example of obvious relevance to gender inequality is differences in pay levels. If a woman in a mixed-sex work group is known to be paid less than her male colleagues, she will be doubly disadvantaged in others' and even her own implicit assumptions about her likely competence in the situation. Her influence and status suffer accordingly.

Performance expectations are also affected by a person's actual behavior in the group. To gain influence, of course, a person must participate and offer task suggestions. In general, simply engaging in more task-oriented participation improves the performance expectation others hold for you (Berger et al. 1974) although backlash can occur, as we will see later. Even more important than how much you say is how you say it, and how you present yourself in general. Verbal and nonverbal behaviors that give the impression of confidence tend to be interpreted as competence (Moscovici 1976; Berger, Webster, Ridgeway, and Rosenholtz 1986; Ridgeway 1978; Ridgeway, Berger, and Smith 1985). A direct gaze, firm voice tone, rapid, fluent speech, erect but relaxed body posture, and consistent arguments have all been shown to increase the perceived competence of a speaker independent of the content of her or his arguments (see Ridgeway et al. 1985 and Berger et al. 1986 for reviews).

Finally, and not surprisingly, clear outside evaluations or feedback on the competence of one's task suggestions have a dramatic effect on performance expectations (Wagner et al. 1986). Evaluations can come from an outside authority or from rewards or costs accruing to the group once it has acted on the suggestion. Such outside tests of "real" differences in the usefulness of interactants' contributions are quite rare, however. Competence in regard to the complex problems dealt with in most goal-oriented interaction is difficult to evaluate in clear-cut terms.

Research On Status Characteristics and Behavioral Status Orders

So a status characteristic like gender is only one of the factors that affects a person's status and influence in goal-oriented interaction. Yet, when a status characteristic is salient, it tends to shape the subsequent display of other factors in such a way as to confirm the status implications of the characteristic (Berger et al. 1977). In this way, status characteristics like gender *govern* task behaviors, nonverbal manner, response to performance feedback, and future reward distributions. This is what makes the status effects of gender such a powerful determinant of interactional outcomes.

Status characteristics have such far-reaching effects on interaction for two reasons. First they have an early impact on the formation of performance expectations. Second, in addition to shaping performance expectations, they set in motion a legitimacy dynamic that affects the normative appropriateness of women's efforts to achieve influence (Meeker and Weitzel-O'Neill 1977; Ridgeway 1982; Ridgeway and Berger 1986). I will discuss each of these in turn.

Shaping Expectations, Behavior, and Standards

People begin to form relative expectations for their own and other's performance from the moment they know they will interact about a shared task or goal. The first information about the other that becomes salient forms the core for these expectations and subsequent information is perceived in terms of that core. Gender, like a few other important status characteristics in our society (e.g., age and race), can be quickly discerned.[1] When you see or hear a person, usually one of the first things you recognize is the person's sex. Of course, it is a testimony to our culture's deep commitment to gender differentiation that people are so careful to follow social rules about how males and females should dress, wear their hair, and gesture, and thus present themselves in a manner that clearly indicates their sex.

When you not only know the other's sex, but it is different than yours, relevant to the task, or similar to yours in being different from that of the authority structure, the status and competence associations of gender are activated. Gender becomes the basis for your initial performance expectations for yourself and the other. Information on other factors such as specific abilities or reward levels is usually not as quickly available as it is on gender and therefore is less likely to shape initial expectations. As a result, interaction proceeds on performance expectations based on gender. The subsequent flow of interaction may actually even discourage the later revelation of inconsistent information on reward levels or specific abilities. They become difficult to introduce into the conversation.

Imagine, for instance, that you, a woman, walk into a business meeting and see that all the other participants are male. Even before anything is said, you feel slightly less confident and the men feel a bit more confident about how well each of them is going to do. As a consequence, you hesitate at first. In that moment, one of the men jumps in and proposes an agenda. You speak up to disagree but your voice betrays your nervousness. Detecting your unsure manner, the men assume you cannot be too certain of your point and quickly dismiss your concerns. Their dismissal shakes you a little and you are silent for a while. In fact, the topic of discussion is something you have experience and skills in. You try to speak up again to tell the others of your expertise, but you have trouble getting the floor for long enough to explain. The others are now dominating the conversation. When the final decision is made, your opinions carry little weight.

There is substantial evidence for this account of gender's impact on interaction. Most comes from experiments explicitly designed to test different aspects of the theory. In order to show that the mere knowledge of someone's gender, when salient, is enough to create differences in performance expectations and influence, some experiments place participants in separate rooms, inform them only of each other's name and gender, and have them push buttons on a console to exchange opinions and make decisions on a shared task (e.g., Pugh and Wahrman 1983; Wagner et al. 1986). Other experiments show the effects of gender status and performance expectations on verbal and nonverbal behavior by recording face-to-face interaction between men and women (e.g., Ridgeway 1982; Wood and Karten 1986). In some of these studies, one participant is trained to act in a particular way, a woman to be assertive, for instance, and the reactions of other group members are recorded.

Such studies demonstrate that gender, once activated, shapes performance expectations that in turn drive verbal and nonverbal interaction. Wood and Karten (1986) showed that in mixed-sex discussion groups, gender did indeed lead to lower competence expectations for women than men and that these expectations led women to have lower rates of active task behaviors and influence in the groups. Similarly, Dovidio, Brown, Heltman, Ellyson, and Keating (1988) studied several verbal and nonverbal behaviors that have been associated with confidence, assumed competence, and power (Ellyson, Dovidio, and Fehr 1981; Dovidio and Ellyson 1982; Ridgeway et al. 1985). In mixed-sex dyadic (i.e., two-person) discussions of a gender-neutral topic, men, as predicted, showed higher levels of these behaviors. They spoke more and tended to initiate more speech, looked less at the other while listening, gestured more, and smiled less than their women partners. I and colleagues similarly found that gender status governed length of initial eye contact and speed of response during interaction (Ridgeway et al. 1985). That is, in mixed-sex groups, women looked away sooner and responded more slowly than men did or than women did when interacting with other women.

In Dovidio et al.'s (1988) study, mixed-sex dyads also discussed a stereotypically male and a stereotypically female topic. Exactly as expectation states theory predicts, during the masculine topic, men showed an exaggerated advantage in competence and power behaviors. They had much higher levels of speaking, initiating speech, eye contact while speaking, and gesturing and much lower levels of looking while listening than their women partners. However, when a few moments later these same dyads discussed a feminine topic, the power patterns of verbal and nonverbal behavior reversed, again precisely as the status expectancy argument predicts. With a feminine topic, women spoke longer, initiated more speech, gestured more, and looked more while speaking and less while listening than their male partners, although they continued to smile more than the men. The fact that in this study the same interactants formed one behavioral status order on the basis of gender and then reversed it, also on the basis of gender, demonstrates three essential points: It shows how strongly status characteristics can govern behavior in interaction. It indicates that they do this through their relevance to the task and the performance expectations this creates. Finally, it underscores the importance of taking a situational approach to face-to-face status and power.

Status characteristics and the expectations they create not only shape behavior. They also shape the way feedback on the interactant's performance is perceived. Foschi (1989, 1990) argues that when interactants differ on a status characteristic, as in a mixed-sex encounter, they activate different standards for assessing the competence of the high-status-characteristic person compared to the low-status-characteristic person. A woman in a mixed-sex group, says Foschi (1989), is held to a stricter standard for proving competence at the collective task and a more lenient standard for showing incompetence. Consequently, a woman must perform better than a man in a mixed-sex context to be perceived as having equal ability to him. An initial experiment conducted by Foschi (1990) supports the operation of such double standards for men and women in mixed-sex contexts.

Foschi's work demonstrates the uphill battle women face in achieving influence and respect when gender status is activated (except when the task is stereotypically female). First, the competence associations with gender cause others to expect little from her and erode her own confidence. This in turn makes it difficult for her to present her ideas effectively. Then even those ideas she does present will be judged by a harsher standard than if from a man and seen as less indicative of status-worthy qualities in her. It is through means such as these that women find themselves without influence in mixed-sex task groups despite their efforts.

Gender and Legitimacy

In addition to their formative effects on performance expectations, status characteristics also control interaction by evoking legitimacy dynamics. As Meeker and Weitzell-O'Neill (1977) pointed out, people with high-status characteristics not only presume themselves more capable, they also act and often are treated as if they had a *right* to achieve high influence and respect in the encounter. Similarly, people with low-status characteristics struggle with the feeling that even if they are competent, they have no right to try for high status. A right to something implies that your possession of it is normative and legitimate and others should support your efforts to earn it. On the other hand, if you do not have a right to something, then your effort to achieve it is illegitimate and subject to others' sanctions. If the activation of women's low gender status creates an assumption that they do not have a right to an influential position in the group, then assertiveness on their part may draw a negative reaction.

Joseph Berger and I argue that a legitimacy process develops when group members hold beliefs about social reality associating an activated status characteristic with the occupation of valued status positions in society (Ridgeway and Berger 1986). For instance, most people believe, correctly, that more men occupy valued status positions in our society than do women. Such *referential beliefs*, as we call them, are activated along with competence expectations when gender is made salient.

These beliefs cause interactants to expect that those with higher status characteristics will also have higher status in the present encounter. They may not wish this to occur, but they expect, as a matter of reality, that it is likely. Since they expect it to be so, they are likely, even inadvertently, to act as if it were true. They do this by treating high-external-status members' claims as appropriate and expected, but low-external-status members' claims as a bit deviant, out of line, embarrassing, to be quickly overlooked. When they act this way and others in the group react similarly or do not challenge them, they take their expectations to be normative in the group. And, in fact, other group members are indeed likely to support or at least not challenge such action since they, too, are likely to share the widely held referential beliefs about the status characteristic. By this means, group members socially construct a normative right for those with external status characteristic advantages to be allowed to earn high status in the group rather than those with status characteristic disadvantages.

If such legitimacy effects occur, and there is suggestive if not yet direct evidence that they do (Meeker and Weitzell-O'Neill 1977; Fennell et al. 1978; Ridgeway 1982, 1988; Carli 1990), then it is easy to see how they will increase the self-fulfilling impact of gender status on interaction. The creation of behavioral inequalities through performance expectations is insidious but essentially voluntaristic. Performance expectations control women's behavior by making them doubt themselves and feel the pressure of others' doubting of them. As a result, they actually behave as expected and contribute less actively to the group's goal activities than they could.

Legitimacy effects are more coercive and take over where performance expectations leave off. If a woman resists the pressure of low expectations and insists on contributing actively and assertively, legitimacy processes can produce a "backlash" reaction against her (e.g., Ridgeway 1982; Butler and Geis 1990; Carli 1990; Ellyson, Dovidio, & Brown 1992). She is seen as strident or embarrassingly off track, wasting everybody's time. Even if she persists, it is not clear that others, who assume that she has no right to be doing what she is, will even seriously listen to her substantive contributions. As a result, her chances of breaking out of the low status implied by her gender and gaining influence and respect in the group are limited.

Status Interventions

If status characteristics so thoroughly shape goal-oriented interaction, are women simply doomed to low status in mixed-sex groups when the task is not stereotypically female? Not surprisingly, expectation states theory has also been used to devise techniques for counteracting the governing effects of status characteristics. These intervention techniques manipulate both performance expectations and legitimacy effects.

One technique is to modify both men's and women's expectations for one another in a given situation by showing that the women, while lower in external status, are higher than the men on a valued skill (Cohen and Roper 1972; Freese and Cohen 1973; Pugh and Wahrman 1983). This increases everyone's performance expectations for the women and lowers those for the men. The result is that the women and men then interact as equals. Convincing the group members that the women really are capable also removes the problems of illegitimacy they would otherwise face as they become influential. Wagner et al. (1986) showed that, even for stereotypically male tasks, clear feedback that the women were more skilled at it than the men resulted in high influence for the women.

For this technique to work, it is not enough to modify women's expectations for themselves. The expectations of the men in the group must also be changed or the newly assertive women will face resistance (Cohen and Roper 1972). Women often lack the power or resources to force a change in men's expectations. Furthermore, the demonstration of superior skills in interactional contexts is difficult, given the double standards that Foschi (1990) has shown. In fact, this technique works best when imposed on the interactants by an outside authority such as an organization within which the group operates. Not surprisingly, its greatest use has been in the classroom (Cohen 1982).

The second technique for overcoming women's disadvantage in mixed-sex groups works by neutralizing legitimacy effects. Meeker and Weitzel-O'Neill (1977) suggest that women may try to defuse the resentment their task efforts arouse by presenting them as an attempt to help the group rather than as a competitive bid for status. Women's efforts to do this may partly explain their higher rates of positive social behaviors compared to men in goal-oriented groups. Subsequent studies have indeed demonstrated that when women who are competent at the group task participate actively, but accompany their task suggestions with positive social behaviors and statements of their cooperative intent, they achieve high influence in the group (Ridgeway 1982; Shackelford, Wood, and Worchel 1989). The advantage of this technique is its wide practical application since the woman has only to modify her own behavior to use it.

Each of these techniques will allow a woman in a mixed-sex group to achieve influence and status. The positive results of this are not trivial. It allows her ideas to shape what the group decides and does. It also gives her access to any rewards or opportunities that result from the group's activities. Furthermore, it shows her as a woman in a position of relative power, which can have salutary effects on others' and her own expectations for women. On the other hand, neither technique directly challenges the basic belief systems that accord men higher status in the first place. The second technique of showing cooperative intent is particularly conserving of underlying status beliefs since it does not challenge the fact that only women are required to engage in the stereotypically female behavior of "being nice" in order to succeed in having their contributions acknowledged by influence and respect.

The Problem of Same-Sex Groups

The account expectation states theory gives for gender's impact in mixed-sex groups appears to work quite well. Tests of its predictions not only by proponents of the theory (e.g., Lockheed 1985; Pugh and Wharman 1983, Ridgeway et al. 1985; Wagner et al. 1986), but also by others (e.g., Wood and Karten 1986; Dovidio et al. 1988; Carli 1990), have demonstrated a strong pattern of support, despite a few nonconfirming studies (e.g., Stewart 1988; Carli 1989). The case of same-sex groups is more complicated. First, what exactly does expectation states theory predict for groups where gender status equates the members? Second, does it match the available data?

I have argued that when gender is activated in an all-female group, either by a stereotypically male task or by a male authority structure, the theory implies that all members start without much confidence in regard to the task and with a feeling that they are not really legitimate candidates for high-status positions (Ridgeway 1988). Consequently, task efforts are likely to be offered cautiously and be peppered with positive social behaviors to assuage their own and the other group members' sense of their illegitimacy.[2] As a result, initial rates of task behavior are likely to be lower and rates of social behaviors higher than in mixed-sex groups. Because this early pattern becomes normative, it may persist after group members resolve initial doubts and evolve a stable influence order. There is some evidence that women's behavior in all-female groups does differ in this way from their behavior in mixed-sex groups (Carli 1989).

When gender is activated in an all-male group (except, of course, by a stereotypically female task), all members are likely to feel like competent, legitimate candidates for high status (Ridgeway 1988). As a result, interaction may be rather competitive, with higher rates of task behavior and lower rates of positive social behavior than in mixed-sex groups. There is some evidence that all-male groups do sometimes behave this way (Meeker and Weitzel-O'Neill 1977; Carli 1989).

The behavioral patterns predicted by expectation states theory for same-sex groups do occur, then. It is not clear, however, whether they always occur or do so only when gender has been activated by a gendered task or authority structure, as the theory requires. A basic aspect of the theory's situational and contextual approach is that gender is sometimes *not* activated in same-sex groups. Since most authority structures are male, gender should be activated quite frequently in all-female groups. According to the theory, however, men sometimes should relate to one another not on the basis of their gender status, but in terms of other individual characteristics. Yet these ideas about same-sex groups have never been directly tested. Until they are, explaining same-sex groups will remain a weakness in the theory's account of gender, interaction, and status.

Feminist Concerns

Now that we understand the expectation states explanation for gender's impact on interactional inequality, we are in a position to step back from the theory and ask some additional questions of it. A number of feminists have pointed out the extent to which sociological theories, even those of gender, have continued to embody male bias (e.g., Stacey and Thorne 1985). How does the status expectancy approach to gender fare in this respect?

Specifically, I would like to consider three questions about the status expectancy approach that a feminist might ask: First, does treating gender as a status characteristic reify women into an abstract cultural stereotype that obscures the diversity of actual women and their experience? Second, does the status expectancy approach portray women merely as passive victims without explaining their resistance as well? Finally, is the theory's strong scientific orientation inherently male oriented?

Turning to the first question, Does treating gender as a status characteristic reduce women to reified cultural stereotypes? I believe the answer is no. The theory's insistently situational approach explicitly recognizes that the status attained by any individual woman depends not only on her gender but on the particular context she is in, her behavior, and her and the other interactants' other identities such as race or class. Furthermore, the impact of gender status itself, whether it is negligible or strong, whether it advantages or disadvantages a woman, depends on the situation she is in. One of the theory's great strengths, from this point of view, is that it provides a context-specific view of individual women's interactional status while still offering general principles to explain gender disadvantage.

In effect, the theory disaggregates one part of existing gender stereotypes, that dealing with the status value of being male or female, and shows how the substantial effects of this on the behavior of real men and women is part of a more general status process that can include many factors in addition to gender. The theory explicitly states that the cultural beliefs that make gender a status characteristic in our society are socially constructed and are therefore subject to historical and social variation (Berger et al. 1980; Wagner 1988). Furthermore, while the theory assumes that most men and women share status beliefs, it acknowledges that this is an empirical question. Some individuals may not hold gender status beliefs. Because of this social constructivist approach, the theory does not reify the status value of gender into an inevitable or unchanging quality of gender relations.

The second question is whether the status characteristics approach portrays women as passive victims of oppression without also accounting for their resistance. The answer is yes and no. The emphasis of the theory is definitely on the way status characteristics cause people to construct themselves and others into behavioral status orders that reflect those characteristics. The theory works hard to explain why and how people behaviorally conform to their oppression in this way. One of the things I personally find most interesting about the theory is the subtlety of the account it provides for how this occurs and for the power it demonstrates in self-fulfilling expectations. On the other hand, it is undeniably true that the theory offers no comparable account of why or when people resist this process, although it acknowledges that they occasionally do so. It does document intervention techniques a woman could use to resist successfully. Its legitimacy argument also describes the sanctions her resistance could arouse.

The third feminist challenge to the status expectancy approach is the most difficult. Expectation states publications espouse the construction of abstract, logically formal theories and the use of laboratory experiments to test them. Is this classic scientific approach inherently male biased? The philosophical issues that arise in the feminist debate over science are too complex and lengthy for me to argue properly here (see, for instance, Keller 1984; Harding 1986; and the paper by Sprague and Zimmerman in this volume). Instead, I will state my personal view, which may be atypical among feminists. I am persuaded with Keller (1982) that the historical dominance of science by men has yielded not only an organizational form that has excluded women, but a choice of questions to investigate and guiding metaphors for theories that reflect men's rather women's concerns (as these are constructed in Western society). I also accept the impossibility of "objective" or perspective-free knowledge. Finally, I believe our society wrongly valorizes scientific (i.e., predictive) knowledge over other forms of knowledge, treating it as a master narrative to which all other forms of knowledge are inferior. The result is a narrowing of our understanding of human experience.

However, these criticisms do not justify throwing the baby out with the bath water.

The scientific method will never yield truth or objective knowledge. However, I believe that the scientific method, by being as explicit as possible about its biases and trying to take these into account in its empirical tests, does provide as good a method as yet devised for distinguishing theories that are more predictive of our experience from those that are less so. Although predictive knowledge is not the only type of knowledge that renders human experience meaningful, it is one such form. Consequently, I think feminists should do science in order to produce a form of that valuable knowledge that is less male biased.

Some feminists also criticize scientifically oriented theories for their detached stance toward the phenomena being studied. This stance separates the perspective of the knower from that of the known. With Keller (1984), Stacey and Thorne (1985) argue that a detached perspective can transform the act of knowing into a morally repugnant and unfeminist exercise of power and domination over the known. There is some truth to this argument. However, I disagree with Stacey and Thorne that subjective or interpretive methods in which the knower seeks to identify with the perspective of the known provide any greater protection against domination by the knower. This is because, try as she might, the knower can never completely or accurately represent the perspective of the known. Interpretive like objective knowledge will always be imbued with the perspective of the knower. But in failing to explicitly represent a split or "otherness" between the known and the knower, subjective knowledge risks absorbing the known into the knower and in that way dominating the known. Thus, in my view, both detached and subjective modes of knowledge carry inherent risks for abuse and domination. Neither is superior to the other in this. Within either mode, it is incumbent upon the feminist researcher to guard against the potential for slipping into a dominating stance toward the known that is inherent in the knowledge strategy. Detached and subjective approaches are indeed the stereotypically masculine and feminine modes of knowledge in our culture. As feminists, we should resist being trapped within either.

From my point of view then, expectation states theory's scientific orientation does not make it inherently unfeminist. This does not make it entirely unproblematic, however. Whatever its validity as a knowledge strategy, the language of formal theory and experimentation is a language of power in our society, a source of power that some expectation states papers can seem to flaunt. As a feminist working in this tradition, I believe such flaunting must be resisted. In my view, however, these problems do not invalidate the theory and the importance of what it can contribute to an understanding of gender inequality.

Conclusion

As a theory of gender and interactional inequalities of power and influence, the status expectancy account has much to recommend it. It documents how our society's belief systems about gender, status value, and competence structure women's and men's expectations in interaction, which in turn drive their behavior and the development of situational legitimacy in a self-fulfilling manner. It shows how women's disadvantage in interactional power and influence can be explained simply by means of social structural systems of beliefs and interactional processes common to all goal-oriented encounters.

There are several distinct advantages to the approach taken by this theory. First, it provides a much needed account of the mediating effect of interactional processes in the production of gender stratification. Interaction is the crucial arena through which individual women and men are directed toward or discouraged from various activities and paths of accomplishment. Interactional outcomes are also the basis on which many of society's rewards of power, position, and respect are distributed. Consequently, no theory of gender stratification will succeed unless it incorporates an account of mediating interactional processes.

A second advantage of the status expectancy approach is that it explains women's interactional disadvantages without recourse to individual women's and men's dispositional traits or gender-specific knowledge. That is, it is a social structural account. Ultimately, this may prove an extreme stand and the theory may have to be modified to incorporate some gender-specific attributes. However, for both sociologists and feminists, it is important to push the status explanation for gender effects as far as it will go. Only by doing so can we know how much of what we think of as gender is in fact the voice of status and power.

A third advantage of the approach is that it combines both a situational and contextually specific account of individual women's power and influence with general explanatory principles about women's systematic disadvantages. It spans the gap between accounts of individual diversity and abstract, generalizing explanations. Furthermore, it does this with an account that is both theoretically and empirically systematic.

The status expectancy account has limitations of course. Despite its successes with mixed-sex interaction, its account of gender's impact on status in same-sex groups is not yet fully adequate. Also, expectation states theory has just begun to broaden its scope to social as well as task behavior (Johnson 1988; Ridgeway and Johnson 1990; Ridgeway 1988). As yet, the theory has only a limited ability to explain such behaviors, despite their probable role in gender-based inequalities in interaction. These are significant shortcomings that must be addressed. Yet, despite them, the status expectancy account remains the most systematic and best documented explanation of gender's crucial role in interactional inequalities.

Notes

1. In our society, race is also quickly known about another. This is partly why gender and race so often interact in their effects on face-to-face influence. But note that, according to expectation states theory, the status and competence associations of race are not activated in racially homogeneous interaction with a non-race-related goal or task.

2. This will not necessarily lead to poorer task performance. In fact, it may be superior for some kinds of tasks (Wood 1987).

References

Bales, Robert F. 1950. *Interaction Process Analysis: A Method for the Study of Small Groups*. Cambridge, MA: Addison Wesley.
———. 1953. "The Equilibrium Problem in Small Groups." Pp. 111–61 in *Working Papers in the Theory of Action*, edited by T. Parsons, R. F. Bales, and E. A. Shils. Glencoe, IL: Free Press.
Berger, Joseph, Bernard P. Cohen, and Morris Zelditch, Jr. 1972. "Status Characteristics and Social Interaction." *American Sociological Review* 37:241–55.
Berger, Joseph, Thomas L. Conner, and M. Hamit Fisek (eds.). 1974. *Expectation States Theory: A Theoretical Research Program*. Cambridge, MA: Winthrop.
Berger, Joseph, Thomas L. Conner, and William L. McKeown. 1974. "Evaluations and the Formation and Maintenance of Performance Expectations." Pp. 27–51 in *Expectation States Theory*, edited by J. Berger, T. Conner, and H. M. Fisek. Cambridge, MA: Winthrop.
Berger, Joseph, M. Hamit Fisek, Robert Z. Norman, and David G. Wagner. 1985. "The Formation of Reward Expectations in Status Situations." Pp. 215–61 in *Status, Rewards, and Influence*, edited by J. Berger and M. Zelditch, Jr. San Francisco: Jossey-Bass.
Berger, Joseph, M. Hamit Fisek, Robert Z. Norman, and Morris Zelditch, Jr. 1977. *Status Characteristics in Social Interaction: An Expectation States Approach*. New York: Elsevier.

Berger, Joseph, Susan J. Rosenholtz, and Morris Zelditch, Jr. 1980. "Status Organizing Processes." *Annual Review of Sociology* 6:479–508.

Berger, Joseph, Murray Webster, Jr., Cecilia Ridgeway, and Susan J. Rosenholtz. 1986. "Status Cues, Expectations and Behavior." Pp. 1–22 in *Advances in Group Processes*, Vol. 3, edited by E. Lawler. Greenwich, CT: JAI Press.

Berger, Joseph, and Morris Zelditch, Jr. (eds.). 1985. *Status, Rewards, and Influence*. San Francisco: Jossey-Bass.

Butler, Dore, and Florence L. Geis. 1990. "Nonverbal Affect Responses to Male and Female Leaders: Implications for Leadership Evaluations." *Journal of Personality and Social Psychology* 58:48–59.

Carli, Linda L. 1989. "Gender Differences in Interaction Style and Influence." *Journal of Personality and Social Psychology* 56:565–76.

———. 1990. "Gender, Language, and Influence." *Journal of Personality and Social Psychology* 50:941–51.

Cohen, Elizabeth G. 1982. "Expectation States and Interracial Interaction in School Settings." *Annual Review of Sociology* 8:209–35.

Cohen, Elizabeth G., and Susan S. Roper. 1972. "Modification of Interracial Interaction Disability: An Application of Status Characteristics Theory." *American Sociological Review* 37:643–57.

Cook, Karen S. 1975. "Expectations, Evaluations, and Equity." *American Sociological Review* 40:372–88.

Dovidio, John F., Clifford E. Brown, Karen Heltman, Steven L. Ellyson, and Caroline F. Keating. 1988. "Power Displays Between Women and Men in Discussions of Gender-Linked Tasks: A Multichannel Study. *Journal of Personality and Social Psychology* 55:580–87.

Dovidio, John F., and Steven L. Ellyson. 1982. "Decoding Visual Dominance Behavior: Attributions of Power Based on Relative Percentages of Looking While Speaking and Looking While Listening." *Social Psychology Quarterly* 45:106–13.

Eagly, Alice H. 1987. *Sex Differences in Social Behavior: A Social Role Interpretation*. Hillsdale, NJ: Erlbaum.

Ellyson, Steven L., John F. Dovidio, and Clifford E. Brown. 1992. "The Look of Power: Gender Differences and Similarities in Visual Dominance Behavior." Pp. 50–80 in *Gender, Interaction, and Inequality*, edited by C. Ridgeway. New York: Springer-Verlag.

Ellyson, Steven L., John F. Dovidio, and B. J. Fehr. 1981. "Visual Behavior and Dominance in Women and Men." Pp. 63–79 in *Gender and Nonverbal Behavior*, edited by C. Mayo and N. M. Henley. New York: Springer-Verlag.

Fennell, Mary L., Patricia Barchas, Elizabeth G. Cohen, Anne M. McMahon, and Polly Hildebrand. 1978. "An Alternative Perspective on Sex Differences in Organizational Settings: The Process of Legitimation." *Sex Roles* 4:589–604.

Foschi, Martha. 1989. "Status Characteristics, Standards, and Attributions." Pp. 58–72 in *Sociological Theories in Progress: New Formulations*, edited by J. Berger, M. Zelditch, and B. Anderson. Newbury Park, CA: Sage.

———. 1990. "Double Standards in the Evaluation of Men and Women." Paper presented at the annual meeting of the Canadian Sociology and Anthropology Association, Victoria, B.C., May.

Freese, Lee, and Bernard P. Cohen. 1973. "Eliminating Status Generalization."
    Sociometry 36:177–93.
Harding, Sandra. 1986. *The Science Question in Feminism*. Ithaca, NY: Cornell
    University Press.
Harrod, Wendy J. 1980. "Expectations from Unequal Rewards." *Social Psychology
    Quarterly* 43:126–30.
Johnston, Janet R. 1988. "The Structure of Ex-Spousal Relationships: An Exercise
    in Theoretical Integration and Application." Pp. 309–26 in *Status Generaliza-
    tion: New Theory and Research*, edited by M. Webster, Jr., and M. Foschi.
    Stanford, CA: Stanford University Press.
Keller, Evelyn F. 1982. "Feminism and Science." *Signs* 7:589–602.
———. 1984. *Reflections on Gender and Science*. New Haven, CT: Yale University
    Press.
Lockheed, Marlaine E. 1985. "Sex and Social Influence: A Meta-Analysis Guided
    by Theory." Pp. 406–29 in *Status, Rewards, and Influence*, edited by J. Berger
    and M. Zelditch, Jr. San Francisco: Jossey-Bass.
Lockheed, Marlaine E., and Katherine P. Hall. 1976. "Conceptualizing Sex as a
    Status Characteristic." *Journal of Social Issues* 32:111–24.
Maltz, D. N., and R. A. Borker. 1982. "A Cultural Approach to Male and Female
    Miscommunication." In *Language and Social Identity*, edited by J. J. Gumperz.
    Cambridge: Cambridge University Press.
Meeker, Barbara F. 1981. "Expectation States and Interpersonal Behavior." Pp.
    290–319 in *Social Psychology: Sociological Perspectives*, edited by M. Rosenberg
    and R. Turner. New York: Basic Books.
Meeker, B. F., and P. A. Weitzel-O'Neill. 1977. "Sex Roles and Interpersonal
    Behavior in Task Oriented Groups." *American Sociological Review* 42:92–105.
Moscovici, Serge. 1976. *Social Influence and Social Change*. New York: Academic
    Press.
Norman, Robert Z., Roy Smith, and Joseph Berger. 1988. "The Processing of
    Inconsistent Status Information." Pp. 169–87 in *Status Generalization: New
    Theory and Research*, edited by M. Webster, Jr., and M. Foschi. Stanford, CA:
    Stanford University Press.
Parsons, Talcott, and Robert F. Bales. 1955. *Family, Socialization, and Interaction
    Process*. New York: Free Press.
Pugh, Meredith D., and Ralph Wahrman. 1983. "Neutralizing Sexism in Mixed-
    Sex Groups: Do Women Have to Be Better Than Men?" *American Journal of
    Sociology* 88:746–62.
Ridgeway, Cecilia L. 1978. "Conformity, Group-Oriented Motivation, and Sta-
    tus Attainment in Small Groups." *Social Psychology Quarterly* 41:175–88.
———. 1982. "Status in Groups: The Importance of Motivation." *American
    Sociological Review* 47:76–88.
———. 1988. "Gender Differences in Task Groups: A Status and Legitimacy
    Account." Pp. 188–206 in *Status Generalization: New Theory and Research*,
    edited by M. Webster, Jr., and M. Foschi. Stanford, CA: Stanford University
    Press.
Ridgeway, Cecilia L., and Joseph Berger. 1986. "Expectations, Legitimation, and

Dominance Behavior in Task Groups." *American Sociological Review* 51: 603–17.

Ridgeway, Cecilia L., Joseph Berger, and LeRoy Smith. 1985. "Nonverbal Cues and Status: An Expectation States Approach." *American Journal of Sociology* 90:955–78.

Ridgeway, Cecilia L., and Cathryn Johnson. 1990. "What Is the Relationship Between Socioemotional Behavior and Status in Task Groups?" *American Journal of Sociology* 95:1189–1212.

Shackelford, Susan, Wendy Wood, and Stephen Worchel. 1989. "How Can Low Status Group Members Influence Others: Team Players and Attention Getters?" Unpublished paper, Department of Psychology, Texas A&M University.

Stacey, Judith, and Barrie Thorne. 1985. "The Missing Feminist Revolution in Sociology." *Social Problems* 32:301–16.

Stewart, Penni. 1988. "Women and Men in Groups: A Status Characteristics Approach to Interaction." Pp. 69–85 in *Status Generalization: New Theory and Research*, edited by M. Webster, Jr., and M. Foschi. Stanford, CA: Stanford University Press.

Strodtbeck, Fred L., Rita M. James, and Charles Hawkins. 1957. "Social Status in Jury Deliberations." *American Sociological Review* 22:713–19.

Strodtbeck, Fred L., and Richard D. Mann. 1956. "Sex Role Differentiation in Jury Deliberations." *Sociometry* 19:3–11.

Torrance, E. Paul. 1954. "Some Consequences of Power Differences in Decision Making in Permanent and Temporary Three-Man Groups." In *Small Groups*, edited by A. P. Hare, E. F. Borgatta, and R. F. Bales. New York: Knopf.

Wagner, David G. 1988. "Gender Inequalities in Groups: A Situational Approach." Pp. 55–68 in *Status Generalization: New Theory and Research*, edited by M. Webster, Jr., and M. Foschi. Stanford, CA: Stanford University Press.

Wagner, David G., Rebecca S. Ford, and Thomas W. Ford. 1986. "Can Gender Inequalities Be Reduced?" *American Sociological Review* 51:47–61.

Webster, Murray, Jr., and James E. Driskell. 1978. "Status Generalization: A Review and Some New Data." *American Sociological Review* 43:220–36.

Webster, Murray, Jr., and Martha Foschi. 1988. *Status Generalization: New Theory and Research*. Stanford, CA: Stanford University Press.

Wood, Wendy. 1987. "Meta-Analytic Review of Sex Differences in Group Performance." *Psychological Bulletin* 102:53–71.

Wood, Wendy, and Stephen J. Karten. 1986. "Sex Differences in Interaction Style as a Product of Perceived Sex Differences in Competence." *Journal of Personality and Social Psychology* 50:341–47.

Chapter 10

Sexuality and Gender:
An Interactionist/Poststructural Reading

Norman K. Denzin

My intentions are to offer a symbolic interactionist/poststructural analysis of the production and meanings of sexuality and gender in everyday postmodern life.[1] The particular version of symbolic interactionism that I present merges poststructuralism and cultural studies with a critical, interactionist tradition (Denzin 1985, 1987, 1989, 1990b, 1990c, 1991). The following issues will be discussed: symbolic interactionism and poststructural thought and their relationship to cultural studies, the production of texts on and about sexuality and gender, the reading and writing of such texts, and the contribution of this tradition to the understanding of gender and gender inequality in postmodern society. My analysis will be divided into the following parts. I will briefly define the terms in my title, offer a historical note on the place of gender and sexuality in the interactionist tradition, discuss the poststructural view of sexuality and gender, and then illustrate the contributions of the interactionist/poststructural position on gender through a discussion of three types of problems: ideology and the political economy of gender production, the textual creation of gendered subjects by social scientists, and the world of lived gender. It will be necessary to discuss how the interactionist and poststructural positions can be combined because these perspectives are not commonly fitted together. Terms first.

Gender Terms: Gendered Identities

Every human being in American culture belongs to a specific sex class, male or female, and this assignment is made immediately upon birth (Cahill 1989, p. 282). Femininity and masculinity are socially defined terms that are added to the biologically determined sex class of the individual (Garfinkel 1967, pp. 116–17, 122–24; Mitchell 1982, p. 2). Gender defines the social and cultural meanings brought to each anatomical sex class; children learn, that is, how to "pass as" and "act as" members of their assigned sexual category. Gender, however, is more than learning masculine and feminine behavior (Deegan 1987, p. 4).

Gender also involves sexuality, sexual desire, and being sexual; that is, enacting a gendered sexual identity with another. As Mitchell (1982, p. 2) argues, the "person is formed *through* their sexuality" and their sexual desires, which become part of their personal sexual identity. Sexuality (being sexual) is culturally shaped (e.g., being sexually alluring, or sexually dominant), and these cultural understandings are fitted to the sexual biography of the individual. This sexual identity has three components (Sullivan 1953): the good sexual me (valued sexual experiences), the bad sexual me (identities that produce anxiety), and the not sexual me (identities that are dissociated from the self).

Emotional codes specific to each gender are learned as language is acquired. These codes interact with the sexual selves and sexual identities that circulate in the various arenas of popular culture in everyday life (Carey 1989). The masculine code in our society represses emotionality, while the feminine code expresses vulnerable and nurturing forms of emotionality. Each code speaks to a body culture that stresses health, beauty, and erotic attraction. Two gender-specific, sexual, and emotional cultures thus exist side by side, with females taught to do the emotional labor work (Hochschild 1983), which males avoid, yet expect.

The gendered identity is an interactional production. It is embedded in those interactional places (home, work) that give recurring meaning to ordinary experience. These are sites where emotional experiences, including sexual practices, occur. In them concrete individuals are constituted as gendered subjects who have emotions, beliefs, and social relationships with others (see Althusser 1971, p. 165). In these sites ideology—beliefs about the way the world is and ought to be—intertwines with taken-for-granted cultural understandings about love, intimacy, sexuality, the value of work and family, money, prestige, status, and the meaning of the "good life." What is represented in ideology "is therefore not the system of real relations which govern the existence of individuals, but the imaginary relation of these individuals to the real relations in which they live" (Althusser 1971, p. 165). Ideology, which works at the level of language and the symbolic (e.g., everyday conversation), also exists as a set of material (economic), interactional practices (e.g., inscriptions by social sciences, popular music and film), which *"hail or interpellate concrete individuals as concrete subjects"* (Althusser 1971, p. 173; italics in original). At the level of the symbolic and the imaginary, ideology consists of the myths, beliefs, desires, and ideas people have in their heads about the way things are and should be. At the material level, ideology works through the interactional structures that bring persons together. In this way ideology recruits sexually gendered subjects through this process of interpellation, or hailing ("Hey, girl, come here!"). Individuals are called to their sexually gendered identities. In Althusser's words (1971, p. 174), "The hailed individual [when called] will turn around. By this mere one-hundred-and-eighty-degree physical conversion, he becomes a *subject*. Why? Because he has recognized that the hail was 'really' to him, and that 'it was *really him* who was hailed' " (italics in original). Daily greetings, requests, and conversational exchanges ("Honey, I need a cup of coffee," "Hey, big fella, give me a hand here") cast individuals in gendered identities. These activities constitute individuals as concrete gendered subjects in the gender stratification order.

It must be understood that an interactional, dialectical relationship connects these material practices to the worlds of experience where gendered identities are produced. Specific systems of discourse and meaning operate within specific sites to create particular gendered sexual versions of the human being. These systems cohere during particular periods of time (e.g., the Victorian era, immediate post–World War II America) to create coherent, consistent images of the gender stratification order (e.g., the return of women to the home after World War II). During other historical moments, these systems fall apart or enter interregnums during which competing images of sexuality, gender, family, marriage, and work conflict (e.g., the 1970s and 1980s in the U.S.), only to be brought back together again during another historical moment (e.g., the 1990s' return of the "traditional" mother and woman as promoted by such magazines as *Good Housekeeping*).

The above terms and their meanings are culturally and historically specific. The sexually gendered human being in late twentieth-century America is a social, economic, and historic construction, built up out of the patriarchal cultural myths that have been articulated in American popular culture for the last two hundred years.

The Interactionist/Poststructural Perspective

A "feminist," interactionist sociological imagination[2] (Balsamo 1989, 1990a, 1990b) takes up the problematics of sexuality, desire, language, gendered selves and identities, and the cultural narratives that work to create the worlds of gendered, emotional experience in contemporary society. Gender and sexuality (as indicated above) arise out of the complex interactions that connect the texts, meanings, and experiences that circulate in everyday life, with the things the members of our culture tell one another about being men and women. Stories in the daily newspaper, in social science articles, comic books, daytime TV soap operas, nighttime family comedies, and melodramas, and in large box-office-drawing films like *When Harry Met Sally, Sex, Lies and Video-tapes, Blue Velvet, Driving Miss Daisy, Working Girl, Biloxi Blues*, and *Everybody's All-American* reproduce the gender stratification order.

Sexuality and gender are situated, interactional accomplishments (Garfinkel 1967; Denzin 1989b; West and Zimmerman 1987), shaped by a surrounding patriarchal culture. Woven through this culture are the myths and beliefs surrounding romantic love, the beautiful woman, the handsome male, the all-American family, and erotic sexuality, which is contained within the monogamous marriage structure (Fiedler 1966, p. 339). The performances of sexuality and gender, like those of race and class, constitute experiences "which shape the emergent political conditions that we refer to as the postmodern world" (Downing 1987, p. 80). These performances, when captured in social texts, constitute what we know about these phenomena. How these texts are written thus requires analysis.

Symbolic Interactionism and Gender Studies

A great deal of caution is necessary when addressing the question, What is the relationship between symbolic interactionism, poststructuralism, and the study of gender and gender inequality? I want to avoid the path that suggests that the topics of women and gender can be easily fitted under the rubrics of standard, conventional symbolic interactionist thought (i.e., Reynolds 1990; Deegan and Hill 1987).[3] Rather, with Clough (1987, p. 4) I want to "emphasize the historical moment at which feminist theory challenges the function of [symbolic interactionism] in the production of" texts on and about sexuality and gender. This challenge to interactionism has occurred as a result of the work of theorists like Levi-Strauss, Lacan, Althusser, Barthes, Derrida, and Foucault, and the reading of this work by feminist theorists (see Clough 1987 for a review) who have taken up Freud's challenge to forge their own theory of sexuality, meaning, and existence within a patriarchal culture. (Recent developments by feminist theorists such as Morris 1988a, 1988b, have attempted to move poststructural-postmodern theory into the field of cultural studies, as discussed above.)

It has been the traditional function of *symbolic interactionism*, along with the other subjective, interpretive social psychologies (phenomenology, ethnomethodology, everyday life sociology, etc.), to offer a theory of self, interaction, and socialization that speaks to the question of how the human being is formed out of the interaction order (see Denzin 1977; Lindesmith, Strauss, and Denzin 1988, Chapter 1). The work of symbolic interaction has traditionally been guided by four basic assumptions: First, humans act toward things "on the basis of the meanings that things have for them" (Blumer 1969, p. 2). Things are termed social objects. Social objects may be as concrete as paper and pencils, as abstract as religious systems of thought, or as cultural as the meanings brought to the terms male and female. Second, the meanings of social objects arise out of social interaction; meanings are not in objects. Third, meanings are "handled in, and modified through an interpretive process" (Blumer 1969, p. 2). That is, people interact with and interpret the objects they act toward. As a consequence the meanings of objects change in and through the course of action. Fourth, everyday reality is socially constructed through the interactions that occur between self-reflective individuals in concrete situations (Blumer 1969, p. 3). Symbolic interactionism, in its interpretive version (interpretive interactionism; Denzin 1989), is the research strategy that implements a critical, cultural studies approach (see below) to the study of how human beings make history, but not under conditions of their own choosing.

For the symbolic interactionist, gender and sexuality are social constructions (Deegan 1987, pp. 4–5) that occur under a patriarchal regime where women are exchanged from male to male, as currencies of exchange (Clough 1987, p. 10). While gender and sexuality entered interactionist thought quite early (e.g., Hall 1898, p. 360; Cooley 1922), Mead's (1934) theory of self, like Blumer's later (1969), was gender free and scarcely took notice of sexuality. The classic textbooks in the tradition (Lindesmith and Strauss 1949) and the revisions of the perspective in the 1960s and 1970s by such authors as Stone (1962) and Goffman (1974, 1979) either treated gender from the perspective of the psychoanalysts (Freud and H. S. Sullivan) or applied a structural reading to the sexual stratification order in American society. By the late 1970s and throughout the 1980s interactionists increasingly turned to the socialization of gender, and the acquisition of gender identities in a variety of settings. These studies mined the inner, developmental side of gender, arguing, in a manner consistent with the origins of their perspective, that society is in interaction and that the meanings of terms like gender, sexuality, male, and female must be found in the meanings persons bring to these categories of experience (see Denzin 1977; Joffe 1977; Cahill 1980, 1986, 1989; Power 1985; Risman 1982; Andersen 1981; Horowitz 1981; Williams 1990; Kanter 1977; Martin 1978; Ferraro and

Johnson 1983; Cho 1990; Blum 1982; Malhotra-Bentz 1989; Deegan and Hill 1987).

Poststructuralism

Poststructuralism is that theoretical position which asks how the human subject is constructed in and through the structures of language and ideology. Two key terms, text and deconstruction, organize this perspective. A text is any printed, visual, oral, or auditory production that is available for reading, viewing, or hearing (e.g., an article, a film, a painting, a song). Readers create texts as they interpret and interact with them. The meaning of a text is always indeterminate, open-ended, and interactional. Deconstruction is the critical analysis of texts. It is a process that explores how a text is constructed and given meaning by its author or producer. Poststructuralists argue that there is only the text; that is, the objective reality of social facts (e.g., gender) is a social accomplishment. This accomplishment is documented through the production of texts about the topic at hand, e.g., gender and sexuality. Deconstruction analyzes how a text produces its subject matter.

Commonly called poststructural, post-Marxist, and postmodern, this work (i.e., Foucault 1982) argues that the microrelations of power in late capitalist societies continually reproduce situated systems of discourse (i.e., social science articles, the law, religion, art, literature), which create particular versions of the human subject (male, female, and child), the family, the state, science, and social control. These systems of discourse have reduced women to the status of socializing agents of society and treated the family as the site of madness.

Women's sexuality and their relationship to children, to their own bodies, and to men have been systematically excluded from this discourse, which until the early 1970s was primarily written by men. A number of feminists have appropriated this theoretical position for their own purposes. Under this new view, the traditional Marxist conception of base-superstructure is displaced. Power is located in a "disciplinary society," which continually transfers individuals from one disciplinary system of discourse to another (schools, colleges, work, family, the courts, mental hospitals, prisons, etc.). The intervention of the state in the economy and the family, under late capitalism erases the distinction between the private and public spheres in everyday life. There is a dialectical relationship "between women's oppression in the home and in her exploitation in the work force" (Clough 1987, p. 20). In both spheres she does unpaid emotional labor (Hochschild 1983), which further increases her oppression and alienation. These subjective states are seen as being produced by the social practices and discourses of patriarchal and bourgeois ideologies, which reproduce the hegemonic order (Clough 1987, p. 20).

Feminism thus becomes a way of reading how sexuality, gender, and subjectivity have been constructed under a bourgeois power structure. This system of power and the orders of knowledge (Foucault 1970) that it has constructed (the human disciplines) have incorporated a psycho-analytic view of sexuality into a theory of science, narration, and representation. This theory of representation presumes the ability to "realistically" map the world out there, within a positivist and postpositivist theory of knowledge (Smith 1979). An Oedipal logic structures the sociological texts that are written about the individual. These texts, whether ethnographic and qualitative, or quantitative, locate subjectivity back in the family, in the male-female relationship (Clough 1987, p. 16; 1988, 1992). The figure of woman emerges in the

> patriarchal culture as a signifier of the male other, bound by a symbolic order in which man can live out his fantasies and obsessions through linguistic command, by imposing them on the silent image of woman still tied to her place as the bearer of meaning, not the maker of meaning. (Mulvey 1982, p. 413)

The poststructural feminist intervention into symbolic interactionist work concludes "that a 'man's discourse' about women thoroughly saturates the discourse of the human sciences" (Clough 1987, p. 18). Feminist knowledge is thus both "implicated in and is an implication of this order of power/knowledge" (Clough 1987, p. 16).

Poststructuralism and Interactionism:
Enter Cultural Studies

A more critical, interactionist, psychoanalytic feminism (Clough 1987, 1988a, 1992) has emerged, which has attempted to bridge symbolic interactionism with the poststructural theories of Lacan, Derrida, and Barthes, and the more recent postmodern arguments of Lyotard (1979) and Baudrillard (1987). The failures of traditional interactionism have been augmented by this poststructural-feminist perspective. Both symbolic interactionism and feminist poststructuralists focus on the production of cultural meanings. Recent work in cultural studies (Denzin 1990a, 1990b) has blended these perspectives through a consideration of the economic and cultural conditions that lead to the reproduction of gender stratification in a society like the United States. This version of *cultural studies* attempts to unravel the ideological meanings that are coded into the taken-for-granted meanings that circulate in everyday life, tracking down "In the decorative display of what-goes-without-saying, the ideological abuse which is hidden there" (Barthes [1957] 1972, p. 111). Cultural studies examine three interrelated problems: the production of cultural meanings, the textual analysis of these meanings, and the study of lived cultures and lived experiences (Johnson 1986/87, p. 72). Each of these problems constitutes a field of inquiry in its own right. When applied to the study of gender and sexuality the production of cultural meanings involves issues of ideology and political economy, as these processes produce recurring meanings that are attached to the gender stratification system in postmodern society.[4] The textual analysis of these meanings involves the implementation of a variety of reading strategies, from semiotics to hermeneutics, psychoanalysis, and feminism. At the level of textuality, the question turns on how a text creates a gendered subject. At the level of lived experience, a central problem becomes the examination of how interacting individuals connect their lived experiences to the cultural representations of those experiences. Interpretive interactionism enters the field of cultural studies and the analysis of gender at the level of lived experiences.

As a distinctly qualitative approach to social research, interpretive interactionism attempts to make the world of lived experience directly accessible to the reader. The focus is on those life experiences, called *epiphanies* (turning-point experiences), which radically alter and shape the meanings persons give to themselves and their life projects (Denzin 1989, pp. 14–15). In the field of gender studies, this strategy seeks those moments of existential crisis when a person's sexuality and gender identity are forcefully and dramatically called into question. This is a matter of extreme theoretical and methodological importance, for in these epiphanic moments the gender order is revealed in ways that are normally not seen.

The Political Economy of Gender

I turn now to the political economy of gender and examine how a social text, which circulates in the popular culture, contributes to the construction of a gendered subject. Consider the following. During late 1988 and early 1989 *Good Housekeeping* ran a series of full-page ads in such publications as *The New York Times* describing the new traditional woman. One such ad read as follows:

The New Traditionalist. She has a mission in life—and it could shape your marketing plan. She has made a commitment. Her mission: create a more meaningful quality of life for herself and her family. She is the New Traditionalist—a contemporary woman who finds her fulfillment in traditional values that were considered "old-fashioned" just a few years ago. She is part of an extraordinary social movement that is profoundly changing the way Americans look at living—and the way products are marketed. The home is again the center of American life, oatmeal is back on the breakfast table, families are vacationing together, watching movies at home, playing Monopoly again. Even the perfume ads are suddenly glorifying commitment. This new quality of life is the embodiment of everything that *Good Housekeeping* has always stood for. These are the values that we have always represented. . . . Who else can speak to the New Traditionalist with that kind of authority and trust. . . . America is coming home to *Good Housekeeping*. (*New York Times*, Nov. 17, 1988, p. 46)

In the center of the ad is a picture of a mother with her arms around her young daughter's shoulders. The mother has her hair pulled back in a bun, as does the daughter. Both are dressed in conservative dark dresses. The daughter's dress has lace around the collar, and she has a bow in her hair. She appears to be about three years old, her mother in her middle thirties. Both wear simple black shoes. The mother is seated in a white wicker chair on the front porch of a traditional house, beside a table with a floral tablecloth. The porch floor is made of finished, simple pine planks. The porch railing behind and the classic turned spindles are painted white, as is the large porch column that frames the mother's head. Trees shade the background, although the sun shines through the leaves.

In this series of ads males were seldom present. A handful changed the race of the mother and child. These ads illustrate Althusser's argument about the constitution of individuals as concrete subjects, for here the new traditional woman is given a set of beliefs (old-fashioned, the home is the center of life, commitment, etc.) and located in a site (home), doing specific things (caring for her children) that embody *Good Housekeeping*. This woman has a mission: to create a more meaningful quality of life for herself and her family. She is the mover of family values, and her daughter is the embodiment of these values. She is a traditionalist, which means paid work is less important than family and home. Furthermore, on the level of sexuality, this traditional woman uses perfume that glorifies commitment, not one-night stands. This mother doesn't rush off into the bed of another man, nor does she leave her children at home to fix breakfast for themselves. Oatmeal is on the breakfast table, and this family takes trips together and even plays that all-American version of capitalism called *Monopoly*.

This ad works at several levels at the same time. On the level of the visual it creates a beautiful image of a favored cultural dyad: mother and daughter. It locates this dyad in an idyllic cultural setting: the classic American home in a rural environ. It says that here is where the new traditionalist takes her stand; no ghetto for her, no expensive condo in the city. She lives in the country, where values run free and pure, like the water in the brook that surely bubbles in the background behind the trees.

At the level of textuality, the ad moves in two directions at the same time. It appeals to two different classes of readers: the new woman who is created by the ad, and the American capitalist who creates and then attempts to sell products to this woman. In a doubly subversive manner the ad intends to sell this woman to herself and to the capitalist, who will sell things to her. But, of greatest importance, both buyers must be induced to buy this magazine, *Good Housekeeping*. The woman will find pictures and stories about herself. The capitalist will find buyers who, in reading these stories, will also read his ads for his products. Both buyers will buy space in and copies of the magazine, if the ad is successful. Everybody wins.

The woman-buyer first. The printed words surround this woman and her child with a cluster of symbols that define what the new traditionalist means: old-fashioned, oatmeal, breakfast table, family vacations, watching movies at home on the TV. (Presumably they watch movies about old fashioned families.) This level of textuality creates a sexually gendered female subject. She as an individual is called forward by this ad and challenged to take a position on the new traditional values. Who could turn their back on these symbols?

Now the capitalist. He must be convinced that this woman exists out there in the marketplace. And, of course, she does exist because here she is with her daughter. She is part of a new "social movement that is profoundly changing the way Americans look at living—and the way products are marketed." Her presence sets the stage for a new marketing plan. This plan must emphasize quality of life, the old-fashioned values (again), home, and family, etc. They must not appeal to women who seek narcissistic self-fulfillment, for this new woman is "other-child" oriented. She is a giver, not a taker. She wants products that will allow her to raise children like this daughter, and keep houses that look like this house.

This woman is the bearer of meaning, the subject of the capitalist's gaze. She is not the maker, not the creator of meaning. The discourse that surrounds her is entirely masculine; her subjectivity has been located back in the home, not in nondomestic work. Her sexuality (motherliness) defines her gendered being. This ad inserts a structure of imaginary relationships (oatmeal breakfasts, family vacations) between this woman (all women) and her daughter (all daughters). As a set of material practices this ad constitutes the new woman as a concrete subject who has these wants, desires, and needs that can be served by this magazine and the capitalists who advertise in it. This ad transforms an already gendered feminine subject into a new subject—the new traditionalist.

By locating itself within history (a new social movement, tradition) the ad argues that a new system of discourse is cohering on the American scene. This discourse is creating a new version of the American woman. The ad challenges earlier versions of this woman. This earlier version of woman didn't value her children, fix breakfasts, or take family vacations, and she used perfumes that didn't invoke commitment. In creating this woman this ad provides a new historical reading of sexuality and gender in American culture. Ideological productions like this, which presume the circulation of a variety of commodities in the political economy of everyday life, including buyers and sellers, create and reify the gender stratification system. At the level of cultural analysis, these ads and their meanings suggest a turn back to an earlier time when women were also urged to return to their homes (post–World War II) and take care of their husbands and children.

If productions like this bring a class of meanings from the popular culture to the figure of woman, consider now another level of textuality, a social scientist writing about a woman. I turn, then, to a case study. This discussion will reveal how a social scientist constructs a representation of a gendered, sexual, female being.

Producing Gender in Lived Experience and in A Sociological Text

This is the strange story of Agnes (Garfinkel 1967). It is a case of how gender is accomplished socially and textually in interaction, in a way that is determined neither absolutely by biology nor by the dominant culture. The details are familiar to sociologists (see Cahill 1989, pp. 281–82). Agnes was referred by a private physician to the Department of Psychiatry at UCLA in October 1958. She appeared as an attractive nineteen-year-old, white, single girl (Garfinkel 1967, p. 119), and was found to have a unique type of a most "rare disorder: testicular feminization syndrome. . . . [T]he patient was completely feminized in her secondary sex characteristics . . . with a nonetheless normal-sized penis and testes" (Garfinkel 1967, p. 285). She requested that her genitalia be surgically transformed so that an artificial vagina could be constructed from the skin of the penis. After intensive investigation of the patient's medical history, this operation was performed.[5] The patient reported that she had been living undetected as a woman for about two years, but that "as far back as her memory reached, she had wanted to be a girl . . . though she was fully aware that she was anatomically a male and was treated by her family and by society as a boy" (p. 286). In October 1966 Agnes returned to her physician, Robert J. Stoller, and revealed during a conversation "with the greatest casualness, in mid-sentence, and without giving the slightest warning it was coming . . . that she had never had a biological defect that had feminized her but that she had been taking estrogens since age 12" (p. 287).[6]

From November 1958 to March 1959 Garfinkel had approximately thirty-five hours of conversation with Agnes. His study of how she accomplished passing in society as a female, even though she was a male, is based on the transcriptions of these conversations. The Appendix to his Chapter 5 contains the above information on Agnes's lie, which Garfinkel did not know when he wrote his chapter. However he uses the Appendix to show how an ethnomethodological study works, because the above news about Agnes shows how "the recognizedly rational accountability of practical actions is a member's practical accomplishment" (p. 286).

There is more going on here than just the practical accomplishment of Agnes's passing, which Garfinkel takes as an instance of his theory that facts are social accomplishments. Behind this question lies another, even more basic, and this involves how Garfinkel produced a text that allowed him (and the reader) to see Agnes as an "intersexed" person with male genitalia who managed to pass as a female. How did this work? How, that is, does Garfinkel's text, which is part detective story (How did she learn to act like a woman?) and part melodrama (How does this poor man/woman find happiness in life?), organize itself so that it gives the appearance of having accounted for Agnes's passing?

From the outset Garfinkel saw Agnes as the person she wanted to be; as an attractive female with a very female shape (38-25-38), who desired and received a "sex change" operation, in actuality a castration. He also saw her as an instance of a person who had accomplished passing (p. 118), and hence she was material for his theory about the accountability of practical actions and their practical accomplishments in everyday life.

Key to Garfinkel's construction of Agnes as a woman was her appearance, which was convincingly female. Garfinkel writes: "She was tall, slim, with a very female shape. . . . She had . . . a young face with pretty features, a peaches-and-cream complexion, no facial hair, subtly plucked eyebrows, and no makeup except for lipstick" (p. 119).

Seeing her thus, he now must create a gendered space for her. He invokes a sense of typical woman to assure himself that she was "a typical girl of her class and age. . . . There was nothing garish or exhibitionistic in her attire, nor was there any hint of poor taste. . . . Her voice . . . was soft" (p. 119). He goes even beyond the "otherness" of typical woman, however, and compares Agnes to male homosexuals. Her speech and delivery "had the occasional lisp similar to that affected by feminine appearing male homosexuals" (p. 119, see also p. 131). Assuring himself (and the reader) that she is not garish, or crude, or vulgar, or homosexual, he now diminishes her standing in the female community: "Her manner was appropriately feminine with a slight awkwardness that is typical of middle adolescence" (p. 119).

Garfinkel has given a masculine reading of Agnes's sexuality, which complements her own notion of being feminine. Now he must tell us how he interacted with her:

> There were many occasions when my attentions flattered her with respect to her femininity: for example, holding her arm while I guided her across the street; offering to hang up her coat; relieving her of her handbag. . . . At times like this her behavior reminded me that being female for her was like having been given a wonderful gift. . . . At such times she acted like a recent and enthusiastic initiate into the sorority of her heart's desire. (p. 119)

Garfinkel is leading Agnes into femininity. His actions call out these characteristics in her, which he then sees and reports upon. Her presence in his text is a social and interactional accomplishment.[7]

Sexuality and Gender at the Level of Lived Experience

The political economy of sexuality is framed around and within the dominant (and subordinate) cultural myths concerning power, domination, masculinity, femininity, homosexuality, and intimacy. It remains to complete the third part of a cultural studies approach to the analysis of gender and sexuality. These terms must be inserted into the world of interactional, lived experience. In such worlds a gendered feminine (and masculine) identity is produced. These enlivened performances create the gendered sexual self. A political economy of sexual differences structures these experiences. When they occur, cultural meanings are illuminated and often forced upon the person. A given epiphanic moment (see below) can deepen the person's internalized oppression to a gendered sexual identity, lead to open rebellion, or produce a deeper commitment to it. Dialectically the individual as a sexual subject acts back on the gender order.

My accounts will be drawn from five sources: young children learning their sexual identities (Cahill 1989), the feminine gaze of the male body (Balsamo 1990b), prostitutes learning how to deal with clients (Heyl 1979), Korean wives being battered and sexually abused by their husbands (Cho 1988), and gay males with AIDS sorting out their experiences with lovers (Kowalewski 1988).

A Young Boy Being a Woman

Cahill offers the following example of how young preschool children experiment with the management of their personal, sexual identities. A fifty-five-month old boy (S) slips into a red "dress-up" dress in a preschool classroom and then walks over to a fifty-one-month old girl (M).

S: "TA-DA-DA" [in an affected high-pitched voice].
M: "Silly."
S: "TA-DA-DA."
M: "You're silly."
S: "DA-TA-TA"[in an affected low-pitched voice while slipping out of the dress], "SUUUPerman!" (Cahill, 1989, p. 292)

M rejected S's silly dress-up behavior. She mocked this version of his sexual self, implying that boys aren't girls. S agreed. He didn't just step out of the dress and into a culturally approved male sexual identity. He became supermale, superman. In the political economy of sexual difference that operates in middle-class American preschools, boys are sanctioned against playing as females. Beyond this they are socialized into the culture's beliefs about fantastic male and female comic book characters. Being Superman is an ordinary occurrence in such settings. In the acceptance of this cultural masculine identity the young male becomes not just man, but *super*man, a man who has extraordinary power and strength, is extremely handsome, and is sexually attractive to females. In this slice of represented lived experience S has enacted a culturally approved masculine sexual identity.

Gazing on the Male Body

A woman finds herself in a nightclub. Male strippers are performing. Her eyes are drawn to Ramone. She writes:

> A dancer named Ramone . . . performed an erotic routine one night. . . .
> He came out dressed in tight blue jeans, a white t-shirt, cowboy boots, and
> bandana. But he was also wearing dark black sunglasses. During his first
> routine he stripped to his waist, never removing those glasses. During his
> second dance . . . off with the shirt, the pants, the shorts, stripped to his
> g-string, he never removed the glasses. . . . During Ramone's act, I be-
> came aroused sexually and silently within myself, in spite of myself. I
> could say now that I desired him. . . . I felt an erotic charge that provoked
> a fantasy of meeting him after the show, dancing, and then leaving with
> him; a dream that stopped short of any sexual encounter. . . . I was
> aroused by this arousal. (Balsamo 1990a, p. 95)

Here the member reverses the usual cultural model of the female being
the object of the male erotic gaze. She is bearer, not the carrier of sexual
meaning and finds herself uncomfortable in this sexual identity. Yet the
presence of the male body, eyes hidden by the dark glasses, sexually
arouses and brings into play an aroused sexual self. This moment of
insight into herself, as she transgresses usual sexual boundaries, even
though they have been culturally prescribed by the occasion, creates
confusion.

Doing Sex for Pay

Here is a house madam (an owner of a house of prostitution) talking
about her early experiences in the trade.

> I can remember a time when I didn't know that I was supposed to hustle.
> . . . When I turned out it was $2 a throw. They got a hell of a fuck. And
> that was it. One Saturday night I turned forty-four tricks! . . . I was so
> tired—I thought I was going to die. And I got my ass whipped for it.
> [Lloyd, her pimp said] "Don't you know you're supposed to ask for more
> money?" Nobody told me that. (Heyl 1979, p. 118).

Here the prostitute sells her body for two dollars a trick. Her enacted
sexuality creates a negative self-impression. The same woman (Ann)
continues talking:

> I call it "turn-out blues." Every girl that ever turns out has 'em. . . . You'll
> wake up one morning and you'll say: "Why in the hell am I doing this. . . .
> [E]verybody gets it. Here's when you'll decide whether you're going to
> stay or you're gonna quit. (p. 125)

In these two epiphanic moments Ann learns to charge more for her body, and to accept this occupation and its demands. Prostitution changes a woman into a paid-for sexual act. Her gender, which is enlivened through her sexuality, becomes irrelevant to the experience at hand. She is there to serve a male client. Her sexuality becomes a commodity, and she the person who delivers that commodity.

Being a Battered Wife

A battered Korean wife speaks:

> I have been beaten so many times severely in the early days of the marriage. But I would tell you the recent one. About 8 months ago, I was beaten badly. In the middle of the beating I ran out of the house. . . . But he followed and caught me. He grabbed my hair and dragged me to the house. He pushed me into the bathroom and kicked my body with his foot. My baby was crying. . . . Now I suffer from headache . . . and I feel dizzy. . . . I can't forgive him! I hate, hate, hate him so much. . . . Is this because I was born a woman? (Cho 1988)

Violently assaulted by the man she married, this woman now hates him and her body. But more importantly she hates being woman, for being woman means being available for male violence. Trapped in her bathroom, beaten nearly to death, days later this epiphanic experience led this woman to attempt to walk away from her marriage and her husband. Her husband's conduct embodies a level of lived sexuality that is pure patriarchal violence.

Gay Lovers

As Kowalewski (1988, p. 211) notes, a double stigma for the gay male has been created by the presence of AIDS within the gay community. The sexual politics that surround this disease reinforces the stereotype of promiscuity that the broader culture attributes to gay men, and also "adds the stigma of disease to the stigma of amoral character" (p. 211). AIDS introduces danger into sexuality, an almost continuous epiphanic moment into gay sexual life, for persons with AIDS (PWAs), are not safe sexual partners. This means that the sexual practices and experiences that connect gay men with one another now take on new meaning. Anal sex has become desexualized and given disease meanings. A gay man speaks:

> Anal sex is becoming more desexualized for me. I learned over the years to be excited by it. Now I don't want it. It's a redefining of what is erotic for me. I want to do things that make me feel safe. (p. 216)

Another gay male describes kissing, a new unsafe sexual practice: "I can't stop kissing, especially if it's someone I care about. I'm willing to take that risk. I can't live my life in fear of what might happen" (p. 217). In these two cases a member is forced, by the AIDS crisis, to modify a sexual practice, which changes his sexually gendered identity.

The political economy of gendered sexuality in American society circulates through a structure of cultured meanings that reinforces masculinity, male domination over females, the stigmatizing of homosexuals, and the valorization of beautiful women (Douglas and Atwell 1988). This system of cultural meanings impinges directly into the world of lived sexuality. This system of meaning and discourse makes sexually gendered males and females in this culture social constructions who reproduce a patriarchal system of domination. This system produces gender inequality that turns females and their sexuality into commodities traded in a male-controlled sexual and economic marketplace. Gay males, doubly stigmatized, signify the normal stigma brought to females, for their sexuality is not only deviant and amoral, it is the carrier of a disease.

In Conclusion: Doing Gender, Sexuality, and the Social Text

Five examples of gender lived through sexuality in the concrete interactional moment have been presented. In each case the lived experience of sexuality departs from or amplifies the mythical beliefs that operate in the popular culture about love, family, eroticism, and the relations between the sexes in late twentieth-century America. The interactionist-poststructural, cultural studies approach to these phenomena has been presented. The study of epiphanic moments has been presented as a strategic method for uncovering the inner worlds of sexually gendered experience. In such moments cultural stereotypes are illuminated and their dominating influence over the person is revealed.

Taking gender inequality as something to be explained, the interpretive interactionist approach moves, at all times, between three levels of analysis: the production of cultural texts, the reading and analysis of these texts, and the relationship between these texts and the everyday world where gender inequality occurs. Stressing the violent, erotic side of gendered life, this perspective argues that a systematic analysis of the cultural myths and beliefs about men, women, sexuality, love, and marriage must occur before inequality will begin to disappear.

I end with another myth. This one is from a feminist theorist (Morris 1988a). It is about the pirate's fiancee. I want to use the metaphor of the pirate's fiancee to describe the relationship between symbolic interactionism, poststructuralism, and feminism. I will assume, however, that the metaphor applies to most, if not all sociological theories about feminism and gender. (I exclude only explicitly feminist theories from this judgment.)

The Pirate's Fiancee

In one of its forms the myth of the pirate's fiancee describes a woman "who lives on the edge of a village with her goods and chattels, her goat, and her bit of high-tech—a tape recorder. She makes money from men, and from cleaning" (Morris 1988a, p. 1). She is spurned by the villagers, who also fear her because of her reputation and sharp tongue. In her house the village men confide in her, depend on her, and trust her, even as they permit vicious attacks on her home.

> She saves their money and with her recorder she has saved their words. One day she leaves. As she sets off on the road, she leaves behind a village listening in horror not to the voice of the curious girl, but to its most intimate secrets and confessions—playing loudly, in public, for all to hear. (p. 1)

Now another version of this story, borrowed again from Morris, who offers the following reading of the Brecht-Weill song "Pirate Jenny" from *The Threepenny Opera*. Pirate Jenny dreams of the day when her ship will come in, commanded by a masculine savior whom she will marry, after which she will be recognized as a pirate queen who has the power to destroy everyone who has ever humiliated her. If Jenny joyfully plays the part of the pirate's fiancee, the woman in the previously discussed version of the myth rejects this position, turning the tables, so to speak, on her male capturer. Seizing her own voice and goods, she leaves town, having undone the oppressive order that scorned her. She doesn't need a male to save her.

Apply these two stories to the topic at hand. Feminism, in many of its forms has been the pirate's fiancee. The pirate, whether on board a rational-choice, world systems, Marxist, psychoanalytic, network, expectations state, ethnomethodological, interactionist, or functionalist ship, has sailed into port, and taken the bereaved, neglected, betrothed figure of woman into the ship's quarters and fashioned a theory that fits her. She in turn has many times worn these garments, and redesigned them to fit the peculiarities of her situation. Too infrequently has she turned her back on the captain of the ship and gone off on her own project (e.g., Daly 1980; Coward 1985). The interactionist/poststructuralist approach to sexuality and gender is a calling for feminist theorists to chart this new course.

Notes

1. After Mills (1959, p. 166) the postmodern age started with the end of World War II and continues to the present. It is marked by increased mass consumerism, a worldwide informational-media system, multinational state-supported, socialist-corporate capitalism, an absorption of third-world labor markets (women and children) into an international economy, and a general confusion of conservative, fascist, democratic-socialist, and communist political ideologies (see Denzin 1991).

2. That is, a version of the sociological imagination (Mills 1959) that asks, "What kind of woman, man, and child is produced in the contemporary historical moment by forces that operate behind people's backs?

3. I borrow this opening from Clough (1987, pp. 1–2).

4. This involves studies on the production, circulation, and consumption of cultural products keyed to sexuality and gender, as well as analyses of the theoretical "knowledges of advertisers [and] persons involved in public relations for large organizations" (Johnson 1986/87, p. 55). Gender-oriented productional studies also ask how members of the popular culture make a commodity recommended to them the object of their own engendered actions, thereby appropriating the sexual identities and body images offered up to them by the marketplace. Such actions reproduce the images of masculinity and femininity that lie behind these representations.

5. It was determined that she had never taken estrogens (p. 286) and that she was "so strongly fixed in a female direction that no forms of treatment could ever make her masculine" (p. 154). This is Stoller's, not Garfinkel's text (see Stoller 1968, p. 135).

6. This meant she duped the doctors and Garfinkel, for she, not nature, induced the changes in her body.

7. Elsewhere (Denzin 1990c) I offer an interpretive reading of Agnes's sexuality that takes account of the psychoanalytic subtext that is buried in the story.

References

Althusser, Louis. 1971. *Lenin and Philosophy*. New York: Monthly Review Press.

Andersen, Margaret L. 1981. "Corporate Wives: Longing for Liberation or Satisfied with the Status Quo?" *Urban Life* 10:311–27.

Balsamo, Ann. 1989. "Imagining Cyborgs: Postmodernism and Symbolic Interactionism." Pp. 369–79 in *Studies in Symbolic Interaction*, Vol. 10; edited by N. K. Denzin. Greenwich: CT: JAI Press.

———. 1990b. "Rethinking Ethnography: A Work for the Feminist Imagination." Pp. 45–57 *Studies in Symbolic Interaction*, Vol. 11, edited by N. K. Denzin. Greenwich, CT: JAI Press.

———. 1990. "Technologies of the Gendered Body: A Feminist Cultural Study." Unpublished Ph.D. dissertation, Institute of Communications Research, University of Illinois at Urbana–Champaign.

Barthes, Roland. [1957] 1972. *Mythologies*. New York: Hill and Wang.

———. [1977] 1982. "From *Writing Degree Zero*." Pp. 31–61 in *A Barthes Reader*, edited by Susan Sontag. New York: Hill and Wang.

Baudrillard, Jean. 1987. *America*. London: Verso.

Blum, Linda M. 1982. "Feminism and the Mass Media: A Case Study of *The Women's Room* as Novel and Television Film." *Berkeley Journal of Sociology* 27:1–24.

Blumer, Herbert. 1969. *Symbolic Interactionism*. Englewood Cliffs, NJ: Prentice-Hall.

Cahill, Spencer E. 1980. "Directions for an Interactionist Study of Gender Development." *Symbolic Interaction* 3:123–38.

———. 1986. "Language Practices and Self-Definition: The Case of Gender Identity Acquisition." *The Sociological Quarterly* 27:295–311.

———. 1989. "Fashioning Males and Females: Appearance Management and the Social Reproduction of Gender." *Symbolic Interaction* 12:281–98.

Carey, James W. 1989. *Communication and Culture: Essays on Media and Society*. Boston: Unwin Hyman.

Cho, Joo-Hyun. 1988. *"A Social Phenomenological Understanding of Family Violence: The Case of Korea."* Ph.D. diss., University of Illinois, Champaign-Urbana.

Clough, Patricia Ticineto. 1987. "Feminist Theory and Social Psychology." Pp. 3–22 in *Studies in Symbolic Interaction*, Vol. 8, edited by No. K. Denzin. Greenwich, CT: JAI Press.

———. 1988. "The Movies and Social Observation: Reading Blumer's *Movies and Conduct*." *Symbolic Interaction* 11: 85–94.

———. 1992. *The End(s) of Ethnography*. Newbury Park, CA: Sage.

Cooley, Charles Horton. 1922. *Human Nature and the Social Order*. New York: Scribner's.

Coward, Rosalind. 1985. *Feminine Desires: How They Are Sought, Bought and Packaged*. New York: Grove Press.

Daly, Mary. 1980. *Gyn/Ecology: The Metaethics of Radical Feminism*. Boston: Allen & Unwin.

Deegan, Mary Jo. 1987. "Symbolic Interaction and the Study of Women: An Introduction." Pp. 3–18 in *Women and Symbolic Interaction*, edited by M. J. Deegan and M. R. Hill. Boston: Allen & Unwin.

Deegan, Mary Jo, and Michael R. Hill (eds.). 1987. *Women and Symbolic Interaction*. Boston: Allen & Unwin.

Denzin, Norman K. 1977. *Childhood Socialization: Studies in the Development of Language, Social Behavior, and Identity*. San Francisco: Jossey-Bass.

———. 1985. "On the Phenomenology of Sexuality, Desire, and Violence." *Current Perspectives in Social Theory* 6:39–56.

———. 1987. *The Alcoholic Self*. Newbury Park, CA: Sage.

------. 1989. *Interpretive Interactionism*. Newbury Park, CA: Sage.

------. 1990a. *Hollywood and the American Alcoholic: 1932–1989*. Hawthorne, NY: Aldine de Gruyter.

------. 1990b. "Reading Cultural Texts." *American Journal of Sociology* 95: 1577–80.

------. 1990c. "Harold and Agnes: A Feminist, Narrative Undoing." *Sociological Theory* 11: 199–216.

------. 1991. *Images of Postmodernism: Social Theory and Contemporary Cinema*. London: Sage.

Douglas, Jack, and Freda Cruse Atwell. 1988. *Love, Intimacy and Sex*. Newbury Park, CA: Sage.

Downing, David B. 1987. "Deconstruction's Scruples: The Politics of Enlightened Critique." *Diacritics* 17:66–81.

Ferraro, Kathleen J., and John Johnson. 1983. "How Women Experience Battering: The Process of Victimization." *Social Problems* 30:325–39.

Fiedler, Leslie A. 1966. *Love and Death in the American Novel*. Rev. ed. New York: Stein and Day.

Foucault, Michel. 1970. *The Order of Things*. New York: Vintage.

------. 1982. "Afterword: The Subject and Power." Pp. 208–26 in *Michel Foucault: Beyond Structuralism and Hermeneutics*, edited by H. Dreyfus and P. Rabinow. Chicago: University of Chicago Press.

Garfinkel, Harold. 1967. "Passing and the Managed Achievement of Sex Status in an Intersexed Person." Pp. 116–85 in *Studies in Ethnomethodology*, edited by Harold Garfinkel. Englewood Cliffs, NJ: Prentice-Hall.

Goffman, Erving. 1974. "The Arrangement between the Sexes." *Theory and Society* 4:301–31.

------. 1979. *Gender Advertisements*. New York: Harper & Row.

Hall, G. Stanley. 1898. "Some Aspects of the Early Sense of Self." *American Journal of Psychology* 9:351–95.

Heyl, Barbara Sherman. 1979. *The Madam as Entrepreneur: Career Managemention House Prostitution*. New Brunswick, NJ: Transaction Books.

Hochschild, Arlie. 1983. *The Managed Heart*. Berkeley: University of California Press.

------. 1989. *The Second Shift*. New York: Knopf.

Horowitz, Ruth. 1981. "Passion, Submission and Motherhood: The Negotiation of Identity by Unmarried Innercity Chicanas." *Sociological Quarterly* 22: 241–53.

Joffe, Carole. 1977. *The Friendly Intruders*. Berkeley: University of California Press.

Johnson, Richard. 1986/87. "What Is Cultural Studies Anyway?" *Social Text* (Winter):38–80.

Kanter, Rosabeth Moss. 1977. "Some Effects of Proportions on Group Life: Skewed Sex Ratios and Responses to Token Women." *American Journal of Sociology* 82:965–90.

Kowalewski, Mark R. 1988. "Double Stigma and Boundary Maintenance: How Gay Men Deal with AIDS." *Journal of Contemporary Ethnography* 17:211–28.

Lindesmith, Alfred, and Anselm L. Strauss. 1949. *Social Psychology*. New York: Dryden.

Lindesmith, Alfred, Anselm L. Strauss, and Norman K. Denzin. 1988. *Social Psychology*, 6th ed. Englewood Cliffs, NJ: Prentice-Hall.

Lyotard, Jean-Francois. 1979. *The Postmodern Condition*. Minneapolis: University of Minnesota Press.

Malhotra-Bentz, Valerie. 1989. *Becoming Mature: Childhood Ghosts and Spirits in Adult Life*. Hawthorne, NY: Aldine de Gruyter.

Martin, Susan E. 1978. "Sexual Politics in the Workplace: The Interactional World of Policewomen." *Symbolic Interaction* 1:44–60.

Marx, Karl. [1852] 1983. "From the Eighteenth Brumaire of Louis Bonaparte." Pp. 287–323 in *The Portable Karl Marx*, edited by E. Kamenka. New York: Penguin.

McCall, Michal M. 1990. "The Significance of Storytelling." Pp. 145–61 in *Studies in Symbolic Interaction*, Vol. 11, edited by Norman K. Denzin. Greenwich, CT: JAI Press.

Mead, George Herbert. 1934. *Mind, Self and Society*. Chicago: University of Chicago Press.

Mills, C. Wright. 1959. *The Sociological Imagination*. New York: Oxford.

Mitchell, Juliet. 1982. "Introduction—I." Pp. 1–26 in *Feminine Sexuality: Jacques Lacan and the ecole freudienne*, edited by J. Mitchell and J. Rose. New York: Pantheon.

Morris, Meaghan. 1988a. "Introduction: Feminism, Reading, Postmodernism." Pp. 1–18 in *The Pirate's Fiancee: Feminism, Reading, Postmodernism*, edited by M. Morris. London: Verso.

———. 1988b. "At Henry Parkes Motel." *Cultural Studies* 2:1–47.

Mulvey, Laura. 1982. "Visual Pleasure and Narrative Cinema." *Screen* (Autumn):412–28.

New York Times. 1988. November 17, p. 46.

Power, Martha Bauman. 1985. "The Ritualization of Emotional Conduct in Early Childhood." Pp. 213–27 in *Studies in Symbolic Interaction*, Vol. 6, edited by N. K. Denzin. Greenwich, CT: JAI Press.

Reynolds, Larry T. 1990. *Interactionism: Exposition and Critique*. 2nd ed. Dix Hills, NY: General Hall.

Risman, Barbara J. 1982. "College Women and Sororities: The Social Construction and Reaffirmation of Gender Roles." *Urban Life* 11:231–52.

Rose, Jacqueline. 1982. "Introduction–II." Pp. 27–58 in *Feminine Sexuality: Jacques Lacan and the Ecole Freudienne*, edited by J. Mitchell and J. Rose. New York: Pantheon.

Smith, Dorothy E. 1979. "A Sociology for Women." Pp. 225–263 in *The Prism of Sex: Essays in the Sociology of Knowledge*, edited by J. Sherman and E. Beck. Madison: University of Wisconsin Press.

Stoller, Robert J. 1968. *Sex and Gender. Vol. 1: The Development of Masculinity and Femininity*. New York: Jason Aronson.

Stone, Gregory P. 1962. "Appearance and the Self." Pp. 86–118 in *Human Behavior and Social Processes*, edited by A. M. Rose. Boston: Houghton Mifflin.

Sullivan, Harry Stack. 1953. *The Interpersonal Theory of Psychiatry*. New York: Norton.

West, Candace, and Don Zimmerman. 1987. "Doing Gender." *Gender & Society* 1:125–51.

Williams, Norma. 1990. *The Mexican American Family: Tradition and Change*. Dix Hills, NY: General Hall.

Chapter 11

You Are Who You Know:
A Network Approach to Gender

Lynn Smith-Lovin and J. Miller McPherson

In one sense, it is impossible to have a network theory of gender. While most social theories characterize actors in terms of their individual attributes, the distinctive feature of the network approach is that actors are only understood in terms of their relationships to one another. In its pure form, network theory views actors as identically endowed, interchangeable nodes. Social processes and individual outcomes are determined only by patterns of relationships among actors (Blau 1989, p. 53).[1] How can we apply a theoretical perspective based on relationships to an individual attribute like gender?

Our argument here will share some features with the West-Fenstermaker chapter in this volume. West and Fenstermaker suggest that gender is an interactional accomplishment; viewing it as an individual attribute effectively reduces gender to biological sex.[2] The network perspective suggests that much of what we characterize as masculine or feminine is the product of social relationships in which men and women are embedded; structural positions defined by patterns of relationships affect perceptions, beliefs, resources, and contingencies. Such effects, taken together with the fact that positions are linked into systematic sequences (one example of which is career ladders), allow network theory to explain how small, seemingly inconsequential differences between males and females in childhood or early adulthood can be transformed over the life course into dramatic levels of gender segregation and inequality.

To understand the uniquely sociological nature of the network perspective, it is useful to contrast it with other major disciplinary models. Both economists and psychologists view the individual as the bearer of significant attributes that affect behavior in response to social situations. Microeconomic theory calls some of these attributes tastes (or preferences). Of course, choices are always made within constraints; the primary types of constraints recognized by economists are endowments and the prices of things in markets. Endowments include biologically inherited abilities (another type of individual attribute) as well as resources one is given by parents or others. Since discrimination within markets is an anomaly for neoclassical economists, men and women are assumed to face the same market constraints. Thus, if microeconomic men and women make systematically different choices, economists see it as because they have different tastes (e.g., from early socialization) or because they are maximizing utility while faced with different endowments (e.g., women may anticipate more discontinuous careers because of childbearing, so they might make rational investment decisions based on this fact).

The network perspective differs from the economic view in at least one key way. In microeconomic models, tastes or preferences are exogenous to the system; they are assumed not to change as the result of one's position or relations with others. Network theory, on the other hand, argues that these preferences are determined by the relationships in which a person is embedded. These relationships (and thus tastes) are endogenous to many phenomena of economic interest (e.g., occupational settings). In addition to this fundamental disagreement, the network perspective also elaborates the economic view in leading us to think about the local rationality created by one's network position. While contemporary microeconomic analysts recognize that people make choices based on limited, imperfect information, they take the distribution of that information as given and typically consider only the cost of acquiring more. Network analysis highlights the highly structured nature of information availability; what we know (and, therefore, what seems rational) is a function of the relationships we have with others. The tastes and information with which we operate constrain our choices in ways much more fundamental and socially structured than economic models typically recognize.

Sociobiological and psychological approaches also see individuals as important carriers of gender-differentiated traits. While sociobiologists regard traits as genetically transmitted and psychologists treat them as encoded in relatively stable personalities by early socialization, both perspectives agree that adult men and women are fundamentally different. In these views, adult gender differences are relatively unchanging traits that lead men and women to respond in fundamentally different ways even when confronted by similar social situations.

In contrast, network theory locates the source of stability of gender differentiation in the stability of network relations and the location of positions in coherent career paths. It assumes that the important individual characteristics remain malleable throughout the life course, and that individuals continue to respond to changes in their structural positions with shifts in their beliefs, attitudes, and behaviors. Changing the set of relationships in which a person is embedded changes the person.

Social network theory thus explains the changes in society and the experiences of individuals in terms of changes in the web of relationships that constitute the social structure. If we broaden the network approach slightly to consider both the distribution of positions *and* the pattern of relations among positions (Blau 1989), we have the potential for a general, powerful perspective that explains how gender differences cumulate, why such differences are often perceived as larger than research indicates they actually are, and how policy interventions might alter the current gender inequality.

In this chapter, we hope to accomplish several tasks. First, we will briefly review the major concepts of network theory. Then we will review the empirical research on gender and networks and mention its shortcomings. In the final section, we will assess the theoretical contributions of this network research for sociological theory and for feminist social change.

Network Concepts

A network consists of a set of *nodes* (also called points), and a set of *relations* linking these points (Knoke and Kuklinski 1982). Often, the nodes in a network are human individuals. In this case, the relations may be connections between these individuals such as "is a friend of," "discusses important matters with," "gives orders to," "goes to for advice," or "goes on a date with." Nodes could represent organizations (e.g., McPherson 1982), face-to-face groups (McPherson 1983), societies (Breiger 1974), or any other unit capable of bearing a relationship to other units. All of the networks we consider in this chapter will have individuals as nodes. Detailed analyses of the structure of ties focus on patterns like transitivity (do the people that X likes like each other?), reachability (does person X have a tie to someone who has a tie to person Y?), centrality (how easily can X "reach" all of the people in the net?), and vulnerability (what would happen if person X was removed from the net?).

When we shift our focus to an entire network rather than dyadic relations, we can represent the system by an adjacency matrix, in which there is both a row and a column for each individual, and the entries in the matrix (often zeros and ones) indicate the presence and absence of connections between the individuals. When we focus on a single person, we essentially abstract a single row and column from the adjacency matrix. When we do this, we are limiting our attention to only connections between the focal person (called *ego*) and the others (*alters*) to whom he or she is connected. This limited slice of the whole network is called an *ego network*.

Ego Networks and Their Characteristics

An ego network is the set of relations defined by an individual and his or her contacts with others. Common ego network variables include the size, density, and heterogeneity of the alters to whom an individual is tied (Marsden 1987, p. 124). Size is simply the number of alters to whom one is linked. An individual who has network connections to more alters is more socially integrated than someone who has few connections. Network density is an inverse measure of the range of alters to whom a respondent is connected. Dense, heavily interconnected interpersonal environments often contain less diverse others and have greater potential than less interconnected ego nets for both social support and social influence. Density is often operationalized by the proportion of possible ties among alters that are present, but also can be measured by the mean intensity or strength of ties among alters. The density measure ranges from zero, when none of an individual's alters know of one another, to unity, when each alter is closely tied to all others.

The heterogeneity of a personal network measures the diversity of persons an individual can contact within his or her interpersonal environment. High diversity indicates contacts with multiple spheres of activity; a diverse network allows one access to information from multiple, nonoverlapping sources, which researchers have found to be advantageous for instrumental purposes like finding a job (Granovetter 1974) or locating an illegal abortionist (Lee 1965). Heterogeneous ties can only occur, of course, when there is heterogeneity in the population. The more diversity there is among individuals, the greater the chance that a network tie will link people who are different from one another. So, a network embedded in a firm consisting mostly of men will have little gender heterogeneity in the ego networks of its workers, while a firm with a 50-50 distribution of men and women could in principle have much diversity in the workers' ego nets.

There is a multivariate character to this relationship between the distribution of attributes and the heterogeneity of ego networks. Blau (1977) pointed out that the correlation among attributes structures the degree to which homogeneity on one characteristic implies homogeneity on others. When, for instance, all women in a system are paid low wages and all men are paid high wages, then all ties between people with similar income will be same sex.

Heterogeneity of contacts is measured in two ways. A concern with diversity per se leads to measures based on differences among alters in a respondent's network (standard deviations or indices of qualitative variation of alters' characteristics). A focus on intergroup relations leads to indicators that assess differences between the respondent and the alters to whom he or she is tied. Perhaps surprisingly, such measures are often not strongly related; Marsden (1990, footnote 7) finds the correlations of diversity-based and difference-based personal network measures range between .47 and .63.

The measures described above all use the individual as the unit of analysis, and translate network characteristics into attribute terms. Often the distinction between relational and attribute analysis becomes blurred as units are characterized in terms of their relational qualities. For example, we can collapse the complete pattern of friendship relations in a business organization into a summary of the sizes of the ego networks of the individual workers, which we may correlate with other characteristics like gender and formal authority level.

Structural Variables

Maintaining the relational character of the matrix of connections between elements allows analysis of network *structure*, or the configuration of ties that are present and absent. Such structures are useful for explaining outcomes for individuals, classes of individuals (like men and women), and the system as a whole. They offer a means for bridging the gap between macro- and microanalysis. It is important to emphasize that the *absence* of ties is just as critical to the structure as the presence of ties; it is these "holes" in the matrix of relations that differentiate structural positions within the system and that affect system operation.

One concept that will have special importance for our discussion of gender differences is *homophily*. Homophily refers to the extent to which similar nodes are more likely to have a relationship than dissimilar nodes. For example, if two whites who work within an organization are more likely to become friends than a white and an African American, then the friendship relationship is homophilous. Similarly, if two Ph.D's are more likely to discuss important matters than a Ph.D. and a high school dropout, then the discussion relationship is homophilous. It is important to note that the homophily concept does not imply that the similarity between linked nodes is a function of individual choice. It may arise as a result of ecological forces (as described in McPherson 1990). Homophily is a pattern of relationships and node characteristics, rather than a statement about the sources of that pattern.

Positions within a network are defined by the patterns of relations among actors. Although actors and their observable relations with others provide the data for identifying positions, the positions themselves are conceptually distinct from the people who occupy them. Therefore, such network positions have much in common with the traditional concepts of role and status in sociology. The contribution of network analysis is a formal definition of social position in terms of the relations it entails, a definition that is distinct from individuals and their attributes.

There are two standard ways to identify network positions (Burt 1978). The first and most commonly used is *social cohesion*, in which actors occupy the same position to the degree that they are connected directly to one another. The cliques or social circles thus identified represent closely interconnected groups of actors (whether their interconnections are exchanges, information flows, sentiment relations, or authority/power relations).

The second technique identifies equivalent positions in the social structure, which are not necessarily connected. In this case, it matters a great deal whether the graphs (or network configurations of nodes and relations) that are analyzed are labeled or unlabeled. In a labeled framework, two actors are said to occupy the same structural position (called *structural equivalence*) when they are connected to the same other actors. For example, two teachers in a university system are structurally equivalent to the extent that they teach the *same* students and have the *same* chairperson and dean. The identity of the people to whom the focal actors are tied is retained; that is why this is called a labeled approach. Cliques are special cases of structural equivalence, in the sense that all of their members are tied to each other in a similar way. Structurally equivalent actors do not, however, necessarily have to be tied directly to one another.[3]

The unlabeled approach examines the *way* that an actor is connected to others, rather than to *which* others he or she is connected. Actors who are isomorphic in this unlabeled sense are said to be *role equivalent* because they have the same types of relations to similar others. For example, two teachers would be role equivalent if they had the same types of relations with students, chairs, deans, and secretaries, even if they were at different universities. In other words, two actors are role equivalent when they are linked in similar ways to the same *positions*.

A very interesting feature of the unlabeled approach is that it is completely structural; actors can be equivalent to one another if they have similar positions even if they are distant or unreachable from each other. If these isomorphic actors have similar social outcomes, it is due to the similarity of their structural position; since their contacts need not overlap, the alternative hypothesis of diffusion or direct social influence is not tenable (Borgatti 1990).

A final network concept that will prove useful to us in describing gender differentiation is *hypernetwork*. Hypernetworks are generated whenever there exists a set of elements (in our case, individuals) linked together by a set of relations (for example, common membership in organizations), when that relation also defines a new set of elements (organizations) that are linked by relations defined by the first set of elements (individuals) (McPherson 1982, p. 227). Hypernetworks relate elements at two levels of analysis, defining the connections between elements at each level in terms of the other.[4] Studies using this conceptualization allow us to examine the differing organizational contexts in which men and women operate, and the implications of these contexts for both the individuals and organizations involved.

Gender-Related Research Questions

The network perspective leads us to several fundamental questions for gender studies. To what extent do women's and men's networks differ? What is the source of these differences? In particular, can differences at later stages of the life course be explained by earlier network patterns? Is there reason to believe that these networks differ enough to account for the differences in women's and men's opportunities, aspirations, and behaviors? How do these patterns influence the macrolevel structures in which men and women are embedded? What are the implications for policies affecting gender inequality?

Below we briefly review the literature on networks and gender. We emphasize the life course differentiation and organizational contexts in which network differences appear. The research suggests that homophily by gender in early ties to playmates and some subtle tendencies to respond differentially to network structures lead males and females to move into very different social worlds during the school years. These different locations in the social structure for young men and women, accentuated by women's greater involvement in childrearing, produce movement by women into kin-related rather than occupationally related flows of information and opportunity. Women, located in regions of the network rich in information about family and household, see the world as organized around these themes. Men, participating in flows of information about career, money, and recreational pursuits, are exposed to vastly greater opportunities for mobility in that world. The core insight of the network perspective is that small differences in access to information will accumulate over the course of a career to produce large differences in attainment. When we observe the system at one point in time, we may observe gender differences in aspirations and values that appear to be affecting their careers; we argue that this relationship is spurious because both beliefs and career outcomes depend on the structure of network contacts. What appears in cross section to be an innate or fundamental difference between men and women is merely a reflection of the fact that men and women are usually located in different regions of the network. We now turn to the development of the first gender differences in networks in early childhood.

Networks in Childhood

By the time children enter school, they have learned that gender is a permanent personal characteristic. At about the same developmental stage, researchers first observe homophily (the choice of similar companions) in play patterns and a tendency for girls to play in smaller groups than boys (Block 1979; Lever 1978). There is disagreement about whether these differences are socialized through the provision of toys that encourage dyadic interaction for girls and team play for boys (Block 1979) or represent some more fundamental tendency.[5]

Hallinan and her colleagues have done the most comprehensive studies of young children's network relationships. They have studied transitivity in sentiment relations and how intransitive relations get resolved. An intransitive sentiment relation is one in which, for any three people in a triad (ABC), A likes B and B likes C, but A does not like C (Hallinan 1974).[6] Children show less tolerance for intransitivity as they get older (Leinhardt 1973; Hallinan 1974). There appear to be gender differences in how intransitivity is resolved. Eder and Hallinan (1978) found that girls are more likely to resolve intransitivity by deleting friendship choices, while boys are more likely to add them. Suppose, for example, that A likes B and B likes C, but there is no liking relationship between A and C. Young boys in the A position are more likely to resolve the intransitivity by developing a liking relation to C; young girls in the same position are more likely to resolve the intransitivity by ceasing to like B.

Intransitivity is more tolerated when it involves cross-sex members (Hallinan and Kubitschek 1990), and is more likely to be resolved by adding a choice if that choice would link same-sex children (Hallinan and Kubitschek 1988). Hallinan's data dramatically demonstrate how sex barriers to youthful friendships influence the resolution of relationship intransitivity and the development of social networks. Children are significantly more likely to resolve intransitivity by deleting a cross-sex friendship than by adding another cross-sex friendship. In fact, most youths are more likely to delete a same-sex choice than to resolve the intransitivity by adding a cross-sex one (Hallinan and Kubitschek, 1990).[7]

The Hallinan results are important primarily because of their implications for the emergence of cliques and larger network structures. Youths tend to have friends who are popular peers of the same sex; this tie is likely to be reciprocated if both youths are popular. This stable dyad is most likely to expand to a stable, transitive triad if the third person is also of the same sex, is popular, and reciprocates the choice. These transitive triads are likely to add more people (creating more triads) to create cliques of the "popular crowd" of more same-sex people who will then form further friendships of their own among the new triads created (Hallinan and Kubitschek 1988, p. 91). Girls are likely to be excluded from these cliques (or to be in smaller versions of their own) because they are less likely to extend or receive friendship ties. Since each new member of a clique creates an intransitive structure (Hallinan and Sorenson 1973) that must be resolved by adding ties if the clique is to grow, girls are less likely to join larger cliques; they tend to resolve intransitivity by dropping, rather than adding, friendships. Simple, small tendencies toward homophily and differences in resolving problems in the structure of their relationships mean that boys and girls will move toward very different social circles. Their worlds become gender segregated, with boys in larger, more heterogeneous cliques.[8]

There is evidence that networks and knowledge coevolve, with the connections between individuals creating shared knowledge, which in turn shifts interaction propensities (Carley 1986a, 1986b). Over time, knowledge overlap increases between network alters and decreases between people not connected in the network. As the networks become more organized around gender, the similarities between males and females, so apparent in the early years (Maccoby and Jacklin 1974), begin to subside as differences emerge. The joint effects of shared knowledge and friendship relationships lead to greater and greater gender differentiation. As boys and girls have less shared information, they have less to talk about, which leads to less contact, and so on. Thus, very small initial differences in physiology, appearance, dispositions, etc., can lead to exaggerated differences in patterns of contact between males and females. If we assume that there is some initial bias in the knowledge that comes to male and female children (e.g., through normative forces or differential contact with same-sex parents), we can see that the homophilous networks that begin early in the school years may greatly magnify the impact of initially trivial differences in information.

An example will illustrate how small differences may be magnified over the childhood years through differential networks. Imagine that Jim and Jane come to preschool with similar endowments. They associate with same-sex friends. As a result, they are in groups largely of their own sex. Jim and his male buddies have a little more contact with their fathers than the girls do (homophily works in child/adult relations too); they talk about the contacts that they have from adult males in their group, combining their information and interpretations. (Of course, both the boys and girls have much more contact with female adults— their mothers and female teachers.) As the school years progress, Jim's group learns male slang, learns boy games, gets exposure to electronics and other male mysteries. Jill doesn't hear about these things, because the few girls that she hangs out with don't hang out with their fathers, and there are simply fewer people from whom to gather such esoteric knowledge. Boys may seem disgustingly different in the early grades and alluringly different at puberty, but they seem like fundamentally different creatures than the girls. As high school progresses, Jane's network has more information about secretarial and nursing jobs; Jim's draws in concrete detail about engineering and military work. Jim hears about schools that are further from home; Jane hears about girl's schools and small, liberal arts colleges that her two friends' sisters have attended. They hear about different majors after they get into college, too. Notice that the network model uses the homophily principle (an empirical generalization) and the spread of information through networks to explain how differences arise and are maintained between boys and girls. The content of the differences is determined by the history of the system; adult men and women have different information to transmit to children. Some of these differences develop because of women's childbearing and the network influences it exerts (see discussion below).

Having discussed how gender differences might arise in childhood and accumulate over the school years, we now review the literature on personal networks in the adult years. Most of this research is descriptive in character; we will learn *how* men's and women's networks differ. But we should keep in mind that such adult differences are considered endogenous in a network perspective. Network researchers view positions in adult networks as the result of a chain of earlier network positions. Who we know and (therefore) what we come to know in early school years determine the educational and personal careers that will lead us to jobs, marriage, families, and friends in adult life. These adult network positions, in turn, influence the opportunities and aspirations that we display to others in a cross-sectional view of the adult population.

Personal Networks in the Adult Years

A crucial change in people's lives as they mature is in the character of the organizations and groups they experience. When children are very young, the family is the major group experienced, with possible minor forays into medical and religious settings. With increasing age come steep increases in the amount of time spent in organizational settings outside the family. From this period until death, life is a sequence of incredibly diverse organizational settings, the coordination of which determines almost all outcomes for the individual. As people pass through these settings, experiences in each change the probabilities of future sequences. Early family and school experiences determine access to later educational organizations, which affect early labor force experiences, which determine career trajectories through the corporate world.

Social networks are generated by organizations, in that organizations provide the settings in which contacts develop (McPherson and Smith-Lovin 1982, 1987). At the same time, networks modify the flow of people from one setting to another because they are the major source of information about, and recruitment to, organizations; networks are also a potent force shaping organizational attrition (McPherson, Popielarz, and Drobnic 1992; McPherson and Popielarz 1990). Since gender differences in network structure could account for gender differences in the vast array of outcomes mediated by organizations, we will sketch some of the relevant research results on gender differences in adult networks.

Men and women usually have networks of similar size in the adult years (Fischer 1982; Marsden 1987), but women have fewer ties to non-kin (Fischer and Oliker 1983; Wellman 1985; Marsden 1987). Networks in adulthood show strong homophily on sex and other characteristics like race, ethnicity, religion, age, and education (Marsden 1988). Women typically have more ties to kin and neighborhood, which tends to increase the age and sex heterogeneity of their contacts while reducing racial, ethnic, and religious diversity. Men, on the other hand, have more ties to coworkers and voluntary group members, which decreases age and sex diversity in those ties (Marsden 1990).

But, of course, these social associations depend heavily on opportunities for social contact (Blau 1977, p. 281). Most of the gender differences in composition disappear when researchers control for variables like employment status, marital status, and family composition; a slight tendency remains for women to have more frequent and more diverse kin ties than men (Hurlburt and Acock 1990). There is also some evidence that even among employed men and women, men are more likely to consider coworkers to be friends (Campbell 1988).

Fischer and Oliker (1983) found that life course factors seem to be particularly important in the development of gender-differentiated networks (see also Marsden 1987, footnote 15). Young, unmarried women and men have personal networks of roughly the same size. Gender differences accumulate, however, as young adults move into marriage and childbearing years. Married women, especially those with children, have fewer people that they can count on for support like personal advice, help with odd jobs, or lending money. The exclusivity with which infant care is usually delegated to women may be a fundamental factor; by the time men become involved with childrearing of older children (Crano and Aronoff 1978), women's networks may be fundamentally altered. Wellman (1985) found that having children significantly reduced cross-sex contacts for women, moving them into a female world of play groups and PTAs. A new study by Lynne Zucker (reported in Aldrich 1989, p. 124) using the "small world" technique showed that female networks were more densely interconnected, while men's are more extensive and less tightly linked.[9] The shortest paths in Zucker's study involved women respondents using female network links to find a female target in a sex-segregated setting.

Let us again use an example to illustrate how the network forces we have been discussing affect gender differentiation. Imagine that Jim and Jane meet (perhaps through mutual, homophilous friends) and marry. Jim is serious about his career as an engineer; Jane is equally serious about her nursing. When their first child is born, however, Jane's mother comes to visit for two weeks; Jane begins to use her sister as a babysitter for daytime care while she is working. Since she is breastfeeding, she spends more time with the baby than Jim; she talks about physical and psychological aspects of this experience with the other women at work and in her family. Jim's experiences as a father evoke less discussion with his fellow fathers. Because more of her time is taken up with the baby, Jane's networks become more centered on neighbor-hood and kin, to some extent at the expense of her work and voluntary association friends. Jim's work and group ties are less altered. He is now more likely to suggest a work friend as a dinner companion than Jane; Jane is more likely to suggest an extended family activity or neighbors with similar-age children.

The conventional wisdom is that women's focus on family is the result of their having lower paying jobs than their husbands. However, a small study concentrating on women in high-prestige careers found that even this select group significantly shifted its reference groups with the onset of childbearing (Zanna Crosby, and Lowenstein 1987). Half of the mar-ried women without children in this study had all-male reference groups; they reported that they compared themselves to these men to assess their career achievement and success. Only 14 percent of those with children used only men as a reference. Almost all of the mothers began to think mostly of other women as the relevant alters to whom they should compare their performance. In fact, the majority of the mothers (59 percent) had all-female reference groups.

Fischer and Oliker (1983) also found that women are much more likely to know people through their husband's coworker networks than men are to know their wives' work friends. On one hand, this finding implies that women benefit more from their spouses' network position than do men; women use their husbands' work contacts to extend their own ties. On the other hand, Aldrich (1989) has suggested that the pattern may indicate that women are more supportive of their husbands' networks than vice versa. Contacts that women make through their husbands may be less useful to women in work-related spheres, and supportive only of their roles as wives.

In a study of recent job changers in four occupations (programmers, personnel workers, real estate agents, and sales workers) Campbell (1988) reinforced the view that women are less tied to occupationally relevant others and more affected by life course factors and geographic mobility than men. She found that women know people in fewer occu-pations than men; in particular, their networks have a "floor" that eliminates lower status occupations. The size and status composition of women's occupational networks are negatively affected by having chil-dren under six years of age and by changing jobs in response to their spouses' mobility. When the women in Campbell's study moved with their husbands, their networks reached fewer high-status and fewer low-status occupations. Men, of course, are much less likely to have moved because of a wife's career; when they do, they are more likely to be involved in national professional networks that do not suffer as greatly with the dislocation. Men also were affected less by the presence of small children in the family.

Campbell argued that these findings indicate that women's networks are less well-suited than men's to job searches and subsequent occupational advancements. Strong ties like kinship are more likely to transmit redundant information; your mother, your father, and your brother are likely to know the same information about the same job opportunities (because their interconnections are so dense). Discussion relations or friendships developed through work or work-oriented voluntary groups are more likely to carry new information that could be useful in the occupational domain.[10] Women's involvement with family, children, and neighborhood exposes them to more localized information; their personal networks are more likely to have high density. Men's ties to a wider variety of occupational settings and work-related organizations gives them important conduits through which information about such matters might flow. There is some evidence that women are less likely to search for and find jobs through their personal contacts or to gain unsolicited information in this way (Campbell 1985). When women gain jobs through female contacts, these jobs are likely to be sex segregated, female, and low paying; women who use contacts with men for locating a job are more likely to find high-status employment (Ensel and Lin 1982).

Aldrich (1989; Aldrich, Reese, and Dubini 1989) has argued that network differences are crucial for the entrepreneurial activities of women. Traditionally, low pay and short career ladders lead workers to break into self-employment. Women are much more likely than men to be faced with these employment circumstances (England and Farkas 1986). But do they have the network resources to move into an independent business environment? Aldrich (1989, p. 103) pointed out that networks are important to entrepreneurial activity in at least two ways. On the demand side, information flowing through work-related and informal networks reveals niches in opportunity structures where environmental resources can be exploited by new businesses. On the supply side, potential entrepreneurs need access to capital and other resources so that they can exploit perceived opportunities. Clearly, the fact that work establishments are extremely sex segregated (Baron and Bielby 1984) and the fact that women are not in high-ranking positions does not aid women's attempts to find entrepreneurial niches and the resources necessary to support them. The fact that women are less likely than men to be encouraged to start their own business by parents and siblings (Kalleberg 1985),[11] taken together with the large number of kinship ties that women have in their networks, means that they might lack the social support or information necessary to begin entrepreneurial activity.

Perhaps the strongest evidence for the importance of networks in entrepreneurship, however, is Aldrich et al.'s (1989) finding that there are very *few* gender differences in network structure among men and women who are already engaged in entrepreneurial activity.[12] In the U.S., Italy, and Sweden, male and female business people spent similar amounts of time developing and maintaining contacts, discussed business with the same numbers of people, and had similarly interconnected networks. The only significant gender difference was in the percentage of network ties with persons of the opposite sex: Both men and women overwhelmingly contacted men to aid their business efforts. In other words, men and women who succeeded at moving into the entrepreneurial world (or at least into organizations designed to help them enter it) were roughly role equivalent. They were connected to the same types of people in the same ways. We agree with Aldrich that these network patterns are probably necessary for successful entry into entrepreneurial activity. In addition, the voluntary organizations in which he found his respondents probably help to develop the network resources to aid the business start. Below we explore some of the organizational sources of these network configurations, and help explain why women are so rarely found in these entrepreneurially advantageous positions.

Organizational Ties and the Networks They Create

As noted above, weak ties in the informal network of relations are important channels through which vital information about the system passes. Boissevain (1974) and Granovetter (1974) showed that the indirect links generated by such informal contacts explain a great deal about the operation of education and employment systems. McPherson and Smith-Lovin (1982) argued that voluntary association memberships are an important source for these weak ties. Voluntary group activities create an opportunity structure for tie information. Earlier research has shown that members who become acquainted through organizational activities influence one another's behavior (Whiting 1980) and provide information about matters outside their immediate environments (Jones and Crawford 1980).

Women are doubly disadvantaged in developing network resources within voluntary associations. First, they belong to fewer organizations than men (Scott 1957; Booth 1972). Perhaps more importantly, however, they belong to much smaller groups and to groups that are organized around social and religious activities rather than work-related activities (McPherson and Smith-Lovin 1982). The size of the organizations to which women and men belong is important because large organizations generate a larger opportunity for weak ties; small women's organizations may also be less salient and politically powerful in the community. McPherson and Smith-Lovin (1982) showed that women's groups are, on the average, one third the size of men's groups.

The hypernetwork created by voluntary organization memberships is, if anything, more gender segregated than the world of work. Nearly one half of the organizations in a study of ten communities were exclusively female, while one fifth were all male (McPherson and Smith-Lovin 1986). From the point of view of the individual, the typical female membership generates face-to-face contact with about twenty-nine other members, less than four of whom are men. Male memberships, on the other hand, produce contact with over thirty-seven other members (because their organizations are bigger), eight of whom are women. Men's contacts are both more numerous and more heterogeneous. Business-related and political groups are more likely to be gender integrated than social, child-centered, or religious groups. From the organizational point of view, the few women who belong to these gender-integrated voluntary associations have key positions, which may provide bridges between male and female domains. Far from integrating men and women, the development of ties within the voluntary sector tends to lower the diversity of contacts (McPherson and Smith-Lovin 1987; Marsden 1990). McPherson and Smith-Lovin (1987) show that choice of friends *within* the groups is a relatively unimportant factor; it is the opportunity structure created by the groups' composition that leads to most gender segregation. Jane's PTA committee and women's bridge club don't do as much for her nursing career as Jim's professional engineer's society and Rotary Club aid his work, although the women's groups may provide more social support.

Networks within Work Organizations

While not as segregated as voluntary organizations, work settings also create an opportunity structure that differentiates men and women. Women and men historically have worked in different occupations (Beller 1984); sex segregation at work is even stronger at the establishment level where workers actually interact (Baron and Bielby 1984). Women are found in positions with shorter career ladders, less authority, and less discretionary power (Kanter 1977; Miller 1975; South, Bonjian, Corder, and Markham 1982). While they may interact with powerful men in other occupations (e.g., nurses with doctors, secretaries with managers), these contacts are likely to be routinized and uniplex; workers in the same job title are more likely to share multiplex relations (two nodes linked by multiple ties like "is friends with," "shares information with," and "goes to for advice").

In addition to these differences in formal position, women are usually less central in informal communication, advice, friendship, and influence networks (Ibarra 1989, 1990; Lincoln and Miller 1979; Miller, Labowitz, and Fry 1975). This finding is understandable since women are underrepresented at upper ranks in businesses, and rank is correlated with centrality in informal networks. There is substantial evidence, however, that even controlling for rank, women are less well-connected in the informal structure. Put differently, women are less able to translate valued personal attributes like rank, authority, education, and job experience into network centrality (Miller et al. 1975; Miller 1986; Ibarra 1989).

The composition and function of women's work groups is important for understanding their networks within businesses. Women in high ranks are more likely to be in a distinct minority and their token position puts them under special interactional pressures (Kanter 1977). Brass (1985) argued that this basic fact of organizational demography might account for the centrality findings. If high-status women are usually minorities, faced with a large number of dissimilar others, they may be less central in informal networks simply because they are different. In fact, Brass (1985) found that men and women were equally central in informal networks when he studied an organization where women were fairly equally represented. However, he found that the informal networks were quite gender segregated and that the women were central in networks of other women. They were much less likely to be integrated into men's networks or to have ties to a dominant coalition (a clique of four high-ranking men) that predicted promotion during the next three years. Brass (1985) and Ibarra (1989, 1990) found that work group composition was very important in shaping women's informal networks. Women who worked in gender-integrated departments had more male contacts (and more subsequent success, in Brass' study). Ibarra (1989) found that department function was much more important for women than for men in determining centrality: Women tended to be more central when they belonged to departments mediating critical organizational contingencies (like accounting) or when their departments had a large number of contacts with outside clients.

All of these findings support the general image developed by Kanter (1977) and Miller (1986) that women and men occupy very different network positions within work organizations, even when they have the same rank or title. If we compare Jim to his fellow engineer, Sally, we likely would see that Jim would be closer friends with his (male) boss and the predominantly male clients on the job. The contractors are more likely to come to Jim for advice, even though Sally has the same degree from the same university. Jim goes out for beer after work with a large group of other engineers (including some at higher and lower ranks), while Sally is close friends with the two other female engineers who work at the firm.

Women generally have less opportunity, influence, and access to the information that affects their ability to get things done. However, we stress that a network perspective would not see these patterns as evidence that some fundamental difference between men and women (whether biological or socialized) leads to these economically disadvantageous network positions at work. Rather, a network researcher would look to earlier structural forces (like network position in education, kinship, voluntary groups, or friendship circles) to explain how men and women came to these gender-differentiated positions within work organizations. Such forces operate to make men and women different, sharing less information and background. These differences then lower the probability that they will interact.

The Effects of Network Position

The research reviewed above shows that there are gender differences in personal networks and network positions in a variety of contexts. To what extent can such contrasts in the social worlds of men and women explain gender stereotypes and inequality? Perhaps the most basic point is that one's network—the relationships in which one is embedded—determine the roles that one enacts in daily life (Stryker 1980, 1987). Women, with more kin and fewer coworkers in their personal networks, will spend more time occupying the identities of daughter, mother, or sister, rather than worker, professional, expert, etc. The behavioral and emotional implications of this allocation are substantial (Smith-Lovin and Heise 1988; Smith-Lovin 1990). Staying tied to kin encourages a traditional approach to many issues, in both gender relations and other areas (Waite, Goldscheider, and Witberger 1986). Attitudes are strongly shaped by such structural positions (see review in Kiecolt 1988, pp. 388–89).

Network ties can affect things as basic as health and wealth. Researchers have found that participation in a variety of relationships leads to better health and longevity (Berkman and Breslow 1983; House, Landis, and Umberson 1988a; Moen, Dempster-McClain, and Williams 1989a, 1989b). Similar results are found for mental health (see review in

Mirowsky and Ross 1989). The mechanism here probably involves care, information, and activity. It operates as a double-edged sword for women, since although their larger volume of kin ties provides them with more social support it also means that they will perform a caretaking role more often than men. Perhaps this is why both men *and* women receive most health benefits from their ties to women; widowers often suffer great decline in mental and physical health after their wives die (House, Umberson, and Landis 1988b, p. 300).

While the homophilic structure of networks benefits women's health relative to men's (because they have more ties to other women), it works against their economic well-being. Extensive, weak ties to nonfamilial sources are most useful for finding a job and achieving higher income (Granovetter 1974; Lin, Ensel, and Vaughn 1981; Lin, Vaughn, and Ensel 1983).[13] Within organizations, centrality in men's networks is more useful for gaining promotion and influence (Brass 1985), probably because men dominate the upper ranks of most businesses.

Kanter (1977) provided the most complete account of how women's positions within organizations shift attitudes, values, and behaviors in a way that reinforces gender stereotypes. She argued that the short career ladders on which women's jobs were located led to attitudinal and behavioral effects that reinforced stereotypes that women were not career oriented. Research on the personality effects of job characteristics reinforces this perspective. Challenging, high-opportunity work enhances workers' cognitive complexity and other positively evaluated characteristics, molding people who have "good" jobs to have the characteristics that we often erroneously think of as prerequisites to such jobs (Kohn and Schooler 1983; Spenner 1988).

Similarly, the lack of discretionary power, influence, and upward mobility of women in Kanter's study led to unfavorable relationships with their subordinates. Employees have much to gain from network ties with a powerful boss. Impressionistic accounts of mentoring and sponsorship indicate that such subordinates are often pulled upward through the structure (Powell 1988, pp. 185–88). At the very least, an upwardly mobile boss creates a vacant position that increases the probability of promotion for employees in the next lower tier, if internal promotion is favored over outside recruitment (Stewman 1988). Finally, Brass (1985) showed that ties to a boss in the "dominant coalition" of a company increases one's centrality, influence, and chances of promotion.

Perhaps the most influential of Kanter's ideas has been her discussion of how proportions of men and women in work groups can affect performance. Kanter (1977, pp. 206–42) put most emphasis on the perceptual effects of being a token; token status makes you stand out in a group. Observers are more likely to remember your actions (including mistakes), and to selectively perceive stereotypic phenomena. However, she also discussed the network effects of such minority representation, noting that tokens are less likely to have the informal relationships with co-workers that buffer stress, make life pleasant, and provide job-relevant information. While later research has shown that being a *low-status* token is a much more serious detriment to interaction and success-ful performance than being a high-status token (see Williams' chapter in this volume; see also Ridgeway's chapter regarding status effects in group interaction), simply being *different* means that one is faced with mostly heterophilous ties to peers in the work group. These distribu-tional characteristics influence the composition and stability of one's network relations with coworkers. On the positive side, there is evi-dence that these heterophilous ties are likely to provide more support for the advancement of women when they are in the minority (as opposed to a more threatening proportion of the group) (South, Mark-ham, Bonjian, and Corder 1987); the ties to male coworkers may also be advantageous for centrality, influence, and advancement (Brass 1985).

The effects of heterogeneity on work group functioning may serve to reinforce gender segregation in work establishments. Homogeneous work groups are characterized by more frequent contact and communi-cation (Pfeffer 1983); turnover is higher in heterogeneous organizations (Wagner, Pfeiffer, and O'Reilly 1984). According to Wharton and Baron (1988), men are less satisfied with their work in settings that have equal numbers of men and women than when the setting is dominated nu-merically by *either* men or women. If work is more enjoyable and effi-cient in settings that are segregated, and if tokens are under interaction-al pressures that make their survival in groups less likely, we can see that homophily processes in social networks will operate as a social control mechanism to continue sex-segregated work establishments. If men and women are exposed to differential information and oppor-tunities based on their network position, they will confront different menus of opportunity. If employers then infer characteristics of individ-ual men and women from modal behavior patterns, a practice called statistical discrimination (England and Farkas 1986, pp. 125–26), the current segregated structure of the system will perpetuate itself even if there is substantial movement of men and women through positions within the system (Jacobs 1988).

Shortcomings of the Network Literature on Gender

While the studies discussed above contribute a great deal to our understanding of how men and women occupy different social worlds, the network literature has some serious shortcomings from a feminist perspective. Perhaps the most frustrating feature of the network approach for a scholar interested in gender segregation and inequality has been the emphasis on technique rather than substance in this literature. A casual survey of the leading journal, *Social Networks*, or the annual meetings of the International Society for the Study of Social Networks reveals that most network researchers devote their attention to developing new formal models or statistical techniques. Applying these techniques to substantively important problems has been an infrequent, less prestigious activity.

The second major shortcoming is an outgrowth of limitations to those modeling techniques, however. Until recently, network analysis typically required a complete matrix of all relations among all elements in the system to study the structure (see discussion in McPherson 1982). This feature effectively limited network studies to small, unrepresentative populations, typically located through a naturally formed group. Since voluntary groups and work establishments tend to be highly sex segregated, choosing such settings for study ensured that most classic network data sets were almost entirely single sex. The tendency to study elites and other "important" collectivities ensured that they were almost always male. Studies of representative populations that allow the systematic analysis of gender differentiation are a recent development (see McPherson and Smith-Lovin 1982, 1986; Marsden 1987, 1988). The limitation of these studies of more representative populations is that such studies almost necessarily focus on ego networks (i.e., the personal network reported by a respondent in a survey). While we can glean much information about network contacts from such an approach, viewing network variables as attributes in a survey context encourages an individualistic view that is antithetical to the unique contributions of the network perspective. Discussion of ego nets leads one easily into the language of choice; we may develop an image that men and women are different because they choose to associate with different types of people (see, for example, the heavily individualistic language of the Hallinan tradition). Researchers analyzing ego nets lose sight of the coevolution of networks and organizational contexts in which they are often generated. We must keep in mind that network ties both reflect the opportunity structure created by the settings in which people operate (McPherson 1990; Marsden 1990) and determine recruitment and attrition into and out of those settings (McPherson et al. 1992). There may be very little choice involved; we cannot have discussions with and become friends with people we don't meet (McPherson and Smith-Lovin 1987).

Finally, most substantive network studies concentrate on one type of relation (e.g., friendship or discussion). Since the few studies that look at more than one type of tie indicate that influence, communication, work flow, and affective networks can have very different structures and very different impact on outcomes, it will be increasingly important to study these features simultaneously (Brass 1985; Ibarra 1989, 1990). Again, to ignore the differentiated nature of people's connections to one another misses the embedded nature of economic and social life that is the major insight of the network perspective. [See Granovetter (1985) for an excellent discussion of the implications of embeddedness for economic action.] To ignore the ways that structural positions are linked in career ladders makes network ties seem to be a matter of personal choice, when they may in fact be determined by earlier structures.

The Potential

As a theoretical perspective on gender, network analysis offers us a rigorous framework within which to study the social influences that create and maintain gender differences. It allows us to organize information about cross-cultural and historical variation in a way that highlights general sociological processes rather than historically particular ones. It allows us to treat multiplex relations of social and economic life within a common structure. Most importantly, it allows us to see how gender differences that seem innate might be the result of a self-maintaining system in which what we know and who we are is fundamentally shaped by our social relations with others.

The network perspective gives an interpretation for why social change is so difficult to instigate. Homophily, beginning in early childhood and reinforced by organizational structures in adult life, means that the majority of social relationships will be with others of the same sex. Therefore, any existing gender differentiation is likely to be transmitted through the network to new generations. Early differences in information available to boys and girls, men and women, will tend to be irreversible and self-maintaining as interaction and knowledge coevolve (Carley 1986a, 1986b). To the observer at any one point in time, these differences will appear to be the result of a rational allocation of individual to positions of differential activity, opportunity, and power (Kanter 1977).

Gender-based inequality differs from other inequalities, however, in the crucial bottleneck of network relations created by childbearing. Women are unique in the impact that childbearing has on their interpersonal environments. Not only do women develop very close ties to a young alter, but childbearing links women to kin in ways that are rare for men. [For an interesting parallel to race, see Stack's (1974) discussion of African American families' use of extensive kin networks]. The birth of a child both arouses the interest of kin and creates a need for support services that kin can often provide. While fathers undoubtedly experience some of this increased contact, the mother's central role in childbearing and early childraising makes the effect much stronger for them.

Childbearing often occurs in the young adult years when people are first moving into organizational settings that will structure their contacts in important ways. We suggest that these crucial events then act to create different pools of information, different opportunity structures, and different choice structures for men and women. The fact that unmarried, childless women often seem quite similar to men in many ways supports the image that childbearing may represent a network bottleneck sending men and women into very different structural career streams (Jacobs 1988). This fact points up the pivotal role that institutionalized alternatives to traditional mother-centered childrearing can play in transforming the sex-segregated occupational system. By allowing mothers to maintain contacts outside the intimate family domain, day care centers and other supports for childrearing are expected to have a large cumulative impact.

The policy implications of the network perspective are intriguing. On one hand, it offers a structural interpretation for apparently essential differences. Inequalities with structural sources can have structural solutions. On the other hand, the imbedded nature of the problem alerts us to the fact that simple interventions are not likely to be effective. [For example, see Kanter's (1977) discussion of affirmative action and the token situation it creates.] Since there is substantial gender inequality in the current system, and since women are unlikely to stop bearing children, substantial change is likely to be difficult.

To end on a more positive note, we observe that changes in the timing of events in the life course (e.g., later marriage and childbearing) can have substantial effects. If extensive networks of non-kin are developed before the strong child-induced kin ties are activated, women may not end up in a different world, just a more crowded one. If patterns of full-time employment and later childbearing continue, we may eventually observe that women have more extensive networks than men, with equal configurations of non-kin as well as a relatively larger number of kin ties.

Acknowledgments

The authors would like to thank Paula England, Herminia Ibarra, and David Krackhardt for helpful suggestions on the topic. Preparation of this chapter was supported by National Science Foundation grants SES-8821365 to McPherson and SES-9008951 to Smith-Lovin.

Notes

1. The interesting question of whether actors should be characterized in labeled or unlabeled terms (i.e., whether two actors must be connected similarly to the *same* others to be considered alike) will be discussed below.

2. Unless gender differences are biological in some sense (e.g., hormonal, instinctive, genetic), they are not truly individual in nature. If they are shaped by socialization or (as this chapter argues) largely elicited by situations, then they are fundamentally relational and/or cultural rather than individual in nature.

3. However, Borgatti (1990) pointed out that structural equivalence carries a strong element of cohesion with it; actors who are structurally equivalent can be no more than network distance two from one another (that is, they must be reachable in two ties through the other actors that lead them to be structurally equivalent).

4. Breiger (1974) has called this conceptualization a dual network.

5. One possibility is that girls' somewhat greater maturation and/or lower activity levels might predispose them toward more intensive, focused play relationships. Evidence on sex differences on such characteristics is mixed, however (Maccoby and Jacklin 1974). Even if one assumes such a difference, the question of its origin would still be open to socialization, personality, and sociobiological interpretations.

6. Balance theories suggest that unbalanced or intransitive sentiment relations cause cognitive distress, are unstable, and are likely to be resolved in favor of a transitive structure (by either removing some of the positive relations or adding the A-C link; Heider 1958; Abelson and Rosenberg 1958), and research has supported this prediction (Holland and Leinhardt 1970; Leinhardt 1973; Hallinan 1974).

7. There is a race-by-sex interaction on the likelihood of resolving intransitivity in this way. Cross-sex friendships are somewhat more acceptable to black boys and less acceptable to white girls, while white boys and black girls occupy an intermediate position (Hallinan and Kubitschek, unpublished).

8. The networks are more heterogeneous primarily because boys are more tolerant of intransivity, and intransitive relationships are more likely to be cross sex and cross race.

9. Respondents are asked to send a message to a contact person they do not know using only people with whom they are acquainted. In Zucker's variant, contact targets were drawn from the male world, the female world, or an integrated setting. In half the cases, the respondent could use any acquaintance; in the other half, respondents were restricted to passing the message only to someone of the same sex.

10. There is abundant evidence on this point, but most of it is collected in studies focusing on males only [see, for example, Lin et al. (1981, 1983) or the classic study by Granovetter (1974)].

11. Spouses, on the other hand, are quite supportive of both men's and women's self-employment aspirations. This finding may be due to selection biases. It may simply not be possible to successfully embark on a self-employment path without some level of spousal support.

12. The respondents were either already self-employed or planning a venture, and were all members attending organization activities supportive of their plans.

13. Bridges and Villemez (1986) provide some counterevidence, however. They find that weak ties produce more income, but the difference is eliminated if other variables (like gender) are controlled.

References

Abelson, Robert P., and M. J. Rosenberg. 1958. "Symbolic Psychologic: A Model of Attitudinal Cognition." *Behavioral Science* 3:1–13.

Aldrich, Howard. 1989. "Networking among Women Entrepreneurs." Pp. 103–132 in *Women-Owned Businesses*, edited by Oliver Hagan, Carol Rivchun, and Donald Sexton. New York: Praeger.

Aldrich, Howard, Pat Ray Reese, and Paola Dubini. 1989. "Women on the Verge of a Breakthrough?: Networking among Entrepreneurs in the United States and Italy." *Entrepreneurship and Regional Development* 1:339–56.

Baron, James N., and Bielby, William T. 1984. "A Woman's Place Is with Other Women: Sex Segregation in the Workplace." Pp. 27–55 in *Sex Segregation in the Workplace: Trends, Explanations, and Remedies*, edited by Barbara Reskin. Washington, DC: National Academy Press.

Beller, Andrea H. 1984. "Trends in Occupational Segregation by Sex and Race, 1960–1981." Pp. 11–26 in *Sex Segregation in the Workplace: Trends, Explanations, and Remedies*, edited by Barbara F. Reskin. Washington, DC: National Academy Press.

Berkman, Lisa F., and Lester Breslow. 1983. *Health and Ways of Living: The Alameda County Study*. New York: Oxford University Press.

Blau, Peter M. 1977. *Inequality and Heterogeneity: A Primitive Theory of Social Structure*. New York: Free Press.

———. 1989. "Structures of Social Positions and Structures of Social Relations." Pp. 43–59 in *Theory Building in Sociology*, edited by Jonathan Turner. Newburg Park, CA: Sage.

Block, J. H. 1979. "Socialization Influences on Personality Development in Males and Females." Pp. 26–55 in *APA Master Lecture Series on Issues of Sex and Gender in Psychology*, edited by M. M. Parks. Washington, DC: American Psychological Association.

Boissevain, Jeremy. 1974. *Friends of Friends*. London: Blackwell.

Booth, Alan. 1972. "Sex and Social Participation." *American Sociological Review* 37:183–91.

Borgatti, Stephen P. 1990. "Comparison of Labeled and Unlabeled Perspectives on Position." Paper presented at the Sunbelt Social Network Conference, San Diego, CA.

Brass, Daniel J. 1985. "Men's and Women's Networks: A Study of Interaction Patterns and Influence in an Organization." *Academy of Management Journal* 28(2):327–43.

Breiger, Ronald. 1974. "The Duality of Persons and Groups." *Social Forces* 53:181–89.

Bridges, William P., and Wayne J. Villemez. 1986. "Informal Hiring and Income in the Labor Market." *American sociological Review* 51 (August):574–82.

Burt, Ronald S. 1978. "Cohesion versus Structural Equivalence as a Basis for Network Subgroups." *Sociological Methods and Research* 7:189–212.

Campbell, Karen E. 1985. "Women's and Men's Job Searches, Job Changes, and Social Resources." Ph.D. dissertation, University of North Carolina, Chapel Hill.

———. 1988. "Gender Differences in Job-Related Networks." *Work and Occupations* 15:179–200.

Carley, Kathleen M. 1986a. "An Approach for Relating Social Structure to Cognitive Structure." *Journal of Mathematical Sociology* 12(2):137–89.

———. 1986b. "Knowledge Acquisition as a Social Phenomenon." *Instructional Science* 14:381–438.

Crano, William D., and Joel Arnoff. 1978. "A Cross-Cultural Study of Expressive and Instrumental Role Complementarity in the Family." *American Sociological Review* 43:463–71.

Eder, Donna, and Maureen T. Hallinan. 1978. "Sex Differences in Children's Friendships." *American Sociological Review* 43:237–50.

England, Paula, and George Farkas. 1986. *Households, Employment and Gender: A Social, Economic and Demographic View.* Hawthorne, NY: Aldine de Gruyter

Fischer, Claude. 1982. *To Dwell among Friends.* Chicago: University of Chicago Press.

Fischer, Claude, and Stacey Oliker. 1983. "A Research Note on Friendship, Gender and the Life Cycle." *Social Forces* 62:124–32.

Granovetter, Mark S. 1974. *Getting a Job: A Study of Contacts and Careers.* Cambridge, MA: Harvard University Press.

———. 1985. "Economic Action and Social Structure: The Problem of Embeddedness." *American Journal of Sociology* 91(3):481–510.

Hallinan, Maureen T. 1974. *The Structure of Positive Sentiment.* New York: American Elsevier.

Hallinan, Maureen T., and Warren N. Kubitschek. 1988. "The Effects of Individual and Structural Characteristics on Intransitivity in Social Networks." *Social Psychology Quarterly* 51(2):81–92.

Hallinan, Maureen T., and Aage B. Sorenson. 1983. "The Formation and Stability of Instructional Groups." *American Sociological Review* 48:838–51.

Heider, Fritz. 1958. *The Psychology of Interpersonal Relations.* New York: Wiley.

Holland, P., and Samuel Leinhardt. 1970. "A Method for Detecting Structure in Sociometric Data." *American Journal of Sociology* 75:492–513.

House, James S., Karl R. Landis, and Debra Umberson. 1988a. "Social Relationships and Health." *Science* 241:545–50.

House, James S., Debra Umberson, and Karl R. Landis. 1988b. "Structures and Processes of Social Support." *Annual Review of Sociology* 14:293–318.

Hurlburt, Jeanne, and Alan C. Acock. 1990. "The Effects of Marital Status on the Form and Composition of Social Networks." *Social Science Quarterly* 71(1):163–74.

Ibarra, Herminia. 1989. "Centrality and Innovativeness: Effects of Social Network Position on Innovation Involvement." Unpublished Ph.D. dissertation, Yale University.

———. 1990. "Women's Access to Informal Networks at Work: An Intergroup

Perspective." Paper presented at Academy of Management meetings, San Francisco.

Jacobs, Jerry A. 1988. *Revolving Doors: Sex Segregation and Women's Careers.* Stanford: Stanford University Press.

Jones, J., and G. Crawford. 1980. "Work and Network: The Relationship of the Social Circle to the Economic Action of Poor Men." Paper presented at the American Sociological Association meetings, New York, August.

Kalleberg, Arne. 1985. *Entrepreneurship in the 1980s: A Study of Small Business in Indiana.* Bloomington, IN: Center for Survey Research.

Kanter, Rosabeth Moss. 1977. *Men and Women of the Corporation.* New York: Basic Books.

Kiecolt, K. Jill. 1988. "Recent Developments in Attitudes and Social Structure." *Annual Review of Sociology* 14:381–403.

Knoke, David, and James H. Kuklinski. 1982. *Network Analysis.* Beverly Hills, CA: Sage.

Kohn, Melvin L., and Carmi Schooler. 1983. *Work and Personality: An Inquiry into the Impact of Social Stratification.* Norwood, NJ: Ablex.

Lee, Nancy Howell. 1969. *The Search for an Abortionist.* Chicago: University of Chicago Press.

Leinhardt, Samuel. 1973. "The Development of Transitive Structure in Children's Interpersonal Relations." *Behavioral Science* 12:260–71.

Lever, Janet. 1978. "Sex Differences in the Complexity of Children's Play and Games." *American Sociological Review* 43:4:471–83.

Lin, Nan, William M. Ensel, and John C. Vaughn. 1983. "Social Resources and the Strength of Ties: Structural Factors in Occupational Status Attainment." *American Sociological Review* 46:393–405.

Lin, Nan, John C. Vaughn, and William M. Ensel. 1981. "Social Resources and Occupational Status Attainment." *Social Forces* 59:1163–81.

Lincoln, J. R., and J. Miller. 1979. "Work and Friendship Ties in Organizations: A Comparative Analysis of Relational Networks," *Administrative Science Quarterly* 24:181–99.

Maccoby, Eleanor E., and Carol N. Jacklin. 1974. *The Psychology of Sex Differences.* Stanford, CA: Stanford University Press.

Marsden, Peter V. 1987. "Core Discussion Networks of Americans." *American Sociological Review* 52:122–31.

――――. 1988. "Homogeneity in Confiding Relations." *Social Networks* 10:57–76.

――――. 1990. "Network Diversity, Substructures and Opportunities for Contact." Pp. 397–410 in *Structures of Power and Constraint: Papers in Honor of Peter M. Blau,* edited by Craig Calhoun, Marsall Meyer, and W. Richard Scott. New York: Cambridge University Press.

McPherson, J. Miller. 1982. "Hypernetwork Sampling: Duality and Differentiation among Voluntary Organizations." *Social Networks* 3:225–49.

――――. 1983. "The Size of Voluntary Organizations." *Social Forces* 61:1044–64.

――――. 1990. "Evolution in Communities of Voluntary Organizations." Pp. 224–245 in *Organizational Ecology,* edited by J. Singh. Newbury Park, CA: Sage.

McPherson, J. Miller, and Pamela A. Popielarz. 1990. "Social Networks and

Organizational Dynamics I: The Duration of Voluntary Memberships." Paper presented at the 1990 Sunbelt Social Network Conference, San Diego, CA.

McPherson, J. Miller, Pamela A. Popielarz, and Sonja Drobnic. 1992. "Social Networks and Organizational Dynamics." *American Sociological Review* 57:153–170.

McPherson, J. Miller, and Lynn Smith-Lovin. 1982. "Women and Weak Ties: Differences by Sex in the Size of Voluntary Organizations." *American Journal of Sociology* 87:883–904.

————. 1986. "Sex Segregation in Voluntary Associations." *American Sociological Review* 51:61–79.

————. 1987. "Homophily in Voluntary Organizations: Status Distance and the Composition of Face-to-Face Groups." *American Sociological Review* 52: 370–79.

Miller, J. 1975. "Isolation in Organizations: Alienation from Authority, Control and Expressive Relations." *Administrative Science Quarterly* 20:260–71.

————. 1986. *Pathways in the Workplace.* Cambridge: Cambridge University Press.

Miller, J., S. Labovitz, and L. Fry. 1975. "Inequities in the Organizational Experiences of Women and Men: Resources, Vested Interests and Discrimination." *Social Forces* 54:365–81.

Mirowsky, John, and Catherine E. Ross. 1989. *Social Causes of Psychological Distress.* Hawthorne, New York: Aldine.

Moen, Phyllis, Donna Dempster-McClain, and Robin Williams, Jr. 1989a. "Social Integration and Longevity: An Event History Analysis of Women's Roles and Resilience." *American Sociological Review* 54:635–47.

————. 1989b. "Successful Aging: A Life Course Perspective on Women's Multiple Roles and Health." Paper presented at the Gerontogolical Society of America, Minneapolis, MN, November.

Pfeffer, Jeffery. 1983. "Organizational Demography." Pp. 299–357 in *Research in Organizational Behavior*, Vol. 5, edited by H. Z. Zopata and J. H. Pleck. Greenwich, CT: JAI Press.

Powell, Gary N. 1988. *Women and Men in Management.* Newbury Park, CA: Sage.

Scott, John Jr. 1957. "Membership and Participation in Voluntary Associations." *American Sociological Review* 22:315–26.

Smith-Lovin, Lynn. 1990. "Emotion as the Confirmation and Disconfirmation of Identity: An Affect Control Model." Pp. 238–70 in *Research Agendas in the Sociology of Emotions*, edited by Theodore D. Kemper. Albany, NY: SUNY Press.

Smith-Lovin, Lynn, and David R. Heise (eds.). 1988. *Analyzing Social Interaction: Research Advances in Affect Control Theory.* New York: Gordon and Breach.

South, Scott J., Charles M. Bonjean, Judy Corder, and William T. Markham. 1982. "Sex and Power in the Federal Bureaucracy: A Comparative Analysis of Male and Female Supervisors." *Work and Occupations* 9:233–54.

South, Scott J., William T. Markham, Charles M. Bonjean, and Judy Corder. 1987. "Sex Differences in Support for Organizational Advancement." *Work and Occupations* 14(2):261–85.

Spenner, Kenneth I. 1988. "Social Stratification, Work and Personality." *Annual Review of Sociology* 14:69–97.

Stack, Carol B. 1974. *All Our Kin: Strategies for Survival in a Black Community.* New York: Harper and Row.

Stewman, Shelby. 1988. "Organizational Demography." *Annual Review of Sociology* 14:173–202.

Stryker, Sheldon. 1980. *Symbolic Interactionism: A Social Structural Version.* Menlo Park, CA: Benjamin/Cummings.

––––––. 1987. "Identity Theory: Developments and Extensions." Pp. 89–103 in *Self and Identity: Psychological Perspectives*, edited by K. Yardley and T. Honess. Chichester: Wiley.

Wagner, W. G., J. Pfeiffer, and C. A. O'Reilly III. 1984. "Organizational Demography and Turnover in Top Management Groups." *Administrative Science Quarterly* 29:74–92.

Waite, Linda J., Frances Kobrin Goldscheider, and Christina Witsberger. 1986. "Nonfamily Living and the Erosion of Traditional Family Orientations among Young Adults." *American Sociological Review* 51:541–54.

Wellman, Barry. 1985. "Domestic Work, Paid Work and Net Work." Pp. 159–191 in *Understanding Personal Relationships*, edited by Steve Duck and Daniel Perlman. London: Sage.

Wharton, Amy S., and James N. Baron. 1988. "So Happy Together? The Impact of Gender Segregation on Men at Work." *American Sociological Review* 52(5, October): 574–87.

Whiting, Beatrice. 1980. "Culture and Social Behavior: A Model for the Development of Social Behavior." *Ethos* 8:95–116.

Zanna, M. P., F. Crosby, and G. Lowenstein. 1987. "Male Reference Groups and discontent among Female Professionals." Pp. 24–41 in *Women's Career Development*, edited by B. A. Gutek and L. Larwood. Beverly Hills, CA: Sage.

PART III

Dialogue and Debate

Chapter 12

Overcoming Dualisms:
A Feminist Agenda for Sociological Methodology

Joey Sprague and Mary K. Zimmerman

Positivism has been the ruling epistemology in sociology since its incep-
tion; however, critical epistemologies, most recently feminist, have
made it clear that positivism holds little promise for sociology's future.
The goal of this paper is to assist the birth of an inclusive feminist
methodology—one that can accommodate a range of research strategies
and will guide the research of all sociologists. To begin, we summarize
the major contours of the critique of positivism and the common feminist methodological responses to this critique. We argue that too often
the methodological alternatives offered by feminists have been simply a
mirror image of positivism. Feminist alternatives, we maintain, must
overcome the problems imposed by dualistic thinking: Otherwise, they
are equally as limiting as positivism for the development of social understanding. We suggest that both positivistic and common feminist approaches are organized around four dualisms—object/subject, rational/
emotional, abstract/concrete, and quantitative/qualitative—but that the
two approaches differ in which half of each dualism is emphasized and
normatively valued. Positivism claims an objective reality, perceivable
independently of subjective experience, and values the rational, abstract, and quantitative. Feminists, in contrast, give priority to actors'
own subjective experience and emphasize the emotional aspects of
social life grounded in concrete, daily experiences. For them, data must
be qualitative in order to reveal these aspects.

We take the position that rather than representing absolute dichotomies, these four oppositions express tensions that we should strive to
integrate in doing research. We propose an inclusive feminist methodology based on the premise that social research is both collective and
processual. Accordingly, we develop specific strategies for implement-

255

ing a nondualist feminist methodology. We suggest working toward the integration of these dualisms at three points of the research process: the development of an agenda, the conduct of specific projects, and participation in discourse. We conclude with the observation that pursuing such a feminist methodology is in the best interests of developing the entire discipline of sociology.

The Feminist Critique of Positivism

Positivism was linked with sociology at the beginning by its major founders, August Comte, the mathematician credited with founding the discipline, as well as Emile Durkheim, who played a major role in establishing the new discipline's credibility. Comte argued we could only be "positive" about knowledge obtained by dispassionately observing empirical data to uncover hidden laws. Disciplined observation could be facilitated through quantifying observations and using statistical principles to detect patterns. Empirical observations were facts; the adoption of specific routines assured the objectivity of the process; the ability to predict was the measure of a model's adequacy (Barzun and Graff 1970, pp. 222–29). Positivistic epistemology has enjoyed hegemony in sociological research up to the present, though not without challenge.

There has been a strong tradition within sociology of contesting positivistic assumptions. The sociology of knowledge has focused on demonstrating the degree to which knowledge is socially constructed (e.g., Berger and Luckmann 1966; Habermas 1979; Mannheim 1936). The Frankfurt school has criticized positivists for (1) a lack of awareness that positivism itself is rooted in a specific social order. (2) emphasis on the reporting of empirical findings isolated from the social processes underlying them, (3) a view of knowledge as inherently neutral, and (4) a blindness to the biases embedded in the observer's point of view (Farganis 1986).

In addition, Habermas (1971) challenges the positivistic notion that predictive power is the fundamental criterion of a theory's adequacy. He argues that simply being able to predict behavior does not enhance our ability to see that behavior from the point of view of the actors or to enable their emancipation from oppressive social relations. Under what circumstances is prediction an adequate criterion of knowing? Habermas suggests predictability is adequate when the goal is to be able to thwart undesirable behaviors or encourage desirable ones. For example, being able to predict what categories of people are most likely to use cocaine is more useful for allocating resources for social control than it is for revealing how drug abusers see themselves and the world or how to create a society in which people are not self-destructive.

Phenomenology and the interactionist school, with roots in the social behaviorism of George Herbert Mead and philosophical pragmatism (Stone and Farberman 1981), have also provided related, though by no means politically self-conscious, challenges to positivism within sociology. The interactionist tradition has placed major emphasis on the extent to which reality is constructed, interpreted, and reinterpreted as an ongoing and emergent process. Interactionism denies a single, objective reality independent of actors' meanings and instead recognizes the likelihood of multiple realities, each subject to renegotiation. Research methods within this tradition have focused on human actors' subjective accounts of experience and therefore have consisted largely of qualitative techniques.

Radical feminist critiques of positivistic notions of science have perhaps provided the most serious and pervasive challenge (Cook and Fonow 1986; Farganis 1986; Harding 1987; Harding and Hintikka 1983; Jaggar 1983; Keller 1982; MacKinnon 1982; Smith 1979, 1987). This work tends to cluster around two interrelated themes: (1) an expanded critique of the notion of scientific objectivity; (2) an analysis of the power relations embedded in the social organization of research.

The Feminist Critique of Objectivity

While other critics have debated the attainability of objectivity, feminists have added the issue of its desirability. Positivistic claims of objectivity are built on the idea that the scientist must be detached from the subject of her/his research. Thus, typically in the social and behavioral sciences, research subjects are treated as objects and the detached or "objective" researcher is privileged as the "knowing" party. In essence, the subjectivity of the researcher as well as that of the "object" of research are ignored. This has raised fundamental problems for feminists—both in terms of biases in the construction of knowledge and in terms of issues of political exploitation and subjugation. First, we consider the problem of bias.

A central argument in feminist epistemology has been that the separation of subject and object has negative consequences for validity (Cook and Fonow 1986; MacKinnon 1982; Ring 1987). The positivist researcher employing quantitative methods often "interacts" with the object of study only through the medium of a questionnaire or some other documentary evidence. In order to quantify, measures are constructed with a fixed set of categorical responses. In the interest of standardization, measures developed in one situation are frequently applied to another. The resultant data are fragments of decontextualized human experience. These fragments are recombined using analytic categories and interpretive frameworks drawn from previous work within the literature, itself built on the unexamined assumptions of a white male perspective (MacKinnon 1982; Smith 1979, 1987). Thus, in employing quantitative techniques the researcher widens the gap between her/him and those s/he is studying to such a degree that in-depth understanding is severely compromised and distortion can easily occur. It follows that research in this tradition is likely to be an expression of patriarchal ideology, useless for understanding and counterproductive for feminist goals.

In response to this epistemological critique, some feminists have advocated that all research and particularly studies of women should reject a priori constructs in favor of privileging the subjectivity of women (Farganis 1986). One argument to support such an approach is that as an oppressed group women have had to develop a dual perspective: the perspective to understand the point of view of their dominators as well as the perspective developed through their own experience. In struggling to overcome their oppression, they are sensitized to the social and psychological mechanisms of dominance (Mies 1983). As people assigned the daily work of meeting people's physical, emotional, and social needs, women have a clearer understanding of their connections with nature and with each other (Hartsock 1985; Smith 1987). Thus, like Hegel's slave, they have the potential to understand more completely and less perversely than their oppressors (Harding 1986).

In fact, a major contribution of feminist sociology has been to uncover and examine domestic life, revealing the intricate and often subtle ways that women's own domestic orientation and the expectations of others for their nurturing role maintain the conditions of gender inequality on a daily basis. Making the personal—and, in male terms, often the mundane—visible as an important part of the social system has been possible because of the development of a feminist standpoint. A way of understanding the world that is grounded in the practical experience common to women (Hartsock 1983) casts light on the connections between social structure and the microdynamics of daily experience (cf. Risman and Schwartz 1989).

This "standpoint" argument has been expanded to assert that gender intersects with class and ethnicity to create unique sets of experiences, giving rise to the development of distinctive perspectives (Collins 1986, 1989; Dill 1979, 1983; King 1988). The standpoints of those who have historically been intellectual outsiders are particularly valuable in revealing the distortions of mainstream white upper-class male frameworks (Collins 1986; King 1988).

Feminists also have insisted on the legitimacy of alternative ways of knowing, including intuition and emotionality (Cook and Fonow 1986). Such sources of knowledge defy conventional notions of rational thought, rooted as they are in the narrow assumptions of positivist science. Mistakenly dismissed as irrational, these alternative paths to knowledge can, in fact, further understanding. Even apart from the feminist critique, successful scientists have voiced understandings achieved through nonrational paths but have failed to recognize or acknowledge them as acceptable sources (Keller 1982).

The contribution of alternative ways of knowing to scholarly research has been hidden in part because positivistic science distinguishes between the *context of discovery* and the *context of justification* (Reichenbach 1938). The context of discovery refers to the origin of research questions. The context of justification refers to the set of processes through which research questions are tested. The context of justification is subject to rationalization and control through the procedural rules of the scientific method. Positivistic assumptions cannot, however, rationalize or account for the context of discovery, the seemingly idiosyncratic and mysterious process through which research questions and creative, novel hypotheses emerge (Harding 1987). Because it lies outside positivistic explanation, the context of discovery and the role of intuition and emotionality in generating insight and creativity are ignored.

If alternative ways of knowing were recognized as valid sources of information, women would be recognized as privileged observers partly because they have developed abilities to understand phenomena through intuition and emotionality (cf. Cook and Fonow 1986). In fact, the subjectivities of researchers would not be the only source for research questions and insightful understandings. Thus, feminists, particularly black feminists, have emphasized that the concepts and explanations of ordinary people can also be valid bases on which to develop our social analyses (Collins 1989; Dill 1983).

The Connection Between Science and Domination

The other dominant theme in feminist critiques of conventional methodology is a recognition of the politics embedded in the social organization of science. Positivist ideology represents science as value neutral both as a set of processes and in its relationship to society. The procedures of the scientific method are assumed to guarantee against the infiltration of politics. The pursuit of knowledge is seen as independent of any political interests that knowledge may serve. Ethics is distinct from epistemology. Feminists have taken issue with these elements of positivist ideology, arguing that traditional science reproduces domination both in power inequities in the research process, and in the way it contributes to the reproduction of broader social inequality. More than that, the very form science takes in our culture equates it with power and domination.

Feminist epistemologists have specifically connected the practice of positivistic sociology with the imposition of social dominance at two levels: First, the conduct of research is carried out through social relationships of differential power with the attendant risks of exploitation and abuse. The researcher typically has more control over the situation—its definition and its outcomes—than does the subject of research. The research group—principal investigator, research assistants, clerical workers—is also organized hierarchically both in terms of decision-making and in the allocation of accrued benefits. Second, research is inherently political in facilitating particular structures of power within the larger society, either those already in existence or those through which the currently oppressed are empowered. The questions asked, the conceptualizations used, the research design, and the criteria for adequate answers all express a specific worldview (Smith 1987). Research expressing a specific worldview and resulting in knowledge claims that reflect this view is inherently value laden and therefore, raises issues of morality and ethics (cf. Reinhartz 1983). To avoid serving dominant interests, researchers must be self-consciously oriented toward the interests and struggles of the dominated. Specifically, research would have to address the dismantling of patriarchy and the empowerment of women (Mies 1983; Cook and Fonow 1986: Smith 1987).

The very orientation of positivistic science makes the subject under study an object of scientific dominance. Keller (1982) sees this as the outcome of a masculine perspective, which includes a high degree of individuation, of separation from the other (cf. Chodorow 1978). This masculine sense of self as cut off from other people and from the natural world is the basis for positivists' preference for a strict separation between subject and object. As Stacey and Thorne put it, "rationality divorced from feelings, and sharp separation between the knower and the known . . . [constitute] an objectifying stance basic to Positivist social science" (1985, p. 309). They ask, quoting Keller: "To what extent does the disjunction of subject and object carry an intrinsic implication of control and power?" (p. 309). It is failing to see ourselves as intimately connected with, as part of the physical as well as social world that allows us to see the world as something for us to use and control rather than to seek to understand how we can improve our harmony with it. It is depersonalizing others, shunning empathy, that makes it possible to ignore the question of the likely impact of our work on their potential for self-determination (cf. Hartsock 1985 for an extended argument).

A Problematic Feminist Response

Feminists have criticized mainstream positivistic science for ordering its world into dichotomies—object/subject, rational/emotional, abstract/ concrete, quantitative/qualitative. In each, positivism places value on only one side of the duality, the first of each pair as given here. In contrast, as we have pointed out previously (Sprague and Zimmerman 1989), many feminist scholars have argued for just the opposite— research centered on the subjectivity of those studied, relying on emotional and intuitive evidence and staying close to the concrete, everyday world. Frequently, this has meant that only qualitative methods have been fully accepted as legitimate for feminist research.

Grant, Ward, and Rong (1987) cite three reasons why qualitative methods are arguably more appropriate for feminist research on gender: First, the topic of gender introduces issues that are not easily quantifiable, like emotions and context-specific events. Second, qualitative techniques allow the "use of emotion and self-reflection as data" (1987, p. 857). Third, they maintain that qualitative methods have more potential for correcting "androcentric bias" embedded in traditional questions, concepts, and theories than do quantitative strategies (1987 pp. 856–58). Grant, Ward, and Rong explicitly allow for the application of quantitative approaches after qualitative groundwork has been done.

Other feminist researchers are less sanguine about the feminist promise in quantitative methods. Reinharz (1983) presents an elaborate framework for a new method for feminist social science, which she calls "experiential analysis." She presents an extensive dichotomous inventory contrasting "conventional/patriarchal" with "alternative/feminist" methods. Her dualistic approach rejects quantification in favor of "nonlinear patterning." It considers survey and archival data as patriarchal as opposed to experienced or witnessed feelings and behavior, which are considered feminist.

The common feminist tendency to idealize qualitative research is not shared by all. Recently, qualitative research itself has been intensely examined, particularly the degree to which it actually achieves the feminist aim of privileging the perspective of women. Proponents of the "new," critical, or postmodern ethnography (Clifford and Marcus 1986;

Marcus and Fischer 1986) point out that where the researcher interprets or reinterprets the views or behavior of women, it is the subjectivity of the researcher that is privileged and not the subjectivity of the women. Warren (1988), for example, reviewed recent work in anthropology that calls into question field notes, viewing them not as representations of facts or objective reality, but rather as texts, themselves data subject to study and analysis.

The question from this perspective becomes one of how women's lives and perspectives can accurately be revealed when the researcher studying them is in any way involved in the interpretation of data. In order to avoid privileging the researcher and to ensure that social scientists' interpretations do not muddy or distort the so-called pure data provided by women talking about themselves, some feminist researchers have advocated what essentially is the simple act of holding the microphone. They call for research that eschews interpretation, or the selective process inherent in the gathering and reporting of qualitative data (cf. McCall and Wittner 1989). The researcher's role is to interview by simply recording the subjects' words and to report results by distributing transcripts or extensive quotations. Advocates of this method fail to acknowledge that the researcher still interprets or edits through the choice of subjects, subject matter, and even decisions such as when to start recording and when to stop. What these strategies can do, though, is to encourage the illusion of an unmediated representation of the world, which is to hide the problem of the researcher's standpoint from view.

This "postmodernist turn" in social science has not gone without critical feminist examination (Harding 1987; Mascia-Lees, Sharpe, and Cohen 1989); and neither has the more basic feminist idealization of qualitative methods (Stacey 1988). We, however, are convinced that even more careful examination of feminist methodological alternatives is required. We argue that any kind of strict reliance on qualitative methods as a response to the problems posed by positivism is of limited value because it is fundamentally inconsistent with three basic principles of feminist theory and epistemology: a skepticism about dualisms, a recognition of the social construction of worldviews, and a commitment to the empowerment of women.

Skepticism about Dualisms

A recurrent theme in the feminist literature is that dichotomies should be viewed with a great deal of skepticism. A key feminist discovery has been the patriarchal character of many dichotomies. Jay (1981) identifies the specific form of dichotomy in question, which she calls a logical dichotomy. The logical dichotomy comprises two categories that are not merely distinguishable from one another but are defined in mutually exclusive and exhaustive terms: everything is in either one or the other category and there is no middle ground between them. Jay argues that the conception of logical dichotomy does not exist in nature and could not have been empirically derived. Rather, it is a social construction motivated by a basic requirement of patriarchal societies: the perception of a clear opposition between men and women. Jaggar illustrates the general feminist skepticism about logical dichotomies by quoting Robin Morgan: "The either/or dichotomy is inherently, classically patriarchal" (Jaggar 1983, p. 367).

O'Brien (1981) describes the structure of Western European thought as dominated by dichotomies like city of God/city of man, master/servant, capitalist/worker. She suggests that these are expressions of the degree to which "male-stream thought" is the result of men as an aggregate mediating their alienation from biological reproduction by opposing themselves to it and constructing social structures to control it. Rosser (1988) reviews feminist critiques of research in animal behavior, neuroscience, and endocrinology and argues that these critiques have all targeted the same underlying assumption: that biological processes can be isolated from contextual effects. She says this assumption is based on conceptualizing a (logical) dichotomy between nature and nurture that is unsubstantiated by the data (see also Tuana 1983).

Others have stressed that dichotomies bias and distort social life because they artificially channel us into thinking that less of one pole implies more of another (England 1989). The well-known criticisms of the masculinity-femininity dichotomy and the polar scales used to "measure" it provide a particularly compelling case in point. Being characterized as strong and assertive, for example, should not automatically indicate that one is not sensitive and nurturing at the same time.

It is instructive to consider these criticisms of dualistic thinking in light of the strong contrast between quantitative and qualitative methodologies and the accompanying polemical ways they are discussed in much feminist discourse. We have argued elsewhere (Sprague and Zimmerman 1989) that feminist critics tend to see quantitative research as it has been historically practiced but advocate qualitative research as it might ideally be practiced. Stacey (1988) observes that we tend to visualize the quantitative researcher as male and antifeminist and the qualitative researcher as female and feminist. In addition, much feminist work communicates the notion that separation (as between subject and object) is bad and connection is good (Sprague and Zimmerman 1989). Our point here is that it is possible to see this form of feminist epistemology

as organized in terms of: quantitative/historical/separate/antifeminist/
male versus qualitative/ideal/connected/feminist/female. Clearly, this itself is dualistic thinking; feminists who adopt such a view are in effect
reproducing the logical dichotomy organized around the opposition
male vs. female. We suggest that to be consistent with established
feminist principles, another answer must be found to the problems
posed by positivistic science.

Worldviews Are Socially Constructed

Another basic principle emphasized in the feminist literature is that
the worldviews of individuals are constructed socially within a particular context. Furthermore, reflecting the social order, the standpoint of
white upper-class males has dominated the discourse. This phenomenon has occurred within the scientific community as well as outside, and
it is instructive to note the degree to which it characterizes the social
sciences.

This bias within social science has been demonstrable partly because
of the explicitness of quantitative methods. By rationalizing techniques
of measurement, codification of resulting data, and processes of evaluation, quantitative strategies provide visible research standards and offer
at least the potential for critical discourse within the community of
scholars. For example, Bourque and Grossholtz (1974) reexamined the
reported data in Campbell, Converse, Miller, and Stokes's classic study
of voter turnout and preference, *The American Voter (1960)*. They found
evidence that lower female participation was not inevitable as the authors concluded but rather could be remedied if males took more responsibility for childrearing. Shabad and Andersen (1979) criticized
masculine bias in the coding of reasons for candidate preference used in
the same study and on reanalyzing the data found that the original claim
that women are more personality oriented than men was an artifact of
coding. Analysis of research on the negative psychological effects of
abortion shows that studies prior to the late 1960s agreed that abortion
caused women psychological harm; however, subsequent studies employing more precise, quantitative methods led uniformly to entirely the
opposite results (Zimmerman 1981).

Earlier we argued that proposed qualitative strategies like simply
holding the microphone cannot escape the interpretive influence of the
researcher's subjectivity in selecting where to point the microphone and
when to turn it on or off. The problem with the goal of these strategies is
not just that it is not attainable, but also that it is based on the assumption that the unmediated worldviews of subjects constitute the best way

to understand the world in which we live. Even if it were possible to gather such pure data, this position is inconsistent with the feminist critique of positivism and contradicts the arguments in feminist analyses of cultural domination.

Feminist and other critics of positivism have pointed out that by representing findings as a simple revelation of "what is," positivists obscure (and therefore help reproduce) the social processes behind the facts. Like positivists, our subjects are also viewing a world in which apparent facts are the outcome of the operation of social relations of domination. Like positivists, our subjects interpret their experience using frameworks provided by their culture.

Feminists and other students of culture have made us acutely aware of the degree to which our culture is dominated and the worldviews available to us to interpret our lives are distorted. Gramsci (1971) argued that "common sense" was the vehicle for hegemonic ideology. Many feminists have pointed out the ways in which the dominant culture gives legitimacy to a patriarchal worldview (Cantor 1987; Dorenkamp, McClymer, Moynihan, and Vadum 1985; Gledhill 1978; MacKinnon 1982). We cannot assume that the views of those we study, including those of women, are undistorted. For example, Bellah and colleagues (1985) have argued that in an individualistic culture we would never get a picture of social structures through interviewing people. Many housewives will testify, among other things that feminists don't necessarily agree with, that the place for women is in the home. To accept this as the only perspective on the situation of women is naive. Sociologists have long cited the example of the slave who claims to be happy and the ridiculousness of accepting such a self-report as an indication that there is no oppression involved in slavery.

The experiences of people who are in the front lines, doing the work of keeping our social institutions, both public and private, going on a daily basis, are an important point of access to the workings of this society (Hartsock 1985; Smith 1987). We cannot afford to disregard their perspectives. Taking a standpoint requires interpretation of these perspectives (Harding 1987), interpretation of the logics they reveal, logics of domination and of struggle against it. Sociological views of violence against women, for example, have been radically changed as a result of such feminist research. While many women report they have never experienced rape, studies asking women about the behavior of their partners show that their partners have, indeed, behaved violently in ways that conform to the definition of rape. Naively relying on women's reports of rape would lead to very inaccurate conclusions about the nature and prevalence of rape (Holmstrom and Burgess 1983). Jaggar contrasts the standpoint of women to the worldviews of specific women:

[T]he standpoint of women is not something that can be discovered through a survey of women's existing beliefs and attitudes. . . . Instead, the standpoint of women is discovered through a collective process of political and scientific struggle. The distinctive social experience of women generates insights that are incompatible with men's interpretations of reality and these insights provide clues to how reality might be interpreted from the standpoint of women. (1983, p. 371)

The concept of a standpoint of women recognizes certain commonalities in experiences of women in a patriarchal society (cf. Smith 1987, pp. 1–2). It is not meant to contradict the reality that women occupy a diversity of social positions, including varying intersections of class and ethnicity, each of which can give rise to the development of distinct insights.

Commitment to Empowering Women

A third basic principle of the feminist project is that it is more than an intellectual stance: it is a commitment to the empowerment of women and other oppressed people. Thus, feminist research is connected in principle to feminist struggle. Making social change possible first requires evidence of what is necessary, specifically, the documentation of oppression in its various forms. For example, we need to demonstrate that recognized social values like equality of opportunity, personal security, and healthy families are not being realized under current arrangements. Arguments for broad change must demonstrate the pervasiveness as well as the seriousness of a problem. Convincing policy proposals are based on an identifiable analysis, an explanation of causes and consequences, and often on comparative research. Quantification can play a valuable role in such work.

Quantitative research has provided statistical data clearly revealing oppression not previously recognized. Diana Russell's epidemiology of sexual assault (1984) makes the extent and seriousness of violence against women difficult to deny. Research by Treiman and Hartmann (1981) and England, Farkas, Kilbourne, and Don (1988) on occupational sex segregation and its impact on wage discrimination and by Lenore Weitzman (1985) on the way in which the implementation of "no fault" divorce legislation has radically reduced the standard of living of women and children provide examples of the kind of information we need to be able to have a clearer sense of how to make conditions more equal across genders.

In fact, it is difficult to see how women can empower themselves without access to quantified information. Further, it is difficult to imagine empowerment without the analytic understanding and dismantling of patriarchal knowledge that comes from feminist analysis and theorizing (such as that encompassed in this volume). To be consistent with the feminist principle of empowerment, one cannot discard the interpretive work of the sociological researcher.

The wholesale rejection of quantitative methods and unqualified acceptance of qualitative ones is a violation of the feminist skepticism of dualisms and would deprive women of an important informational and persuasive resource in their struggles for empowerment. The discrediting of the project to develop general feminist social analysis flies in the face of our awareness that the worldviews of our subjects are also socially constructed and ignores the need for such an analysis to guide feminist political struggle.

A few feminist epistemologists have called attention to the irony in the postmodern position that all truth is rhetorical, a narrative, a text, an act of faith. Haraway says this position subjects feminism to the "epistemological electroshock therapy" of peeling away layer after layer of social construction, a practice that instead of getting women into "the high stakes tables of the game of contesting public truths, lays us out on the table with self-induced multiple personality disorder" (1988, pp. 577–78). Mascia-Lees and coauthors (1989) cite Sara Lennox's observation that just when Western white males realize they can no longer define the truth, they decide there is no truth to be discovered. Just as feminists have begun to challenge traditional patriarchal knowledge with their own quantitative tools, these tools are declared useless. Just as feminists have broken out of the constricting framework and conceptual language of patriarchal sociology to forge their own, such theoretical work is devalued.

Harding's distinctions among method, methodology, and epistemology can further clarify the nature of the mistake being made. A *method*, she notes, is a way of gathering data, including listening to respondents in interviews or through written answers to questions, observing behavior, and examining documents. A *methodology* is "a theory and analysis of how research does or should proceed" (1987, p. 3), including how a theory should be applied in a specific research area. An *epistemology* is a "a theory of knowledge," a set of beliefs about what can be known, who can be a knower, and what are legitimate ways of knowing.

Harding (1987) observes that positivist philosophy of science has collapsed epistemology and method, made beliefs about what is knowable identical with a specific set of techniques. This elision is expressed in the term *the scientific method*. It allows positivist researchers to avoid critically evaluating their methodological assumptions by narrowing their debates to technical issues. Feminists reintroduced the issues of methodology and epistemology but, we submit, have too often repro-

duced the positivist equation of method and epistemology in the process. They have linked their denial of the possibility of objective outcomes, in Harding's terms an epistemological argument, with a denial of
the desirability of quantitative techniques, a stance on method.

Integrating The Dualisms

We argue that a more careful reading of feminist theory and epistemology would recognize that the apparent duality of subject/object,
abstract/concrete, and rational/emotional is the product of a history of
social domination. Thus, rather than dichotomies between which we
must choose, they identify tensions that we must struggle to integrate.
For sociologists, this integration will require new ways of thinking about
qualitative and quantitative methods. Rather than dualistic thinking that
forces us into valuing one over the other—or viewing one as always a
preliminary step to the other—we must recognize that both present a
different yet equally fundamental view of what is ultimately the same
social phenomenon.

Integrating Subject with Object

An important feminist contribution to integrating subject and object in
social research has been an insistence on awareness that the objects of
our research are themselves subjects. Whether we are studying individual consciousness, small-group interaction, social organizations, or
world systems, the empirical bottom line is people acting in concert with
others, responding to real or imagined others, making sense out of their
lives (Smith 1987). Further, these are not interchangeable instances of
some abstract universal subject, they—and we—are actual, embodied
subjects, struggling with the constraints of a specific gender/class/ethnic
intersection and developing perspectives out of that struggle (Collins
1989; Dill 1983). This means that we must anticipate the likelihood that
categories and relationships developed in one intersection are not directly applicable in another. For example, the conceptualizations of middle-
class, professional, white, female researchers—for example, their notions of work or leisure or community or even reproductive rights—are
not likely to match those of the people they study in other social
contexts.

Many have argued that the standpoints of those at the bottom of
various social hierarchies have more potential for revealing the social
world than do the standpoints of the dominant (e.g., Collins 1989;

Hartsock 1983, 1985; King 1988; Lukacs 1971; Smith 1987). For one thing, those at the bottom of social hierarchies are more engaged in the day-to-day workings of society, know what needs to get done and how it is accomplished. Also, the survival of those who are in vulnerable social positions depends in part on an ability to anticipate the reactions of those able to exercise power over them. There are many examples of ways in which our thinking has been changed through analyses taking the standpoint of the dominated. Feminists have revealed the way masculine notions of work were blind to domestic labor (cf. Molyneux 1979; Hartsock 1985), volunteer work (Daniels 1987), and emotional labor (Hochschild 1983) and that the traditional distinction between work and leisure is irrelevant for those who do not work outside the home (Oakley 1974). Black feminists have shown the degree to which our understanding of slavery was based in male experience (Davis 1981; Hooks 1981); have noted that white feminist identification of employment as an emancipator is not true for all women (King 1988) and that the distinction between work and family is not applicable to the experience of most black women (Collins 1986); and have demonstrated that additive models of oppression hide the experience and interests of black women (Dill 1983; King 1988).

To take a standpoint is not the same as to reproduce the subjectivity of those who occupy it, however. A standpoint is "achieved rather than obvious, a mediated rather than immediate understanding" (Hartsock 1985, p. 132). Haraway argues that to see clearly from any position requires a kind of dual orientation, not being fully identified with that position, but rather being partially connected and at the same time maintaining some distance. "Splitting, not being, is the privileged image for feminist epistemologies of scientific knowledge" (1988, p. 586).

Integrating Abstract with Concrete

Abstraction is important for feminist analysis because it reveals the underlying patterns in social life, allowing the dynamics of social relations to be examined across contextual differences. Developing a feminist standpoint itself raises questions about integrating the concrete or idiosyncratic with the abstract. As we pointed out earlier, concrete worldviews of specific women are essential for a feminist standpoint, but such a standpoint is developed out of a collective process—a level of abstraction that is grounded in daily experience but that does not invalidate the unique experiences of different groups of women.

The integration of abstract and concrete is suggested by considering the meaning of the Latin root of the verb *abstract*: to draw from. The theoretical and/or quantitative abstraction that engages feminist criticism is abstraction that is severed from the concrete phenomena, existing in its own plane. The abstraction that is informed by feminism would retain the marks of its embeddedness in the concrete circumstances from which it has been drawn.

Haraway (1988) uses human vision as fact and as metaphor to describe this integration at the level of theory. We see the world through concrete instruments—biological and technological—each from our own concrete position, point of view. This concreteness is, in fact, what gives material reality, objectivity, to our knowledge. The idea that any subject is free of a specific context, can see everything, can have totalized knowledge, is the illusion. If we own our vision as embodied, we will understand our knowledge as situated, meaning both partial and associated with a particular location. Theory is formed through "webs of connections" and "shared conversations" among people translating across local knowledges (Harraway 1988, pp. 587–89).

Integrating Rational with Emotional

Emotions and feelings are an integral facet of human social life, an expression of relationship and the means of human connectedness. The separation of rational and emotional is itself an artificial construct, an abstraction that is not grounded in everyday experience, but that has been useful in maintaining traditional, patriarchal science. Integration of rational and emotional can occur through recognizing their interplay in the motivation behind research, in the generation of specific hypotheses, and in the evaluation of evidence. This is not in itself a new idea, but to challenge the gloss imposed by positivism and to acknowledge the emotionality and mystery of this process is new.

Harrison (1985) argues that to distrust emotions shows disregard for the very way we connect to the world. She specifically urges us not to be afraid of anger, which expresses both connection and indignation. Anger is a signal that something is wrong in a relationship; as such, it can empower us to improve the relationship. This suggests a strategy for generating research questions: Being sensitive to what angers us about the social world will not just provide the emotional fuel for our work, it might point to an important gateway to understanding the crux of a social problem.

In the evaluation of evidence, procedures that integrate established scientific protocols with emotionality would embrace "nonrational" information, including folk understandings, intuition, and emotionally based logic. This is possible because there is no universal rationality independent of goals or values. We evaluate rationality either explicitly or implicitly with regard to a specific set of values or goals. Ruddick's (1980) account of "maternal thinking," for example, is the identification of a rationality emerging out of the goal of fostering the growth and development of children. Her analysis demonstrates the disparity between these values and those underlying dominant conceptions of scientific rationality.

A key to the feminist integration of rational and emotional lies in Smith's (1987) argument that we take everyday life as our problematic, our puzzle to be solved. Daily life appears episodic, unconnected, because it is organized by social relations external to people's direct experience. Smith discusses the extralocal relations of monopoly or even global capitalism; we certainly could add relations of patriarchy and racism. We begin, she says, by taking the standpoint of women and other frontline actors, those directly involved with the work of production and reproduction. We make the apparent irrationality in their lives understandable by uncovering the ways their actions are structured and constrained by relations of subordination to others outside their own immediate experience. In terms of this discussion, the process Smith is advocating could be described as uncovering the goals underlying the dominant rationality and developing alternative rationalities oriented toward feminist goals. These alternative rationalities would be based on the practical knowledge of frontline actors.

Integrating Quantitative with Qualitative Methods

The dichotomy between quantitative and qualitative methods overstates the degree to which these two methods are independent of each other. Often both methods present valid perspectives on an area of sociological inquiry. Each method informs the other and there are frequent occasions when quantitative research moves to qualitative concerns and vice versa.

Integrating quantitative with qualitative methods can be pursued both within and among specific research projects. In implementing quantitative methods we can draw our measures, analytic categories, and hypotheses by comparing previous quantitative and qualitative findings. At the same time we are quantifying and segmenting experience we can examine ways to generate data presenting actors' own views using themes and meanings drawn from their own words and conceptualizations. We can discuss our findings by going beyond speaking in coefficients to talking about the real human social processes inferred from them. In doing qualitative work we can strive to be explicit about the rationale behind our analytic categories and even deduce the implications of our findings for future quantitative work. We should not be afraid to present quantifiable data in quantitative terms within an otherwise qualitative study.

Substantive questions can be addressed by intentionally and carefully triangulating quantitative with qualitative projects. When we encounter apparently different findings from each method, we need not immediately assume that one should be refuted and the other accepted. We can entertain the possibility that, given that each involves selection and interpretation, the outcomes are each "partial truths," which need to be woven together for a more complete representation.

Working Toward A Feminist Methodology

In this section, we move out of the critique mode and into a practical framework by using the above arguments to make concrete suggestions for social researchers. In what follows we suggest ways of working toward the integrations of subject with object, of abstract with concrete, of rational with emotional, and of quantitative with qualitative methods in three phases of the research process: (1) the development of an agenda, (2) the conduct of a specific investigation, and (3) participation in discourse about the research.

Development of an Agenda

There are two aspects to a research agenda: the selection of a question and the development of a strategy for pursuing it empirically. Standard methodological discussions devote a great deal of attention to the latter—the *context of justification* or how hypotheses are tested—and none to the former—the *context of discovery* or where our questions come from (Harding 1987, pp. 6–7). If the source of questions is defined as a nonquestion, if there is no logic applied, then the choice appears to be exempt from criticism. The idea that research questions emerge "from the literature," as though knowledge pursued its own teleology, denies not only the subjectivity of the researcher but also the degree to which gatekeeping—preferences of funders, reviewers, editors, senior colleagues, etc.—has been a factor in the generation of literatures. Attributions of unbiasedness or even nonrationality in the process of selecting questions do not make sense given the regularity of the outcome: We end up asking specific kinds of questions, those of the managers not the workers, of the professionals not their clients, those of the ruling elites not ordinary people (Hartsock 1983; Smith 1987).

Integrating subject with object in the development of our research agendas seems more likely if we keep in mind that "There is no such thing as a problem without a person (or groups of them) who have this problem: a problem is always a problem *for* someone or other" (Harding 1987, p. 6). Harding suggests that our research agendas would look very different if we pursued the questions of the dominated, who are likely to be interested primarily in how to improve the conditions of their daily lives. We choose the standpoint or standpoints we want to operate from and generate questions from there.

This ties into the integration of rational with emotional. Agendas are about goals and goals imply values. We do not simply choose a standpoint—we make a commitment to a group of people, we own a relationship with them. We let our anger and theirs lead us toward our priorities. We may not ask the same questions they are asking. In fact, if we who are in relatively privileged social positions take the standpoints of those who are at the bottoms of social hierarchies, it is unlikely that our questions will be the same as theirs. Smith's suggestion that we take everyday life as our problematic is an important gateway, but not everything is knowable from even the standpoint of frontline actors. If we want to claim to be doing feminist research, however, we should be able to see how addressing our questions will facilitate their answers.

The integration of abstract and concrete will require reinterpreting our existing understandings, "the literature," as embodied knowledge, the local knowledge developed out of specific standpoints, often those of dominant groups. This is not to say we can afford to disregard existing knowledge; it is to insist that the value of that work can only be realized though seeing it contextually. We can critically assess the research questions posed, conceptualizations used, and the interpretation of findings, on the basis of their relation to lived experience. Gaps or questions of fit to the lived experience of a range of people can produce new research questions that better integrate concrete experience with the abstractions of the research process.

Integrating abstract with concrete and subject with object means we will have to broaden our notions of the existing literature. We will need to integrate understandings developed through quantitative with qualitative methods. We will also have to be prepared to learn from those who have been denied an academic voice and are speaking instead through the channels to which they have had access: literature, music, folk wisdom, ritual, and so on. Finally, the biases inherent both in quantitative and in qualitative methods mean that our research agendas should incorporate techniques of each.

As described here, implementing a feminist research agenda appears a daunting, if not impossible, task. That is probably the case if we maintain the ideology of research as individual enterprise. If, instead, we consciously build on what we know to be the case—that any piece of completed work is the product of many hands and minds—by constructing collaborative research agendas, these goals are achievable. We can form research teams consciously constructed of people from diverse social backgrounds (e.g., gender, ethnic, class, disability) and competent in a range of quantitative and qualitative methods, and develop team agendas. To be truly collaborative, communication and integration of efforts would have to be democratic, consensus based, and ongoing. For that to be practical we must train a diversity of scholars in our graduate programs and require training in both quantitative and qualitative methods.

Conducting Specific Projects

In working toward the integration of subject with object in a specific project, we can learn from an insight offered by Jean Baker Miller (1976). Miller observes that all hierarchical relationships are not the same. Some are organized in such a way that the relationship of inequality is maintained or exacerbated. These are the ones that usually come to mind when we discuss inequality. However, Miller notes, we have close at hand several models of a very different hierarchical relationship, one that is organized to reduce the degree of inequality between the members, or even to erase it. The relationships between a parent and a young child or between a teacher and a student are ideally constructed along this logic. If researchers, those working for them, and those whom they study cannot begin as equals, we can certainly organize the research process so that the skills of subordinates are developed and the dignity of those we study is affirmed.

One way to do the latter is through working toward integrating abstract and concrete. We should be careful to make sure that our quantitative measures, as well as our qualitative categories, are indeed drawn from concrete experience. Since the structure of domination means that the dominated are assigned the tasks of implementing the decisions of the dominators, the best sources of concrete categories are those at the bottom of hierarchies of power (Hartsock 1985; Smith 1987). This suggests the importance of quantitative practices like developing closed-ended items from an analysis of open-ended responses from a diversity of women and/or ethnic minorities of both sexes and a range of classes. Open-ended information could be obtained either from previous work or pretests. At the point of analysis, reliabilities of constructed scales could be compared across gender/class/ethnic groups within a sample. Stratified sampling strategies could assure adequate representation of minority segments. These recommendations also raise the question of how readily we can use scales and indices developed in previous research. We should be extremely cautious about the validity claims of these measures, and their grounding in the everyday experience of an adequate range of subjects.

Integrating rational with emotional in each research project means never being blind to the reality of emotional life and labor and the importance of subjective, intuitive, emotional evidence. As we look for relationships among variables or linkages between categories of meaning, we must remain open to discovering affective logics. Gilligan's (1982) work on the patterns of moral development in women and men and Keller's (1983) study of the work of an unconventional biologist are excellent examples of the benefits obtained from maintaining an openness to a different logic, the logic of connectedness.

Participating in Discourse

Working against these dualisms in our discourse requires attention to the form and content of our communication as well as the forums in which we participate. First, we must pay particular attention to our use of language. Discussions that, because of the predominance of technical, statistical, or esoteric theoretical jargon, operate at such a level of abstraction that even the highly trained specialist in a neighboring tradition cannot comfortably follow them are exacerbating the split between subject and object rather than facilitating a constructive reconnection. The feminist goal should be that a concerned, thinking individual totally outside the literature (e.g., a feminist activist) should be able to comprehend and make use of the information. A reasonable first step would be to write so that practicing feminist sociologists are empowered to do their/our work in more feminist ways. To do otherwise amounts to textual domination. We can all help not just by working on our own discursive style, but also by refusing to perpetuate the stereotype that the more obscure a text is, the more we should be in awe of it.

In addition to avoiding free-floating abstractions in our texts, we need to make our own concreteness visible. We should own our personal standpoints and be explicitly self-critical about the limits on our view. Similarly we need to remind ourselves and our readers of the standpoints of those we study. Specifically, we can alter the format of reporting results. We can spend time acknowledging the context of discovery by discussing the origins of the research and acknowledging the alternative ways of knowing involved. We can also address a specific section of our articles to the question of the real-world significance of the research, linking it to the broader aims of the feminist project.

We should review the journals in which we communicate in light of integrating these oppositions. We should make sure that evaluations of the significance of a manuscript are not made merely on the basis of standards like "cutting edge," which, given the history of our discourse, may signal the remoteness of its topic from the daily lives of most people. Rather we should weigh significance by the degree to which it helps us understand those lives. We should question the degree to which our journals are segregated by method, whether it be primarily quantitative or qualitative or even abstractly theoretical.

One way of integrating rational and emotional in our discourse is by expressing our advocacy. If we have connected with a group, we identify with them; we care about their outcomes. Commitment to a group implies a duty to facilitate their development. In academic discourse, the least we can do is express the implications of our work for their lives and life choices, to bring their humanity to the fore. Full commitment implies moving outside academic discourse, at least periodically, into conversations in the mainstream, by participating in popular discourse. The group to whom we have committed will determine the venue: We need to speak where they can hear in language they will hear. We must make this communication a dialogue by creating an atmosphere of collegiality and openness so that questions will be asked, answered and discussed. And, ideally, so that the agenda for future research will be a product of the mutual participation of researchers and subjects.

Conclusion

It may be true, as Rosser (1988) has argued, that a feminist science is impossible to achieve in a social context that is sexist. But we do have choices; some ways of doing science are more feminist than others. Feminist methodology along the lines developed here promises to be in the best interests of our profession. At a time when funding for social research is strained, public support should increase as we focus on problems that are meaningful outside narrow subdisciplines and communicate findings in ways that benefit ordinary people. At a time when universities have begun to question the importance of sociology, feminist sociology can provide the answer: scholarship that is passionate, committed, and engaged in the kinds of questions people care about, using strategies that carefully build on a diversity of skills and standpoints.

Acknowledgments

We would like to thank Sandra Albrecht, Shirley Harkess, Mary Elizabeth Kelly, Joane Nagel, William Staples, and Carol Warren for their comments on earlier drafts of this paper and Cindy Wallis for a wide range of clerical help. We would particularly like to thank Paula England for her combination of contagious enthusiasm and incisive critique.

References

Barzun, Jacques, and Henry Graff. 1970. *The Modern Researcher*, rev. ed. New York: Harcourt, Brace & World.

Bellah, Robert N., Richard Madsen, William M. Sulllivan, Ann Swidler, and Steven M. Tipton. 1985. *Habits of the Heart: Individualism and Commitment in American Life*. Berkeley: University of California Press.

Berger, Peter L., and Thomas Luckmann. 1966. *The Social Construction of Reality: A Treatise in the Sociology of Knowledge*. New York: Doubleday.

Bourque, Susan, and Jean Grossholtz. 1974. "Policy and Unnatural Practice: Political Science Looks at Female Participation." *Politics and Society* 4:225–66.

Campbell, Angus, Philip E. Converse, Warren E. Miller, and Donald E. Stokes, 1960. *The American Voter*. New York: Wiley.

Cantor, Muriel G. 1987. "Popular Culture and the Portrayal of Women: Content and Control." Pp. 190–214 in *Analyzing Gender: A Handbook of Social Science Research*, Edited by Beth B. Hess and Myra Marx Ferree. Newberry Park, CA: Sage.

Chodorow, Nancy. 1978. *The Reproduction of Mothering: Psychoanalysis and the Sociology of Gender*. Berkeley: University of California Press.

Clifford, James, and George Marcus (eds.). 1986. *Writing Culture: The Poetics and Politics of Ethnography*. Berkeley: University of California Press.

Collins, Patricia Hill. 1986. "Learning from the Outside Within: The Sociological Significance of Black Feminist Thought." *Social Problems* 33:514–30.

———. 1989. "The Social Construction of Black Feminist Thought." *Signs: Journal of Women in Culture and Society* 14(4):745–73.

Cook, Judith A., and Mary Margaret Fonow. 1986. "Knowledge and Women's Interests: Issues of Epistemology and Methodology in Feminist Sociological Research." *Sociological Inquiry* 56:2–29.

Daniels, Arlene Kaplan. 1987. "Invisible Work." *Social Problems* 34(5):403–15.

Davis, Angela Y. 1981. *Women, Race, and Class*. New York: Random House.

Dill, Bonnie. 1979. "The Dialectics of Black Womanhood." *Signs: Journal of Women in Culture and Society* 4:545–55.

———. 1983. "Race, Class, and Gender: Prospects for an All-Inclusive Sisterhood." *Feminist Studies* 9:131–48.

Dorenkamp, Angela G., John F. McClymer, Mary M. Moynihan, and Arlene C. Vadum, 1985. *Images of Women in American Popular Culture*. San Diego: Harcourt Brace Jovanovich.

England, Paula. 1989. "A Feminist Critique of Rational-Choice Theories: Implications for Sociology." *American Sociologist* 20(1):14–28.

England, Paula, George Farkas, Barbara Kilbourne, and Thomas Dou. 1988. "Sex Segregation and Wages." *American Sociological Review* 53(4):544–58.

Farganis, Sondra. 1986. "Social Theory and Feminist Theory: The Need for Dialogue." *Sociological Inquiry* 56:50–68.

Gilligan, Carol. 1982. *In a Different Voice: Psychological Theory and Women's Development*. (Cambridge, MA: Harvard University Press.

Gledhill, Christine. 1978. "Recent Development in Feminist Criticism." *Quarterly Review of Film Studies* 3:457–93.

Gramsci, Antonio. 1971. *Selections from "The Prison Notebooks,"* edited by Quintin Hoare and Geoffrey Nowell Smith. New York: International Publishers.

Grant, Linda, Kathryn B. Ward, and Xue Lan Rong. 1987. "Is There an Association Between Gender and Methods in Sociological Research?" *American Sociological Review* 52:856–62.

Habermas, Jurgen. 1971. *Knowledge and Human Interests*. Boston: Beacon Press.

———. 1979. *Communication and the Evolution of Society*. Boston: Beacon Press.

Harding, Sandra. 1987. "Introduction: Is There A Feminist Method?" Pp. 1–14 in *Feminism and Methodology*, edited by Sandra Harding. Bloomington: University of Indiana Press.

Harding, Sandra, and Merrill B. Hintikka (eds.) 1983. *Discovering Reality: Feminist Perspectives on Epistemology, Metaphysics, Methodology and Philosophy of Science*. Boston: D. Reidel.

Haraway, Donna. 1988. "Situated Knowledges: The Science Question in Feminism and the Privilege of Partial Perspective." *Feminist Studies* 14:575–99.

Harrison, Beverly Wildung. 1985. "The Power of Anger in the Work of Love: Christian Ethics of Women and Other Strangers." Pp. 3–21 in *Making the Connections: Essays in Feminist Social Ethics*. Boston: Beacon Press.

Hartsock, Nancy C. M. 1983. "The Feminist Standpoint: Developing the Ground for a Specifically Feminist Historical Materialism." Pp. 283–310 in *Discovering Reality: Feminist Perspectives on Epistemology, Metaphysics, Methodology and Philosophy of Science*, edited by S. Harding and M. B. Hintikka. Boston: D. Reidel.

———. 1985. *Money, Sex and Power*. Boston: Northeastern University Press.

Hochschild, Arlie R. 1983. *The Managed Heart: Commercialization of Human Feeling*. Berkeley: University of California Press.

Holmstrom, Lynda Lytle, and Ann Wolbert Burgess. 1983. "Rape and Everyday Life." *Society* (July/August):33–40.

Hooks, Bell. 1981. *Ain't I a Woman? Black Women and Feminism*. Boston: South End Press.

Jaggar, Alison M. 1983. *Feminist Politics and Human Nature*. Totowa, NJ: Rowman and Alanheld.

Jay, Nancy. 1981. "Gender and Dichotomy." *Feminist Studies* 7(1):38–56.

Keller, Evelyn Fox. 1982. "Feminism and Science." *Signs: Journal of Women in Culture and Society* 7:588–602.

———. 1983. *A Feeling for the Organism: The Life and Work of Barbara McClintock*. New York: Freeman.

King, Deborah K. 1988. "Multiple Jeopardy, Multiple Consciousness: The Context of Black Feminist Ideology." *Signs: Journal of Women in Culture and Society* 14(1):42–72.

Lukacs, George. 1971. *History and Class Consciousness*. Cambridge, MA: MIT Press.

MacKinnon, Catharine. 1982. "Feminism, Marxism, Method and the State: An Agenda for Theory." *Signs: Journal of Women in Culture and Society* 7:515–44.

Mannheim, Karl. 1936. *Ideology and Utopia*. New York: Harcourt, Brace & World.

Marcus, George, and Michael Fischer. 1986. *Anthropology as Cultural Critique: An Experimental Moment in Human Sciences*. Chicago: University of Chicago Press.

Mascia-Lees, Francis E., Patricia Sharpe, and Colleen Ballerino Cohen. 1989. "The Postmodernist Turn in Anthropology: Cautions from a Feminist Perspective." *Signs: Journal of Women in Culture* 15:7–33.

McCall, Michal, and Judith Wittner. 1989. "The Good News About Life Histories." Pp. 46–89 in *Cultural Studies and Symbolic Interaction*, edited by Howard Becker and Michal McCall. Chicago: University of Chicago Press.

Mies, Maria, 1983. "Towards a Methodology for Feminist Research." Pp. 117–39 in *Theories of Women's Studies*, edited by G. Bowles and R. Klein. Boston: Routledge and Kegan Paul.

Miller, Jean Baker. 1976. *Toward a New Psychology of Women*. Boston: Beacon Press.

Molyneux, Maxine. 1979. "Beyond the Domestic Labor Debate." *New Left Review* 116:3–27.

Oakley, Ann. 1974. *The Sociology of Housework*. New York: Pantheon.

O'Brien, Mary. 1981. *The Politics of Reproduction*. Boston: Routledge and Kegan Paul.

Reichenback, Hans. 1938. *Experience and Prediction*. Chicago: University of Chicago Press.

Reinharz, Shulamit. 1983. "Experiential Analysis: A Contribution to Feminist Research." Pp. 162–91 in *Theories of Women's Studies*, edited by Gloria Bowles and Renate Duelli-Klein. Boston: Routledge and Kegan Paul.

Ring, Jennifer. 1987. "Toward a Feminist Epistemology." *American Journal of Political Science* 31:753–72.

Risman, Barbara J., and Pepper Schwartz. 1989. *Gender in Intimate Relationships: A Microstructural Approach*. Belmont, CA: Wadsworth.

Rosser, Sue V. 1988. "Good Science: Can It Ever Be Gender Free?" *Women's Studies International Forum* 11:13–19.

Ruddick, Sara. 1980. "Maternal Thinking." *Feminist Studies* 6(2):342–67.

Russell, Diana E. H. 1984. *Sexual Exploitation*. Newbury Park, CA: Sage.

Shabad, Goldie, and Kristi Andersen. 1979. "Candidate Evaluations by Men and Women." *Public Opinion Quarterly* 43:18–35.

Smith, Dorothy E. 1979. "A Sociology for Women." Pp. 135–187 in *The Prism of Sex: Essays in the Sociology of Knowledge*, edited by Julia A. Sherman and Evelyn Torton Beck. Madison: University of Wisconsin Press.

———. 1987. *The Everyday World as Problematic: A Feminist Sociology*. Boston: Northeastern University Press.

Sprague, Joey, and Mary K. Zimmerman. 1989. "Quality and Quantity: Reconstructing Feminist Methodology." *American Sociologist* 20(1):71–86.

Stacey, Judith. 1988. "Can There Be a Feminist Ethnography?" *Women's Studies International Forum* 11:21–27.

Stacey, Judith, and Barrie Thorne. 1985. "The Missing Feminist Revolution in Sociology." *Social Problems* 32:301–16.

Stone, Gregory P., and Harvey A. Farberman (eds.) 1981. *Social Psychology Through Symbolic Interaction*. New York: Wiley.

Treiman, Donald J., and Heidi I. Hartmann (eds.). 1981. *Women, Work, and Wages: Equal Pay for Jobs of Equal Value*. Washington, DC: National Academy Press.

Tuana, Nancy. 1983. "Re-fusing Nature/Nurture." *Women's Studies International Forum* 6(6):621–32.

Warren, Carol A. B. 1988. *Gender Issues in Field Research. Qualitative Research Methods Series #9*. Newbury Park, CA: Sage.

Weitzman, Lenore. 1985. *The Divorce Revolution: The Unexpected Social and Economic Consequences for Women and Children in America*. New York: Free Press.

Zimmerman, Mary K. 1981. "Psychosocial and Emotional Consequences of Elective Abortion: A Literature Review." Pp. 65–75 in *Abortion: Readings and Research*, edited by Paul Sachdev. Toronto: Buttersworth Press.

Chapter 13

With Many Voices:
Feminism and Theoretical Pluralism

Nancy Tuana

Feminist theorists have recently begun to recognize the problematics of the concept of "woman." As feminists we theorize about gender. But to talk about the ways in which a woman becomes gendered or to speculate about woman's roles seems to require that we focus on those things that all women have in common, and to look beyond the peculiarities of a woman or group of women—their race, class, age, sexual orientation, and so on. But any such attempt to talk about women in terms of characteristics or experiences we all share precludes a recognition of our differences. It assumes that the differences among women are less important than what we have in common. This diminution of difference has too often hidden the fact that most descriptions of what women purportedly have in common are descriptions of the experiences of white, middle-class, heterosexual women. Thus we have what Elizabeth Spelman has labeled "the paradox at the heart of feminism" (Spelman 1988, p. 3). That is, how can we recognize the importance of the differences between women without losing sight of what we have in common?

What many feminist theorists, including myself, are concluding is that we must abandon the quest for a unitary theory, for a "master narrative"—one account that will describe and explain all aspects of women's oppression. Alison Jaggar argues that "the time has perhaps come to emphasize the multiplicity of female expressions and preoccupations so that from the intersection of these differences there might arise, more precisely, less commercially, and more truthfully, the real fundamental differences between the two sexes" (Jaggar 1983, p. 353). Feminist theorists must thus be able to draw on the experiences of all women. But since the lived experiences of women are multidimensional, arising out of the complex intersections of a variety of sources, it is perhaps time to recognize that no one theory, no one method, is sufficient to adequately represent the fullness of gender. Our differences as well as our similarities are best realized through a commitment to pluralism. Abandoning the Enlightenment quest for one unitary theory to explain the oppression of women, we can best acknowledge the diversity of women's experiences by embracing theoretical diversity. Similarly we must avoid the tendency to posit unitary notions of "womanhood" or "female gender identity." Gender is one relevant aspect of an individual's social identity, which interacts with many others such as race, class, sexual orientation, and age. Thus our concern must be to develop conceptions of social identities that allow for such complexity.

Our task then as feminists is to carefully examine the strengths and weaknesses of each theory, to expose the presuppositions and prejudices of one theory through the lens of an alternative theory, which is in turn offered up for critical examination, and to look for the variety of intersections between theories, as well as their points of divergence. Such a commitment would leave us not with the Truth about Woman, but with a fluid, flexible understanding of varieties of women's lived experiences, the multiplicity of truths about genders.

Thus my charge to you, the reader, is not to search out the methodologies presented in this text for that which comes closest to the truth, but to find the truths and the limitations of each of the perspectives presented; to think about the ways in which the experiences revealed by one approach shift our understandings of those uncovered by another; to clarify the standpoint of each author in order to reveal what has been included as well as what has been omitted. A difficult charge, but one that can be entered into in many ways by each of us, joining together into a community of inquirers. I offer the following comments in this spirit.

Sprague and Zimmerman offer a feminist standpoint theory and do an excellent job of articulating the specific nature of a sociological methodology based on such a theory. Rejecting positivistic claims of objectivity on the grounds that knowledge arises out of human experiences, they encourage us to turn to the experiences arising from the activities assigned to women. According to feminist standpoint theorists (Hartsock 1983; Rose 1983; Smith 1974, 1987) looking at the nature of social relations from the perspective of women offers a more complete and less distorted source of knowledge because of woman's "dual perspective," that is, that women work within and comprehend the patriarchal worldview, yet in being excluded from men's conception of culture find that their experiences are different from those valorized in patriarchy. The gender-specific perspective of women as the excluded and exploited other is thus offered as a preferable ground for feminist inquiry since, as Sprague and Zimmerman put it, women "have the potential to understand more completely and less perversely than their oppressors."

There is much of value to such an approach. A feminist standpoint theory clearly rejects the traditional notion of objectivity as the "view from nowhere," reminding us that all knowledge arises out of experience. It makes it impossible to forget that the purportedly objective knowledge of traditional positivism arose out of the experiences of white, middle-class, academic males. But at the same time, it avoids relativism in arguing that a less distorted representation of reality is possible. Nevertheless we must be sure to remember that any feminist standpoint will be partial. It cannot represent the experiences of "woman," because such a being does not exist. Similarly we must carefully examine the claim that "a standpoint of women recognizes certain commonalities in experiences of women in a patriarchal society" (Sprague and Zimmerman). There is danger in expecting to find a common core of shared experiences, for such a quest will tend to blind us to the differences between women. I would suggest that it is more realistic to expect pluralities of experiences that are related through various intersections or resemblances of some of the experiences of some women to some of the experiences of others. In other words, we are less likely to find a common core of shared experiences that are immune to economic conditions, cultural imperatives, etc., than a family of resemblances with a continuum of similarities, which allows for significant differences between the experiences of, for example, an upper-class white American woman, and an Indian woman from the lowest caste.

Furthermore, such a standpoint theory assumes that those who are "on the margin" have a *privileged* access to reality. Why assume that such perspectives are less distorted (a value claim) rather than different? Might it not be the case that the oppression experienced by those who are in the position of "other" can so damage them that their experiences represent a different "distortion"? Granted Sprague and Zimmerman clearly deny the view that the perspectives of those on the margin are *undistorted*. But unless these perspectives are viewed as less distorted, they could not be seen as providing "an important point of access to the workings of this society" (Sprague and Zimmerman). Notice too that this theory seems to support the traditional epistemological claim that reality has a (unitary) structure of which humans can have undistorted (or less distorted) knowledge.

The notion of being on the margin, although a helpful tool, is also problematic. We must not forget to ask Which margin? lest we forget whose knowledge we are discussing. That is, a person, say a woman whose primary role is as mother and homemaker, can be on the margin in certain respects (her gender, her work) but be firmly "center" in other respects (her race, her class, her sexual orientation) and thus her experiences may be distorted by her participation in relations of domination rooted in social relations of race, class, or homophobia.

Johnson offers us an interesting twist on this notion of being on the margin. In discussing her application of Parsons's evolutionary model of social change to the development of the feminist movement, Johnson (in this volume) argues that those women who were most critical of and recognized the social construction of gender were "middle-class white feminists, who were privileged in terms of race and class and therefore were more able to see their disadvantaged position as women." If Johnson is correct, the position of the margin is a source of insight only if one is sufficiently center in other aspects of one's life. Reading Johnson together with Sprague and Zimmerman thus suggests that this notion of being on the margin is complex and in need of further research.[1]

Sprague and Zimmerman argue for an integration of dualisms: reason/emotion, separation/connection, quantitative/qualitative. It indeed appears that in an attempt to reject the patriarchal privileging of certain qualities over others by reversing the valuation (stressing emotions over reason, qualitative research over quantitative), feminists simply reproduce the very dichotomization under question. To glorify traditionally feminine ways of being (connectedness, empathy, nurturance) perpetuates the equation of woman and the body (and the body and emotions), sounding dangerously similar to the traditional rhetoric.

Johnson's discussion of Parsons's instrumental-expressive distinction is an example of an attempt to reverse (or at least balance) the privileging of instrumental actions over expressive. However, the instrumental/expressive distinction ends up preserving the reason/emotion dichotomy rather than undermining it. Just as reason is valued over emotion, although emotion is given its place (for example, the importance of Sophie's nurturance and emotional support of Emile in Rousseau's *Emile*), so is instrumental valued over expressive. Neither Parsons nor Johnson questions the claim that expressive action cannot "mov[e] a system in its environment." That is, they fail to see expressive action as contributing to a group's accomplishment of a task involving a manipulation of its external environment. Yet if, as Johnson, says, expressive leaders encourage group solidarity, does this not often get the task done?

Simply arguing as does Johnson that the instrumental/expressive distinction is not *inherently* sexist is not sufficient. There is a long history of defining the emotions (and thus expressive action) in opposition to reason, and defining reason as masculine (Lloyd 1984). We cannot simply affirm expressive actions without also carrying over the centuries-long tradition of viewing the female mind as different from (and inferior to) the male. Patriarchy has never denied the importance of the expressive role (the notion of the feminine complementing the masculine), even while continuing to view it as inferior. We cannot simply ignore this intellectual tradition, for any valorization of the emotions must occur in the conceptual and institutional space already in place. Although Johnson's goal of advocating "greater recognition of the expressive work women . . . do" is an admirable one, I find her solution too simple.

What is needed is not a reversal in which the emotional is valued over the rational or a rebalance where both are valued but are still seen as separate, but a transformation of values in which we rethink our categories and concepts. For example, developing a theory of rationality in which what we now artificially isolate and call reason and emotion are reconceptualized as aspects of the same process.[2] Sprague and Zimmerman suggest that the experiences of those whose histories and experiences have been denied or unexpressed will assist us in this process of transformation. Denzin, in his interactionist/poststructural reading, advocates a similar emphasis on lived experience as a source of illumination of the cultural construction of gender and sexuality. While not privileging those who experience social relations from the margin, Denzin proposes that certain types of experiences, what he calls "epiphanic moments," offer points of entrance into the social construction of gendered sexuality. There are interesting similarities between Denzin's epiphanic moments and the experiences of those on the margin.

The reason why feminist standpoint theorists see the lived experience of those on the margin as less distorted is because of what Dorothy Smith (1979) calls a "line of fault" between their experiences and the dominant conceptual schemes. She sees the recognition of this lack of fit as a source of insight for feminist sociologists (and theorists in general), that is, a springboard for analysis. Similarly Denzin's epiphanic moments involve a similar line of fault, which he offers as a valuable resource for investigations of the construction of gendered sexuality.

Consider the unnamed woman watching Ramone doing a striptease. She reports: "I became aroused sexually and silently within myself, in spite of myself. I could say now that I desired him . . . I felt an erotic charge that provoked a fantasy of meeting him . . . a dream that stopped short of any sexual encounter" (Denzin, in this volume). For Denzin this is an epiphanic moment because it reverses the usual cultural model of the female being the object of the male erotic gaze. Thus the line of fault appears from the tension between what the woman is experiencing and her social script. Through the careful study of such experiences, Denzin suggests that we can perceive cultural stereotypes and examine their dominating influence over individuals.

While reminding us of the value of such epiphanic moments, Denzin also, both intentionally as well as inadvertently, reminds us of the intricacies of their interpretation. Discussing Garfinkel's study of Agnes, Denzin argues that when sociologists turn their gaze upon the lived experiences of another, they carry with them their own stereotypes and expectations through which they "read" the experiences of the other. Denzin carefully and persuasively uses the case of Garfinkel's study of Agnes to illustrate that in addition to the practical accomplishment of Agnes's passing, there is also Garfinkel's construction of a text that enabled him and his readers to see Agnes as a person with male genitalia who passed as a female. In other words, Garfinkel imposed his own "masculine" conceptions of what constitutes a woman in constructing his representation of Agnes.

The moral we can derive from Denzin's discussion of Garfinkel is that in learning from the experiences of others we must be sensitive to the ways in which our own social scripts carry over into our interpretations. Denzin unintentionally reinforces this lesson when he turns to his own analysis of epiphanic moments. Look again at his description of the house madam. She says simply that there was "a time when I didn't know that I was supposed to hustle. . . . When I turned out it was $2 a throw." Denzin concludes, from the fact that she turned out for $2, "Her enacted sexuality creates a negative self-impression." But why conclude this? She clearly states that her customers "got a hell of a fuck." Interpreting this latter statement as a sign of a positive self-impression, that is, that she perceived herself as doing her job well, it seems equally possible that the "fault" was her naivete concerning the rules of prostitution ("I didn't know that I was supposed to hustle"). But Denzin implies that either the existence or amount of the price degrades her and lowers her self-image. This same interpretive bias can be seen in how Denzin expresses her work: "the prostitute *sells her body* for $2 a trick" (my emphasis). The prostitute no more sells her or his body than does a beautician or a chiropractor. A prostitute sells a sexual service. Denzin slips into using a slang phrase that carries a negative connotation, thus reinforcing our culture's negative views about sex.[3] But it would be incorrect to conclude from this that Denzin was simply doing "bad science," that is, that it is possible to set aside all our biases. We cannot avoid carrying out values and concepts over into our interpretations of the experiences of others, thus the need for a community of scholars who will reveal our biases and their implications, and whose work will in turn be so examined by others.

Comparing Williams's psychoanalytic interpretation of gender differ-

ences at work to West and Fenstermaker's ethnomethodological interpretation of Hochschild's research on the activities of women and men
who work as flight attendants reinforces the importance of theoretical
pluralism. In her discussion of male nurses,[4] Williams (in this volume)
comments that they "actively strive to set themselves apart from their
female colleagues," pointing out how this is different from the situation
of female marines who do not strive to be seen as different. She argues
that an object-relations analysis is helpful in understanding this asymmetrical experience of men and women who enter nontraditional occupations, seeing it as the result of men's greater need for separation and
differentiation, particularly from anything feminine.

West and Fenstermaker's discussion of women and men flight attendants covers a similar area—men entering nontraditional occupations.
But in comparing the analyses, we find significant differences. Whereas Williams stresses the conscious choices of male nurses to differentiate themselves and their skills at nursing from those of female nurses,
West and Fernstermaker focus on the ways in which the airlines' train-
ers as well as the passengers expect different roles and abilities from
the women and men attendants. West and Fenstermaker note that
Hochschild found that "women trainees were told to treat their passengers as they would treat guests in their living room," and that "[b]y
contrast, men flight attendants were used as authority figures, charged
with tasks such as managing 'uncontrolled' passengers."

West and Fenstermaker see gender as an interactional accomplishment in which individuals both hold themselves accountable and are
held accountable for their performance of any activity as women or as
men. They look beyond individual choices to stress the interactional
nature of any activity such as being a flight attendant. Their perspective
makes us aware of the ways in which what appear to be individually
motivated choices are often a complex response to the expectations of
others and of the demands of institutions.

West and Fenstermaker thus open up new ways of looking at the
experiences of male nurses. We need to look not only at what they say,
but also at the nature of their training, the responses of those they
interact with, and so on. That is, we should become sensitive to the
differences in the ways that male nurses and female nurses are held
accountable for their enactments of gender.

But Williams in turn opens up additional perspectives on the theory of
West and Fenstermaker. West and Fenstermaker simply note that "sex
categories are omnirelevant circumstances of action." But this leaves us
with the question, What causes gender to be relevant to the accomplishment of any activity? For a feminist this is a crucial question, for it is just
this "fact" that most feminists would want to change. West and Fenster-

maker's ethnomethodological approach simply assumes the omnirelevance of sex categories and phenomenologically describes it, but does
not offer an explanation of its causes. Williams's psychoanalytic approach begins to fill this gap by looking at the ways in which the
assignment of parenting to women affects the development of masculine and feminine personalities of children reared in such families.

Williams does an excellent job of offering an overview of Nancy
Chodorow's theory, *The Reproduction of Mothering* (1978). I will not repeat
it, but rather will offer two criticisms, one concerning essentialism, the
second dealing with the absence of sufficient attention to economic
structures. The first concern applies only to such psychoanalytic theories of the formation of gendered personalities. The second applies to
psychoanalytic theories as well as to ethnomethodological theories.

The assumption of heterosexuality is an essentialist underpinning of
feminist object-relations analyses that can be best revealed through the
question of the place (or lack thereof) of male homosexuality.[5] One of the
basic points of Chodorow's theory is that under the present state of
affairs in which women perform the majority of childcare, the primary
object of all desire is woman. That is, both sexes "carry" a longing for
the original (pre-Oedipal) union with a woman. Heterosexuality is thus
seen as natural for a man. Heterosexuality is more difficult for a woman
in that she must displace her primary love for women, making woman's
desire for women perhaps more natural than desire for a man.
Chodorow, however, pays scant attention to lesbianism, simply saying
that "lesbian relationships do tend to recreate mother-daughter emotions and connections, but most women are heterosexual" (Chodorow
1978, p. 200). Her theory provides no explanation of why most women
are heterosexual. But it is with male homosexuality that Chodorow's
lacuna is even more apparent: Her theory offers no explanation for a
man's sexual desire for a man.

The second objection is the lack of attention devoted to an analysis
of the influences of economic conditions on gender arrangements. Williams gives a passing nod in this direction when she notes that
Chodorow turned to theorists of the Frankfurt school for "a model for
integrating a critique of domination into the psychoanalytic approach."
But a throughgoing critique of the effect of postindustrial capitalism on
the family and on the construction of gender is missing from most
psychoanalytic analyses, including Williams's. Such a critique also applies to West and Fenstermaker's ethnomethodological approach, and in
fact may provide a fertile resource for explaining their unquestioned
claim that "sex categories are omnirelevant circumstances of action." A
psychoanalytic critique is also open to the charge that the type of family

seen is paradigmatic, that is, the middle-class, white, heterosexual, nuclear family, is only one of many forms of the family.

Johnson argued for the importance of a multidimensional approach for rethinking gender, an approach that will include, but not be limited to, biological, psychological, social, economic, and cultural issues. I strongly concur with her emphasis on a multicausal analysis, but I think it is an error to seek one theoretical framework that will do so. The importance of a text like the present one is that in bringing together a variety of theorists on gender, we can begin to perceive the strengths and weaknesses of the various approaches, to recognize areas still omitted, and to begin to speculate about new ways of synthesizing approaches.

Notes

1. I find Johnson's analysis of the feminist movement problematic. She argues that the feminism that developed in the 1960s represented a concern by women for *inclusion* in the mainstream of society (one of Parsons's categories). She claims that the sexual revolution can be considered an example of this for "women wanted inclusion in the sexual freedom taken for granted by men." I find this a questionable analysis. Women were questioning the institution of sexuality, demanding not inclusion but transformation of the values and practices of gendered sexuality. Additionally, women did not simply want to become like men (included in male activities and roles) but wanted a change in men and women alike. An example of this is the emphasis at this time on the goal of androgyny.

2. For examples see Keller (1987) and Holler (1990).

3. We see similar impositions of Denzin's own conceptual framework when he tells us that the Korean woman who is battered by her husband hates her body and hates that she was born a woman and in the judgmental comment that Agnes's sex change operation was "in actuality a castration."

4. In keeping with each author's terminology I will use the qualifier *female* or *male* when referring to nurses and marines, and *woman* or *man* when referring to flight attendants.

5. I am influenced in this critique by the writings of Diana Fuss (1989).

References

Chodorow, Nancy. 1978. *The Reproduction of Mothering.* Berkeley: University of California Press.

Fuss, Diana. 1989. *Essentially Speaking: Feminism, Nature and Difference.* New York: Routledge.

Hartsock, Nancy. 1983. "The Feminist Standpoint: Developing the Grounds for a Specifically Feminist Historical Materialism." Pp. 283–310 in *Discovering Reality*, edited by S. Harding and M. Hintikka. Dordrecht: Reidel.

———. 1985. *Money, Sex, and Power*. Boston: Northeastern University Press.

Holler, Linda. 1990. "Thinking with the Weight of the Earth: Feminist Contributions to an Epistemology of Concreteness." *Hypatia: A Journal of Feminist Philosophy* 5(1):1–23.

Jaggar, Alison. 1983. *Feminist Politics and Human Nature*. Totowa, NJ: Rowman and Allenheld.

Keller, Catherine. 1987. *From a Broken Web*. Boston: Beacon Press.

Lloyd, Genevieve. 1984. *The Man of Reason: "Male" and "Female" in Western Philosophy*. Minneapolis: University of Minnesota Press.

Rose, Hilary. 1983. "Hand, Brain and Heart: A Feminist Epistemology for the Natural Sciences." *Signs: A Journal of Women in Culture and Society* 9(1):73–90.

Smith, Dorothy. 1974. "Women's Perspective as a Radical Critique of Sociology." *Sociological Inquiry* 44:7–13.

———. 1987. *The Everyday World as Problematic: A Feminist Sociology*. Boston: Northeastern University Press.

———. 1979. "A Sociology for Women." Pp. 135–187 in *The Prism of Sex: Essays in the Sociology of Knowledge*, edited by Julia A. Sherman and Evelyn Torton Beck. Madison: University of Wisconsin Press.

Spelman, Elizabeth. 1988. *The Essential Woman: Problems of Exclusion in Feminist Thought*. Boston: Beacon Press.

STANDPOINTS AND THEORY: REPLY TO TUANA

Joey Sprague and *Mary K. Zimmerman*

Tuana's insightful essay raises two questions we want to address, not because we have the answers but because the questions are so important. The first question centers on the privileging of specific social standpoints. The second challenges the desirability of unitary theory.

In a sense, *standpoint* is an unfortunate term because it connotes two very different meanings. One meaning, the meaning we take and the meaning we read in the work of such "standpoint theorists" as Hartsock, Haraway, and Smith, is that of a place to stand, a point from which to view a phenomenon. The other meaning, which often seems to underlie criticisms of standpoint theory, is the equation of standpoint with the definition of the situation developed by people in a specific social position. There is a big difference between the *descriptive* notion of the kind of consciousness developed by people in a particular intersection of gender/class/ethnicity and the *analytic* notion of standpoint, as what can be seen by critically viewing the social world from a particular social position. A specific social position is a point of departure, its standpoint is the goal of analysis.

Identifying standpoints, Tuana correctly notes, often goes hand in hand with claims that some standpoints are better places than others from which to clearly see the social world. The preferred standpoints are not on the margins of society, however. Tuana identifies the andro-centric bias revealed in identifying the position of most women as "on the margin." We agree. The word *margin* does not appear in our text. Rather, we use the term *frontline actors* to suggest, much as Tuana does, the theoretical and political importance of the positions of the people who, by virtue of taking care of people, making social relations work, getting ideas implemented, and so on, are at the center of social action (Smith 1987). It is for this reason that standpoints developed from their social positions have such value. Not everything can be seen from these localized positions, but what can be seen is likely to be an alternative to the hegemonic view, a standpoint developed from the perspective of those in positions of dominance. This is not to say that the view from any specific location is complete. We can make arguments that the standpoints of the dominated have more potential because of their pragmatic content or because the dominated must understand more about their oppressors than vice versa. But, in the final analysis, recog-nizing that all standpoints are partial, thus distorted, leaves one the choice between relativism and intentional selection of bias. The choice among standpoints is not intellectual but political. Relativism cannot guide action. As academics we can enjoy comfortable lives debating the fine points of the social construction of consciousness and the complex-ities of epistemology while all around us others struggle daily for life and often lose. Or, we can consciously choose to stand with those for whom the experience of social dominance and the need for social change are more than abstractions.

While women are not on the margins of social life, however, they/we are on the margin of official, hegemonic, discourse. Women of all classes and ethnicities, though certainly some more than others, are denied full participation in socially legitimated discourse. This brings us to the second issue suggested in Tuana's essay.

Tuana questions the desirability of any unitary theory, doubting that any theory can validly describe the diverse experiences of gender. We agree that gender is not a monolithic experience. Yet we are not ready to give up on the idea that there is value to the goal of identifying broad structures and social processes that permeate social life.

We have inherited from a masculine epistemological tradition the notion that knowledge is a thing that an individual possesses and that truth is a property of an individual theory. In malestream epistemology, there are three terms: the (abstract male) knower, the knowledge, and the object known (Genova 1983). In the real world, however, knowledge is bound inextricably to relationships among knowers. What is knowledge besides the intersubjectivity we need in order to act in concert with one another, beyond social agreement on how to make sense of the world? The intersubjectivity we call knowledge is negotiated in interactions with one another, interactions that are rarely, if ever, diverse and egalitarian. When the interactions are narrow and/or dominated, the intersubjectivity produced in them is biased toward the standpoint of the most powerful party.

Truthfulness is not and probably will never be a property of an individual knower or an individual theory. Truthfulness is better understood as a property of a discourse. We need to move the center of gravity from individual knowers and individual theories to a conversation among us, among occupants of a standpoint and students of it and among students of varying standpoints. We need to recognize and consciously constitute ourselves, in Tuana's words, as a "community of inquirers". Communities are constructed through shared discourse, motivated not just by an exchange of localized perspectives but by a belief that some new understanding is or at least potentially can be achieved through it.

The limitations on each of our perspectives and the specificity of each of our experiences make the attainment of a unitary theory seem improbable. Nevertheless, our best hope for understanding and working against social domination is that we simultaneously remain skeptical of any theory's universalistic claims while we continue to press on as though such a theory were eventually possible.

The recognition of knowledge as the product of a conversation among us is elegantly illustrated in Tuana's use of the analysis presented in one paper as a lens on another. It is expressed in the structure of this book, which presents itself as a dialogue among authors and reviewers of texts. It is expressed more broadly in the mission of this book, which is to integrate discourses that have been segregated: feminist and mainstream sociology.

References

Genova, Anthony C. 1983. "The Metaphilosophical Turn in Contemporary Philosophy." *Southwest Philosophical Studies* IX:1–22.
Smith, Dorothy E. 1987. "The Everyday World as Problematic: A Feminist Sociology." Boston: Northeastern University Press.

REIGNING IN DIVERSITY: REPLY TO TUANA

Miriam M. Johnson

Nancy Tuana suggests that "we can best acknowledge the diversity of women's experiences by embracing theoretical diversity." She goes on to give examples of the diversity of an individual's social identity besides his or her gender, such as race, class, sexual orientation, and age, i.e., the other bases our society uses for prejudice and exclusion. I would argue that we can only come to grips with diversity with a systematic theory, a theory that can in itself, encompass both similarity and diversity, and a theory that can understand social relations as more than the interlocking of oppressions.

Thus while I agree with Tuana that recognizing diversity is important and taking something from every theory is desirable, I think we must go farther and attempt to put it all together—not in one unitary theory but in a general framework. I certainly agree with Tuana's implication that premature closure would be bad, but I think she dismisses neofunctionalism as a framework too easily, especially since one of its main points is to avoid such closure and to see theory building as an ongoing process.

Let me comment on a few specific matters. Tuana argues that the instrumental/expressive distinction ends up preserving the reason/emotion dichotomy. This is discouraging, since I and my colleagues have been at great pains to show that this is not the case. In a sense our research (Gill, Stockard, Johnson, and Williams 1987) was aimed at doing exactly what Tuana calls for, "a transformation of values in which we rethink our categories and concepts." We were able to show empirically that instrumental and expressive categories are not complementary or opposite but rather that the main sex difference is that men saw themselves as less expressive than women while women saw themselves as being both expressive and instrumental. Beyond this we attempted to theorize expressivity in a new way that combined it with rationality and that could lead to a more positive vision of the "work" of social integration that women do.

In a footnote, Tuana questions my statement that the feminist movement was first motivated by a desire for "inclusion" in mainstream (malestream) society, noting, as evidence for her doubts, the early feminist emphasis on androgyny. I would argue that the early emphasis on androgyny tended to accept a male-oriented definition of femininity (as being childlike and/or a sexual temptress) rather than a definition created by women themselves. For example, Bem's androgyny scale, much used by psychologists, included *shy*, *childlike*, and *yielding* as stereotypical measures of femininity. Also Mary Daly argued against androgyny a long time ago on the grounds that combining John Wayne and Brigitte Bardot (a man's man and a man's toy) hardly solved the problem of male dominance. It was only later that women themselves were able to develop a more positive definition of femininity based on the maternal virtues of active caring, nurturance, responsibility, non-violence, and nondualistic, nonhierarchical thinking. Once women were more able to define themselves, it became possible to generalize these virtues beyond the private sphere and for women to ask that men become more like them, in both roles and values. Parsons would call this process "value generalization," i.e., creating an overarching value system that can be shared by both sexes and become a basis for increasing gender dedifferentiation.

References

Gill, Sandra, Jean Stockard, Miriam M. Johnson, and Suzanne Williams. 1987. "Measuring Gender Differences: The Expressive Dimension and Critique of Androgyny Scales." *Sex Roles* 17:375–400.

WORKING WITH THE CRITIC I: REPLY TO TUANA

Norman K. Denzin

If sociological feminists are to chart a new course of theorizing that breaks free from the demands the pirate places on the fiancée, they must turn their backs on scientific sociology. This will require the systematic deconstruction of those sociological myths that surround the meanings brought to work, men, women, sexuality, love, and marriage. It will also require a willingness to examine how the lived experiences of sexuality depart from or amplify the mythical beliefs that circulate in the popular culture above love, family, eroticism, and the relations between the sexes in late twentieth century America.

The current postmodern moment is conservative to the core. It is defined by a nostalgic longing for the past where old patriarchal traditions hold sway. It is characterized by a pornography of the visible; the commodification of sexuality and desire; and a consumer culture that objectifies a set of masculine cultural ideals that celebrate the cult of Eros. This is a violent sexual culture. It is a culture that codes personal identity and social worth in terms of the decisive performances attached to sexuality, gender, class, and race.

Cultural power turns on the ability to define and shape the meanings brought to these performances. Feminist theory is not located at the center of cultural power (Bordo 1990, p. 141). It is a system of discourse born from an outsider status in the mainstreams of academic and everyday political and economic life. As an outsider discourse, feminist thought has been especially attuned to the problems of marginality, exclusion, and invisibility (Bordo 1990, p. 141).

This is where Nancy Tuana's text, "With Many Voices: Feminism and Theoretical Pluralism," enters the picture. Balancing the tension between essentialism and difference, and abandoning the search for a master narrative, Tuana, like Fraser and Nicholson (1990), calls for feminist discourses that emphasize the multiplicity of female expressions, voices, and experiences; the multiplicity of truths about gender. Understanding that all glimpses are partial, she argues against the privileging of one voice over another, including the voices from the margins. However, she follows Sandra Harding in suggesting that those on the margins have experiences that expose a fault line, thereby producing a challenge to the privileged interpretations of their situations.

Here is where my text becomes problematic. In privileging the epiphanic moment as a way of entering the world of gendered sexuality, I offered a series of readings of lived experiences where sexuality is made problematic. These included the cases of an intersexed individual, a young boy playing the part of a woman, a woman gazing on the body of a male dancer, a woman learning how to be a prostitute, a battered Korean wife, and gay lovers in the age of AIDS. In reading such moments, scholars must be sensitive to the problem of constructing the subject in their own image. This may happen unintentionally. Tuana may well be right that, in my attempts to read the experiences of Ann, the house madam, I erred in interpreting her statements as examples of negative self-experience. In applying phrases that implied negative connotations, I may have perpetuated certain cultural myths concerning the prostitute and her experiences, including the association of the work with negative self-images, crime, and illicit sex (see Jenness 1990). Indeed, Barbara Heyl's (1979, pp. 113–28) analysis of Ann's situation locates the experiences I examined under the headings "Learning the Trade" and "Madam as Teacher." Ann was using her experiences to teach other young women how to turn out, to sell a sexual service. I misread the account.[1]

A nonessentialist, historically specific, locally grounded, democratic-socialist-feminist pragmatism (Fraser 1989, pp. 105–8), works outward from the race- and gender-segmented labor markets that define contemporary multinational capitalism. It seeks a utopian vision defined in terms of the relations between human beings in multicultural societies "without racism, sexism or heterosexism—an international society of decentralized, democratic, self-managing collectivities" (Fraser 1989, p. 108). How to get from the present moment to this utopian site is what the present discourse is all about.

Note

1. Barbara Heyl, in conversation, supports Tuana's reading.

References

Bordo, Susan. 1990. "Feminism, Postmodernism, and Gender-Skepticism." Pp. 133–56 in *Feminism/Postmodernism*, edited by Linda J. Nicholson. New York: Routledge.

Fraser, Nancy. 1989. *Unruly Practices: Power, Discourse, and Gender in Contemporary Social Theory*. Minneapolis: University of Minnesota Press.

Fraser, Nancy, and Linda J. Nicholson. 1990. "Social Criticism without Philosophy: An Encounter between Feminism and Postmodernism." Pp. 19–38 in *Feminism/Postmodernism*, edited by Linda J. Nicholson. New York: Routledge.

Heyl, Barbara Sherman. 1979. *The Madame as Entrepreneur*. New Brunswick, NJ: Transaction Books.

Jenness, Valerie. 1990. "From Sex as Sin to Sex as Work: COYOTE and the Reorganization of Prostitution as a Social Problem." *Social Problems* 37: 403–20.

PSYCHOANALYSIS AND PLURALISM: REPLY TO TUANA

Christine L. Williams

I heartily concur with Nancy Tuana's call to embrace theoretical pluralism in feminist studies. Unitary notions of womanhood are not only empirically suspect, they are oppressive to the many they exclude. Unfortunately, psychoanalytic theory has been a main offender in this regard: Freud defined "normal" femininity according to his own middle-class ideals of propriety, and he devised a therapeutic technique that has been used to force women to conform to this ideal.

In my contribution to this collection, my goal was not to present an apologia for Freud's unitary model of femininity. Rather, I attempted to salvage elements of the theory that I believe can bridge gaps in our understanding of the reproduction of gender differences. It was part of my "assignment" to focus on the particular strengths of this theory and contributions it could make to feminist studies. But I agree with Nancy Tuana: The theory cannot and should not stand alone.

Tuana notes correctly that psychoanalytic theory ignores the interactional component to gender identity maintenance, as well as the role that economic factors play in the reproduction of gender differences. In fact, I do include these additional factors in my analysis of men and women who work in nontraditional occupations. I assure the reader that space considerations, rather than theoretical hegemony, dictated the focus of my paper.

In my book, *Gender Differences at Work* (Williams 1989), I attempt to show how certain ideals of masculinity and femininity are enforced on individuals by people in positions of power in society. Since most of these people in powerful positions are white, rich, heterosexual men, their irrational needs concerning gender differences are institutionalized in law and organizational policy. My case studies of the Marine Corps and the nursing profession illustrate this process. For example, this marine described to me how the irrational interests of her commanding officer were institutionalized on the post where she worked:

> We couldn't wear jeans around the compound . . . because we'd look less feminine . . . and for a long time women couldn't . . . ride motorcycles to work. I've seen a lot of trash going on; that's just some of the games we [female marines] put up with. But that general is not going to be around forever. People like him are going out of the Marine Corps. People with new, better outlooks are going to be in charge.

To this marine and her female colleagues, these regulations were "stupid" and, even worse, hurtful. Femininity meant something very different to these women, yet their contrary viewpoints were not reflected in official policy. Psychoanalytic theory, I think, helps to explain the origins of the irrational interests behind the general's policies. But other approaches are needed to explain why his particular interests were the ones that were institutionalized and enforced on others. In my view, psychoanalytic theory is not incompatible with other approaches; it simply focuses on issues ignored by the alternatives (and, in turn, it ignores issues that are the focus of other theories).

Tuana is also critical of Nancy Chodorow's work for its assumption of heterosexuality, and the little attention it pays to homosexual and lesbian relationships. Chodorow does not examine or explain homosexuality, as Tuana correctly observes. However, this silence reflects her book's focus (the reproduction of the unconscious desire to mother in girls), not any inherent biases in the theory. Others have explored the etiology of male heterosexuality and homosexuality in ways that are consistent with Chodorow's overall approach (See Johnson 1988, pp. 148–50). In my opinion, one of the strengths of psychoanalytic theory is that it views adult heterosexuality (or homosexuality or bisexuality or asexuality) as a social "accomplishment," not a taken-for-granted outcome of human anatomy.

Furthermore, psychoanalytic theory is not incompatible with other explanations of homosexuality or lesbianism. For example, Adrienne Rich's (1983) analysis of "compulsory heterosexuality" draws upon insights from psychoanalytic theory (even though she is very critical of Chodorow's work). In her view, lesbian attachment is primary in women because of the fact that women mother in our society. It is only through a long process of cultural brainwashing backed up with the threat of violence that women ever "become" heterosexual. Once again, we can see how both the rational and irrational interests of the dominant group in society (white, heterosexual, rich men) are enforced on women. In my opinion, psychoanalytic theory elucidates the sources of these emotional, irrational interests.

I agree with Tuana that there can be no unitary theory of gender, and the goal of this book should not be to attempt to construct one. Indeed, the goal of my essay was not to put forward psychoanalytic theory as the "one right way." Rather, I hope that my discussion of its strengths and weaknesses will provoke those who have rejected the theory outright to reconsider the potential—albeit partial—contribution it can make to the project of "rethinking gender" that Tuana urges us to pursue.

References

Johnson, Miriam. 1989. *Strong Mothers, Weak Wives.* Berkeley and Los Angeles: University of California Press.

Rich, Adrienne. 1983. "Compulsory Heterosexuality and Lesbian Existence." Pp. 177–205 in *The Powers of Desire*, edited by Anne Snitow, Christine Stansell, and Sharon Thompson. New York: Monthly Review Press.

Williams, Christine L. 1989. *Gender Differences at Work: Women and Men in Nontraditional Occupations.* Berkeley and Los Angeles: University of California Press.

THE OMNIRELEVANCE OF SEX CATEGORY:
REPLY TO TUANA

Candace West and Sarah Fenstermaker

As a response to Tuana's comments on our chapter, we will clarify some possible points of confusion. We do not "simply note that 'sex categories are omnirelevant circumstances of action'," as Tuana states. Instead, we note that "to the extent that sex categories are omnirelevant circumstances of action (Garfinkel 1967, p. 118), they provide others with an ever-available resource for interpreting those actions". We imagine and have every reason to believe that the salience of sex category to human interaction is subject to variability. Tuana's question about this point ("What causes gender to be relevant to the accomplishment of any activity?") appears to confuse *sex category* with *gender* (see our reiteration of the distinction between the two in our reply to Wilson). We do not claim that gender is omnirelevant to the accomplishment of any activity. Rather, we claim that the potential omnirelevance of sex category provides a *resource* for doing gender in the course of any activity.

Still, Tuana is correct in her observation that we do not explain *why* sex category would be potentially omnirelevant (other than our reference to Garfinkel's work, of course). We do not pursue this question because it is in one sense, irrelevant: the power of our framework does not depend on a "theory of origin." As we stated in our chapter, the accountability of persons to sex categories is interactional in character, drawing its idiom from the institutional arenas in which social relationships are brought to life. Thus, changes in existing institutional arrangements may result in changes in the *idiom* of gender's accomplishment but they cannot prevent the doing of gender. The further reason we do not explain why sex category might be omnirelevant is that we are not convinced of Tuana's claim that "it is just this 'fact' that most feminists would want to change." As we noted in our chapter, *sex categorization* consists of the ongoing identification of individuals as girls or boys and women or men in everyday life. Is the possibility of such identification truly what "most feminists would want to change"? We think the point arguable, and instead call for renewed rigor in articulating *how* the accomplishment of gender determines gender inequality—what most feminists would want to change.

References

Garfinkel, Harold. 1967. *Studies in Ethnomethodology*. Englewood Cliffs, NJ: Prentice-Hall.

Chapter 14

Toward Integrating Micro and Macro, Structure and Agency, Science and Feminism

Linda D. Molm

The authors contributing to this volume were selected to represent a diversity of perspectives. While that diversity is evident among the papers on which I was asked to comment, the potential for integration is substantial. The papers by Dunn, Almquist, and Chafetz on macrostructural perspectives, Smith-Lovin and McPherson on networks, and Ridgeway on expectations and status all propose structural explanations of gender inequality. Together, they provide a composite of structural effects across different levels of analysis, from macro to micro. Friedman and Diem's paper on rational choice may appear at first glance to present an opposing perspective, one based on individual choice rather than structure. I will argue, however, that it contributes to a more complete theory, which takes account of both structural constraint and individual agency.

One reason for the coherence of these four papers is that all share, implicitly or explicitly, a common philosophy of science and methodology. All accept the use of the scientific method, quantitative analysis, and—in some cases—formal theory construction. This position has been criticized by many feminist theorists, and the feminist debate over science is the explicit topic of the Sprague and Zimmerman paper. These issues are also addressed, albeit more briefly, in the Ridgeway and the Friedman and Diem chapters.

I will organize my comments on the five papers around these three topics: linking structural theories of gender inequality across micro- and macrolevels, integrating theories of structure and individual choice in explanations of gender inequality, and the feminist debate over the scientific method.

My choice of these topics and my evaluations of the papers are un-doubtedly influenced by my own theoretical and methodological preferences. I am a structural social psychologist, working in the tradition of social exchange theory. I use the experimental method to test fairly abstract theories of the relations between structural power and social interaction, including structural explanations of the relation between gender and power. Both the theoretical and methodological characteristics of this tradition have been criticized as male biased. I would argue, instead, that social exchange theory and the experimental method contribute to one of the most fundamental of feminist concerns: testing theories of male dominance based on access to power resources. In short, my own theoretical propensities lead me to favor structural explanations of gender, and my methodological propensities make me less sympathetic to the position on the scientific method taken by Sprague and Zimmerman than by the other authors.

Structural Theories of Gender Inequality: Macro to Micro

Dunn et al., Smith-Lovin and McPherson, and Ridgeway all propose structural theories of gender inequality, at different levels of analysis. Dunn et al.'s chapter focuses on theories at the macrolevel of analysis, where structural variables are characteristics of aggregate units such as communities or nations. Ridgeway's analysis shows how macrostructures are reproduced in microstructures of interaction, through the mechanism of performance expectations. Smith-Lovin and McPherson propose that network theory, which explains gender inequality by the patterns of relationships among social actors, can bridge the gap between macro- and microlevels.

Dunn et al. begin their paper by stating that "macrostructural theories differ fundamentally from social psychological and other microlevel perspectives on gender. The latter focus primarily on the process of learning gendered self-concepts, personality, emotional, and cognitive traits by individuals, and on individual-level choices and behaviors as they reflect and affect gender roles and gender inequality." As the papers by Smith-Lovin and McPherson and Ridgeway illustrate, however, structural analyses of gender are not restricted to the macrolevel. There are many levels of structure between the society and the individual, and not all microlevel analyses are based on individual characteristics. Both Ridgeway and Smith-Lovin and McPherson emphasize the difference between their structural explanations of gender inequality, which view gender differences as the product of changeable situations and structures, and socialization explanations, which view gender differences as the product of relatively unchanging traits internalized early in life.

Analyzing these three papers together offers an excellent opportunity to discuss the interrelationships among these different levels of analysis and different approaches to structure. The result is a more comprehensive picture than can be achieved by any single perspective, and the beginnings of a micro-macro integration.

I agree with Dunn et al. that structural explanations of gender inequality can appropriately begin at the macrolevel. The intersection of economic, political, and family structures at the societal level produces a system of stratification that determines many of the "givens" with which the other theories, operating at lower levels of analysis, begin. Dunn et al. provide a comprehensive and very readable overview of this literature. Their chapter is a useful introduction for anyone who wants to know the major arguments of this perspective. Unlike the other chapters, no single theory is presented. The macroperspective consists of a number of different theories that tend to focus on similar variables, but propose different relations among them (e.g., the debate over the causal priority of material structures or ideological belief systems), or place different emphasis on their relative importance.

As Dunn et al. repeatedly note, the weakest feature of the macroperspective is the paucity of empirical research testing the theories. In addition, most research does not live up to the promise of the theories. As theory, the macroperspective has the advantage of breadth. Gender inequality is conceptualized as multidimensional, and theories span historical eras, societal types, and multiple causation. But in practice, most researchers study contemporary industrial societies, and focus on fewer variables. System-level variables like kinship structures are neglected in favor of more easily measured aggregates of individual variables (e.g., the percentage of women who are married). The authors recognize this problem, and comment on the difficulty of testing this approach. But they offer little in the way of solutions. Is the difficulty merely one of lack of data availability? If so, what data need to be collected, and how might this be done? If the issue is a failure of linking concepts and measures, what improvements do the authors suggest? These are questions that I would like to have seen addressed, even if only in a preliminary way.

Whereas some macrotheories attempt to explain the origins of gender inequality, the network perspective is most useful in explaining the maintenance, perpetuation, and strengthening of existing inequalities. Much of the empirical literature on gender differences in networks is descriptive in nature. Smith-Lovin and McPherson skillfully use this literature, in combination with a few important principles and assumptions, to make a convincing causal argument. By taking a life course perspective, they show how very small gender differences in childhood network relations can accumulate over time to produce substantial levels of gender inequality in different spheres.

Their analysis is based primarily on the principle of homophily—the tendency of an individual to interact with others like oneself (in this case, with members of one's own sex). Beginning in childhood, and continuing in adulthood, homophily produces networks in which males and females primarily interact with their own sex. That, in and of itself, would not produce inequality. The inequality arises from two main sources: differences in the information that is shared by individuals in the male and female networks, and the tendency for small differences to accumulate over time as the result of sequential network effects.

What accounts for the different information—the "different social worlds"—that male and female networks represent, even in childhood? Like many of the macrotheorists, Smith-Lovin and McPherson place major emphasis on women's childbearing and child care responsibilities. They argue that child care permanently alters women's networks, linking women to other women, kin, and neighbors, and restricting their outside contacts. These differences in adult networks are then passed on to children through socialization, creating gender differences in children's networks as well.

Because the theory rests on women's primary responsibility for the care of children (not just childbearing), I think it is more effective at explaining the maintenance of inequality than its origins. Women's biological capacity to bear children and lactate is insufficient to explain the contemporary persistence of women's responsibility for child care. Macrotheorists usually link the effects of women's reproductive role with particular patterns of social organization, most of which do not apply to contemporary industrialized societies. And, as Chafetz and Friedl note (as discussed by Dunn et al.), women's domestic and maternal involvement may in part be a response to exclusion from more socially valued roles in the economy. Thus, the causal priority of inequality in childcare and other roles is unclear.

One of the compelling features of network theory is its reliance on relatively few principles and assumptions. Nevertheless, I believe it would be strengthened by greater consideration of how network ties *between* men and women contribute to gender inequality. While homophily is undoubtedly the rule in friendship networks, voluntary organizations, and occupations, it is equally true that very important relations occur between the sexes. Of greatest importance are the relations between husbands and wives, and the relations between men and women in the workplace. Although men and women are segregated in occupations, they are not necessarily segregated in work settings (as Smith-Lovin and McPherson recognize). For example, interactions between managers and secretaries, doctors and nurses, or flight attendants and pilots are often cross-sex. I would like to see more discussion of how the unequal distribution of power in cross-sex network relations affects gender inequality. Such an analysis might help to explain why women continue to be the principal child rearers, and why occupational sex segregation persists.

While Smith-Lovin and McPherson emphasize networks as the bridge between society and the individual, Ridgeway asserts the importance of interaction processes as an intermediate level of analysis. She proposes that expectation states theory and its concept of status characteristics can explain why women are disadvantaged in goal-oriented interaction. Through the mechanism of performance expectations, macrolevel gender stratification and the cultural belief systems that support it are transformed into behavioral inequalities at the microlevel. Without some account of mediating interactional processes, Ridgeway argues, theories of gender stratification are incomplete.

The theory of expectation states (discussed by Ridgeway) links up particularly well with Chafetz's theory (discussed by Dunn et al.). Chafetz argues that patterned belief systems emerge out of material structures (primarily economic), and serve to legitimate the existing structural arrangements. Although this logic is not explicit in Ridgeway's chapter, some of her other writings (e.g., Ridgeway 1991) include similar arguments. What expectation states theory does is to explain how these inequalities in power and ideology are perpetuated through interaction in groups, such as we might find in work settings, families, and voluntary organizations.

The idea that societal beliefs about gender affect individual performance expectations might suggest an individual-level, socialization-type explanation (i.e., individuals internalize societal beliefs about gender, which then govern interaction). Expectation states theory avoids this by arguing that gender beliefs are only activated in particular situations, in which gender is salient as a status characteristic. Gender becomes salient when some aspect of the situation—such as the presence of both men and women—triggers a gender comparison.

Originally, the theory predicted gender inequalities only in mixed-sex groups. Thus, comparing same-sex groups with mixed-sex groups was the traditional test of the expectation predictions. Empirical studies show some differences between men and women even in same-sex interaction, however (e.g., Anderson and Blanchard 1982; Carli 1982). In an effort to account for these findings, Ridgeway has proposed that gender can be activated by other conditions in same-sex groups: a gender-linked task, or a gender-linked authority structure. Empirical tests of her predictions remain to be conducted. Even if supported, however, the addition of new activating conditions runs the risk of weakening the theory's major strength. The situational emphasis of expectation states theory requires that there be some conditions under which gender is not activated as a status characteristic, and in which men and women do not differ in their behavior. These conditions must occur in same-sex groups, because mixed-sex groups will always activate gender status. As the conditions predicted to activate gender in same-sex groups increase, it becomes more difficult to find conditions under which gender differences are not predicted to occur. Consequently, as Ridgeway notes, explaining interaction in same-sex groups remains one of the weaker parts of the theory. If men and women interact extensively in same-sex groups, as Smith-Lovin and McPherson argue and as a good deal of empirical research suggests, addressing this weakness is an important task for future development of the theory.

The network and expectation states approaches differ in their policy implications for changing gender inequality. Smith-Lovin and McPherson see gender inequalities arising from the relatively sex-segregated nature of networks, beginning in childhood and increasing in adulthood, and the advantageous informational resources in men's networks. Because of the imbeddedness and sequential effects of networks, Smith-Lovin and McPherson suggest that change might be difficult. Interventions would require integrating networks by sex, or changing the source of informational differences. In contrast, Ridgeway views gender inequalities as resulting from the situational activation of cognitive beliefs. Interventions consist of modifying these beliefs (both performance expectations and beliefs about legitimation). For particular groups, this approach appears to be quite feasible. An applied branch of expectation states theory has demonstrated that interventions based on the theory can reduce or eliminate the effects of status characteristics on interaction. These interventions are unlikely to have more broad-based effects, however, because they do not change the cultural belief systems that are at the root of the problem. These belief systems, like the information in networks, are transmitted to new generations through socialization. If belief systems are linked to material resources, as Chafetz proposes, then redistribution of resources may be necessary for any fundamental change.

Individual Choice and Structural Constraints

Rational-choice theories place the locus of causation in the individual actor rather than the social structure. Often, rational-choice theories are presented as if they were in direct opposition to structural theories. For rational-choice explanations that rest solely on the mechanism of preference, that evaluation would be correct. But when rational-choice explanations incorporate external forces in the form of institutional constraints and opportunity costs, as Friedman and Diem do, they link the perspectives of structure and agency.

Friedman and Diem's paper does two things: first, it addresses feminist criticisms that rational-choice theory is sexist in its assumptions, and second, it shows how rational-choice theory can be used, or has been used, to explain gender inequality.

Feminist critiques of rational-choice theory rest on some of the same issues that are involved in feminist critiques of positivist methods. That is, the theory is said to be based on the perspectives of men rather than women. Such an argument rests on the assertion that men and women, for whatever reasons, are different. Sprague and Zimmerman call this "dualistic thinking" and argue that it is not productive. The specific dualism that is at issue in the critique of rational choice is different conceptions of the self: a separative, individualistic model of the self for men, and a connective, emotionally embedded model of the self for women. Chodorow's (1978) work is perhaps most associated with this notion, and both Keller (1986) and England and Kilbourne (1990) draw on it.

Friedman and Diem argue persuasively that the assumptions of rational-choice theory are not based on a separative model of the self. They point out that the assumption of self-interest made in rational-choice theory does not necessarily imply selfishness, as critics of the separative model of self imply. Moreover, they do not reject the possibility of making interpersonal utility comparisons, nor do they agree that such comparisons, if possible, require empathy (a stereotypically feminine trait). A desire to compete (traditionally associated with males) might also motivate one to compare expected and actual outcomes with those of others.

While Friedman and Diem demonstrate that rational-choice theory does not assume a separative, masculine self, they do not comment on the more basic issue of whether evidence supports the assertion that men and women differ in how separate or connected their sense of self is. I am not convinced that women are more connected to others than are men, at least not in ways that are relevant to rational-choice theory. If one looks only at emotional connections in intimate relations, then women may, on the average, fit the connective model more than the separative model, and vice versa. But if one looks at social connections in friendship and work relations, then different conclusions can be drawn. The network literature reviewed by Smith-Lovin and McPherson suggests that adult men and women usually have networks of similar size, although their content differs. Men have ties to a wider variety of occupational settings and work-related occupations, and women to family. Women's networks do tend to be more interconnected, while men's are more extensive and less tightly linked. Is this sufficient evidence to suggest a fundamental gender difference in connectedness to others? I don't think so.

The second issue that Friedman and Diem confront is how well the theory of rational choice can explain gender inequality. Inevitably, this evaluation raises issues of whether any individual-level theory becomes a "blame the victim" or at least a "change the victim" theory of inequality. I think rational-choice theory, at least the version proposed by Friedman and Diem, potentially fares much better in this regard than socialization theories. It does so when it is used to explain the mechanisms of choice within existing structural constraints. When used in this way, rational-choice theory explains the linkages between social structure and individual behavior, and shows the reciprocity between structure and human agency. But I'm not sure that all rational-choice theorists would say, as Friedman and Diem do, that "it does not follow from the rational-choice approach that we would hold women to blame for their position in the socioeconomic structure. The root cause of their position rests with the constraints that they face, not with the choices that they make." That is a statement of structural causation, and rational-choice theory is left to explain the mechanisms of choice within structural constraints.

I am less satisfied with some of the particular illustrations that Friedman and Diem choose to show how rational choice can contribute to explanations of gender inequality. In particular, the illustration of institutional constraints raised the very specters that Friedman and Diem are trying to lay to rest. Gender inequality in the labor market is the result of both gender differences in human capital, and structural constraints operating at different institutional levels. Most research suggests that human capital explains less than 50 percent of the gender gap in pay (e.g., Corcoran and Duncan 1979), and some studies suggest that structure has a greater effect (e.g., Beck, Horan, and Tolbert 1978, 1980). Structure is, without question, an "institutional constraint." Yet, Friedman and Diem choose to illustrate the effect of institutional constraints on human capital—an effort that suggests, even if unintentionally, an acceptance of the economic arguments that human capital differences account for the gender gap in wages. While their illustration shows very convincingly that human capital differences are not entirely a matter of individual choice and preferences, it may nevertheless contribute to the assumption that rational-choice theories minimize the role of other structural constraints.

The illustration of opportunity costs has similar strengths and weaknesses. The analysis of the different opportunity costs that men and women face in making choices about employment is very convincing. But it takes as givens the conditions that only structural theories can explain. Friedman and Diem begin their analysis by stating, "Choosing homemaking is an option much more available to women than it is to men, for many social and historical reasons. . . . [T]his means that women who choose employment bear greater opportunity costs of deciding to be employed than men do." Certainly, that is true, and an analysis of how these different opportunity costs affect decisions is enlightening. But the explanation is incomplete. To explain gender inequality, we must explain that initial assumption: Why is homemaking an option that is much more available to women than it is to men? What are those social and historical reasons?

The macrostructural theories of Dunn et al. provide some answers to those questions. And the network theory of Smith-Lovin and McPherson addresses some of the other factors that rational choice takes as given: preferences, information, the existing structure of relations. In short, these theories have the potential to complement each other in interesting ways. They need not be viewed as competing. The givens of one theory are the dependent variables of the other. Together, they provide one possible picture of the linkages between structure and individual choice. I believe network theory and rational-choice theory are particularly complementary for the very reasons that Smith-Lovin and McPherson use to distinguish the network perspective from economic models. In rational-choice theory, tastes or preferences are exogenous to the system; in network theory, they are determined by the relationships in which a person is embedded. Thus, networks determine the preferences with which rational-choice theory begins. Similarly, Smith-Lovin and McPherson explain how the networks of men and women provide different information about choices and create structures of relations in which opportunity costs are different. Rational-choice theory takes information and structure as givens, and explains the mechanism of choices within them. While rational-choice theory is certainly not the only microtheory that can explain the mechanism of choice, and Smith-Lovin and McPherson might prefer a different theory (or, more likely, no theory of individual choice), the two are potentially compatible.

Science and Feminism: Misinterpreting Dualisms

Sprague and Zimmerman do three things in their chapter: They present the feminist critique of positivism, they show that this critique is based on the very logic it seeks to destroy—dualistic thinking, and they propose a feminist methodology that is intended to integrate the dualisms. Some of these efforts are more successful than others.

Sprague and Zimmerman effectively point out a number of the fallacies of past feminist critiques of positivism. They show, for example, that qualitative work in no way prohibits the biases of the researcher from influencing interpretation of results, that eliminating the researcher's influence on the data is impossible, that subjects' self-reports are no less biased by a patriarchal culture than those of the researchers, and that quantitative research has provided some of the most important and influential data documenting inequality. Ridgeway makes many of the same points in her chapter, and I agree with them.

The main point that Sprague and Zimmerman are making, however, is that the methodological choices preferred by some feminists are based on the same dualistic thinking that feminists criticize. Associating objective, rational, abstract, and quantitative with male, and subjective, emotional, concrete, and qualitative with female, accepts the basic notion of an opposition between men and women that is a requirement of patriarchal societies.

I think it does even more than that. It poses the very real danger of placing women in a methodological ghetto that will undermine, rather than advance, women's status in the profession. Women have fought for a long time to avoid being associated with such "trait" labels as subjective and emotional. Associating one group of these attributes with males and another with females does nothing to change the lower valuation that has traditionally been placed on the female-associated traits. If women's subordinate position in society has created a different way of seeing, thinking, or understanding, then basing research on those differences simply maintains them. Sprague and Zimmerman are quite right to criticize this approach.

But their proposed integration does not solve the problem. It is too vague and idealistic to promote a new methodology, it is too heavily weighted toward the allegedly feminine side of the dichotomies, and it ends up leaning strongly in the direction of applied research. We are left with a vision of research in which teams made up of representatives of different social groups study problems suggested by the needs and everyday experiences of those groups, use a wide range of methods, and write research reports that are understandable to the general public. That may be a useful approach for some purposes, but I don't think it's a general model that we can use to conduct basic research.

My own assessment of these issues is that criticism of male bias in research has concentrated on the wrong part of the research enterprise. It is not the scientific method that is male biased, but the choice of research questions and, in some cases, the origin of theories. As Sprague and Zimmerman correctly point out, the context of discovery— the origin of research questions—is not subject to control through the procedural rules of the scientific method. It is wide open to bias from a variety of sources, including patriarchal ideology. That those biases have influenced research is quite evident. Male researchers have placed greater emphasis on those spheres of society and experience that men are best acquainted with and place the most value on: paid work, organizations, political and economic institutions, and the like. In studying those spheres, they have predominantly studied the experiences of men in them. The spheres that women have traditionally been more acquainted with—and that therefore have been valued less in our society—have been relegated to lower status in the discipline: family, household work, education, health, friendships, everyday life. All of these topics carry lower status as research subjects in our discipline. That is a direct product of male bias, and a worthy target of feminist criticisms.

But to suggest that research methods are also "male" or "female," and to throw out those deemed "male" (or rather, to leave them to men, thus aiding stereotyping) seems, as Ridgeway suggests, to be throwing out the baby with the bathwater. The procedures associated with the scientific method are designed to do precisely what feminist critics of positivism are most concerned about: guard against bias influencing the collection, analysis, and interpretation of data. Obviously, no methodology can completely eliminate bias. But methods based on subjectivity, emotion, and qualitative measurement are far more susceptible to it than those based on objectivity, rationality, and quantitative measurement. The opportunities for selective observing, selective reporting, and subjective interpretation are all far greater with qualitative field methods. There are more opportunities for researchers' biases to enter in, and no way to safeguard against them. Therefore, rejecting the scientific method in favor of more subjective alternatives might have the unintended consequence of increasing, rather than decreasing, ideological bias— including patriarchal ideology.

References

Anderson, L. R., and P. N. Blanchard. 1982. "Sex Differences in Task and Social-Emotional Behavior." *Basic and Applied Social Psychology* 3:109–39.

Beck, E. M., Patrick M. Horan, and Charles M. Tolbert III. 1978. "Stratification in a Dual Economy: A Sectoral Model of Earnings Determination." *American Sociological Review* 43:704–20.

————. 1980. "Industrial Segmentation and Labor Market Discrimination."
     Social Problems 28:113–30.
Carli, L. L. 1982. "Are Women More Social and Men More Task-Oriented? A
     Meta-Analytic Review of Sex Differences in Group Interaction, Reward Al-
     location, Coalition Formation, and Cooperation in the Prisoner's Dilemma
     Game." Unpublished manuscript, University of Massachusetts at Amherst.
Chodorow, Nancy. 1978. *The Reproduction of Mothering: Psychoanalysis and the
     Sociology of Gender.* Berkeley, CA: University of California Press.
Corcoran, Mary, and Greg Duncan. 1979. "Work History, Labor Force Attach-
     ment, and Earnings Differences between the Races and Sexes." *Journal of
     Human Resources* 14:3–20.
England, Paula and Barbara S. Kilbourne. 1990. "Feminist Critiques of the
     Separative Model of Self: Implications for Rational Choice Theory." *Ratio-
     nality and Society* 2:156–71.
Keller, Catherine. 1986. *From a Broken Web: Separation, Sexism, and Self.* Boston:
     Beacon.
Ridgeway, Cecilia L. 1991. "The Social Construction of Status Value: Gender and
     Other Nominal Characteristics." *Social Forces* 70:367–86.

THE METHODOLOGICAL THORN IN THE THEORETICAL ROSE:
REPLY TO MOLM

Dana Dunn, Elizabeth M. Almquist and *Janet Saltzman Chafetz*

Linda Molm presents a perspective on sociological theory, with which
we heartily concur: emphasizing the need to meld theory and research.
She also rightly places the theories in our chapter within the context of
providing the "givens" with which other, more microlevel theories must
begin. After noting our repeated discussion of the paucity of empirical
tests and the difficulties inherent in conducting them, she asks why we
offered so little by way of possible solutions to the problems we enumer-
ated. The answer is both simple and humbling: we have not yet been
able to completely resolve a series of thorny methodological issues.
These include data availability, data comparability, and the operational-
ization of theoretical constructs. For example, we know of no aggregate,
cross-national data that capture such dimensions of gender stratification
as physical coercion and social restriction. Useful indicators might include frequencies of assault and rape of women, and limitations on
women's freedom of movement. Such indicators are problematic because they are not comparable across societies. In Saudi Arabia legislation prohibits women from driving; in some Latin American countries
women are discouraged from leaving the domestic compound unless
escorted by a man.

One solution to the data comparability problem might be to define
women's status on each dimension of statification as a percentage of

men's status, and then to aggregate case studies into a meta-analysis. Almquist, Poston, and Ward use this approach in a forthcoming book, which examines gender inequality in minority groups within thirteen countries. In more developed countries (e.g., United States, England, Australia) women's share of managerial and professional occupations serves as an indicator of gender inequality in the workplace, but in predominantly agricultural countries (e.g., India, China) women's shares of cultivator positions and emerging manufacturing jobs are more appropriate indicators of status in the workplace. Racial, ethnic, religious, caste, and immigrant groups are incorporated into the research, thus capturing each country's own definition of minority groups. The authors then ask how gender inequality in occupations varies across minority groups with differing class locations. Similar studies of other dimensions of gender inequality such as political status and freedom from coercion can provide more rigorous tests of the macrostructural perspective.

This type of multiple–case study approach is capable of recognizing the unique cultural and historical features of societies, as Folbre recommends in this volume. It also resolves the problem of data comparability by permitting diverse operational definitions across different societies. But the case study approach does not resolve the problem of operationalizing inherently difficult theoretical constructs such as the strategic demand for women's labor. The multiple–case study approach is grounded in the scientific/empirical paradigm that Molm so eloquently defends, and that we view as the only productive approach to furthering knowledge and refining macrostructural theories of gender stratification.

References

Almquist, Elizabeth M., Dudley L. Poston, Jr., and Kathryn B. Ward. Forthcoming. *Minority Women and Work in Thirteen Countries.* Albany State University of New York Press.

SOME *DIS*INTEGRATING THOUGHTS ON STRUCTURE AND AGENCY: REPLY TO MOLM

Lynn Smith-Lovin and *J. Miller McPherson*

Molm skillfully integrates our network perspective with other theoretical approaches by arguing that (1) the theories can be arrayed along a micro-macro continuum and (2) a structural view and rational choice are

compatible bedfellows, each dealing with the questions that the other
eschews. We'd like to push our argument a bit further (proving Molm's
point that we probably would prefer no theory of choice at all).

Several of Molm's points illustrate what we think is a perceptual
tendency to translate network properties into individual properties
when we consider interpersonal interaction. For example, she suggests
that we need to pay more attention to the unequal distribution of power
in cross-sex network relations. We certainly agree that network relations
between men and women seldom are equal power. But why is this so?
Perhaps a sociobiologist would argue that power is a genetically selected
male trait, but most reasonable people would look to resources external
to the relationship to determine whether a male-female interaction is
power equal or unequal. There is an extremely productive literature on
social exchange that demonstrates how the network structure of exchange relations affects the relative power of two exchange partners.
While this literature often is phrased in terms of negotiated, marketlike
transactions, Molm has shown in her own work (Molm 1990) how
generally these exchange concepts can apply to social interaction. We
would follow the network exchange literature, and argue that power
within male-female relationships is a direct function of network ties to
other people. The only central aspect of interpersonal power that this
conception leaves out is the control over material resources (which also
can produce differential power in relationships). We, of course, would
argue that material resources are acquired through network structures.
We come into the world with no material wealth; we acquire both
human capital and other resources through our contacts with others.

We are puzzled by Molm's implicit assumption that information is
something external—carried on the network, but not affected by it. In a
network perspective, my information is a function of the contacts I have
with others. The fact that contacts are occasionally transmitted through
sources like print or other media changes the pattern of transmission,
but does not remove the network process. We have access to a great deal
of social scientific work, but we are more likely to read the work of
people that we know. We often find new references because a friend
recommends them to us. In short, most of the information that flows
through men's and women's networks is shaped by those networks.
Networks don't just explain the continuity of content in homophilous
social groups; they explain its content as well.

Molm brings up another potentially individual characteristic of connectedness in her discussion of the Friedman and Diem paper; we agree
with her assessment, based partially on data that we review, that there
is no compelling evidence of fundamental gender differences in connectedness to others. A network perspective would argue against the image

that network ties might vary in some important way based on a property of the node (individual) sending the tie. Instead, we would think it more likely that the individual is shaped by the ties that he or she has. Women seem inherently more connected and emotionally tied to others because more of their network relations are multiplex rather than simplex. A tie to a co-worker one sees only at work is inherently more simple than a tie to a husband who is also a colleague, co-author, recreational partner, etc. Multiple role relationships with the same alter demand more attention to the connection; one may be able to engage in zero-sum competition with a simple co-worker in the best separatist, masculine tradition. The same competition with a co-worker who is also one's recreational buddy, neighbor, and friend will have costs that greatly outweigh the advantage gained. The emotions aroused by winning such a competition will be a simple glow of success in the former case; the gratification will be tempered by mixed emotions (elicited by the multiple role identities involved) in the latter.

The greater likelihood that women will be involved in close, intimate, multiplex relationships leads us to the topic of women's childbearing role. Molm points out that childbearing does not equal child raising, and that women are more likely to take on the lifelong child raising task (with all of its network implications) if they have lower power. The absence of attractive alternatives leads women to make rational choices to stay home and care for the children. We agree but, of course, have a different framing of the problem. It is true that the biological act of childbearing implies only a short period in which the mother's connection to the child is stronger and more time intensive than the father's.[1] Indeed, we all know women whose network ties to work or other extrafamilial domains pull them back into public life as soon as they are physically able (a matter of days, in some cases). Typically, however, this happens to new fathers more quickly than to mothers. It is the mother's relatives who visit to help out. She is more likely to have the network ties to people who have child care expertise. She is less likely to have the ties to good jobs, non familial recreation, etc. Rosaldo (1974) linked the universal inequality between men and women to the fact that women are placed in the domestic sphere by their childbearing role, while men are engaged in more public activities. In our terms, those with the boundary-spanning, extensive networks will know more about what's going on and get more of the goodies. Throughout all of human history, it appears to be the men who have had these extensive, simplex networks. Women may make the choice to be closer to their children, but we don't need much of a theory to explain their micro-level behavior, once we understand the system-level inequalities between men and women.

Molm would argue that this structural effect is more a matter of inequality maintenance than inequality creation. To some extent she is correct. The childbearing function implies child rearing to a much lesser extent in modern societies than it did in the less technologically advanced societies that feature prominently in Rosaldo's argument. But remember the tendency of small differences to accumulate over time as a result of sequential network effects. If the tie to children is stronger for most women for at least a short time, if at least a few women who disengage from unacceptable partners end up bearing children who have no close tie to a father, and if networks are homophilous (so that women are more likely to interact with other women), we will find that women as a social group will seem more knowledgeable and involved in child raising. They will seem more emotional and connected, because they have close, multiplex ties to children and other kin. And they will have less power, because their ties will be less extensive.

Note

1.   The fact that breastfeeding extends this period is a source of some frustration to fathers who would prefer to share equally in child raising activities. Breastfeeding dictates that the midnight feedings remain the woman's domain; it creates a closer tie between mother and child into the second or third year, in some cases.

References

Molm, Linda. 1990. "Structure, Action, and Outcomes: The Dynamics of Power in Social Exchange." *American Sociological Review* 55:427–47.
Rosaldo, Michelle Zimbalist. 1974. "Women, Culture and Society: A Theoretical Overview." Pp. 17–42 in *Women, Culture and Society*, edited by Michelle Zimbalist Rosaldo and Louise Lamphere. Stanford, CA: Stanford University Press.

SAME-SEX INTERACTION AND THE SITUATIONAL APPROACH:
REPLY TO MOLM

Cecilia L. Ridgeway

As Molm notes, we share a common philosophy of science and methodology. Perhaps it is not surprising, then, that I largely agree with her analysis and find her efforts at integration useful. For similar reasons, her criticisms of my expectation states account are telling, pointing to what I must admit are genuine, if not unsolvable problems. She focuses on the theory's acknowledged weaknesses in accounting for gender's effects in same-sex contexts and notes that the solutions I propose to address these weaknesses have their own problematic implications.

I certainly agree that whatever the theory's successes with mixed-sex interaction, it must also come to grips with gender's impact in same-sex contexts, given the importance of the latter for the gender structure of society. This may not be easy for the theory and may require acknowledging additional gender processes beyond the scope of a theory of status processes. As a partial solution, I have suggested that the status characterisitc of gender may sometimes be activated in same-sex situations by the organizational context in which the interaction occurs, allowing expectation states theory to explain some effects of gender in that context. Molm comments, however, that this solution, by increasing the likelihood that gender status will be activated in any situation, blunts expectation states theory's claim to be a situationally specific theory that differs from conventional "master role" or socialization analyses that view gender's impact on interaction as relatively constant across situations.

Molm is essentially correct here, but I am not convinced that the "blunting" is severe enough to seriously weaken the theory's claim to a situational approach. It is important to note that the situational activation idea still does not imply the gender status is *always* activated in every situation, even for women. There will still be some situations when it is not, preserving the basic idea that status relations are socially constructed and situationally specific. Further, it suggests that, given the predominance of male authority structures in organizations, while gender status may quite often be activated for women in same-sex groups, this is much less true for all-male groups. Thus, this theoretical approach suggests that women must more often confront their (low-) gender status than men must confront their (high-) gender status. Men are more often in situations where they are free to deal with one another as "just people" rather than in terms of the gender status of men. While women are sometimes in this relation to other women, they are more likely than men to have to deal situationally with one another as fellow victims of their (low-) gender status. This is a theoretical implication of the situational activation concept that would not be suggested by master role or socialization approaches. That expectation states theory, modified to include the situational activation of gender status, makes empirical predictions that alternative master role or socialization approaches do not indicates that a clear theoretical distinction still remains between them.

In fact, gender indeed may be unusual among status characteristics in that it is activated in more situations than other characteristics (e.g., race) because men and women interact with one another much more frequently than do, say, whites and blacks [although individual blacks must deal with whites much more frequently than whites interact with blacks, as Blau (1977) notes]. Gender divides the population into two groups of roughly equal size and the usual tendency to homophily is moderated by a predominance of heterosexual interest (Ridgeway 1991). These factors together mean men and women deal with one another in one context or another all the time, activating gender status. This surely does greatly strengthen the processes by which gender maintains its status significance and salience in the culture. That, in turn, is likely to increase its carryover effects to same-sex contexts, effects that are as yet poorly understood.

References

Blau, Peter, M. 1977. *Inequality and Heterogeneity*. New York: Free Press.
Ridgeway, Cecilia L. 1991. "The Social Construction of Status Value: Gender and Other Nominal Characteristics." *Social Forces* 70:367–86.

CONSTRAINED CHOICES AND CONNECTED SELVES: REPLY TO MOLM

Debra Friedman and *Carol Diem*

Molm's criticisms often left us puzzled. This is because what she takes to be failings we take to be successes. For instance, where she criticizes us for *merely* explaining the mechanisms of choice within structural constraints, we are enormously pleased to be able to understand those variations. If it is a modest accomplishment, so be it. So too with her evaluation of our demonstration that human capital differences are not a matter of individual choice and preference.

It is the case, as Molm points out, that we do not discuss the effect that structural constraints have in producing gender inequality in the labor market apart from the consequences that such constraints have on the formation of human capital. Nevertheless, the example of human capital seems particularly well suited to the task of demonstrating the importance of structural constraints and the constrained choices of women, as opposed to unconstrained individual choice, in shaping gender inequality. If it can be shown that structural constraints have an impact on human capital, then the one source of gender inequality that might at first glance appear to stem from the unconstrained choices of women can be shown to be a result of structural constraints, and one of the strongest potential reasons for blaming women for their position in the labor market is eliminated. Furthermore, that this argument is fashioned from rational-choice principles was intended to show the incompatibility of rational-choice theory and the sexism with which it frequently has been charged.

We agree wholeheartedly with Molm that these explanations are incomplete, and that much of the most interesting work lies ahead in the investigation of the origins of the unequal structures and unbalanced choices. There is recognition of this particular theoretical lacuna among rational-choice theorists (see, for example, the various studies contained in Hechter, Opp, and Wippler 1990).

Molm's charge that we do not "comment on the more basic issue of whether evidence supports the assertion that men and women differ in how separate or connected their sense of self is" also leaves us baffled. What evidence? If there were sufficient evidence, then we would be in a position to test competing hypotheses derived from alternative theories, rather than in the more preliminary position of formulating the theories from which such hypotheses are drawn. Yet there is an interesting question that can be asked of rational-choice theories: What hypotheses might rational-choice theory offer about variations among men and women in the degree to which their sense of selves is separate or connected?

To answer this we must begin by acknowledging that if one of the distinguishing characteristics of a sense of self is an abiding orientation to the world that implies a *given set of means* for dealing with others, then rational choice rejects a sense of self in favor of a sense of selves. Here, selves is meant in the Simmelian sense of the modern individual whose identity is constructed from her affiliations, which are not necessarily each circumscribed by the other. The self chosen by the actor and observed by the social scientist depends entirely on context. For the rational-choice theorist, the means by which the individual seeks to be efficacious in her world will be chosen in order to enhance the probability that she will achieve her ends. If dealing with her associates is best done with a self that adopts a separative orientation, then this kind of self will dominate in that environment. Here then is the prediction that rational-choice theory would make: When women are systematically and consistently channeled by social processes into situations in which the most advantageous means of achieving goals call upon a connected self, women will adopt connected selves. So, too, for men: When men are systematically and consistently channeled by social processes into situations in which the most advantageous means of achieving goals call upon a separative self, men will adopt separative selves. These are hypotheses that speak to frequencies rather than to preferences, and we would expect to observe systematic differences in self-definition between men and women. However, if women and men both exist in a world in which their self-definitions must be more fluid in order for them to be efficacious in different situations, we would not expect to find such systematic differences in self-definition by gender.[1] These hypotheses imply that the connective-self/separative-self differentiation *derives from* rather than causes observed gender differences, particularly institutional ones.

Note

1. It may be instructive to consider how the hypotheses derived from rational choice would differ from those proposed by those in the tradition of Chodorow (1978). One difference would be, we believe, that these other perspectives would predict greater cross-situational consistency: This consistency emanates from the realms of difference, relevant to parenting, that develop between women and men as a result of their different childhood experiences. (These stem from the fact that women usually mother.) Consistency in this perspective takes the place of efficaciousness in the rational-choice model.

References

Chodorow, Nancy. 1978. *The Reproduction of Mothering.* Berkeley: University of California Press.
Hechter, Michael, Karl-Dieter Opp, and Reinhard Wippler. 1990. *Social Institutions: Their Emergence, Maintenance, and Effects.* Hawthorne, NY: Aldine de Gruyter.

SEEING PAST SACRED SCIENCE: REPLY TO MOLM

Joey Sprague and Mary K. Zimmerman

Linda Molm's discussion of our paper, while sometimes in acknowledged agreement with our arguments, takes on for the most part a critical tone. In her introductory paragraphs, Molm cites her own methodological stance as an experimentalist as making her "less sympathetic to the position on the scientific method taken by Sprague and Zimmerman." She fails to explain why her preference for the experimental method should place her at odds with our viewpoint. We have stressed in our writing that quantitative *methods* must not be equated with positivistic *epistemology*. It may be that Molm is conflating the experimental method with positivistic epistemology. Her major criticism appears to rest with our proposals for integration of the dualisms we cover in the paper (subject/object, abstract/concrete, rational/emotional, and quantitative/qualitative research methods). It is revealing that she does not dispute our basic argument about dualistic thinking and its role in obstructing the aims of feminist research.

While our paper makes points with which Molm might agree, there is a clear difference in how she and we view science, especially the issue of dualistic thinking. Sandra Harding (1986) describes the common understanding of scientific method as a mythical construct (which she calls "sacred science"), a set of moral norms, rather than rules that accurately represent the practice of science. Thus, what we think of as the scientific method is just one way of configuring the methodology of science, not the only way. This idea, according to Harding, is perhaps the most difficult part of the feminist critique of knowledge to grasp—even for feminist scholars themselves. So pervasive and taken for granted is the dominant epistemology that many researchers cannot visualize a science that is not positivistic.

In the paper, we state that both sides of each duality we discuss "present a different yet *equally fundamental* view of what is ultimately the same social phenomenon" (emphasis added). Nonetheless, our suggestions for integrating these pairs are viewed by Molm as "too heavily weighted toward the allegedly feminine side of the dichotomies" and our integration "ends up leaning strongly in the direction of applied research." Her position is intriguing because we said nothing about relative weights. Apparently any divergence from the philosophy of logical positivism is unacceptable. It is ironic that Molm is imposing the application of masculine/feminine and applied/basic as mutually exclusive categories, evoking the very dichotomous thinking both she and we agree is problematic. Her critique provides yet another illustration of the dominance of sacred science.

The description of our proposal as "applied" is particularly disturbing. "Applied" generally refers to research that sets out to solve a particularistic and concrete problem largely devoid of theoretical relevance. We assume Molm is referring to our recommendations that researchers pursue questions that address the conditions of the dominated, that they carefully choose their standpoints, that they evaluate the significance of research by the degree to which it helps them understand daily lives in a gendered world, and that researchers maintain a commitment to the development of those groups whose standpoints they have taken. Whose interests does it serve to obscure the political and theoretical value of this research agenda by invoking the pejorative label of "applied research"? The basic/applied research distinction is itself a logical dichotomy founded on the assumption that social research cannot both advance theoretical understanding and take the standpoints of those who do not hold social power.

Molm falls deeper into dualistic thinking when she eventually ascribes to us the very point of view we set out in our paper to criticize. By the time she reaches her concluding paragraph she has inexplicably categorized us with the very feminists we have criticized—those who view research methods as gendered and who advocate "female" or qualitative methods—and has taken up a defense of the other side of this false dualism: "methods based on subjectivity, emotion, and qualitative measurement are far more susceptible to [bias] than those based on objectivity, rationality, and quantitative measurement." While in the end Molm appears to have missed the point of our paper, in so doing she underscores the need for arguments like the one we are making.

References

Harding, Sandra. 1986. *The Science Question in Feminism*. Ithaca, NY: Cornell University Press.

Chapter 15

Micro, Macro, Choice, and Structure

Nancy Folbre

My primary network is political economy, not sociology. If, as network theory suggests, I am who I know, I am also who I write about, and therefore have become someone new in the course of writing these comments. Still, the socialist/feminist/economist I started out as prevails. In commenting briefly on each of the essays, I have selfishly (or perhaps only self-interestedly) assessed their relationship to my own theoretical concerns. I believe that feminist theorists must develop better links between their conceptualization of individual agency (what economists term a micro foundation) and its theory of macro structures. And I believe that macro structures can't be reduced to one dimension of gender inequality. Three of these essays, it seems to me, are particularly relevant to the former, three to the latter. I've organized my discussion of them around a larger effort to clarify this micro/macro issue. I've paused in the middle, and at the end, to indulge my own priorities.

How do we interpret the choices of individual men and women and how they differ? Christine Williams espouses a Chodorowian psychoanalytic approach, arguing that the organization of child rearing creates a gendered distribution of preferences and priorities in the next generation. Lynn Smith-Lovin and J. Miller McPherson develop a network approach, arguing that preferences are determined by the "relations in which an individual is embedded." Debra Friedman and Carol Diem, on the other hand, defend the economists' traditional emphasis on rational choice. These approaches are not mutually exclusive: The family could be conceptualized as the first "network" that affects subsequent involvements. Once their preferences are set by childhood experiences and social networks, individuals may proceed to act as rational maximizers. The specifics of these arguments, however, are not so easily reconciled.

Williams provides a cogent defense of feminist object relations theory, summarizing much recent research pro and con. I appreciate her discussion of Parson's early appropriation of Freud, and Chodorow's feminist reappropriation. I am convinced by her most general point, that psychoanalytic theory can complement analysis of forms of discrimination embedded in social institutions. And I agree that many positivist critiques of psychoanalytic theory are unfair. But object relations theorists often seem reluctant to risk specific claims—the generalities they invoke are not even contestable.

Williams often equates the broad argument that men and women have disparate ways of relating to the world with the more specific claim that the disparity can be attributed to the organization of child rearing. The work of Lillian Rubin and Evelyn Fox Keller (discussed by Williams) strongly supports the former, but not necessarily the latter. Similarly, Williams's description of her own research dwells on the devaluation of femininity by male nurses, without discussing the childhood experiences of the individuals involved. I wish she had speculated more on the ways we might explore the relative influence of mother rearing (the factor emphasized by Chodorow) and cultural norms, transmitted through reinforcement or cognitive learning.

Also, the possible role of biological factors is slighted by the suggestion that this inevitably implies "determinism"—a word feminist social scientists often seem to brandish like garlic to keep vampire sociobiologists at bay. I mean this as self-criticism, as much as commentary on Williams's arguments—all of us should try to be less territorial. Biological differences between men and women may shape the social construction of gender identity—the tendency to rule them a priori out of order is antithetical to the ideals of interdisciplinary research.

Similar concerns surfaced as I read the essay by Lynn Smith-Lovin and J. Miller McPherson, which focused rather narrowly on the precepts of network theory. I kept wanting to ask the authors what alternative theoretical perspectives might predict the same results. They contrast their assumptions with those of neoclassical economic theory, but not those of object relations theory. In the network view, preferences are not exogenously given, as generally assumed by neoclassical economists, but "determined by the relations in which a person is embedded." I agree, parting company with most of my fellow economists. But could some relationships (such as those with parents) be more important than others? Aren't individuals more than the sum of their network nodes? If neoclassical economic theory overstates the role of individual choice, this theory seems to eliminate it.

Many of the descriptive tools of network analysis are interesting, and the vocabulary is a lot of fun. I now realize that I'm prone to homophily, but involved in at least one intransitive sentiment relation. Pillow talk aside, there are some important insights here—especially the notion that very small differences in the size and character of a network can have a cumulative and therefore quite significant effect on the flow of information over the life cycle. However, as the authors themselves emphasize, network theory puts more emphasis on measurement than explanation, and leaves many questions unanswered. Why are women more prone to homophily than men? Why are women less tolerant of intransitivities? Would Smith-Lovin and McPherson be willing to splice in some object relations theory here? Or some biology? Or could these patterns represent rational responses to constraints imposed on women's roles, constraints that do not all flow from network locations?

Debra Friedman and Carol Diem do a good job of arguing the latter. As an economist, I applaud their eloquent defense of rational choice. However, they exaggerate a bit when they assert that feminist scholars "have typically assumed that rational-choice theory is a fundamentally sexist theory." That statement slights the work of those who have sought to reinterpret the meaning of rational choice, to modify orthodox conceptualizations by suggesting that information is imperfect, preferences are partially endogenous, and utilities are partially interdependent (England 1989; McCrate 1988; Folbre 1988). I love the rational baby, but want to throw out the reductionist bathwater. And I want economists to admit that even grown-up Rational Economic Man succumbs to temper tantrums.

The strongest point of the Friedman/Diem essay, it seems to me, is its distinction between effective and ineffective choices. They argue that individuals may avoid certain commitments to collective action, not because they selfishly want to free ride, but because they judge them ineffective. It is rational and efficient for individuals to ask not only, Is this the right thing to do? but also, Will it make a difference? Still, I think Friedman and Diem understate the extent to which the game-theoretic dilemma, what economists call "the coordination problem," is affected by the level and persistence of altruism. A person who makes a commitment on a purely moral basis, irrespective of the consequences, reduces uncertainty for other decision-makers, and makes it more likely that their commitments will be effective. Whether you call it altruism, leadership, or just plain old strength of character, it's usually an important catalyst to more instrumental forms of collective action.

Friedman and Diem are correct to emphasize that rational-choice theory begins with the assumption that individuals are self-interested, not selfish. Individuals are assumed to maximize utility, not wealth, and they may gain utility from others' happiness as well as their own. Hence the possibility of altruism. However, the theory is seldom applied, at least by neoclassical economists, without the related, very convenient assumption that there are no interdependent utilities. This latter assumption means that your utility does not affect mine, and thus does imply complete selfishness. Indeed, suspension of this assumption would wreak havoc in introductory microeconomics classes, where students are asked to prove that demand curves slope downward. If, for instance, the consumer's invisible utility function encompassed the welfare of Central American peasants, he or she might buy more cups of coffee, rather than less, when their price increased.

Rational economic man isn't what he used to be, having been beaten about the head by economists, as well as sociologists. John Elster (1979), Geoffry Hodgson (1988), and Robert Frank (1990), to name a few, have demonstrated the complexity—and occasional irrationality—of what we call rational behavior. Similarly, game theorists like Robert Axelrod (1984) and rational-choice sociologists like Michael Hechter (1987; Hechter, Opp, and Wippler 1990) have begun to develop plausible stories about the evolution of cultural norms and institutions as solutions to coordination problems. In my opinion, these institutionalist approaches offer a more constructive microeconomic foundation than neoclassical theory—one that is actually more consistent with Friedman and Diem's larger agenda.

Rather than "choosing" between individual rationality and cultural/ social determination, we should move beyond this traditional dichotomy to ask how preferences are socially constructed, and why individuals sometimes actively choose a set of "metapreferences" (preferences about preferences, such as What should I want? and What would I like to enjoy?). Such questions are inherently less tractable than those which begin with a fixed assumption that tastes and preferences are exogenously given, or that individual choice is irelevant. The possible answers are less predictable, less certain, but far more relevant to our understanding of reality.

The appropriate metaphor is a strategic game in which the rules and rewards themselves are subject to negotiation, a game with both cooperative and noncooperative aspects. In traditional neoclassical economic theory, individuals merely choose to buy or sell, subject to income and prices. They have perfect information, and the consequences of their choice are clear; given perfect competition, the parameters are unaffected by others' decisions. In a game-theoretic world, choices are much more difficult, because they are strategic. Outcomes hinge on the simultaneous decisions of other participants.

Decisions to buy or sell are far less important than decisions to accept or contest cultural norms, to reinforce or weaken certain social institutions, to free ride or to pay up. Family, gender, race, ethnicity, citizenship, class, all represent vectors of collective identity and action that can empower certain individuals more than others, often in contradictory ways. Formal mathematical models offer only limited insights, because the game can't be reduced to the simple question, Who wins? What does it mean to win? Does the winner define it, or the other way around? The contest takes place on a microlevel, but its rules, outcomes, and rewards are defined on a macrolevel.

The macrolevel is the locus of what we social scientists tend to describe as "structures" of inequality. Yet we are a long way away from any comprehensive, even consistent theory of such structures. In my opinion, Beth Anne Shelton and Ben Agger are grossly overconfident of Marxist theory. On the other hand, the essay by Dana Dunn, Elizabeth Almquist, and Janet Chafetz on macrostructural perspectives seems too atheoretical and empiricist, almost taxonomic in its approach. I feel more affinity with Kathryn Ward's criticisms of world systems theory, but it doesn't quite deliver on its promise of "reconceptualization."

I have great respect for the Marxist tradition, which has informed my own work. It angers me to see it simplified and distorted. Shelton and Agger endorse a naive epistemology akin to the very positivism they criticize when they write "a theory's validity is proven by the extent to which it is successful in changing the world, not in terms of whether data support the hypotheses derived from the theory." If Hitler had won World War II would that have validated his theories? If the former Soviet Union becomes a capitalist state (if it has not already) will that invalidate Marx? No, and that's not what Marx and Engels meant when they wrote, in their *Theses on Feuerbach*, that the point was not to understand the world, but to change it. There's a big difference between statement of purpose and the assertion that there is some simple arbiter of truth.

These authors assert that Marxism and feminism are not fundamentally different or opposed traditions, that they have "a common enemy." However, they never explain exactly what this common enemy is. The ruling class? Capitalism? All systems of domination? All those who are privileged by systems of domination? Isn't it possible that the correct definition of "the enemy" depends on which struggles are being fought where by whom? Other scholars have developed stronger (though, to my mind, still unpersuasive) arguments in feminist defense of Marxism. Lise Vogel, for instance, argues that male domination is functional for the social reproduction of capitalism (1983). Fraad, Resnick, and Wolff develop the very different argument that men exploit women through a "feudal" class process (1989).

Feminist strands strengthened the fabric of the early Marxist tradition, particularly in the writings of Friedrich Engels and August Bebel. Similar strands traversed early neoclassical theory via Jeremy Bentham, Harriet Taylor, and John Stuart Mill (Folbre and Hartmann 1988). The distinct feminist approach that began to emerge in the late nineteenth century wove many of these strands together in a distinct cloth, emphasizing the collective interests of men and women across classes, conflicts among family members, and the importance of household production. Feminist theory cannot simply be reduced to or subsumed within Marxist theory, especially by pronouncements such as Shelton and Agger's that "Marxism is the more global and more agile analytical strategy because it offers a perspective on the interrelatedness of the totality."

Ironically, the essay by Dana Dunn, Elizabeth Almquist, and Janet Chafetz makes me appreciate the force of Marxist theory on my own thinking. They start out asking "Who gets what? And why?" but focus exclusively on gender, hardly alluding to other dimensions of inequality, such as nation, race, or class. They miss what seems to me the most vital aspect of a macrostructural perspective—the conflicts and complementarities between different structures of inequality that reflect contradictory collective interests. Class differences divide women, just as gender differences divide classes. To take just one example, in countries where a large percentage of women work as domestic servants, a large percentage of affluent women are freed from more onerous requirements of housework and child care.

This essay provides a very useful review of the sociological and anthropological literature on gender stratification, and it gracefully acknowledges the unresolved differences between the materialist approaches represented by Blumberg and Chafetz and the culturalist approach represented by Sanday. Reading along, however, I get the uneasy feeling that feminists have become the establishment, citing authoritative tomes ("the following all argue that . . .") rather than questioning authority. Sometimes the intent seems to find correlations, rather than to provide explanations. Terms like *predictors* and *indicators* make me nervous because they seem to privilege facts that can be quantified, aggregated, and compared "panhistorically and cross-culturally."

These "facts" are all culturally constructed, and many are emblematic of gender bias. Labor force participation rates are notoriously inaccurate, because they underestimate women's participation in the market through family enterprises and informal work. They implicitly devalue nonmarket work as "nonparticipation." Marriage rates mean something quite different in a polygamous than in a monogamous culture. The proportion of women in manufacturing, like the proportion of men, reflects patterns related to the timing and pace of economic development, not merely gender dynamics. Not that such "indicators" are entirely spurious—rather that their interpretation, outside any historical context, as "major independent variables" is macroempiricist, not macrostructural.

Some of Kathyrn Ward's earlier work (1984), focused on aggregate measures of fertility and integration into the world system, falls into the same category, simply defining a different set of major independent variables. In her essay in this volume, however, Ward promotes a more convincing historical perspective, calling for more attention to race and class and more exploration of dynamics between men and women inside the household. As she points out, Immanuel Wallerstein and those of his school have simply subsumed women within households whose fate has been largely determined by the requirements of the global capitalist economy.

Her criticisms of the world system approach are well taken, though I would take them even further. As she points out, exclusive emphasis on relations of exchange and market labor obscures the importance of child rearing and household work. In their emphasis on European capitalist hegemony, world systems theorists overlook the influence that indigenous structures of governance exert over forms of articulation with the world market. No collective interests, coalitions, or political struggles within peripheral nations are theorized, so it's hardly surprising that patriarchal interests and institutions remain invisible. Ward correctly points to the "persistent presence of precapitalist forms of informal and household labor" and argues that men have actively sought to perpetuate the traditional sexual division of labor. She cites research that substantiates this point, such as Jean Pyle's (1990) case study of Irish government policies that effectively restricted female labor force participation.

How then to reconstruct the theory? Ward's recommendations are right on. We can't just add women and stir. Yes, gender, race, and class need to be analyzed in a holistic manner. Yes, we need to look at overlapping relations of production and the distribution of resources. But we need to go beyond these exhortations to develop a conceptual vocabulary that can clarify the relations between different dimensions of collective identity and action. We need to talk more about systems, modes, structures. We need to move beyond critique.

A lot of possible paths are open; I'm not sure I'm headed in the right direction or that I'm carrying the right tools. One thing I like about the Marxist tradition is its emphasis on forms of collective identity and action. This needs to be extended to nation, race, gender, family, and probably some other dimensions, as well as class. This implies that most individuals are in contradictory positions—privileged as men, but exploited as workers, exploited as women, but privileged as citizens of the

United States. Complicated, but, I think, accurate because it helps explain why individuals often join coalitions that are inimical to some of their interests (feminist Republicans, for instance).

One thing I don't like about the Marxist tradition is its economism, reflected in a tendency to reduce social structures to relations of production or distribution. I think social institutions, including implicit and explicit rules, laws, and cultural norms, set the stage and define the context for both production and distribution. In my work, I describe these as structures of constraint that reflect the interests and power of shifting coalitions (Folbre 1991). No balanced pluralism is implied, rather a picture in which patriarchal, capitalist, and white U.S. citizens' interests often converge in oppressive cultural and political, as well as economic hegemony. My intent is strategic—to study the potential for realignments that might empower the groups with which I identify.

Structures of constraint define the context of individual choice; they shape individual tastes and preferences, self-images and affections, networks, affinities, and commitments. But the microlevel is not predetermined. Individuals are still free to exercise their developing capacities for rational action, free to devise new strategies of conflict and cooperation, free to choose. The best choice, in my opinion, is commitment to a feminist theory that is based on principles broader than gender justice alone.

References

Axelrod, Robert. 1984. *The Evolution of Cooperation*. New York: Basic Books.

Elster, Jon. 1979. *Ulysses and the Sirens: Studies in Rationality and Irrationality*. London: Cambridge University Press.

England, Paula. 1989. "A Feminist Critique of Rational-Choice Theories: Implications for Sociology," *American Sociologist* 20(1, Spring):14–28.

Folbre, Nancy. 1988. "The Black Four of Hearts: Towards a New Paradigm of Household Economics," Pp. 248–64 in *A Home Divided, Women and Income in the Third World*, edited by Daisy Dwyer and Judith Bruce, Stanford: Stanford University Press.

———. 1991. *Who Pays for the Kids? Gender and the Structures of Constaint*. Manuscript in progress, Department of Economics, University of Massachusetts, Amherst. Forthcoming, London: Routledge.

Folbre, Nancy, and Heidi Hartmann. 1988. "The Rhetoric of Self Interest and the Ideology of Gender," Pp. 184–206 in *The Consequences of Economic Rhetoric*, edited by Arjo Klamer, Donald McCloskey, and Robert Solow. Cambridge: Cambridge University Press.

Fraad, Harriet, Stephen Resnick, and Richard Wolff. 1989. "For Every Knight in Shining Armor, There's a Castle Waiting to Be Cleaned: A Marxist-Feminist Analysis of the Household." *Rethinking Marxism*, 2 (4, Winter):10–69.

Frank, Robert. 1990. "Rethinking Rational Choice," Pp. 53–87 in *Beyond the Marketplace: Rethinking Economy and Society*, edited by Roger Friedland and A.F. Robertson. Hawthorne, NY: Aldine de Gruyter.

Hechter, Michael. 1987. *Principles of Group Solidarity*. Berkeley: University of California Press.

Hechter, Michael, Karl-Dieter Opp, and Reinhard Wippler (eds.). 1990. *Social Institutions: Their Emergence, Maintenance and Effects*. Hawthorne, NY: Aldine de Gruyter.

Hodgson, Geoffry. 1988. *Economics and Institutions. A Manifesto for a Modern Institutional Economics*. Philadelphia: University of Pennsylvania Press.

McCrate, Elaine. 1988. "Gender Difference: The Role of Endogenous Preferences and Collective Action," *American Economic Review* 78(2):235–239.

Pyle, Jeanne. 1990. *The State and Women in the Economy: Lessons from Sex Discrimination in the Republic of Ireland*. Albany: State University of New York Press.

Vogel, Lise. 1983. *Marxism and the Oppression of Women*. New Brunswick, NJ: Rutgers University Press.

Ward, Kathryn. 1984. *Women in the World-System*. New York: Praeger.

NEITHER BIOLOGY NOR SOCIAL LEARNING: REPLY TO FOLBRE

Christine L. Williams

Folbre raises three criticisms of psychoanalysis in "Micro, Macro, Choice, and Structure." First, she is concerned that the possible influence of biology on our gender arrangements is ignored by the theory. Ironically, it was Freud who popularized the "anatomy is destiny" slogan, and he based his theory of "penis envy" on innate differences between the sexes. Feminist versions of psychoanalytic theory reject this simple biological determinism. Although feminist psychoanalytic theorists do carefully consider the influence of the mother-child relationship on the social organization of gender, they view this essentially biological bond as mediated by culture, personality, and social structure. Our gendered identities are not guaranteed outcomes of our biological natures.

The second concern Folbre raises is that the generalizations drawn from psychoanalytic theory are not "contestable," that is, no one can disagree with them. In fact, several sociologists dispute Chodorow's claims, including her assertion that women have greater emotional needs for connection and more developed relational capacities than men (e.g., Risman 1987; Epstein 1988; Molm in this volume, Ridgeway this volume, Smith-Lovin's reply to Molm in this volume). In my opinion, the evidence supports Chodorow's claims, but not everyone agrees with me!

Finally, Folbre questions whether the psychoanalytic account is any more compelling than alternative cultural conditioning or social learning theories of gender socialization. I think Chodorow makes a convincing argument that these alternatives are insufficient because they lack an analysis of the mediating role of the unconscious in acquiring and sustaining our gendered identities. As Chodorow notes:

> We do not just react to our contemporary situation or conscious wishes, nor can we easily change values, feelings, and behavior simply if we have an encouraging social setting... [Role-training theories and social learning theories] suggest that changing the social setting and nature of reinforcement should automatically change behavior, which we know from experience is not true. (Chodorow 1989 p. 171)

It is precisely because psychoanalysis offers an explanation for the tenacity of our gender arrangements—without relying on biological determinist accounts—that I find the theory more compelling than alternative models of gender socialization.

References

Chodorow, Nancy. 1989. "Feminism, Femininity, and Freud." Pp. 165–177 of *Feminism and Psychoanalytic Theory*, edited by Nancy Chodorow. New Haven, CT: Yale University Press.

Epstein, Cynthia Fuchs. 1988. *Deceptive Distinctions: Sex, Gender, and the Social Order*. New Haven, CT: Yale University Press.

Risman, Barbara J. 1987. "Intimate Relationships from a Microstructural Perspective: Men Who Mother." *Gender & Society* 1(1, March):6–32.

ELIMINATING CHOICE: REPLY TO FOLBRE

Lynn Smith-Lovin and *J. Miller McPherson*

There's an old joke about economists studying how people make choices and sociologists studying how they have no choices to make. Folbre accuses us of being sociological to the core, of developing a theory that eliminates choice. One senses that she is somewhat repelled by the notion; she asks "Aren't individuals more than the sum of their network nodes?"

We plead guilty to her charges. We argue that the question should be, Where do the preferences, tastes, utilities, values, language, norms, etc., come from? If you think that they come from other people, then you are in essential agreement with us. Other than biology, divine inspiration, or the material manifestations of culture, it's difficult to imagine another answer. The really important difference between our perspective and rational choice is that the unit of analysis for us is the connection, rather than the actor. The configuration of those connections determines the outcome, rather than the internal states of actors. To take an individual at a single slice in time and to analyze the influence of preferences and information on choices misses the social process underlying these outcomes.

If one believes, as we do, that both the menu of available alternatives and the tastes/utilities/preferences that the individual uses to judge them come from social relationships, then the independent explanatory power of any theory about choices is vanishingly small. To take an example from our own work, we might try to argue that rational choice dictated our decision to join the 4th Street Mothers' Play Group rather than the Sam Hughes Historical Preservation Society. Fair enough. We will acknowledge that rational choice might give us some insight into this decision (although even here the utilities may be determined by whether or not we have a close network tie to a young child, whether we have friends interested in historic architecture, or whether friends in the neighborhood led us to move into that area to begin with). Alternatively, take the structural-network perspective. We are first led to ask how many groups there are to join; the number available to us in Tucson is in the hundreds of thousands. On the face of it, therefore, we conclude that the explanatory power of a structural approach must be at least one hundred thousand to one in comparison to rational choice.

A rational reader will be objecting at this point. Why are we unfairly including groups outside the neighborhood, even outside the city? Why are we including bowling leagues in Nebraska and men's clubs in New York City, and so on? But that's just the point. The rational-choice perspective must assume a finite number of choices, which have to be bounded in time, space, language, norms, and all of the other baggage that comes from even the most primitive notion of social structure. The vividness of choices that we have to make gives these questions an inappropriate weight in our thinking about social life. As sociologists, the question is, What acounts for this social form? rather than Why did I do that? In answering this question, we immediately have to consider all of the possibilities, rather than only the ones we spontaneously trip over. When we broaden our perspective in this way, we immediately see that the distribution of possibilities in society is constrained almost totally by the power of time, space, and the institutional structure of society. Why don't you belong to every one of the millions of groups that exist in the United States? The answer to that question is obvious to us all. But rational choice wants us to forget that answer, to focus on the two or three choices we're looking at today.

THE IMPORTANCE OF ALTRUISM AND THE INTERDEPENDENCE OF UTILITIES: REPLY TO FOLBRE

Debra Friedman and *Carol Diem*

If there is a recurring theme in critiques of rational-choice theories—particularly theories of collective action—it is that they underestimate the degree to which behavior is motivated by moral rather than by strategic considerations. Folbre reiterates the point. Like most, we would rather live in a world populated more by altruists, leaders, and those demonstrating plain old strength of character than by rational actors concerned only with their own well-being. Yet there is no evidence to support the claim that we live in a world where people are altruistic regardless of the efficaciousness of their actions (see Hechter and Friedman 1984a, 1984b, for extended discussions of this point).

Ultimately, though, this is a pointless debate. Substituting other assumptions for rational behavior will not move us farther along; nor will indiscriminately adding nonrational factors to the utility schedule. The question really must be turned toward what sorts of conditions foster altruistic motivations and the actions that result from them. What kinds of institutional designs produce the most morally appealing behavior on the part of the greatest number of citizens? As Folbre notes, game theories may offer some hints: Iterative games, where players know that they will engage in repeated interactions with the same partners, often lead to more socially optimal outcomes than one-shot plays. So, too, may experimental work: Dawes and his associates, for instance, have done experiments in which simple discussion among subjects promotes subsequent cooperative behavior (see Dawes, van de Kragt, and Orbell 1990). Theoretical work outside game theory can also be instructive: Solidarity, a socially desirable state of affairs by most standards, rests, according to Hechter's (1987) analysis, on dependence and social control. Whether theoretical or empirical, the aim of such research in each case is to understand the processes that lead to different types of social outcomes.

If we all have within us both the capacity for selfish behavior and for socially responsible behavior (as we believe that all individuals do), the compelling undertaking is to understand when we draw on one kind of motivation or the other.[1] Framed in this way, we can begin to ask when individuals or groups are likely to "accept or contest cultural norms, to reinforce or weaken certain social institutions, to free ride or to pay up." These decisions take place within the constraints of existing laws and social institutions. Yet even if our aim is to explain how the existing laws and institutions arose in the first place, or how we ended up with the preferences and goals that we hold individually or as a society, we would need to start with the underlying (and ugly reductionist) question of what motivates these behavioral variations.

This kind of inquiry might lead us back into the questions of the independence and interdependence of utilities, and interpersonal comparisons of utility. It is important to note that here there are two separate choices to be made for any theoretical model: One about whether the model will assume independence or interdependence of utilities, and the other about whether the model will allow interpersonal comparisons of utility.[2] Thus, any theoretical model will have one of four combinations, and it is important to note that none of the four combinations are ruled out entirely in rational-choice analyses, though some occur with more frequency than others.[3] Folbre suggests that most rational-choice theorists reject the assumption of interdependence of utilities, but we can think of at least one enormously important literature involving hundreds of authors—that concerned with issues of social choice, especially emanating from Arrow's (1951) classic work—in which the subject was explicitly conceived as concerned with problems of interdependence of utilities.

Unlike Folbre, as sociologists we do not have to be concerned about what will wreak havoc in introductory microeconomics classes.[4] In the advanced classes they are teaching Sen (1979) and Coleman (1990), neither of whom rejects the possibility of interpersonal comparisons of utilities.[5] In fact, for reasons that are broached in the following paragraph, the study of social inequalities, such as those of gender, can be served by theoretical advance in the understanding of interpersonal comparisons:

> [I]nterpersonal comparison is not the passive concept that is implicit in economists' definitions of utility. Intrinsic to it is a notion of political power. ... Thus the idea of interpersonal comparison of utility actually implies two comparisons. First, since the very concept of the utility of a good implies a willingness to sacrifice something to obtain the good, any interpersonal comparison must include a manifestation of the actor's willingness to sacrifice something, deriving from the utility he stands to gain or lose from the outcomes. ... But the interpersonal comparison must also include a test of the relative efficacy of the actors' resources for realizing their goals. This dual comparison may take the form of conflict or the form of exchange; but whatever form it takes, *it generates systemic outcomes through social processes.* (Coleman 1990, p. 775, emphasis added)

Whatever it is that contributes to further theoretical progress on all-important questions of how gender inequalities originate and how they are sustained is, it seems to us, worth pursuing. There is nothing in rational-choice theory that stands in the way of contributing to this endeavor; more than this, the explicit concern of rational-choice theory with the complex link between individual action and social outcomes may make it an ideal approach.

Notes

1.   Very few theorists have attempted to address this question. Two exceptions are Margolis (1982) and Emerson (1987).
2.   An analytic approach to the problem of interdependent preferences would seek to understand the internal structure of a holistic preference relation for a given set of preferences. This could be either the set for an individual or for a group (as in the case of issues of social choice; Fishburn 1987, p. 874). The question of interpersonal comparisons is quite distinct. Here the question is whether an individual is able to make meaningful comparisons of utility levels among others, or in more limited theoretical constructions, to make meaningful comparisons of utility differences (see Harsanyi 1987, pp. 955–57, for a clear recitation of the specifics of the use of interpersonal comparisons of utility).
3.   There are exceptions to this statement among subgroups of rational-choice theorists. Ordinalists, for instance, cannot admit of interpersonal comparisons of utility differences, though they can assume interpersonal comparisons of utility levels.
4.   Folbre's quip about the consumers buying more coffee if they considered the welfare of Central American peasants misses the point on several grounds. First, a rational actor would always realize that buying a cup of coffee would have a negligible effect on the welfare of any Central American peasant. Second, we are much more interested in explaining collective decisions (political policies) like tariffs on coffee than we are on a single person's buying behavior.
5.   A discussion of the economic conception of interpersonal comparisons of utility is found in Coleman (1990, Chapter 29).

References

Arrow, Kenneth. 1951. *Social Choice and Individual Values*. New York: Wiley.
Coleman, James S. 1990. *Foundation of Social Theory*. Cambridge, MA: Harvard University Press.
Dawes, Robyn M., Alphons J. C. van de Kragt, and John M. Orbell. 1990. "Cooperation for the Benefit of Us—Not Me, or My Conscience," pp. 97–110 in *Beyond Self-Interest*, edited by Jane J. Mansbridge. Chicago: University of Chicago Press.
Emerson, Richard M. 1987. "Toward a Theory of Value in Social Exchange," Pp.

11–46 in *Social Exchange Theory*, edited by Karen S. Cook. Newbury Park, CA: Sage Publications.

Fishburn, Peter. 1987. "Interdependent Preferences," Pp. 874–76 in *The New Palgrave*, edited by John Eatwell, Murray Milgate, and Peter Newman. New York: Norton.

Harsanyi, John C. 1987. "Interpersonal Utility Comparisons," Pp. 955–58 in *The New Palgrave*, edited by John Eatwell, Murray Milgate, and Peter Newman. New York: Norton.

Hechter, Michael. 1987. *Principles of Group Solidarity*. Berkeley: University of California Press.

Hechter, Michael, and Debra Friedman. 1984a. "Does Rational Choice Theory Suffice? Response to Adam," *International Migration Review* 18(2):381–88.

Hechter, Michael, and Debra Friedman. 1984b. "Response to Dickie-Clark," *International Migration Review* 18(2):171–73.

Margolis, Howard. 1982. *Selfishness, Altruism, and Rationality: A Theory of Social Choice*. Chicago: University of Chicago Press.

Sen, Amartya. 1979. "Interpersonal Comparisons of Welfare," Pp. 183–201 in *Economics and Human Welfare: Essays in Honor of Tibor Scitovsky*, edited by M. Boskin. New York: Academic Press.

DIFFERING WITH FEMINIST DIFFERENCE:
REPLY TO FOLBRE

Beth Anne Shelton and *Ben Agger*

Nancy Folbre's comments on our chapter are predictable enough. For us to appear to ingest feminism by Marxism invites all sorts of aversions to territoriality—as we acknowledge in the paper itself. But she misses our basic point: What passes for Marxism and feminism theoretically reflects politically invested readings that have a stake in producing these versions as hostile discourses and practices. We are not the first to make this argument. The Frankfurt School's critical theory attempted to theorize the relationship between production and reproduction in much the same way.

Our point is that Marxism and feminism become the same discourse/practice, in Foucault's sense, when we rethink what it means to be a Marxist and feminist in theoretical and political terms. Notably it means that one opposes *the hierarchy of production over reproduction—the valued over the seemingly valueless*. In our terms, Marxism, as the more self-consciously totalizing perspective, affords us a language (e.g., production/reproduction) with which to expand Marxism/feminism into the totalizing critical theory aimed at by Horkheimer and Adorno in *Dialectic of Enlightenment* (and, of course, by Marx in *Captial*).

To note that Marxism has ignored important questions raised by feminists, notably about the politics of the personal, is to repeat the obvious. Historically, most Marxisms have been oblivious to the politics of personality, sexuality, and reproduction. But we argue that this is not in the nature of Marxism, just as the Frankfurt School argued that an expanded, revitalized Marxism can comprehend the roles of the state and the culture industry in prolonging capitalist domination. We try to read a feminism—attention to the politics of reproduction—into Marxism because it could and should have been there all along, whether one talks about the visionary critique of alienation in the 1844 manuscripts or the critique of political economy laid out in *Capital*.

Folbre does not appear to understand the historicity of our question: She does not appear familiar with the attempt to produce a feminist critical theory (e.g., Fraser 1989) that expands Marxism through feminism. Ignorant of this theoretical project, it is reasonable that one respond to our attempt to conflate Marxism and feminism with some trepidation, if not downright incredulity.

Folbre is angry that we have "simplified and distorted" Marxism. She accuses us of developing "a naive epistemology" that relates a theory's validity to its practical intent. "If Hitler had won World War II would that have validated his theories?" she wonders, rhetorically. She then goes on to *misstate* the eleventh thesis on Feuerbach. She not only misstates the eleventh thesis, she misreads our epistemological argument and misses its obvious grounding in the logic and by now well-explicated tradition of western Marxism. Although Folbre expresses "great respect for the Marxist tradition" she does not understand it very well. In fact, we seriously doubt the extent of her respect for Marxism where, later in her essay, she dismisses Marxism as "economism," a tired stand-up line in the repertoire of both liberals and the right.

To correct the record: Marx argued (we think correctly) that one cannot verify validity claims outside social history; he opposed the ideological notion that there are invariant "laws" of social motion. The "truth" of Marxism can only be assessed with respect to the unfolding of the telos or logic of history—for him, the inescapability of socialism. One cannot "test" Marxism (according to Marx, Lukacs, the Frankfurt School, and us). Rather, Marxism is a philosophy of history the validity of which cannot be evaluated with respect to data in the here and now. Socialism is "true" because its unfolding is contained in the "rational kernel" of history's logic. The project of theory (or "science," for Marx) is to hasten the unfolding of history—not to verify validity claims with reference to static (inessential) data. Otherwise, ideologists would have long ago "proved" the inevitability of capitalism, sexism and racism.

Folbre goes on to say that we do not spell out the "common enemy" of a Marxism/feminism. Actually, we do. We argue that the common enemy of our Marxism/feminism is all hierarchies of the valued over the devalued and valueless. That is our central theoretical claim and one that Folbre fails to refute.

Finally, Folbre simply rejects our claim that "Marxism is the more global and more agile analytical strategy because it offers a perspective on the interrelatedness of the totality," But virtually no version of feminism (differentiated from Marxism as a separate discourse/practice) aims at totality in the way that Marx did. On the other hand, Marxism provides an explanation of the social relations of production and reproduction. The social relations of reproduction reinforce the social relations of production because they reinforce women's subordination to men in the labor force and provide unwaged labor to keep the costs of the reproduction of labor low (see also Smith 1983). This is an interpretive question that must be resolved with reference to texts themselves. If Folbre can find many totalizing feminist texts, fine.

It is risky to combine Marxism and feminism, especially where Marxism is claimed to be the more totalizing theory and practice. This is especially risky at a time when totality itself is suspect, impugned by postmodernists as the epitome of the project of modernity. But we take these risks because we believe that the differentiation of Marxism and feminism inevitably leads to liberalism. It should be obvious by now that feminism is a valid, valuable project that does not need to be defended jealously against integration with other oppositional projects. These integrations change both feminism and the projects with which it is combined. It should be equally obvious that Marxism is incomplete with respect to the politics of reproduction. For feminism to entrench itself in its difference fails to feminize oppositional projects like Marxism as well as to inform feminism with the totalizing critique of political economy ambitiously outlined by Marx in *Capital*.

References

Fraser, Nancy. 1989. *Unruly Practices: Gender, Discourse and Power in Social Theory*. Minneapolis: University of Minnesota Press.

Smith, Joan. 1983. "Feminism and Analytic Method: The Case of Unwaged Domestic Labor," *Current Perspectives in Social Theory* 4:205–23.

THROWING OUT THE BABY WITH THE BATH WATER:
REPLY TO FOLBRE

Dana Dunn, Elizabeth M. Almquist, and *Janet Saltzman Chafetz*

Nancy Folbre offers three criticisms of our chapter on macrostructural theory: (1) it is "too atheoretical and empiricist"; (2) by ignoring forms of stratification other than gender, it misses "the most vital aspect of a macrostructural perspective"; and (3) the "facts" used are "emblematic of gender bias." We take exception to all of these criticisms.

We conceived of our task in this chapter as explicating the central theoretical logic and basic constructs of the major macrostructural gender theories *and* demonstrating the extent to which existing research supports/refutes these theories. Macrostructural theories, unlike most of the others discussed in this book, are eclectic in their choice of theoretical constructs. They draw upon more than one of the broader, more general metatheories (e.g., Marxist, Freudian, Weberian) that constituted the basis for other chapters and add constructs that may not flow specifically from any of the discipline's metatheoretical approaches. What makes them "theories" rather than empirical generalizations (or as Folbre erroneously suggests, taxonomies) is that they all posit causal orderings between the various constructs they include. Indeed, the central differences among the theories we reviewed concern causal ordering and relative emphases among a set of constructs on which the various theories generally agree.

The empirical flavor of the chapter is therefore the result of two things. First, it reflects our decision to include a review of the theoretically relevant empirical literature. Second, we organized the chapter around the central constructs that appear in most of the theories, but whose precise theoretical role varies among theories. These decisions reflect our understanding of "theory" as empirically testable, but abstractly stated explanations of some specified phenomenon, in this case, level of gender stratification.

The second criticism Folbre raises is our failure to include a discussion of the other forms of structured inequality (e.g., race, class, nationality). She rightly points out that women are divided along these lines and that there are therefore conflicts and complementarities between different structures of inequality. Indeed, she goes so far as to conclude her comments by arguing that "commitment to a feminist theory [should be] based on principles broader than gender justice alone." Our understanding of the purpose of this book was that chapters were to review extant gender theories, not to create new ones. To date, there is no macrostructural theory that systematically integrates the various structures of inequality into a coherent explanation of anything. There is an abundance of case-oriented, descriptive work that addresses the "intersection of class, race and gender," but the highly difficult theoretical work has barely begun. The research that does exist is either Marxist or more microlevel in focus, both topics for other chapters.

We would argue that in order to develop a theoretical understanding of the interaction of three (or more) systems of inequality, each must first be understood substantially well in its own right. The theories discussed in our chapter are of two types: (1) those developed by anthropologists concerning small and simple societies where nongender forms of structured inequality are absent or minor; (2) those developed by sociologists who *explicitly* ignored other forms of inequality as a conscious strategy, in order to focus on developing as complete an explanation as possible of gender stratification as a macrolevel construct. Neither we, as chapter authors, nor probably the theorists whose work we discussed, would dispute the need for a next step: to develop macrolevel theories linking the various forms of structured inequality that characterize societies.

The third and final point raised by Folbre criticizes us for "citing authoritative tomes. . .rather than questioning authority." She is "nervous" with "terms like *predictors* and *indicators*. . .because they seem to privilege facts that can be quantified, aggregated, and compared 'panhistorically and cross-culturally.' " How these two points are related logically is not clear to us, but nonetheless, we plead guilty. We along with the theorists whose work we discuss, share a view of sociology that rests on the assumption that patterned regularities exist in social life, and that they can be observed and measured—although often crudely as we pointed out on numerous occasions in our chapter. If the "indicators" cloak meaningful and substantial diversity across time and/or space, then the data will fail to show any meaningful patterns. As of now, it seems more a matter of personal bias than evidence to reject the possibility of such explanations and empirical tests.

It has become fashionable among many feminist scholars to proclaim that the approach to sociology manifested in our chapter is "masculinist"; that empirically oriented theory and quantitative data are antithetical to a "feminist consciousness." Linda Molm's discussion of the chapters in this book cogently addresses the fallacies associated with precisely this kind of criticism. Folbre dismisses the macrostructural approach on the basis of personal preference, which we see as equivalent to throwing out the theoretical baby with the dirty methodological bathwater.

REFRAMING THEORIES: REPLY TO FOLBRE

Kathryn B. Ward

I agree with Folbre's comments and look forward to her work on structures of constraint. She works with an interactive approach that does not privilege any oppression over the others. She moves away from narrow economistic notions of determination and into how people shape their lives and structures.

However, a problem for all of us is how to transform and reframe theories when we are steeped in them. Our vocabularies and ideas about how the world works reflect our training and our own personal identities in regard to our race, class, gender, and geographical location. Some solutions to our dilemmas come from some of the new work on race, class, and gender. (See, for example, the prescriptions on research and epistemologies in Aptheker 1989; Collins 1990; Minnich 1990; Hooks 1990.) Aptheker notes the importance of intellectually (and physically) removing oneself from older theoretical orientations to come up with a new bedrock from which to build our theories. She suggests that we use women's standpoints and pivot around them so as to gain a complete picture of their daily lives. Further, she honors women's narratives and poetry as a source of knowledge from which to build our theories. Collins' black feminist epistemologies complement this work. She calls for adding new ethics of caring, emotions, compassion, and connection to our research. As experts, we need to take our work back to the community from which our work is drawn. Minnich suggests that researchers need to be willing to float theoretically for a while and look for experts in unexpected places. Hooks (1990, p.54) calls for white feminists to account for the process by which they transformed themselves and their intellectual lives to include race, class, and gender. Simply acknowledging that we are white is not enough anymore. As such we can begin to map some of the socioeconomic mosaic of race, class, and gender, which we are only beginning to understand.

References

Aptheker, Bettina. 1989. *Tapestries of Life*. Amherst: University of Massachusetts Press.

Collins, Pat Hill. 1990. *Black Feminist Thought*. Boston: Alwyn and Unwin.

Hooks. Bell. 1990. *Yearning*. Boston: Southend Press.

Minnich, Elizabeth. 1990. *Transforming Knowledge*. Philadelphia: Temple University Press.

Chapter 16

The Subject Woman

John Wilson

"Sociologists and feminists will not give the same accounts of social relations unless they share the same political priorities" (Ramazanoglu 1989, p. 439).

The object of feminist theory is to place women and their lives in a central place in understanding social relations as a whole. Feminists recover and explore the aspects of societies that have been suppressed, unarticulated, or denied within male-dominated viewpoints. Questions central to feminist theory are: What is gender? How is it related to anatomical sexual differences? Are there more or less universal attributes of masculinity and femininity and, if there are, what are their origins? How is gender identity organized and sustained in the day-to-day reproduction of social relationships in different forms of society? How is gender constituted and sustained in a person's lifetime? Does gender have one history or many? What causes gender to change over time? What are the relations between heterosexuality, homosexuality, and gender? Is there anything distinctly "male" or "female" in modes of thought and social relations? How does gender relate to other sorts of social relations, such as class and race? How is the fact that men hold more power than women to be explained?

Feminist theory is more comprehensive than sociological theory. Some, but not all, feminist theorists believe that women have a distinctive standpoint, a mode of experience, and assume that theory will be informed by that experience. Some, but not all, feminist theorists believe that theory must be normative, rethinking ideas of excellence and justice, and are committed to a theory that produces knowledge for, rather than of, women. They believe a feminist approach implies sympathy and political commitment on the part of the writer, where the idea is to study in a critical fashion in order to provoke change.

Each of the essays under review addresses the question of the relation

343

between feminist theory and sociological theory. All answer this question differently because their authors occupy different standpoints with respect to feminism and sociology. This essay, likewise, reflects the socialist feminist perspective from which it is written. From this perspective, there is little point in considering the relation between feminism and social theory unless the goal is to improve our understanding of, and ability to change, social relationships. Feminism's contribution to sociological theory must therefore be measured against its ability to distance itself from what is, to distinguish between appearance and reality, and on that basis to offer a critique of existing social practices. Socialist feminism also seeks the middle course between essentialism and nominalism.[1] It rejects alike the feminism that would propose an essentialist formulation of what it means to be a woman, and the feminism that absolutely rejects the reality of gender in favor of a cultural-discursive determinism. The tendency toward essentialism is betrayed by its biologism and psychologism. The tendency toward nominalism is more insidious, however, because it presents "woman" as a fiction, a locus of pure difference and resistance to logocentric power. If, as this implies, there is no woman as such, then the very issue of women's oppression would appear to be obsolete and feminism would have little reason to exist. Sociology must embrace feminism's focus on difference without going so far as to situate this difference entirely at the level of the text.

To be considered a theory at all, feminism must say more than that women are *typically* subordinated to men. The domination must be a systemic regularity. Unfortunately, much of what passes for feminist thinking in sociology is simply saying, for example, that market workers dominate nonmarket workers, categories that conceivably could be filled by either gender. For gender theory to be systemic it must be logically inconceivable for the categories "male" and "female" to be reversed. Compare, for example, the role of classes in Marxist theory: capital and labor could not conceivably change places. Thus, if women's position is explained as the result of exploitation in the household, what is to prevent men and women changing places? To establish that many men will gain an advantage from their relationship with women restates what is already known rather than demonstrating the existence of a system of patriarchy. An essay in feminist theory should therefore be asking how the subordination of women is produced, maintained, and changed. This is not the same as, and goes much further than, simply asking how gender is involved in the processes and structures that previously had been conceived as having nothing to do with gender.

Feminist theory in the 1990s sees itself grappling with a number of problems of considerable relevance for sociological theory:

1.   What is the nature of the difference between men and women? How well does theory enable us to distinguish among categories of men and women?

2.   What is the relation of gender to other constituents of human identity, such as class and race, and what is the nature and source of the power men have over women?

3.   What is the meaning and significance of theory in feminism? How are the conventional dualisms of sociological theory to be deconstructed and redefined? Does a woman-centered perspective call for a new approach to investigation and analysis?

The remainder of this essay will assess the contribution of each of the chapters under review to answering these questions.

The Nature of Difference

The search for a distinctively feminist theory, in which the difference between men and women is the focal point, inevitably raises the question of whether or not men and women are essentially different. Is there an essentially female sexuality? Are sexual differences to be celebrated, or are they contingent, to be denied?[2] Some feminists believe it is legitimate to write of women as a social category distinct from men: The creative and nurturant aspects of femininity devalued in a patriarchal society are thus revalued. From this also flow attempts to discover a feminist ethics, epistemology, esthetics, and the like.

Few sociologists could embrace essentialism in any guise, and the contributors to this volume are no exception. Characteristics supposed to be essentially feminine, such as restraint, dependence, and passivity, are not regarded as traits at all but as consequences of circumstances that encourage women to act or feel dependent. West and Fenstermaker argue that the important thing is not whether sex/gender differences are real or imaginary, but how the process of assigning facticity and significance to gender works, how biological categories are deployed to render social encounters intelligible. They are interested in gendering rather than gender.

From an ethnomethodological point of view, femininity and masculinity are not invariant idealizations of human natures uniformly distributed in society; rather, what is invariant is the *notion* that men and women possess different natures. There could be no more radical challenge to the essentialist argument from a sociological point of view because its most salient question is "bracketed": Not only gender, but sex is a social construct. Gender is a situated accomplishment, one means (among many) of making interaction intelligible, and thus possible. But what is the consequence of "suspending" the question of the real or material differences between men and women? Is it not merely to reinstate essentialism in a different (ideal) form? Ethnomethodology furnishes no theory as to why gender can perform its accounting function so ubiquitously and powerfully. West and Fenstermaker clearly believe that "doing gender" is central to the organization of human conduct but they neither provide nor draw upon a theory to explain why or when it will be more or less central. Thus the fact of essential difference has been replaced by the idea of essential difference: "Doing gender is unavoidable." Biological and psychological determinism have been replaced by an idealist determinism, quite consistent with the structuralist foundations of ethnomethodology.[3] In short, ethnomethodological feminism runs the risk of becoming too formal, reducing gender to a binary opposition, a tool to think with, and thus reintroducing essentialism by the back door. It seems to assume the inevitability that notions about gender will be used to set up standards of accountability in interaction. Ethnomethodology therefore cannot answer the kinds of feminist questions listed at the beginning of this essay. For example, we need to know whether or not the language of gender changes. Under conditions of race or class conflict gender differences might diminish; under certain economic conditions a woman's identity might be more closely tied to her motherhood than her participation in the labor force. The facticity of difference clearly changes over time, as does the role of gender ideas themselves. In the early 1970s, feminist politicians emphasized the vulnerability of motherhood; difference was a handicap. In the late 1970s, motherhood came to be seen by some women as a focus of power: difference was now an advantage. This coincided with a shift in emphasis in feminist thinking from *production* (where motherhood would be a handicap) to *reproduction and sexuality* (where motherhood is a source of strength). How would ethnomethodology account for these shifts?

Denzin's essay draws from interpretive symbolic interactionism and poststructuralism. He finds fault with essentialism because it merely reiterates existing ideologies of gender. In Denzin's view, the search for an authenticating female subject is an unwitting replication of a patriarchal desire to regulate the instability of language and reflects a nostalgia for first causes, a naive view of the category *woman* as a stable construct. Oppression, for Denzin, lies in fixed meanings—and this includes the meaning of sexuality. Against this view of gender, Denzin counterposes a concept of the feminine as that complexity and indeterminacy that resists and undermines the patriarchal desire for mastery, repression, and control.

Denzin's critique of essentialism takes theory in a different direction to that of conventional sociology. After all, the masculine language of universalization and objectification Denzin rejects is quintessentially sociological. He objects to the practice of seeing social phenomena as objective facts that can be analyzed independently of the contextual meanings in which they are embedded (e.g., "a suicide"). Denzin does not take difference for granted, but sets out to deconstruct it, looking for ways of thinking about gender without either simply reversing the old hierarchies or confirming them, teasing out the negations and repressions contained in historical concepts like "nature" and "female." Denzin ties the meaning of gender to many kinds of cultural representation, and these in turn establish terms by which the relations between women and men are organized and understood.

From a sociological point of view, the relevance and purpose of this exercise depends on the extent to which the terms by which men and women are related are contextualized historically. Unfortunately, Denzin does not provide much help in this regard. The concept of difference *itself* must be politically situated. Whether or not women as a group are seen as different depends on one's political agenda:

> In relationship to a labor history that had typically excluded women, it might make sense to overgeneralize about women's experiences, emphasizing difference in order to demonstrate that the universal term "worker" was really a male reference that could not account for all aspects of women's job experiences. In relationship to an employer who sought to justify discrimination by reference to social difference it made more sense to deny the totalizing effect of difference by stressing instead the diversity and complexity of women's behavior and motivation. (Scott 1988, p. 44)

The difference between women is not invariant, but neither is its variation simply determined by other cultural representations. Denzin's approach to difference is not helpful sociologically because he tends to substitute the analysis of "text" for the analysis of class and gender relations, collapsing all levels of reality into one level of representation. Sociologists must accept neither the relativism implied by Denzin's position (which would permit women to become more like men), nor the essentialism of the radical feminists (which would imply acceptance of the positivist principle that individual right is presocial). Although Denzin rightly rejects essentialism, the end result of his efforts is remarkably similar to quite conventional sociological treatments of sex/ gender differences that assume an essential theoretical *sameness* between men and women. Both treat equality and difference as if they were antithetical. The opposite of equality is not difference, however, but inequality. Equality is simply a deliberate indifference to specified differences, not a denial that differences exist. Denzin ends up by weakening the feminist impact on sociology. Politically, the need is to recognize both equality and difference or, more sociologically, the pursuit of equality in light of historically situated differences. Identifying and accounting for the latter requires a sociology Denzin does not provide.

The Power of Gender

Feminist theory rests its claim for attention on the significance of gender in social life. In this sense, it competes with other theories that would subordinate gender to other sources of social identity (e.g. Marxism) or reconceptualize gender so as to render it equivalent in theoretical significance to other social attributes (e.g., functionalism, expectation states theory). Of all these competing claims, those of Marxism has attracted the most attention because Marxism and feminism share a commitment to critique and social change. Feminism, like Marxism, is committed to a transformational model of social activity, which, opposed to reification and voluntarism alike, allows us to sustain the conjoint dualities of structure and praxis. Feminist emancipation means structural transformation, a change of structure rather than social relationships, a development of other structures rather than escape to a realm that marginally eludes determination.

The similarities between feminism and Marxism do not stop there. Feminism, like Marxism, is structural, its ontology relational, neither individualist nor collectivist. Gender, like class, is a structure based on social production and sustained by ideology. The question, is, How are gender relations organized as a going concern? Finally, both Marxism and feminism depend upon a dialectical theory of consciousness, a theory of human self-activity or objectification as social world–creating within a preexisting space of materiality. Both see people as beings in relation to and dependent on others. Both apply this theory of consciousness to their own practice of social investigation.

The impact of feminism on Marxist sociology is thus potentially greater than it is on any other sociological paradigm. But as both Shelton and Agger and Ward demonstrate, the relationship between feminism and Marxist sociology is not an easy one. Ward argues for the equivalence of gender as a structure of power; Shelton and Agger seek to situate gender within what they see as the larger framework of class analysis.

For Shelton and Agger, the position of women should be theorized as a product of class relations. Capitalist society, with its concomitant wage labor, implies a separation between the reproduction of workers and the production of goods and services and, insofar as gender is used to decide who will do reproductive labor, and this is unpaid, a segregation and denigration of women follows. Their perspective on capitalism puts the production of people on a par with the production of objects, except that even more surplus is extracted from those who produce people. Shelton and Agger concede that both production relations and market forces can be mediated by other factors, but nevertheless, they see gender inequality deriving from capitalism. It is a by-product of capital's dominion over labor. Women's subordination to men results from their exploitation by capital rather than vice versa. Shelton and Agger downplay the tension that exists between patriarchy and capitalism because they do not see them as "separate orders of being."

The position adopted by Shelton and Agger would make it very difficult for feminist theory to have much impact on sociological theory. Many feminists would respond that class neither exists independent of nor determines gender. Gender is an independent and determining factor in the organization of society. Who could deny that patriarchal structures predate capitalism and survive in socialist societies? Moreover, while the unequal value of male and female labor in the market makes it rational in household economic terms for women to stay at home if one of the adults must do so, how can Shelton and Agger explain the fact that women do most of the housework even if both spouses are employed, without recourse to a notion of patriarchy not depending on class relations? This arrangement is clearly not in the woman's interest. And, although the greater economic power of the male might explain his ability to impose this arrangement, it does not explain why he does so.

Shelton and Agger do not seem inclined to acknowledge that the meaning of class is affected by gender relations. In the nineteenth century, certain concepts of male skill rested on a contrast with female labor, which was seen as being, by definition, unskilled. The organization and reorganization of work processes was accomplished by reference to the gender attributes of workers, rather than to issues of training, education, or social class. And wage differentials between the sexes were attributed to fundamentally different family roles that preceded, rather than followed from, employment arrangements. Far from accepting Shelton and Agger's advice to subordinate gender to class, sociology would do well to pay more attention to the impact of gender structure on class. Studies of stratification and mobility still use conceptual schemes based on occupational structures that are already gendered, shaped by a prior sexual division of labor (occupational classifications are male). Similarly, men's mobility processes are predicated on women's immobility (Crompton 1986). Class and gender are therefore both important. In Shelton and Agger's account, gender is reduced to a divide-and-conquer strategem. True, capitalists have exacerbated gender conflict in their own interests and changed its form, but the meanings and patterns of patriarchy were there before and explain much of what happens when this strategem is employed.[4]

Shelton and Agger's Marxism promises to bring the insights of feminist theory deep within the sociological camp but, in arguing against patriarchy, they blunt this promise. Ward, discussing world system theory from a perspective sympathetic to both feminism and Marxism, has the same agenda but, unlike Shelton and Agger, she argues forcefully for the autonomy of gender. It is true, as Ward claims, that most followers of Marx believe that capitalism is indifferent to the kind of labor it uses and will either drive to ignore ascriptive, status-based criteria or opportunistically co-opt whatever extraeconomic oppressions (such as gender) are historically and culturally available to divide workers. There is no specific structural necessity for gender oppression in Marx's theory. Job structures can be defined and reproduced by a pattern of sexual harassment and threats of violence at work but capitalist relations do not depend upon it.

World system theory has simply transferred to global analysis the gender blindness inherent in Marx's analysis of capitalist accumulation. Ward's essay reminds us that capital accumulation on a global scale will be structured by gender relations. Women do not become integrated into the capitalist system in the same manner as men. Nor do they become marginalized in the same fashion or to the same extent. The problem with world system theory is that it builds upon assumptions about the private and public sphere, household and work, that are themselves the product of patriarchy. Ward questions the habit of treating women as either housewives or workers as if these were mutually exclusive categories. This ignores the evidence that many Third World women constantly juggle these contradictory areas of work. It is precisely because not only Marxism but also the functionalism described by Johnson treat the concepts of housework and waged work as universals and apply them uncritically across time and space that the "problem" for women in the non-Western world was initially defined as one of lack of integration into development.

Ward points out that world system theory ignores the historical variation in the meaning of the categories on which it rests. In this argument the combined power of Marxism and feminism is apparent. It is also clear in her argument that men and women enter the informal economy for different reasons and derive different benefits from it. But what is the *relative* significance of class and gender? Perhaps Marx did not anticipate the growth of the informal economy under advanced capitalism, but how much does its appearance depend on gender differentiation? Could Ward, anxious to reaffirm the claims of feminism, be right when she argues that households of a certain gender structure (e.g., single mother) give rise to the informal sector? Does the very distinction between the informal and formal sectors presuppose a gender difference? Or would the weight of evidence suggest that the informal sector is the result of managerial strategies that, incidentally, and in different ways under different class conditions, trade on different (gendered) household forms?

Ward is equally concerned with how world system theory deals with the division between wage labor and household labor. Where capitalist market relations begin to replace old local market relations, men push women out of the market: men are recruited as laborers and women assume more responsibility for subsistence and household production. Ward implies that world system theory, and the Marxism on which it draws, cannot account for this development adequately because it has no theory of gender. But this pattern of development is not (as Ward implies) an aberration of capitalism (and of Marx's theory of capitalism) to be rectified by feminist theory. It is a necessary precondition and result of capitalism's spread. Capitalism, contradictorily and simultaneously, leads to the generalization of wage labor *and* the generalization of nonwage labor. Subsistence is not "outside" capitalism but an integral part of it. Subsistence production and the production of use values remain important in Third World capitalism, which means the household survives as a production unit.

The essays by Shelton and Agger and Ward jointly reaffirm the need for a social theory in which the multiple determination of social relationships is acknowledged, although the target of their criticism is different because they press their claims from different starting points. Women's class interests are embedded within their relationships as men and women (e.g., inheritance rules). Conversely, the oppression of women is enmeshed in other forms of oppression: just as the creation of a middle class of women depended on a class of female domestic servants in the nineteenth century, so today the domestication and consumerism of women in the First World calls for a new class of women producers in the Third. Neither Marxists nor feminists provide a "complete" theory of power.

Ways of Knowing

The feminist project of structural transformation is predicated on the philosophical notion that there is a difference between the world of appearance and the world of reality or, more properly, that there are different levels of reality (Walby 1990).[5] Feminists in sociology should therefore be careful to maintain the distinction between social structure and social relationships. Social relationships are the effect of the articulation of structures. Thus far, only two irreducible social structures have been discovered and these are class structure and the sex-gender structure. Neither is reducible to something else. Neither is explicable in terms of an anterior relationship. Neither can be reduced to the other, although they always produce their effects through, or in articulation with, each other. Feminism does not contribute significantly to sociological understanding if it focuses our attention solely on the intermediate or reducible levels of relationship. It must, in short, reject the positivist limitation of ontology to the observable.

Misplaced emphasis on the level of individual appearances tends to trivialize gender. All forms of methodological individualism, of which expectation states theory is an example, impoverish the contribution feminism can make to sociology because they deny difference. They do so by positing the self as a presocial, self-sufficient unity. The theory begins with individuals who come together to form groups. Gender exists prior to interaction (although it can help change the course of that interaction once "triggered"). Thus expectation states theory tells us that expectations are reinforced by rewards and punishments but it does not tell us why they apply. Nor does it explain whose expectations prevail. How are departures from expectation explained systemically? How does the system engender changes in expectations?

Functionalism, in its holism, its focus on abstract rather than concrete systems, would appear to supply a sociological paradigm fit for the feminism Walby (1990) describes. At least it could be said that there is an overall theory of the function of the gender system and the household in the larger system, a theory that, moreover, acknowledges the tensions between the demands of the occupational and kinship systems in industrial societies, a systemic or structural tension rather than an intra- or interpersonal one. But functionalism's preoccupation with evaluative and normative factors and the role they play in "adaptive upgrading" effectively neutralizes gender conflict (indeed, all conflict) into a "system problem" or "dysfunction." The underlying reality is not structural conflict but a set of equilibrating mechanisms, as if system "efficiency" could be measured without reference to that conflict, as if "processes of differentiation" contained no element of (gendered) power but were of interest only because of their effect on women. Women are seen as the outcome of differentiation rather than its cause. But social reproduction does not just happen. It is the goal of the powerful, not a system need. The solution Johnson provides for this theoretical problem (functional for whom) undermines the whole causal logic of functional analysis (Wilson 1983).

A feminist ontology of realism must be complemented with an epistemology that acknowledges the concept dependency of social life without, however, falling into that conceptual reductionism characteristic of more hermeneutical feminisms. In short, feminist theory must be reflexive and it must impart this reflexivity to sociology. This means rejecting the (masculine) idea of a transcendental reason able to separate itself from the body and from historical time and place.

At this point, the relation between feminism and sociological theory becomes tenuous indeed. Many sociologists have a very impoverished notion of subjectivity, as something fixed, unique, or coherent, taking for granted conceptual distinctions between object and subject, individual and society, emotion and reason. This universalizing strategy, adopted by Ridgeway, for example, has political consequences because it delegitimates differences between men and women (Harding 1990). More radical feminists argue that subjectivity is the product of society, constantly being reconstituted in discourse. It is precarious and contradictory.

Feminism, in its interrogation of ideas of the self as a stable, reliable, integrated unity, of the privileged place accorded to epistemology in conventional science (truth lies in correct method), of the assumption that reason is the path to truth, poses a radical critique of conventional sociological theory and methods. The knower, in feminism, is always situated in the particularity of the everyday world. Objectifications are always at odds with the lived actuality in which they are accomplished. Reciprocally, the subject is another human being rather than a means to a research end. There is no dialogue between researcher and researched in the investigations Ridgeway reports. This sociology shuts off the "feminine" relational emphasis on developing increasingly complex and intense forms of cooperation and intimacy in human relationships and on developing the empathy and sensitivity necessary for taking the role of the particular other. Feminism requires a different kind of rationality for the conduct of sociology, in which the ability to empathize and connect with particular others is highly valued, contrasting with the "masculine" desire to separate, make decisions independent of subjects, develop autonomy, and assume the role of the generalized other.

Theory and Practice

Socialist feminists believe that the task of social theory is to provide conceptions of the nature of human social activity and the human agent that can be placed in the service of practical activity. They reason that social theory is derived from a committed standpoint. Thought is a socially organized practice, taking place in real time in real places under definite material conditions. Theory is not an abstract "stance" analyzable as a metaphysical transcendent, but a practical achievement essentially no different from the thought of ordinary people.

Feminism is thus a species of critical theory seeking to enable its subjects to see through appearances to understand the structure underlying and giving (distorted) meaning to their lives. The purpose of critical theory is to enable people to gain a much clearer picture of who they are and of the real meaning of their practice, a first step in the process of becoming different sorts of people with different sorts of social arrangements. The purpose of theory, in short, is to engender self-knowledge (not to manipulate others in the name of social policy) and to liberate people from the oppressiveness of their social arrangements.[6]

Just as practice must be informed by theory, so the road to knowledge is through practice. Knowledge is a function of engagement with the world. The best way to get at the underlying mechanisms, to see through appearances, is to push hard at the fabric of social institutions so as to better feel the unyielding frame beneath. Practice is therefore the way to test theories. This means that theories must be meaningful to their subjects, as well as their authors. For critical theory to work, for it to help overcome resistance, it must be translatable into the ordinary language in which the experience of the actor is expressed. Resistance (of the subject, too) can be overcome only by revealing the truth to the subject, uncovering hidden meanings, and making explicit a new self-conception. Domination does not depend upon coercion alone but on the interaction of the powerful and the powerless. Critical social theory has to sunder this relationship.

Little consideration of the relation between theory and practice is present in the essays under review. By implication, Ridgeway and Johnson reject the more radical feminists' position that theory means commitment; West and Fenstermaker and Denzin bracket the issue of how the claims of competing theories can be adjudicated and by whom; Shelton and Agger and Ward have more sympathy for this position but their essays are, by the same token, further removed from the mainstream of sociological theory. This stream has not been diverted significantly by feminism. Sociologists listen most attentively to the claims of a liberal feminism, which is willing to acknowledge the roots of theoretical questions in practical activity but reluctant to locate the criteria of truth there.

Conclusion

It is clear from these essays that feminist theory has redirected sociological attention toward the level of social relations and away from
individual characteristics, toward the level of variable social organization and symbolic meaning, and away from sex categories. Sociology, on
the other hand, has helped feminism shift analysis from abstract and
binary differences to examine social relations and contexts in which
multiple differences are constructed and given meaning. Feminism has
had to learn from sociology that not all gender differences are deeply
rooted or immutable.

On the other hand, it is also clear that feminism and sociological
theory remain at arm's length. For most sociologists, women are the
object of study; feminists see women as the subject, the world from the
standpoint of women. Sociologists seek visibility for women, an equal
presence; feminists assert the difference between the genders. Sociologists embrace gender oppression within existing theories of power;
feminists want us to think about power in broader terms, as enabling as
well as limiting. Sociologists abide by a correspondence theory of truth,
as the expression of a correspondence between concepts and the facts or
objects they represent; feminists are more open to conventionalist theories of truth in which the relation between internal and external referents of discourse is largely arbitrary and changeable. Sociologists remain
wedded to an objectivism that reifies either the autonomous individual
or an encrusting social structure; feminists encourage subjectivism in
which such ideas are reduced to rhetorical devices. Sociologists pursue
the goal of a value-free science shielded from political bias by the
vigilance of the scholarly community; feminists believe that a gender-
specific approach is preferable because the experience and perception of
women as the excluded and exploited other is more inclusive and
critically coherent. Sociologists sift from their concepts all cultural and
historical specificity in search of universally valid categories; feminists
do not decry cross-cultural or transepochal study but believe it must be
comparativist rather than universalizing, attuned to changes and contrasts rather than covering laws.

Feminism should not seek an alliance with a sociology divorced from
moral philosophy. Feminism is about denial of humanity, most conspic-
uously in being regarded as physical beings with bodies but not minds.
Sociology should not seek an alliance with a feminism that denies the
social. This is especially important in an era when politicians are all too
ready to declare their belief that society does not exist at all, that policies

should be devised on the assumption that individual choice is the cornerstone of a healthy society. The resulting "enterprise culture" signals a victory for unfettered capitalism and a shift of resources from poor to rich. It also has profound gender implications. It means, for example, a family policy in which women are given a choice of whether or not to do paid work, but only after the conditions that would make that choice realistic for them, such as adequate child care services and convenient public transportation, have been destroyed, or privatized beyond the reach of all but a few.

Notes

1. Essentialism is a species of that realism which locates concepts, such as gender, in our minds, but the something of which they are a concept is not in our minds. Nominalism is the view that only particulars exist, and that all a class of things (e.g., male) has in common is the name we give to it. Feminists show essentialist tendencies when they argue the case, on whatever grounds, for the irreducibility and permanence of gender differences. For an excellent discussion of these issues, see Fuss (1989).

2. It is not only intellectual curiosity that inspires these questions. The shift from viewing women as new objects of investigation to viewing women as subjects coincides with a shift from the political goal of equality of opportunity (with its assumption of sameness) to the celebration of difference and the rejection of male criteria of excellence and achievement.

3. The strategy ethnomethodologists use of linking interpretive procedures and surface rules presumes a generative model such as that used in structural linguistics (Leither 1980, p. 59). Deep structure forms the ability to produce surface sentences. While in ethnomethodology, as opposed to structural linguistics, rules have the status of interpretive aids as opposed to being causal agents, this is nevertheless a version of idealism.

4. Shelton and Agger, at least in this essay, write as if the structure of the household were unimportant or meaningless. Theories that attach women to their husbands or families ignore their subordination in the home, just as those that identify them by their labor force job ignore the domestic labor most women perform. Regarding the household as a black box also means treating it as the gender-blind completion of the circuit of capital. This ignores the fact that women were "given" the task of safeguarding the integrity and current functioning of the consumer market early in the twentieth century. Consumption became a serious business, needing commitment and a concern for the good of society. Many early suffragist claims were based on the management and marketing skills deployed in the home, especially as domestic households became rationalized. There is today a hierarchy of consumption within households structured along gender lines. Different resources are available that carry different valuation. These resources are not distributed according to criteria of need but according to their familial status, and the value attached to a resource is dependent upon the status of the person who enjoys it. Even the same object can have different meaning, depending on its use and user. Driving a car is more

valuable than being driven. Cooking a meal and eating it is less valuable than eating a meal cooked for you.

5. At one level of reality is situated intransitive objects, those whose existence and characteristics are independent of the knowing subject. Intransitive objects do not have to be perceivable, but their presence is evident from the effect they have on perceivable (transitive) objects (Wilson 1983). Neither magnetic fields nor social structures are perceivable, yet their effects are ubiquitous. Social structures thus exist whether or not they are present in the minds of those involved. Appearance is but one dimension of reality, the form in which reality expresses itself.

6. This is not to be achieved by interpersonal consciousness-raising. Not only ideas but conditions must be changed. Critical theory will free people by uncovering causal mechanisms that had hitherto determined their existence in some important way, revealing both the existence and precise nature of those mechanisms and thereby robbing them of their power. This political commitment to theory-guided change distinguishes research for women from research on women (which is not necessarily feminist).

References

Crompton, Rosemary. 1986. *Gender and Stratification*. Cambridge: Polity Press.

Fuss, Diana. 1989. *Essentially Speaking: Feminism, Nature and Difference*. New York: Routledge.

Harding, Sandra. 1990. "Feminism, Science and the Anti-Establishment Critique". Pp. 83–106 in *Feminism/Post Modernism*, edited by Linda Nicholson. London: Routledge.

Leiter, Kenneth. 1980. *A Primer in Ethnomethodology*. New York: Oxford University Press.

Ramazanoglu, Caroline. 1989. "Improving on Sociology." *Sociology* 23:427–42.

Scott, Joan. 1988. "Deconstructing Equality-Versus—Difference." *Feminist Studies* 14:33–50.

Walby, Sylvia. 1990. *Theorizing Patriarchy*. London: Blackwell.

Wilson, John. 1983. *Social Theory*. New York: Prentice Hall.

ETHNOMETHODOLOGY AND "IDEALIST DETERMINISM":
REPLY TO WILSON

Candace West and Sarah Fenstermaker

In our view, the distinctive potential of ethnomethodology for understanding social relations among women and men lies in its proposal that "the facts" of social life are actually situated accomplishments of members of society (Zimmerman 1978). From this perspective, we can examine seemingly objective, apparently transsituational properties of social life—such as gender—as achievements of local processes. Ethnomethodology's insistence on the study of *local* processes and the analysis of *situated* conduct means that we cannot establish the significance of a particular "fact" to social action apart from the context in which it is accomplished (Fenstermaker, West, and Zimmerman 1991). Thus, Wilson's complaint that our ethnomethodological formulation replaces biological determinism with "idealist determinism" implies some fundamental confusion about our argument.

Below we reiterate our formulation, highlighting points that Wilson appears to have misunderstood. Following this reiteration, we address his specific criticisms regarding "idealist determinism" and show how these are misplaced. Finally, we assess the utility of our perspective to answer the "central questions" Wilson poses at the beginning of his chapter.

"Doing" Gender Reiterated

The key to our argument is recognizing the analytical independence of *Sex*, *sex category*, and *gender*. In Western societies, *sex* is determined through the application of socially agreed upon biological criteria for classifying human beings as females or males. What makes this determination possible are the firmly entrenched cultural beliefs that there are two and only two sexes and that everyone is either one or the other (Garfinkel 1967, pp. 116–18). Initial placement in a *sex category* is achieved through application of the criteria for sex, but in everyday life, sex categorization is established through the requisite identificatory displays (e.g., hairstyle, clothing, gestures) that announce a person's membership in one or the other category. So, while sex category may serve as a proxy for sex, the two *can* vary independently of one another (e.g., situations in which persons "pass" as bona fide members of a category, despite their lack of biological credentials). What makes sex categorization possible in everyday life is our cultural view of women and men as unequivocally and naturally defined categories of being (Garfinkel 1967, pp. 116–18; West and Zimmerman 1987, pp. 127–28) whose psychological and behavioral tendencies follow from their reproductive functions.

By contrast, *gender* is a situated accomplishment: the local management of conduct in relation to normative conceptions of appropriate attitudes and activities for particular sex categories. This formulation rests on the notion of *accountability*, that is, the possibility of describing actions and circumstances in serious and consequential ways (Heritage 1984, pp. 136–37). We contend that insofar as members of society know their actions are accountable, they will design their actions in light of how others might see and characterize them. Moreover, insofar as sex category is omnirelevant to social action (Garfinkel 1967, p. 118), it offers an ever-ready resource for interpreting those actions. Thus, a person engaged in virtually *any* activity can be held accountable for her or his performance of that activity as a woman or a man.

"Idealist Determinism" and the Accomplishment of Gender

Wilson argues that our formulation of gender as an accomplishment "reintroduc[es] essentialism by the back door." Here, he seems to be confounding gender with sex category, faulting us for offering "no theory as to why gender can perform its accounting function so ubiqui- tously and powerfully." But as we noted in our chapter, it is sex cate- gory—not gender—that is potentially omnirelevant to the arrangement of human affairs and hence affords a ubiquitous resource for gender's accomplishment. The task of *rendering* actions accountable arises again and again across different situations and different particulars of con- duct. What this means is that we must locate gender's emergence in *social situations*, rather than in some external theory of social action.

Wilson also remarks on our failure to explain why or when the accomplishment of gender "will be more or less central" to the organiza- tion of human conduct. As we noted in our chapter, persons inhabit many different identities that may be stressed or muted, *depending on the situation*. While some standardized occasions almost seem created for the purpose of celebrating "essential differences" between women and men, other seem conventionally expressive in themselves. Although any situation can be adapted to the accomplishment of gender (Goffman 1977), it is *that adaptation* that makes gender relevant to interaction and the operation of social institutions. Thus, we must look to how people adapt their situations to gender's accomplishment in order to explain when that accomplishment will be "more or less central" to the organi- zation of their conduct. We have already indicated one direction that seems promising in relation to this question: the examination of social situations in which people face issues of allocation (who will do what, get what, plan or execute an activity, give directions or take them). Given that our existing institutional arrangements rest on the conviction that women are essentially different from—and essentially inferior to— men, the resolution of such issues conditions the exercise of power and manifestation of inequality between women and men, as well as the centrality of gender's accomplishment.

Wilson's final complaint about our chapter is what he sees as our neglecting that "the facticity of difference clearly changes over time." For example, how could we explain the fact that in the early 1970s motherhood was seen as a source of vulnerability, while in the late 1970s, it was seen as a source of power? In posing this question, Wilson notes that the shift in conceptions of motherhood "coincided " with a shift in feminist thought: from production to reproduction and sexuality. We would invite readers to observe that in Wilson's example (as in the examples we provided in our chapter), the sex category *woman* is invoked to discredit the activity of mothering at one point in time, and to legitimate it at another. The particulars of the situation (i.e., an earlier emphasis on production, a later focus on reproduction) are not merely coincidental to the story as Wilson tells it, but *adaptations* to gender's accomplishment. As we see it, it is not the fact that "difference" shifts from handicap to advantage that begs for explanation here, but the fact that difference is invoked *in both cases*. As we argue in our chapter, what is invariant is the idea that women and men *have* essentially different natures, for which they are accountable in human affairs.

The "Central Questions"

In closing, we would like to point out the utility of our perspective for answering what Wilson deems the central questions for feminist theory. First, our perspective addresses "the nature of the difference between women and men" through its explicit distinctions among sex assignment, sex categorization, and the accomplishment of gender. As we have noted, there is no necessary relationship between sex assignment (on the basis of anatomical differences) and sex categorization (on the basis of identificatory displays) in everyday life. However, sex categorization provides the resource for rendering actions accountable (e.g., as "womanly" or "manly") across different situations and different particulars of conduct. This perspective allows us to "distinguish among categories of men and women" through the systematic examination of their situated conduct.

Second, our perspective affords us a means of addressing "the relation of gender to other constituents of human identity, such as class and race," through the analysis of how gender is accomplished under different circumstances. As we attempted to show in our discussion of De-Vault's (forthcoming) work, normative conceptions of "essential womanliness" can be brought to bear on the activities of women in very different material conditions. And as we tried to demonstrate in our discussion of Hurtado's (1989) work, the doing of gender may involve something very different for white women and women of color, given differences in their relational positions to white men. In accord with the basic assumptions of ethnomethodology, we cannot determine the relevance of race or class to social action apart from the context in which *these* are accomplished. Hence, our attention turns once again to the situated conduct of societal members.

Third and finally, our perspective offers an answer to Wilson's question "How are the conventional dualisms of sociological theory to be deconstructed and redefined?" We contend that bifurcating gender into femininity and masculinity in effect reduces gender to sex (Gerson 1985), while treating gender as a role obscures the work involved in its accomplishment. By contrast, we provide an ethnomethodological understanding of gender: an emergent feature of social situations that results from and legitimates the most fundamental division of our society.

References

DeVault, Marjorie. 1991. *Feeding the Family: The Social Construction of Caring as Gendered Work.* Chicago: University of Chicago Press.

Fenstermaker, Sarah, Candace West, and Don H. Zimmerman. 1991. "Gender Inequality: New Conceptual Terrain." Pp. 298–307 in *Gender, Family, and Economy: The Triple Overlap,* edited by Rae Lesser-Blumberg. Newbury Park, CA: Sage.

Garfinkel, Harold. 1967. *Studies in Ethnomethodology.* Englewood Cliffs, NJ: Prentice-Hall.

Gerson, Judith M. 1985. "The Variability and Salience of Gender: Issues of Conceptualization and Measurement." Paper presented at annual meeting of the American Sociological Association, Washington, D.C., August.

Goffman, Erving. 1977. "The Arrangement between the Sexes." *Theory and Society* 4:301–31.

Heritage, John. 1984. *Garfinkel and Ethnomethodology.* Cambridge: Polity Press.

Hurtado, Aída. 1989. "Relating to Privilege: Seduction and Rejection in the Subordination of White Women and Women of Color." *SIGNS* 14:833–55.

West, Candace, and Don H. Zimmerman. 1987. "Doing Gender." *Gender & Society* 1:125–51.

Zimmerman, Don H. 1978. "Ethnomethodology." *American Sociologist* 13:6–15.

WORKING WITH THE CRITIC II: REPLY TO WILSON

Norman K. Denzin

> "Men, women and children make and perform their gendered sexuality, but not under conditions of their own doing" (paraphrase of Karl Marx).

I think John Wilson would agree with the above paraphrase of Karl Marx. We both seek a nonessentialist, historically grounded, democratic-socialist feminism; a theory of praxis that speaks to the worlds of lived oppression; a utopian, nonsexist, nonracist social order. We both understand that the material conditions of everyday life set the foundations for the infrastructures of class, race, and gender domination. And we both understand that it is the structure of social relations between human beings that must be changed, if this utopian vision is to be achieved. The problem turns, then, on how class, race, and gender operate behind our backs, so as to produce particular subjectivities ideologically coded within the systems of patriarchy and capitalism.

My strategy is to work back and forth between social texts and lived experiences. Wilson works from visible and invisible structures, appearances and reality, to critiques of existing social practices. He and I both want to understand how the subordination of women is produced, maintained, and changed. We both seek a theory that makes a difference. We hold, however, to different epistemologies, and this difference explains my difficulties with his criticisms of my project. He suggests that my approach to difference is "not helpful . . . [because it collapses] all levels of reality into one level of representation."

Wilson rejects my position, contending that an obdurate world out there exists below or beneath the world of appearances. This is the level of reality where situated intransitive objects exist. These objects, their existence and their characteristics are independent of knowing subjects (see Wilson's note 5). Social structures exist beneath the world of appearances. Social relationships exist in the world of appearances; in the structures of these relations can be seen the systems of domination that exist in any society. Apparently it is possible to push at the hard fabric of social institutions (structures) so "as to better feel the unyielding frame beneath."

Wilson eschews a strict correspondence theory of truth, but he is not going all the way over to a conventionalist (feminist) theory, which holds that the relation between "internal and external referents of discourse is largely arbitrary and changeable." He is a social realist. His realist epistemology holds that the world out there exists independent of our perceptions of it. His theory of praxis calls for investigations that expose this oppressive, invisible world.

As a social realist Wilson takes his place in a long tradition that has been simultaneously positivist and post-positivist, or interpretive. From Weber to Durkheim, Mead to Watson, Blumer to Lazarsfeld, Marx to Althusser, this tradition has maintained a commitment to a science that renders the invisible world visible. It has maintained a commitment to the production of a series of realist, melodramatic, social problems texts, which has created an identification with the powerless in society. These works of realism reproduced and mirrored the social structures that needed to be changed. They valorized the subjectivity of the downtrodden individual. They made a hero of the sociological theorist who could write moving texts about the powerless. They created a body of textual work that kept the private/public divisions alive and well in American sociology.

Social realism in sociology continued the narrative, realist traditions of Romantic and Victorian fiction and in the twentieth century quickly grafted itself into mainstream scientific-positivist realism. However, this realism was short-lived, to be replaced by the new governing esthetics and philosophies of science peculiar to modernism and postmodernism (see Jameson 1990). Thus Wilson's text moves uneasily between old-fashioned correspondence theory positivism, and the new poststructuralisms that come with the postmodern period.

Today social realism is under attack. It is now seen as but one narrative strategy for telling stories about the social world out there. In its place comes poststructuralism and grammatology; new writing and reading styles grafted into the cinematic society, where a thing exists if it can be captured in a visual or printed text. Poststructuralism undermines the realist agenda, contending that things do not exist independent of their representations in social texts. Accordingly, if we want to change how things are, we must change how they are seen. How they are seen is itself determined by the older realist and modernist agendas, which presumed worlds out there that could be mapped by a realist, scientific method.

It is this hegemonic vision that must be challenged and Wilson refuses to take up the challenge. He still wants a world out there that proves his theory right or wrong. But how does he find that world and bring it into existence? How does he record what it does when he pushes against it? Unfortunately he never answers this question. Hence the poverty of his theory, for social realism will not produce the utopian society the two of us seek. Nor will social realism furnish the political foundations for the project Wilson pursues. It is that philosophy that got us into this mess in the first place.

References

Jameson, Fredric. 1990. *Signatures of the Visable*. London: Routledge.

ENGENDERING CLASS: REPLY TO WILSON

Beth Anne Shelton and *Ben Agger*

Our introductory and concluding comments to Folbre apply to Wilson as well. Like Folbre, he objects to our effort to create a feminist Marxism, and like Folbre, he misses our basic point about the politically invested nature of feminism and Marxism. We refer the reader to our reply to Folbre for a fuller discussion of this issue.

Wilson criticizes us for blunting the promise to bring the insights of feminist theory into Marxism by arguing against patriarchy. What we try to do, however, is bring the insights of feminist theory into Marxism so that they can be part of a more theoretically grounded analysis of domination. A feminist Marxism does not deny the importance of gender, but rather allows us to understand gender relations as part of class relations. This does not mean that we deny that men may benefit, at least marginally, from the subordination of women in the household and in the labor market, but that we can better understand this subordination with the tools offered by Marxism than with those offered by so-called patriarchy theories. As Smith (1983) argues, by failing to distinguish the differences in gender relations of precapitalist societies from those in capitalist societies, we fail to see the important differences in the form of women's subordination to men and we fail to see how the household and the set of relations to which it is subject "became an outcome of the capitalist wage relationship" rather than its precondition.

We can explain why men impose their will on women and have them do most of the housework by understanding capitalism's need for unwaged labor to lower the cost of reproduction and to use low-waged labor when the need arises. Likewise, that men's labor force participation and occupation mobility depend on women's subordination only indicates the need to develop a feminist Marxism, not a separate theory of gender. Thus, we do recognize gender inequality—we only attribute it to different forces.

Finally, Wilson also suggests that we "downplay the tension" between patriarchy and capitalism. What tension? Historically, the subjugation of reproductive labor has gone hand in hand with (and made way for) the subjugation of productive labor. Indeed, we argue that *there is no such thing as unproductive labor*, enabling us to develop a new conception of the totality that blends Marxism and feminism to the point of indistinguishability.

References

Smith, Joan. 1983. "Feminism and Analytic Method: The Case of Unwaged Domestic labor." *Current Perspectives in Social Theory* 4:205–23.

THE IMPORTANCE OF THE INTERACTION OF GENDER, RACE, AND CLASS IN THE RECASTING OF SOCIOLOGICAL THEORY: REPLY TO WILSON

Kathryn B. Ward

Wilson asks that the theoretical perspective I develop address "the *relative* significance of class and gender." I argue that we should not make a hierarchy of such categories, but instead should look at how race, class, and gender interactively affect socioeconomic phenomena. To do otherwise returns us to the old ways of rank ordering oppressions or allowing them to drop out of discussions. For example, Wilson ignores my arguments on race. Likewise, socioeconomic phenomena such as informalization of the labor force rarely work in additive ways (Collins 1990). Thus, we need to look at the interactive and dialectic relationships among race, class, and gender when we look at the connection between informalization and household survival strategies. Here poor women may engage in informal labor to meet household demands, while some capitalists use informalization to maintain competitiveness and flexibility.

Wilson adopts the misleading binary categorization of all work into wage and household labor when he argues that capitalism increases both waged labor and unwaged household labor. Here he ignores the fact that the informal sector involves waged labor and that a continuum of labor exists from formal to informal to household labor. He fails to recognize that most labor in the world is performed in the household and informal sector, and the failure of the informal sector to disappear *is* inconsistent with world system and other Marxist theories (Mies 1986). Capitalism and Marxism falter by not having women's daily and diverse labors at their theoretical core.

Although Wilson states that "neither Marxists nor feminists provide a 'complete' theory of power," I argue that emerging inclusive feminist theories that have questions of race, class, and gender at their core will provide more accurate *ways* of looking at our world. As such these theories do not seek to provide a "complete" picture of the world, but outline various standpoints/perspectives as provided by combinations of race, class, and gender. Part of the problem with mainstream sociological theories is that most of them seek to provide the complete picture. Where did this picture come from? I suggest that this picture emerged from European white male sociologists whose perspective was only one viewpoint, yet was depicted as the only viewpoint—a logical fallacy (Minnich 1990).

Now with growing critiques of mainstream sociology for its inability to map how race, class, and gender shape socioeconomic phenomena, midrange theories are required. Building such theories requires input from their subjects and reflection on the daily lives of these subjects. In this way, we can avoid reinventing one-sided perspectives that masquerade as the whole picture (Collins 1990; Aptheker 1989). To this end, I recommend putting women of color at the core of our theories, because if we can explain the lives of women of color, then we will do a much better job of theories on men of color, white women, and ultimately white men. Otherwise, our theories will adequately explain white Western middle- and upper-class men's lives and little else. Furthermore by examining the dailiness of women's lives, we tie our theory to practice. All these prescriptions for sociology come from the growing literature by and about women of color. It is past time to take this literature seriously and transform theories that do not have race, class, and gender at their core. The add and stir approach to gender does not work any longer.

References

Aptheker, Bettina. 1989. *Tapestries of Life*. Amherst: University of Massachusetts Press.
Collins, Pat Hill. 1990. *Black Feminist Thought*. Boston: Alwyn and Unwin.
Mies, Maria. 1986. *Patriarchy and Accumulation on a World-Scale*. London: Zed.
Minnich, Elizabeth. 1990. *Transforming Knowledge*. Philadelphia: Temple University Press.

DOMINATION VERSUS FUNCTION: REPLY TO WILSON

Miriam M. Johnson

I found much to like in Wilson's analysis of the papers. He brings up important questions and gets to the heart of issues. I generally agreed with his critique of every theory but functionalism, and every paper but mine! Indeed as I read, I thought, Ah, surely he will see the virtues of functionalist analysis for feminism: And indeed he does, but he also sees what he considers to be serious and irremediable flaws in it. For Wilson, the virtues of functionalism for a socialist feminist are "its holism, its focus on abstract rather than concrete systems," the presence of "an overall theory of the function of the gender system and the household in the larger system," which "acknowledges the tensions between the demands of the occupational and kinship systems in industrial societies, a systemic or structural tension rather than an intra- or interpersonal one." He also seems to find the instrumental-expressive distinction useful and applies it effectively both to and for women.

So far so good, but Wilson then rejects functionalism because its "preoccupation with evaluative and normative factors and the role they play in 'adaptive upgrading' effectively neutralizes gender conflict (indeed all conflict) into a 'system problem' or 'dysfunction.' " Obviously he was not taken with my explanation that functionalists see conflict as ubiquitous and stability as the theoretical problem to be investigated, as opposed to the goal to be attained. I agree that functionalism does not stimulate radical action, but I think functionalist perspectives can help understand conflict as a result of structural tensions. Because functionalists and critical theorists tend to be talking past each other, I believe the best way to explain, and partially defend, neofunctionalism is to address what I see to be even more fundamental problems with critical theory or neo-Marxist alternatives to functionalism.

What Is Social Structure?

I have often had the feeling in talking to Marxists that we are using the term *social structure* differently. Wilson clearly states that "feminists in sociology should therefore be careful to maintain the distinction between social structure and social relationships." He goes on to say that "Thus far, only two irreducible social structures have been discovered and these are class structure and the sex-gender structure." First, I question the sense in which class can be called "irreducible" in view of the historical development of classes in the agricultural period. Why isn't kinship an irreducible structure? Certainly all societies construct gender and kinship systems, probably in conjunction with each other, whereas classes are of more recent origin. Aside from the question of irreducibility, however, the deeper point is that for functionalists, social structure means *any* organized set of regularly occurring patterns of social relationships. These may or may not be hierarchical, may or may not involve domination. For critical theorists, however, structure seems to refer only to a structure of domination.

Moreover, critical theorists speak of social reproduction as the goal of the powerful. Functionalists would say that social reproduction is necessary for *any* social system to remain ongoing. The survival of any culture—egalitarian or authoritarian—depends upon passing on the social heritage and its legitimations. Such social reproduction may indeed be a way of exploiting some of the population, but at the same time those who espouse putting an end to exploitation are also products of social reproduction. I would argue, for example, that nineteenth- and twentieth-century feminists could not have "seen" or articulated their oppression without a tradition of liberal individualism upon which to base their claims. We are all cultural products: Social reproduction is far more than a means to pull the wool over the eyes of the oppressed; it can also foster progressive change.

The Purpose of Theory

The above differences in definitions of social structure and social reproduction derive from more fundamental differences in assumptions about the purpose of theory. Critical theorists tend to see the purpose of theory as being to uncover the reality of class domination or gender domination underneath the appearance of free choice and justice. The problem with this assumption is not that domination does not exist, but that domination cannot explain how a social system works. Suppose all domination ended: Would this automatically create the perfect society that would sustain itself forever? Would this put an end to the need to examine social system functioning? Surely, functional problems of adaptation, goal attainment, integration, and social reproduction would still have to be met.

Prior to the question of domination is the question of how any social system "functions" and how gender and gender oppression fit into the larger system. A functionalist can ask both about the function of gender differentiation in the social system *and* about who stands to gain or lose in the current system. The latter is one question, not the entire question. Thus I would contend that my suggestion that we ask Functional for whom or what? does not, as Wilson suggests, "undermine the whole causal logic of functionalist analysis." Rather it is a question one can ask, and needs to ask, within a larger functionalist framework.

Theory and Practice

I am very taken with the position that theory construction itself is a social practice. Theory is constructed by real people with real "interests." this is true for all theories. No modern functionalist, or Parsons himself for that matter, would claim that theory is not value or "interest" driven. Modern functionalists, however, need to recognize this more fully and are in the process of doing so. But Wilson goes much further and says that not only does theory come out of practice but that "practice is . . . the way to test theories." What this seems to mean for Wilson is that "to see through appearances" we must "push hard at the fabric of social institutions so as to better feel the unyielding frame beneath." Real people, not just social feminists, must test the system and find for themselves the domination that is there in order to free themselves. This gets us back to domination being the central issue for Wilson. The critical theorist already "knows" it is there but others need to test it. Wilson suggests that I "reject the more radical feminists' position that theory means commitment." If he means by this that one's theory is tested by one's commitment to it, then he is right, I don't believe that. What one wants or desires should be separable from the truth claims of propositions derived from one's theory. One must always be willing to see that validity does not depend on its coinciding with one's wishes. One could make a very big mistake that would jeopardize one's cause if one took this position. The question of who decides truth claims is complex and "objectivity" has become a suspect term, but certainly in the last analysis, the establishment of truth must be separable from what we want to find.

In spite of these seemingly irreconcilable differences between critical theory and functionalism, I would contend that at an abstract level their goals are the same and are rooted in the major intellectual themes of the Enlightenment. Functionalists and critical theorists do agree that the point of theory is to understand reality and that understanding can (and usually does) lead to human progress. Functionalists would describe a belief in individual self-realization and human "progress" as characteristic of modern Western society and use this as a criterion for identifying evolutionary change. Critical theorists do not problematize these humanistic goals but rather take them for granted. Instead they see the problem as being to understand how such goals of individual self-realization are thwarted by powerful interests. I agree that this is an important question but would put it in a larger context that problematizes more than domination. This is the context that functionalism can provide.

PROBLEMS OF THEORETICAL STANCE: REPLY TO WILSON

Cecilia L. Ridgeway

Wilson's critique of my chapter is metatheoretical, deriving from his definition of the goals of feminist inquiry and how it may best inform sociology. Consequently, it is the theoretical stance of expectation states theory that concerns him, rather than its substantive claims. Wilson makes one focused criticism of the chapter and a number of comments in passing. I will address the focused criticism first since it raises a number of larger issues about Wilson's essay that put in context his comments in passing.

Wilson criticizes expectation states theory as an example of methodological individualism because it posits "the self as a presocial, self-sufficient unity." This criticism is based on a misreading of expectation states theory that sets the stage for a number of Wilson's concerns about what the theory can offer feminism. Wilson misses the social-constructivist approach of expectation states that views the self and identity as something that is formed and sustained in interaction and, thus, entirely social. I note the dependence of the self on interaction in the first paragraph of my chapter. Thus the self is hardly presocial or self-sufficient in expectation states theory and the approach is not an example of methodological individualism.

In fact, the self is seen as so interactionally dependent that expectation states theory hardly focuses on the individual's self at all, concentrating instead on the causally more powerful process of interaction. This is what it means to take an *interactional* level of analysis, rather than either an individual or a social-structural level of analysis. Wilson may have failed to grasp the interactional level of analysis in my chapter because his own analysis of feminism focuses so heavily on gender as a question of individual identity and difference.

For theoretical purposes, the self in expectation states theory is reduced to a carrier of the cultural knowledge (also socially constructed and historically specific) that society (but not necessarily the actor) deems men more worthy than women and men and women to have different skills in regard to certain gender-related tasks. I say "for theoretical purposes" because expectation states theory does not deny the richness of real selves. Rather, the theory argues that one need know no more than the above minimal information about individual selves to predict a great deal about how they will organize their interaction in regard to status and influence. Because of expectation states theory's focus on interaction and Wilson's focus on gender as individual identity, the two analyses speak past one another.

In the beginning of his essay, Wilson wisely exchews both essentialism and nominalism in the analysis of gender, identity, and social relationships. Yet his insistence throughout on gender as an irreducible category inadvertently collapses back toward essentialism. He notes, for instance, that for "gender theory to be systemic it must be logically inconceivable for the categories 'male' and 'female' to be reversed." He later asserts the only two "irreducible social structures have been discovered," class and sex-gender.

Wilson seems to confound the treatment of patriarchy as an independent social system not logically reducible to class with the idea that gender is an irreducible category. I, like most feminists, am persuaded of the first but not the second. To argue that the sex-gender structure is socially constructed and lacks an inherent, essentialist referent, one must argue that it develops its meaning in relation to other social processes (e.g., power, status, the division of labor, or violence). To make such a relational argument is *not* to say that gender is reducible to any other process. Gender is no more reducible to the processes in relation to which it acquires meaning than a word in a language is reducible to the linguistic structure and context that gives it meaning. Wilson does wish to take a nonessentialist, socially constructed approach to gender and states that gender must be understood in relation to class and race, but cannot be reduced to either. Yet in his discussion of the "power of gender" he criticizes approaches, including expectation states theory, that do not treat gender as a thing-in-itself. Here he contradicts himself and accidently slides toward essentialism.

Expectation states theory does not argue that gender can be reduced to status or that status processes are prior to gender. Rather, it argues that one of the most important ways gender leads to inequalities in interaction is through the status processes it sets in motion. As I note in that chapter, expectation states theory is not and does not claim to be a theory of gender. Rather, it is a theory of status that can illuminate some important effects of gender in interaction and show their relationship to other aspects of power and inequality.

An additional comment that Wilson makes in passing about my approach is that it employs a universalizing strategy based on an impoverished notion of subjectivity taking for granted conceptual distinctions between object and subject, individual and society, emotion and reason. This criticism as well seems to arise from Wilson's failure to understand the social constructivist view of self and subjectivity adopted by expectation states theory. I have already noted that because of this view, the theory does not take as given a distinction between society and individual.

The theory does take the stance of the observer, focusing on behavior rather than the subjectivity of interactants. Although behavior is assumed to be cognitively driven, the theory does not speculate on what the subjective experience of these cognitive and behavioral processes is like for interactants. But to fail to speculate is not to deny the subjectivity and interest-based (and thus emotional as well as rational) point of view of either the interactants or the researcher. As I note when discussing feminism and science, the theory does not argue for the possibility of a classically "objective" or value-neutral stance that implies an inherent difference between knower and known, subject and object. Rather, subject and object are self-conscious stances of an always socially embedded self.

In my view, objective and subjective knowledge strategies both produce valuable but distinct contributions to understanding by providing different angles of refraction on experience. Wilson, on the other hand, finds the work I discuss in my chapter problematic because it lacks an emphasis on the subjective. This, he laments, "shuts off the 'feminine' relational emphasis." As feminists, we all agree on the importance of revaluing the "feminine." But surely Wilson sees the irony of criticizing feminist work for being insufficiently feminine.

Lastly, Wilson assumes that the scientific stance of expectation states theory implies that theory is divorced from political commitment. He seems to assume that the scientific effort to take into account as best you can the ways that your interests bias your perceptions implies that the basic goal of your work is not driven by a deep commitment to understanding how gender oppression works. Again, he is in error in this regard.

There is one legitimate criticism that Wilson does not make of expectation states theory, but I suspect is part of what bothers him about it. This is that it does not explain how gender acquires status value in the first place, only explaining how, once this has happened, it creates interactional inequalities. As a theoretical strategy, it is legitimate to start with certain assumptions and develop from there. But to us a feminists, it means that the theory only explains part of the processes that we are interested in. In my view, the theory must expand to explain processes by which characteristics such as gender could acquire status value in a culture. My own recent work in the area attempts to begin this project (Ridgeway 1991).

Since Wilson raises questions about the political implications of the metatheoretical stance of researchers, I cannot resist commenting on the stance implied by the voice he himself projects in his comments. He notes the commitment of feminism to pluralist views and multiplex voices. Given this, I found it startling and ironic that Wilson, in a firm, universalizing voice reminiscent of Lacan's "voice of the father," defines feminist theory for us. He then measures the feminist contribution of others in terms of the extent to which they meet his definition. Rather than this rather unfeminist approach to feminist theory and the feminism of others, I would like to have seen a more thorough discussion of substance.

References

Ridgeway, Cecilia L. 1991. "The Social Construction of Status Value: Gender and Other Nominal Characteristics." *Social Forces* 70:367–86.

Index

373